MONTEREY BAY AND BEYOND

THE BEST OF CALIFORNIA'S CENTRAL COAST FROM SANTA CRUZ TO SAN SIMEON

BY LUCINDA JACONETTE

CHRONICLE BOOKS

SAN FRANCISCO

For my mom, Joe and Tim

Page 320 constitutes a continuation of the copyright page.

Printed in the United States of America

Jaconette, Lucinda.
   Monterey Bay and beyond: the best of California's Central Coast from Santa Cruz to San Simeon/by Lucinda Jaconette.
p.   cm.
Includes index.
ISBN 0-8118-0488-7
1. Monterey Bay Region (Calif.)—Tours. 2. Monterey Bay National Marine Sanctuary Region (Calif.)—Tours. 3. Pacific Coast (Calif.)—Tours. I.Title.
F868.M7J33 1994
917.94'7—dc20

93-42999
CIP

Editing: Carey Charlesworth
Book and cover design: Amanda Bryan
Cover art: Francois St. Clair
Illustrations: Jeff Siner and Wendy J. Wibbens

Distributed in Canada by Raincoast Books, 112 East Third Ave., Vancouver, B.C. V5T 1C8

10 9 8 7 6 5 4 3 2 1

Chronicle Books
275 Fifth Street
San Francisco, CA 94103

Contents

ACKNOWLEDGMENTS

I am truly grateful to the many people who contributed to this book. Not only have they enriched the pages with their knowledge and understanding, they have touched us all with their kindness.

My deepest thanks are accorded to Bill LeBlond, Carey Charlesworth, Judy Lewenthal, and Leslie Jonath at Chronicle Books for their pertinent questions, careful readings, and encouragement.

For information about the Monterey Bay Aquarium I am grateful to Julie Packard, Steven Webster, and Ken Peterson, as well as numerous other members of the Monterey Bay Aquarium staff and its cadre of volunteers, especially Sheila McMahon. They greatly deepened my understanding, and they continually work overtime to improve the future of our oceans. Gary Greene of the U.S. Geological Survey demystified the theories surrounding the origins of the Monterey Bay Canyon. I hope my words do his studies justice. Alan Baldridge, distinguished librarian of the Hopkins Marine Laboratory, provided sources on the sanctuary and details on its natural history. Todd Bliss added knowledge of geologic formations.

For historical background of native peoples and cultures David Breschini, Rob Edwards, Don Howard, and Patrick Orozco provided a strong foundation and much clarification. Elmer Lagorio, archivist at the Pebble Beach Company, along with several other members of the Pebble Beach Company found answers to difficult questions. James McNaughton, Command Historian of the Defense Language Institute, provided information about the Presidio. Rohanna LoSchiavo walked me through the history of Cannery Row. Ross Gibson provided me countless hours of his own research on the history of Santa Cruz. Craig Barker recalled the spirit of Boulder Creek. Cole Weston shared his art and recollections, bringing Carmel and Big Sur into focus. Geoff Welch, of the Pacific Grove Heritage Society, read early drafts and provided insight into Pacific Grove history. Polly Archer, Lisa Maddalena, and Marjory Cameron, Pacific Grove librarians, and Janice Rodman, Monterey City reference librarian, provided countless sources, often in record time. Pat Hathaway contributed data of the past from his museum-quality files.

Annette Lindstrom shared in much of the early manuscript planning. Joe Strang and Terry Corrigan read and clarified chapters.

This book is greatly enhanced by the fine eye and pen of Jeff Siner, whose landscape and architectural etchings catch qualities unspoken. Wendy J. Wibbens breathed life into the pages with her drawings of fauna and flora. Everett Christopher of Everett Designs provided the drafts for needed maps.

I am indebted also to the *Monterey County Herald* for permission to quote articles from its back issues. Adam Weiland, editor of the *Board and Batten*, newsletter of the Pacific Grove Heritage Society, deserves special regards for his research and permission to use his compiled writings. Bill Bates allowed use of his originals.

My heartfelt thanks are given to my family: To my husband Joe for his understanding, patience, humor, expertise, and company. To our son Tim for his insights and hugs. To my mom for her unconditional love, hours of help, and creative additions. To my brothers Al and Lincoln and their wives Pam and Lennie, for encouragement and reading of numerous drafts.

Finally I would like to thank the hundreds of people I interviewed, for the stories they shared with me. Beyond a doubt, one of the greatest treasures on the Monterey Bay landscape is its remarkable people.

INTRODUCTION

Along the Central Coast of California the Pacific Ocean curves into the beautiful crescent of the Monterey Bay. The core of the Monterey Bay National Marine Sanctuary, this peaceful bay is also the historical center of the Western United States. Gliding above, pelicans ride the winds alongside hang gliders who seek out the seaside updrafts. At the surface a whale salutes with the whack of his flukes, while relentless waves crash to foam against rocks a hundred million years old. Hidden beneath the surface is the deepest of the marine canyons gouged from the ocean bottom off the mainland of the United States. Within and beyond Monterey Bay numerous other marine canyons reach into the sanctuary waters where wrecked ships and a dirigibleshare the Central Coast ocean floor with one of the most diverse marine habitats found anywhere in the world. In what visitors find to explore surrounding the sanctuary, there is equal diversity.

What creatures are at this moment floating on the waves or treading the forested range? Why is that volcano severed in half? Who were the first people here, and where are their descendants? Where can I see the best views, the definitive architecture? Where can I try out a hang glider or a kayak, or learn to cook with the regional masters? Where can I find a serene cove, Victorian garden, or forested glen? And that important question for any traveler, what's there to eat?

You will find the answers here. This guidebook covers the stretch of the Central Coast that is bounded by the Monterey Bay National Marine Sanctuary, a treasure not only for its natural beauty but also for the commitment of residents to maintain it, to act as responsible stewards of the land for generations to come. This stretch extends north and south through four counties. From the traditional northern boundary of the Central Coast, at the northern coastal borderline of Santa Cruz County, it extends to Cambria near the southern boundary of the Monterey Bay National Marine Sanctuary. From the shore this area extends east through the coastal range, the Carmel and Salinas valleys, and the outskirts of the rolling Gabilan Mountains.

The visitor capital of this area is the Monterey Peninsula, one of the top five conference locations in the country. The city of Monterey is often referred to as the "Mother of the Western United States." Historic adobes serve as museums and business locations in this city of firsts in modern California history: first public building, first capital of California, site of the first official raising of an

American flag in declaration of manifest destiny over seven Western states, first hotel, first theater, first billiard tables. For this book the city of Monterey is the first destination, and the one from which travel radiates.

"The greatest meeting of land and water in the world" is the description by artist Francis McComas of the lands around Point Lobos, at the southern end of the peninsula. Four distinct communities on the Monterey Peninsula share the scenery of this phrase, each of them within close proximity of the Monterey Bay Aquarium.

The Monterey Bay Aquarium is the single greatest attraction here at present. Mysteries of the underwater world and new, deeper connections with life, such as those made during eye contact with a gentle octopus, attract visitors.

Half of the Monterey Bay Aquarium is built in Monterey and half in "The Last Hometown," Pacific Grove. Known for its love of the monarch butterfly and preservation of buildings and families, this town boasts Victorian inns and a lovely scenic ocean border. Pebble Beach, the world-renowned golfing and forest resort and residential area, lies to the south, between Pacific Grove and Carmel.

Quaint homes, shops, artist studios, and galleries cluster in the one-mile-square village of Carmel, surrounded by little-known walking trails. Beyond, to the south, the rugged Big Sur Coast extends the length of the Santa Lucia Mountains. South of Big Sur lie the opulent Hearst Castle and Cambria, an artists' colony and one of the few coastal small towns left south of the Monterey Peninsula.

Afternoon winds blow marine air that is cooled over the depths of the Monterey Bay Canyon into the Salinas and Carmel valleys—reminding inland dwellers of their connection with the sea. Inland lakes can be reached by rural Carmel Valley Road or even by horseback expeditions through the Ventana Wilderness Area. Other inland excursions bring you to the caves in the Pinnacles National Monument and close-by San Juan Bautista, a town from another time with wooden sidewalks and a mission plaza.

A collage of communities as well as the ecologically very important Elkhorn Slough frame the journey from Monterey north to Santa Cruz. In early summer, while standing under oak trees at the slough you can see the fins of sharks cut through the water.

In summer, a historic train carries visitors from the shade of thousand-year-old redwoods in the Santa Cruz Mountains to the Santa Cruz Beach Boardwalk. After nature tore out the heart of downtown in the 1989 earthquake, the subtle and sometimes roaring rift between the students of the University of California at Santa Cruz and the town's population seemed to heal. Many former students are employed in the community. Frank Zwart has returned to his alma mater as campus architect. When asked about his decision to return, Zwart echoed many of the residents' feelings: "The variety and liveliness attract me, hold me, and seem to be getting even better."

My own discoveries of the Central Coast began in my childhood, when the highlight of each summer was a trip to Santa Cruz. Today the redwoods are just as tall and the mountain air enlivens my body just as much. I still scream on the roller coaster, I just don't put my hands in the air. I had long thought this would be the ultimate place to live; when the opportunity presented itself twenty years ago, I accepted without hesitation. During those two decades I moved out of the area, staying away for a few years. In short, I have acquired the perspective to offer an insider's guide and also point out the uniqueness in what some residents eventually overlook as ordinary.

Each chapter begins with a short overview of the area visited. This is followed by a Getting Ready section, which tells what to plan for there. Prior planning will help you create glorious days. The set of topics that start off each chapter helps with the details of daily life. When times, prices, and buying information are included they are guides only, as these data change over time. Before you definitely include a place of interest in your plans it is best to call first for the latest information, especially as concerns dining and lodging.

The Directions section in each chapter, before the introduction to the tours, guides you from major highways and the aquarium. With these directions you can start your trip from any point in the area. Historical background in the introduction to the tours offers extra dimensions to the places you visit. A beach feels different when you realize it was once a Chinese abalone village and later a hidden rum-runners hide-out. Along with harboring a history, the Central Coast is continually making its future; it changes every day. This guide facilitates but does not replace the thousands of discoveries that you will make, beginning with these pages.

GETTING READY

THE BEST TIMES TO VISIT AND THE SPECIAL EVENTS

Most people visit the Central Coast during weekends in summer and on three-day holiday weekends throughout the year. The area attracts international, national, and statewide visitors. In addition, people from nearby metropolitan areas escape here for the weekend. Make reservations before you visit in summer or on holiday weekends—well in advance if you have a "special place" in mind. The Friday evening incoming and Sunday outgoing traffic can be quite heavy. None of the segments of the Central Coast is a metropolis, so even when the crowds are shoulder to shoulder in the central tourist locations you can still find a secluded serene beach or wooded glen, even one just a few blocks away.

Some visitors prefer the warm days of spring and autumn, when the crowds are few. Many hotels, motels, and resorts have special off-season rates (November through March). In addition, many motels and hotels offer winter specials, which are advertised in *Sunset Magazine* and the *San Francisco Chronicle*.

When you are in the mood to celebrate, this is the place: the festival capital of California. Steinbeck's birthday, a calamari festival, a welcome-to-the-monarchs butterfly parade, a begonia festival, an unbirthday party, a migration festival, and a garlic extravaganza are just a few of the many. (The unbirthday? It seems Robert Louis Stevenson, who lived and wrote here many years ago, gave his away to a little girl who was born on Christmas and wanted a birthday of her own.) For private celebration, the area excels in quantity and quality of restaurants as well as in private beaches and wooded nooks, for the most romantic of candlelit dinners. A Calendar of Events is included at the back of this book to aid your planning.

CLIMATE AND CLOTHING

The Central Coast of California is one of the few places where you can experience four seasons on the same beach in any one day, sometimes in less than an hour. Ten minutes' drive from the beach, or from anyplace else in the area, you may encounter temperatures very different from where you started. When Pebble Beach is cool and foggy the Carmel Valley may be sunny and hot. Notes below, expanded in each chapter under this heading, describe three general climate areas. Remember that these notes are generalities and that heat waves do occur in cool coastal environs, usually a few times each summer, sometimes with more regularity.

COASTAL AREAS. Spring and autumn are usually the sunniest seasons. When California's inland valleys heat up in July and August, the trees and dunes along the coast disappear in fog. During any season, winds pick up quickly and moist fog can blow in almost as fast as you can get out of your car. Pack a jacket. By the time you put on your jacket, the bright sun may burn fog away for the day. Pack suntan lotion and a hat.

The Big Sur Coast generally follows the coastal weather pattern but with its own set of small bays and microclimates that create variable conditions. On Monterey Bay the central section around Moss Landing and Castroville is historically the foggiest. In general, the warmest stretch of beach is located in the northern arc of the bay from Seacliff through Santa Cruz. In the middle of the arc an eddy effect creates a shelter from northwesterly winds and attracts warmer inland air with less fog. Monterey, Seaside, Marina, and the eastern half of Pacific Grove are generally the sunniest stretches of beach along the southern arc. Even farther south, however, when everywhere else is foggy, Carmel is sometimes gloriously sunny.

Winter is the cooler, unpredictable rainy season. Storms can follow blissful 70 degree days. Snow and heavy frost are extremely rare, although snow did blanket the Pebble Beach "Crosby" golf tournament in 1962.

INLAND VALLEYS. Spring is balmy, at an average 70 degrees with occasional rains. Wildflowers are abundant. In summer, fogbound coastside residents head into nearby valleys to swim at resort and club pools or river beaches. The farther inland you go, the hotter it gets, with some 90 and 100 degree afternoons. The southern lake regions are much hotter, with 90 to 100 degree temperatures common.

Winters are mild and occasionally wild. Flooding can occur during heavy rains. Snow blankets the hills occasionally. Call ahead about conditions if you are entering Los Padres National Forest on routes that lead from Carmel Valley Road or traverse the Santa Lucia Mountains, such as the Nacimiento-Fergusson Road.

MOUNTAINS. The mountains can reach 90 degrees and even 100 during summer months. The evenings cool down, so bring a jacket with you. Summer extends through October. In many years the kids have gone trick-or-treating before days feel crisp. Winter storms can be treacherous. Common sense dictates extreme caution when driving a mountain road in a storm.

CLOTHING. Comfortable, casual attire is the norm for the Central Coast. Bring shorts, long pants, short sleeves, and long sleeves. Capitola Beach and the Santa Cruz Beach Boardwalk are the most casual and the Pebble Beach lodges are the most formal of the spectrum. Prepare for all types of recreation possibilities. Layer your clothes, so when a cold, drizzly, foggy morning turns gloriously sunny you can enjoy it in short sleeves. Most visitors comment that the summers are cooler than they expected. Every location offers pleasant walks, so wear or bring a good pair of hiking shoes with you.

TOUR LENGTHS

The geographical area of each chapter is close enough to the rest to be approached as a day trip from a central location along the Monterey Bay. You might also want to read through this guidebook, pick your favorite places, and stay a couple of nights in each. To explore the Central Coast well you will need at least a week.

WILDLIFE WISDOM

The Central Coast abounds with opportunities for getting close to nature. Every town and city in the area has walking paths. Some, like Ocean View Boulevard in Pacific Grove, bombard your senses with nature's spectacular displays; others, like the Frog Pond Area in Del Rey Oaks, gently prod your soul. This is Ansel Adams and Weston country. Bring a camera. Bring binoculars. For the fossils in the cliffs and close-up looks at tidepool creatures, bring a hand lens.

Black Legged Tick

Poison Oak

The grizzly bears are gone from this section of the coast, but other elements of nature still necessitate a few warnings. Almost every summer there is a report of some young visitor (sometimes not so young) who delivers a beautiful bouquet of bright red "flowers" to the dinner table or tent site. The bright red "flowers" turn out to be the foliage of poison oak, and the visitor spends a miserable two weeks slathered in anti-itch cream. Poison oak, *Rhus diversiloba*, is very common along hiking trails throughout the Central Coast. It is identified by its clusters of three shiny leaves in the spring and early summer, bright red foliage in late summer and autumn. When its leaves are gone in winter, the barely noticeable twigs are still potent. Nature couldn't have provided a better watchdog for tree seedlings and easily trampled flowers than the poison oak that keeps hikers on the paths. The itch from poison oak is caused by the plants' irritating oil. Ask a ranger or a local to help you identify this plant if you are not familiar with it.

When hiking in grasslands it is important to be aware of the Western black-legged tick, *Ixodes pacifica*, the carrier of Lyme disease. In its adolescent stage the dark tick is the size of the head of a common pin. A fully engorged adult is no bigger than a small kernel of corn. California's Western fence lizards, commonly known as blue belly lizards, can stop the spread of the disease by inhibiting it in their blood. Domestic cats have reduced the lizard populations, and the disease has begun to spread in California, although it is still uncommon.

Two-thirds of Lyme disease victims develop a ringlike rash on the skin where the tick attached. Other early signs include low-grade fever, fatigue, and muscle aches. The second stage of symptoms occurs weeks or months later and can include paralysis of facial muscles, severe headaches, and abnormal heartbeat. Call your doctor if you suspect you have the disease.

The best way to avoid Lyme disease is to avoid ticks. Stay on the trails. Tuck your pant legs into your socks. Wear light-colored clothing so that ticks are maximally visible. Apply insect repellent, and check your body frequently to stop ticks before they can attach to you.

VISITOR INFORMATION

Visitor information in each chapter includes phone numbers of major visitor services. Resources in local newspapers are also recommended. For area-wide listings of specialized tours, sports facilities, wineries, and other particular interests, see the Resource Guide near the end of this book.

PARKING AND RESTROOMS

The more densely visited and also exclusive an area is, the more troublesome is finding a reasonable parking place and a restroom. With this in mind, recommendations are given for only the more populated coastal towns and problematic areas. (Parking rates are current as of this writing.)

ALTERNATE TRANSPORTATION

One of my favorite ways to travel is by train. I love destinations where, after arriving, I can walk to the places I want to visit. For these preferences Monterey is one of California's best visitor destinations. Although the Amtrak rail service to the hub city of Monterey is by way of connecting buses from the Amtrak facilities in San Jose, Gilroy, and Salinas, the connections are quite good.

The transit plaza in Monterey is not a building but does have a covered area. It is located at triangular Jules Simoneau Plaza bounded by Munras Avenue and Pearl and Tyler streets in the pleasant center of the city's revitalized historic downtown. Several hotels are within easy walking distance. At the plaza you can catch local bus service (Monterey-Salinas Transit, MST, 408/424-7695 or 408/899-2555) to other downtown locations, Fisherman's Wharf, Pacific Grove, and Carmel. The plaza flies the flags of the United States, Mexico, and Spain plus the California Bear Flag and pennant of the downtown association. These can serve as landmarks for travelers in the downtown.

Bike rentals are available nearby. You can bike along the entire coastline from north of Monterey to Cambria. In summer, for a very reasonable price, MST buses service Highway 1 south along the coast to the community of Big Sur. Several tour companies, most notably Otter-Mobile Tours & Charters on the Monterey Peninsula (408/625-9782), provide any extra sightseeing you might desire. Pebble Beach can not be reached by regular transit bus service.

PLACES TO STAY

Listings provide a variety of accommodations, including bed and breakfasts, resorts, hotels and motels, and campsites (when especially appropriate). The rates cited are for summer weekends. Some places maintain the same rates all year; other places have a variety of rates depending on the day, season, or special event. Weekday rates are sometimes less than weekend rates. Whenever you call to make reservations, inquire about special rates that may apply.

Where should you stay? It is always frustrating to spend any vacation time changing your reserved location. As you read the chapters in this book decide which areas especially appeal to you.

RESTAURANTS

I have selected restaurants to provide a variety of choices and to honor particular restaurants' commitment to quality and service. This region abounds with fabulous restaurants, far too many to include. The abbreviations for credit cards are: AX, American Express; MC, Master Card; V, Visa.

TOUR: POINT OF WELCOME

When I visit a place for the first time, I like to head for the spot with the best view. Some locations where you can experience breathtaking overviews of the Monterey Peninsula include: the summit of Highway 17, for those traveling south from the San Jose area; the summit of Highway 152, west of Gilroy, an alternate crossover for those traveling south on 101; from Jacks Peak, for those traveling north on Highway 68; the Sloat Monument area on the Presidio Hill, for those who have already arrived in the Monterey Peninsula; Shepherd's Knoll and Huckleberry Hill, for Pebble Beach visitors; and Pogonip Park, accessible from Highway 9 or High Street, for those on the Santa Cruz side of the Monterey Bay.

CHAPTER 1

THE MONTEREY BAY AQUARIUM AND THE MONTEREY BAY NATIONAL MARINE SANCTUARY

A PARTNERSHIP

The Monterey Bay National Marine Sanctuary stretches three hundred miles, from the Farallon Islands off the coast of San Francisco south along the enclaves of Monterey Bay and, farther south, along the Big Sur Coast, to Cambria. Located on the border of the cities of Pacific Grove and Monterey, the Monterey Bay Aquarium provides visitors with a close-up view of the life and wonders of the Monterey Bay National Marine Sanctuary.

GETTING READY

This chapter provides a general overview of the sanctuary and highlights the wildlife that visitors may encounter at the destinations in any of the chapters. The tour that this chapter leads is of the Monterey Bay Aquarium; all of the "Getting Ready" information here is for your aquarium tour.

THE BEST TIMES TO VISIT AND THE SPECIAL EVENTS

The aquarium is open daily (except Christmas) from 10 a.m. to 6 p.m. Crowds are smallest on weekdays and, any day of the week, either first thing in the morning or late afternoon. Weekends usually offer a wider variety of free shows. Special shows such as Otter Feeding and Kelp Forest Fish Feeding and Tidepool Divers are offered throughout each day. Call before you arrive for show times: 408/648-4888. During summer a wider variety of interpretive programs is offered. The Monterey Bay Aquarium Research Institute's (MBARI) remotely operated vehicle (ROV), a submersible that travels to the depths of the

Marine Sanctuary, broadcasts live shows only on Mondays, Tuesdays, Thursdays, and Fridays as weather and exploration allow.

The aquarium offers educational classes throughout the year. Weddings and other private social and business gatherings can be arranged before 10 a.m. and after 6 p.m. On-site catering is available through the Portola Cafe. To arrange a private event call 408/649-6466.

TICKET INFORMATION

The current prices of tickets are $10.50, adults; $7.75, seniors, students, and military personnel; $4.75, children ages three to twelve. Children under three are admitted free of charge. Groups of twenty or more qualify for group rates. In summer and during major holiday weekends, the lines to enter the aquarium at peak hours are sometimes subject to delays of an hour. Advance ticket sales allow you to enter with no waiting.

Memberships support ongoing aquarium programs, educational services, and new exhibits. Memberships are especially recommended for those who visit the aquarium more than once during the year. Membership rates are: $55.00, family; $45.00, couples; and $39.00, individuals. If you are purchasing a membership on site, go directly to the membership express entrance. Memberships entitle guests to unlimited express-entry visits, admission to special evening and event programs throughout the year, a 10 percent discount on any aquarium purchases, and the opportunity to participate in aquarium travel excursions.

Advance tickets and memberships can be ordered by calling 800/756-3737 or the main information line, 408/648-4888. A $3.00 service fee is added to ticket orders. Many Monterey Peninsula hotels sell advance tickets to their guests (with no fee).

CLIMATE AND CLOTHING

Wear comfortable walking shoes in the aquarium and casual clothes. You may need to sit on the floor during crowded shows and get wet up to your elbows at the touch tanks. Indoor exhibits extend to several outdoor areas.

TOUR LENGTHS

Allow at least three hours to explore the aquarium. If you need a break, the aquarium will stamp your hand so that you can return any time during the day.

VISITOR INFORMATION

The main aquarium information number is 408/648-4888. An information booth is set up inside the entrance to the aquarium. Volunteer docents are stationed at exhibits throughout to answer your questions. Volunteers with orange jackets have finished a series of training courses. Many volunteers with and without the orange jackets have specialized preparation, such as backgrounds in oceanography, diving, or teaching. The aquarium's Education Division provides a rich grounding of information in various topics related to the Monterey Bay National Marine Sanctuary.

Still and video cameras are welcome. Flash can be used except at posted exhibits where it would disturb the animals. Visitors can also borrow a camera from the information desk. Commercial photography must be arranged in advance through the Public Relations Department, 408/648-4800.

PARKING

A city-owned parking garage on Foam Street off Prescott Avenue and Wave Street, about three blocks from the aquarium, offers twenty-four hour parking at a fee of $1.00 per hour. A city-owned lot located on David Avenue, within a half-block of the aquarium, offers parking at $1.00 per half hour. Metered parking is available on the street for twenty-five cents for each twenty minutes, up to twelve hours. Some streets, such as David Avenue, offer free curbside spaces, but it's a rare day when a space is available.

ALTERNATE TRANSPORTATION

Traffic and parking in the Cannery Row and aquarium areas are often congested. The WAVE shuttle bus, available from 9 a.m. to 9 p.m. daily during summer and on selected year-round weekends, links the aquarium with downtown Monterey, the Monterey Simoneau Transit Plaza, and waterfront locations. One fee covers unlimited rides all day. The WAVE offers excellent connections, and friendly service every fifteen minutes (408/899-2555).

For pedestrians and bicycles, the Monterey Peninsula Recreation Trail passes beside the aquarium. Bike rentals are available in the Monterey Plaza and at the Fisherman's Wharf area.

PLACES TO STAY

The Monterey Bay Aquarium's location is convenient to lodging in any of the surrounding areas. Monterey and Pacific Grove's lodgings (pp. 49 and 74) are only steps away, as these towns border the aquarium. Santa Cruz is a forty-five minute drive. Many visitors stay in the community of Big Sur, which is a little more than an hour south.

RESTAURANTS

Cannery Row restaurants are within a short walking distance of the aquarium. The aquarium also offers on-site dining at the Portola Cafe.

PORTOLA CAFE, (on the first floor of the aquarium). At this beautiful location, overlooking the bay, diners have choices. Dine in a quiet full-service restaurant with linens and flowers, in a self-service cafeteria with a selection of fish, burgers, soup, and salads, or at an espresso, drinks, and oyster bar with menu selections.

Reservations are suggested for the full-service restaurant, as its pasta and fresh fish selections as well as friendly service and ocean views make it a popular choice for aquarium visitors and locals alike. The full restaurant serves from 11 a.m. to 3 p.m.; the oyster bar and cafeteria remain open until 5:30 p.m. 408/648-4870. AX, MC, V. A la carte cafeteria selections, mostly under $5.00. Entrees in restaurant, mostly under $15.00.

DIRECTIONS

The aquarium looks like an industrial building, with two tall smokestacks. Use these smokestacks as landmarks when you are in the Cannery Row area.

From the Central Valley, Highway 156 connects to 101 just west of San Juan Bautista, leading to the continuation of 156 west to Highway 1. Take 1 south to Monterey. For southbound travelers, the aquarium can be reached by traveling scenic Highway 1 from the San Francisco Bay Area, or by Highway 17 to Highway 1 from the San Jose area. Also, Highways 101 and 280 to Highway 1 from San Francisco (through the south bay and San Jose areas) connect to 17 and so to 1 at Santa Cruz. Highway 17 is a curvy mountain route. It can be circumvented by taking 101 from the San Francisco and San Jose areas farther south, to Prunedale (which is twenty minutes south of Gilroy and ten minutes south of the San Juan Bautista exit). From Prunedale take Highway 156 (the "Monterey Peninsula" exit) west to Highway 1, and continue south to Monterey.
Exit Highway 1 at "Del Monte Avenue / Pacific Grove" and go straight, following the brown signs. (The Monterey Visitor's Center can be reached by turning left at Camino El Estero.) Beyond Fisherman's Wharf veer right, and continue through the tunnel. Past the tunnel, turn right at the first street, to follow historic Cannery Row to the aquarium. After five blocks you may want to turn left at Hoffman Avenue, then right on Foam Street for the parking garage entrance.

From Southern California, travel northbound on Highway 101 or coastal route Highway 1. Most people who take Highway 1 as part of a loop with Highway 101 prefer to drive Highway 101 north, then travel the ocean side of Highway 1 on the southbound return trip.

From northbound Highway 101, take the "Monterey Peninsula" exit in Salinas to Highway 68. (For a more scenic parallel route see the Inland Excursions chapter, p. 185.) Follow Highway 68 west to Highway 1 south and exit immediately at Fremont Street. Turn right on Camino El Estero (the Monterey Visitor's Center will be to your right in the second block) and travel to Del Monte Avenue. Then turn left and follow the brown signs through the tunnel. Past the tunnel, take the first right turn to follow historic Cannery Row to the aquarium. After five blocks, you may want to turn left at Hoffman Avenue then right on Foam Street for the parking garage entrance.

From northbound Highway 1, take the Munras Avenue exit in Monterey. Turn left at Soledad Drive and then right at Pacific Street. Continue on Pacific Street until it becomes Lighthouse Avenue. Turn right on Cannery Row, which leads to the aquarium.

Highway 1 north- or southbound travelers can also take the Highway 68 / Pacific Grove exit, then travel 10 minutes north to the second traffic light in Pacific Grove. Turn right at David Avenue. David Avenue merges with Wave Street in front of the aquarium.

INTRODUCTION WITH HISTORICAL HIGHLIGHTS

"When that little ball of fur tentatively pats my face and sniffs at me with its fresh squid breath I just melt." Sheila McMahon, a sea otter rescue volunteer at the Monterey Bay Aquarium, watches as a scuba diver swims underwater in a shallow tidal area nearby. A young southern sea otter whines like a puppy, twists and glides through the water, then slides on the diver's back as if she were its mother. The otter was orphaned in the ocean as a pup and brought to the aquarium for round the clock care by aquarium staff and a group of volunteer adoptive mothers, like Sheila McMahon. They nursed the baby otter with a rich formula of clams, squid, half-and-half, fish oil, and vitamins and minerals. To keep the pup clean and buoyant, volunteers constantly combed and brushed its hair. Now the diver is helping the pup to acclimate to life on its own in the ocean by teaching it to forage for its food. The aquarium staff keeps the otter's name secret so that any divers and anglers with the wrong intentions will not take advantage when it finally cuts its bonds with humans and swims free. The otter is tagged for electronic tracking and observational identification.

Monterey Bay Aquarium

Just as the Monterey Bay Aquarium diver introduces the young otter to its place in the vast ocean, the aquarium introduces nearly two million visitors each year to the wonders of the Monterey Bay National Marine Sanctuary. On any afternoon several hundred of these visitors sit in a dark auditorium at the aquarium and gasp as they watch live broadcasts of events "Live from Monterey Canyon," such as a rare vampire squid getting sucked into a transparent cylinder—the catch of the MBARI ROV, the submersible remotely operated vehicle.

The aquarium sits on the rocky shores on the southern side of Monterey Bay. Right offshore, the ocean bottom drops into the twisting and branching abyss of the Monterey Canyon. Imagine the Grand Canyon of the Southwest flooded with seawater and toured by hundreds of types of fish, assorted sea mammals, and bouquets of sea plants. Imagine sharks, mackerel, whales, giant kelp, and red algae. Sea stars cling to crevices, and colorful sea anemones hold fast to sheared cliffs. Your mental vista of all this would resemble the thirteen mile-wide, mile-deep canyon off the coast of Monterey.

THE ORIGINS OF THE CANYON AND THE SANCTUARY

The canyon is the largest of several canyon systems that cut the ocean floor along the Central Coast. Just south of Carmel at the beach off San Jose Creek, the head of the Carmel Canyon is so close to shore, you can wade into it at low tide. (However easy wading there appears, the force of the water through the canyon often sends large sneaker waves against the shore, sweeping away anyone or anything it meets.) According to Gary Greene, a geologist with the U.S.Geological Survey, rock types from the various canyons match. This matching shows that many of the separate canyons in the area may be severed parts of the greater Monterey Canyon.

What caused the canyon? In the words of Greene, "The answer to that question is not straight facts but involves complex processes, and still perplexes us." Scientists have searched for clues ever since the canyon was discovered in 1890 by pioneer scientist George Davidson, who was astonished to find it while taking soundings with a hand line and lead weights. For many years scientists theorized the canyon was carved when it was above the surface, perhaps as a former drainage of the San Joaquin–Sacramento River Basin, thus making Monterey Bay the original repository of the waters now forming San Francisco Bay.

Between 1938 and 1940 geologist Francis Shepard used electronic echo sounders to define the canyon's several heads, the nearest and largest beginning only a hundred meters offshore from Moss Landing. Shepard reasoned that the canyon could not have been formed above land because, at the time of his study, no evidence existed that at any time in the twenty-five million years of the canyon's history was sea level ever low enough to expose such depths. Shepard hypothesized that a force beneath the ocean was responsible for the great chasm. According to Shepard, "Turbidity currents" provided the answer to the canyon's puzzle. Rocks, mud, and sand are continually washed from the land to near the continental shelf. When the weight of these accumulating sediments reaches a critical mass—whoosh! The seaward edge of the mass sags and the mass slides over the brink. The sudden precipitous movement forms the turbidity current. Depressions that form along the continental shelf in areas of more frequent sliding become the heads of turbidity-charged underground canyons. Undersea landslides then continue to widen and deepen the canyons. Shepard's theory held exclusive weight until the San Andreas Fault put it on shaky ground.

Since the 1960s the plate tectonics theory has convincingly portrayed the Pacific plate of the Earth's crust as colliding with the North American plate. California's Central Coast is located on the Pacific plate. Massive collisions, with the Pacific plate caving beneath the North American plate and causing its uplift, created volcanoes along the the edge of the continent to form the arc of the Sierra Nevada. About twenty million years ago the Pacific plate off Central California stopped diving beneath the North American plate and started to inch its way northwest, along the fracture now known as the San Andreas fault.

Name your left hand the North American plate and your right hand the Pacific Plate. Now press your fingertips together and push hard; your fingers will rise from the conflicting pressures. The Santa Lucia mountain range along the Pacific Coast is still growing upward by a similar impingement of the Pacific plate against the North American plate. Continue pressing your fingers together as you move your right hand sideways, and fold it slightly beneath your left. A model of land movement along the Central Coast is at your fingertips.

Geologists named the land west of the fault in Northern California "Salinia." Granite composes its basement rock, as contrasted with the metamorphic and sedimentary rocks on the east side known as the Franciscan Formation. Although the movement of the fault is now primarily horizontal, over millions of years the movement has alternately been vertical—which accounts for the shark's tooth fossils people find around Boulder Creek, a thousand feet high in the Santa Cruz Mountains. Gary Greene cited the vertical movement as the possible and, actually, well-accepted explanation for how a canyon could have been be cut hundreds of feet in depth near or above sea level, by streams or submarine currents, but also have been dropped well below the surface and cut as well by turbidity forces.

People still ask, however, "What river cut the canyon?" About fifteen years ago I took a series of courses about the California coast from the late Herb Strongin, a geologist with San Francisco State University. Once, with a gleam in his eye, he picked up a rock at Point Lobos, south of Monterey, and dared us to find matching rocks anywhere north of where we were standing. Then he pointed to a place on the map inland from San Luis Obispo and told us to take the rocks with us down there and we would find their match. Why? Because the land we were standing on was moving north at the average rate of eight centimeters a year. East of the San Andreas fault, where Strongin had pointed on the map, the land was stationary.

Upon seeing the resemblance of the Monterey Bay Canyon to the southwestern Grand Canyon, Robert Lloyd Allen, a Navy officer attending the Naval Postgraduate School in Monterey in the early 1980s, hypothesized that the entire Monterey Canyon had moved north from the Colorado River Basin. He used a computer to simulate the movement of the Monterey Canyon and the San Andreas fault and found that twenty million years ago the site of the Monterey Bay would have been west of Bakersfield. The Gulf of California, where the Colorado River now empties, is relatively new, geologically speaking, and did not exist twenty million years ago. Allen theorized the Colorado River may have once followed a more northwesterly course and carved a southern end to the Grand Canyon through uplifted Salinian landscape.

Greene and other geologists place the origin of the Monterey Canyon near present-day Santa Barbara. Most geologists reject the Colorado River hypothesis because of the mountain ranges that are also in the area and the time sequence, among other factors. In fact, I was told by one geologist, who wishes to be left anonymous, that he'd rip this page from the book if I printed such hogwash. The most accepted theory claims that the major carver of the canyon's walls and depths was probably turbidity currents rather than any one powerful river.

Oil exploration wells drilled in the 1960s at Elkhorn Slough, which bisects the midpoint of the Monterey Bay coastline, indicate a massive build-up of ten-million-year-old sediment that covers the ancestral head of the Monterey Canyon. According to Greene, recent explorations of the canyon have yielded "exotic rocks—volcanic rocks matching those on the Franciscan side, and everyone's excited about what this means, but no one has the answer."

The Monterey Bay Aquarium Research Institute (MBARI) submersible research vehicle enhances further exploration of the canyon. About the size of a Volkswagen bug, the sub has an array of cameras, sampling devices, and instruments that record temperature, depth, and other variables. Officially called the Remotely Operated Vehicle (ROV), the unmanned sub is tethered to a research vessel from which scientists operate it by remote control to depths of three thousand feet in waters that brim with creatures as small as microscopic plankton, as large as blue whales, and as exotic as the predacious siphonophore, a shimmering string of gelatinous beads measuring 120 feet long that devours any organism in its path.

The canyon is the centerpiece of the Monterey Bay National Marine Sanctuary, the nation's newest and largest marine preserve. The range of the species and underwater environments it hosts makes it one of the richest, most incredibly varied aquatic communities in the world. Extending along more than 300 miles of coast south from the Farallons, by San Francisco, and ending near Cambria, the sanctuary boundary encompasses an area the size of the state of Connecticut. Different zones of the 5,300 square mile sanctuary contain the deepest and largest underwater canyons on the West Coast, expansive ocean waters with a sandy and muddy floor, kelp forests that support an abundance of life, rocky shores dotted with tidepools, miles of beaches, and fragile wetlands.

A marine sanctuary is similar to a park, in that its natural beauty is protected by the federal government and that conservation of its resources is balanced with research, recreational, and commercial uses. In 1992, after two decades of work, the residents and supporters cheered as the Monterey Bay National Marine Sanctuary was officially established. Twenty-two endangered species find refuge in its waters and along its shore. The sanctuary is home to 27 species of marine mammals, 94 seabird species, at least 345 fish species, 450 species of marine algae, and thousands of invertebrate animal species. The numbers of known species keep growing. One of several scientists on the cutting edge of marine research, George Matsumoto, a MBARI researcher, has discovered ten new species in recent years.

The pristine coast also supports thousands of people who are employed in marine research, coastal agriculture, and fisheries. In addition to MBARI, eight other key research facilities are located in the Monterey Bay region. Millions of people use the sanctuary waters as a place for recreation. Swimming, diving, sailing, surfing, kayaking, birding, sport fishing, whalewatching, tidepooling, and beachwalking are among the pleasures enjoyed by residents and visitors alike.

The indigenous populations in California before European contact are estimated to have been nearly a third of the inhabitants of the Americas north of

Mexico. Over three hundred languages and dialects were chronicled by Spanish and later settlers. The first groups who settled along the California Central Coast relied on the ocean for a major part of their food supply. They discarded shells and bones in mounds that remain as the primary evidence of their use of the environment. On trips to beaches throughout the sanctuary you might sit near one of these shell middens, layers of chipped shells and stones, interspersed in the sand. Most middens, even though they have been disturbed, are not roped off from the rest of the beach. Overall, mussels are the most abundant shells found in middens. Abalone, too, was especially important along the Monterey Peninsula.

Several major tribes and numerous tribelets of the Hokan, Penutian, and Chumashan (southern coastal region) language groups inhabited the land areas around the present sanctuary. Natural resources were abundant and there was little intertribal conflict. Artifacts unearthed in Scotts Valley, north of Santa Cruz, show that people possibly lived there 10,000 years ago when a now-dry lake covered the valley floor. Farther south, the earliest archaeological evidence shows that ancestors of the Hokan-speaking Esselen tribe lived near Moss Landing 9,500 years ago. By 4,500 years ago the Esselen had moved to the south, along the Big Sur coast, and inland, to the present-day town of Soledad. New tribes moving into the area and climatic changes are thought to be the reasons for the shift in the tribe's location. In the 1700s some thirty groups of Penutian-speaking people lived north of Big Sur. Tribes and tribelets such as the Rumsen, Mutsun, and Kalendaruc were grouped by European settlers and later archaeologists as the "Costanoan," derived from the Spanish for "of the coast." The descendants of the tribal groups sometimes prefer the encompassing tribal name "Ohlone."

Baskets and arrow points are the most commonly found artifacts. The largest "quarry" and stoneworking area was located at Año Nuevo Point. Although few completed arrow points are still found, purposely chipped rock is found in the middens throughout the dunes of the area. The Penutian groups were gatherers of acorns and seeds. They cooked by dropping heated stones into watertight baskets. The groups sailed the bay and river areas on reed rafts. Sea mammals such as otters, seals, and sea lions, as well as inland mammals, contributed to their diets.

The cultures and populations of these tribes were largely wiped out, directly and indirectly, by Spanish missions and later settlements of the area. The cultures of the first peoples were often dissimilar from each other, but they practiced a common stewardship of the land. Archaeological evidence continues to be studied, redefining which tribes lived where and brought what customs to the lands. Awareness of the old ways is growing among descendants, who continue the stories and traditions of tribes who lived for over two hundred generations in harmony with each other, the land, and the ocean.

Human imprints from a wider range of the world's cultures began with Spanish explorer Juan Rodriguez Cabrillo, who led the first European expedition into Californian waters. English explorer Sir Francis Drake, who first sailed the sanctuary waters in 1579 aboard the ship the Golden Hinde, called the lands defined by cliffs such as those north of Santa Cruz "Nova Albion," meaning New England. This was forty years before the Pilgrims landed at Plymouth Rock, and so designated California as the first New England. Vizcaino stepped ashore at Monterey and claimed the land for Spain in 1602. The land lay in the hands of the Esselen, the Rumsen, the Ohlone, and surrounding tribelets when otter fur traders brought an influx of Russian sailors to sanctuary waters. In the late 1700s, as a reaction to the fur traders' use of Central Coast waters, the Spanish settled the area with a progression of missions and presidios.

Whaling, the fur trade, gold prospecting, and the opening of the Western frontier for settlement brought new people from diverse cultures to sanctuary waters and surrounding lands. Chinese residents pioneered many of the fisheries, including squid. Gennosuke Kodani, a Japanese immigrant, established the first abalone cannery at Point Lobos in 1898. Sicilians brought fishing techniques that helped Monterey become the world's busiest fishing port. Knut Hovden, a Norwegian, built the largest of the canneries, and Cannery Row boomed.

Diverse groups of immigrants and the needs of the United States continue to influence the uses of the sanctuary. By the 1960s most of the canneries had closed, due to diminishing sardine populations. Then and in the 1970s concern along the coast shifted from the economic impact of fishing to that of offshore oil wells. Citizens' efforts and federal scientific surveys provided the evidence of the rich biological diversity in the area and so of the need for a sanctuary to protect the marine life.

The National Oceanic and Atmospheric Administration (NOAA) manages the Monterey Bay National Marine Sanctuary and other sanctuaries. To protect the resources within the Monterey Sanctuary the following activities are prohibited: exploring for, developing, or producing oil, gas, or mineral resources, and designating new dredged-material disposal sites.

For visitors, in general, the rules and regulations prohibit the moving, injuring, or possession of historical resources and the taking, injuring, or harassing of marine mammals, turtles, or seabirds. As the Marine Mammal Protection Act specifies, people must stay one hundred yards from whales, stay fifty feet from otters, and must not approach harbor seals. Future regulations may change, and visitors are advised to consult information boards at beaches, marine attractions such as the aquarium, and harbor master's offices.

EVOLUTION OF AN AQUARIUM

Even before there was a designated sanctuary, two-year-olds in strollers and nonswimmers could explore the biodiversity of the kelp forests, the ocean floor, and other zones of the sanctuary through their re-creation in the Monterey Bay Aquarium.

Exhibit environments range from a kelp forest thriving in a 335,000 gallon tank of water to an outdoor atrium of sand dunes and mudflats. Visitors pet the silky skin of bat rays, feel the tickle of sea star legs at the indoor tide pools, and visit eye to eye with sharks, giant octopi, and even human divers who clean exhibits and offer feeding demonstrations in the kelp forest.

No one remembers who first came up with the idea for the aquarium. In the 1970s, following decades of dwindling sardine catches, the closed and boarded-up Hovden Cannery stood as a wooden ghost, at the west end of Cannery Row. In 1977 Nancy Burnett, her husband Robin, who taught at Stanford University's Hopkins Marine Laboratories, just a stone's throw west from the old cannery, and friends and fellow professors Chuck Baxter and Steven Webster brainstormed ideas for its future. "That boarded up cannery just caught our imaginations, and it was the topic of discussion at many a dinner," remembers Steven Webster, now education director at the aquarium. It wasn't just any aquarium they finally envisioned, but an aquarium that would showcase and educate people about the habitats of the local Monterey Bay, which heretofore were visible only to divers or lay shrouded in unexplored depths.

At the same time the four scientists were drawing plans for the habitat-based aquarium, Nancy's parents, David and Lucile Packard, were searching for a focus to their family foundation. David Packard, with his partner William Hewlett, had built the Hewlett-Packard electronics giant in Northern California and had amassed fortunes. According to daughter Julie Packard, executive director of the aquarium, David Packard had challenged the foundation board members to come up with a substantial project. "The two ideas happened at the same time. It was a serendipitous event."

Webster smiled as he told me about the early plans. "We were naive with the first ideas we submitted for consideration. We thought we'd be able to wedge a series of aquariums in the old cannery." After a tour of every major aquarium in the country David and Lucile Packard offered a beginning one-time gift of fifty-five million dollars from the family to the public for a top-notch facility. David Packard's vision and an extra gift of thirteen million dollars provided for the world-class Monterey Bay Aquarium Research Institute. Separate from the aquarium, its purpose is to design oceanic research technology and uncover the mysteries of the ocean. The nonprofit Monterey Bay Aquarium Foundation was created in 1978 to oversee aquarium operations and construction.

"Everyone wants to know how this project started," according to Julie Packard, who is also a marine botanist. "The final product was so much greater and richer than the original idea. What we have today is the result of all the ideas and work of all the creative people who have contributed through the years." She began working on the aquarium project with the four other scientists, as a volunteer, to prepare the proposal. She became more and more involved with the aquarium in the early days of slide shows and speaking engagements to gain community support, eventually turning her management skills to the executive directorship.

Many people question why the aquarium looks so industrial. Most of the original cannery was dismantled, its walls and foundation too weak for the proposed aquarium—but there was a great desire that the feel and spirit of Cannery Row remain. For seven years, specialists transformed architectural blueprints into a system of complex seawater systems and giant exhibit tanks within 216,000 square feet of structures that complement the style of the old canneries. Towering fiberglass smokestacks were even added to give a complete feeling of authenticity.

As the buildings rose, exhibits were created. Sixteen-foot-tall acrylic windows, over seven inches thick and eight feet wide, were fitted together to form a sixty-six-foot-long home for an indoor kelp forest habitat where schools of sardines swim together as phantom large fish and sharks glide among the numerous other species. No one knew whether the kelp would survive. There were backup plans with plastic kelp. An open seawater system was created to pump up to two thousand gallons of fresh seawater per minute through the exhibits. The kelp and its habitat dwellers flourished.

David Packard not only provided financial support but worked at his forge in Big Sur to create exhibits for the aquarium, including the gears and pulleys of a simulated tide machine. Scientists and craftspeople worked together to offer an undersea world unparalleled in the country. Sculpted offsite, a parade of life-size whale models saluted the old Cannery Row establishments, abandoned buildings, and onlookers as they were hoisted through aquarium doors to suspension cables above walkways. Local veterinarian Tom Williams cheered at the completion of the thirty-foot otter exhibit. Prior to the aquarium's construction, he had kept orphan pups in his bathtub.

More than 6,500 specimens, representing 525 species of animals, plants, and birds found in Monterey Bay, are housed in the aquarium. The first level showcases the habitats of the Monterey Bay. The second floor houses rotating specialty exhibits such as the internationally recognized "Planet of the Jellies" and "Mating Games." A third-floor observation deck overlooks the Monterey Bay.

A new aquarium wing will open to the public in 1996 to further the mission of the Monterey Bay Aquarium: "To stimulate interest, increase knowledge, and promote stewardship of Monterey Bay and the world's ocean environment through innovative exhibits, public education, and scientific research." This new wing, devoted to the mysteries of the deep sea and open ocean, is being built adjacent to the main aquarium.

"This project is a tremendous challenge," according to Julie Packard. "The deep sea and ocean cover more than two thirds of our planet. Yet they've never been presented on the scale we're planning because the technology and marine science didn't exist to allow an aquarium to exhibit them."

The new wing will expand the aquarium's total exhibit space by almost 50 percent. Its centerpiece will be a one-million-gallon exhibit that showcases the outer bay waters. Blue and thresher sharks, ocean sunfish that can grow to be ten feet long, green sea turtles, barracuda, pelagic stingrays, and schools of fast swimming albacore, yellowfin tuna and other open-ocean fishes are expected to awe spectators in the thirty-four-foot-tall exhibit. Another permanent gallery will house the world's largest collection of mesmerizing jellyfish. A bank of microscopes will introduce visitors to the intricate life forms that exist as plankton—the microscopic base of a food web that supports all life in the sea. Deep-sea galleries will feature fishes and animals that live in the perpetual darkness of the more than two mile deep Monterey Canyon.

THE MONTEREY BAY SANCTUARY TODAY

You will probably first view sanctuary waters from a high vantage point, whether it be an airplane window or the summit of Highway 17 in the Santa Cruz Mountains. The deepest of these waters is found in the Monterey Bay Canyon, the heart of the sanctuary. The canyon cuts into the ocean floor beginning just a few hundred meters offshore from Moss Landing on the inner crescent of the Monterey Bay. Canyon walls plunge more than a mile deep just outside Monterey Bay, then spread out to join the ocean floor, 12,000 feet deep, at the canyon's seaward end. Over sixty miles in length, the long underwater canyon harbors life as large as endangered blue whales and as small as microscopic plankton. Divers explore the upper reaches of the canyon. A guided tour organized as a pleasure cruise or for whalewatching, fishing, or a semisubmersible expedition can take you to the surface of the sanctuary's most extensive habitat—the open ocean. (See tour listings, pp. 291–292.)

About thirty-five species of marine mammals occur along the California coast. These species are grouped in three orders: Cetacea, which includes whales, dolphins, and porpoises; Pinnipedia, which includes sea lions, fur seals, and true seals; and Carnivora, with the southern sea otter, which is related to minks, weasels, skunks, and badgers, as its one representative.

The sanctuary waters have long been noted for their whales. "It is impossible either to describe the number of whales with which we were surrounded, or their familiarity. They blowed every half a minute within half a pistol shot from our frigates," wrote Jean Francois Galaup de La Perouse on a 1786 early exploring expedition of the Monterey Bay area.

Biologists place the whales into two major categories, the Mysticeti (literally translated, "moustached") or baleen whales, and the Odontoceti, or toothed whales. Baleen whales, which are well represented in the ocean waters off the California coast, feed by filtering water containing shrimplike krill and other zooplankton into their mouths using brushlike strainers, called baleen. The gray whale, *Eschrichtius robustus*, which migrates farther than any mammal, is the best known to whalewatchers in the area. Roughly the size of ten elephants, the thirty-five- to fifty-foot-long, forty- to fifty-ton gray whale is marked by light gray splotches and a prominent midline ridge that melds to a series of bumps near its tail. The light splotches on the whale's skin are colonies of thousands of hitch-hiking barnacles. Whale biologists often tell whales apart by their different patterns of barnacle clusters.

The gray whale feeds on bottom-dwelling amphipods in the Bering Sea from late spring until early autumn. Then some twenty-one thousand gray whales begin a ten-thousand-mile migration to Baja California, where the mother gray whales give birth to their young in the lagoons, the only whale known to do so in shallows. Gray whales are most often seen throughout the sanctuary in a southbound migration, from December to mid February. Pods of gray whales most often swim in groups of four or five, but during the peak of migration, from January seventh to seventeenth, it is possible to see pods with up to fifteen individuals. Early birthings of calves in and near Monterey Bay have been reported each January.

The northbound migration spans mid-February to mid-May. Mothers and slow-swimming calves are the last to pass north. Sometimes the whales turn into the relatively calm waters of the Monterey Bay at the southern tip by Point Pinos. Whale sightings in the northern bay are unusual. You can see pictures in movies and books, but nothing quite equals the close eye-to-baseball-size-eye contact you make with these barnacle-covered giants while standing on the deck of one of the whalewatching boats that you can arrange to take out of Santa Cruz, Monterey, or San Simeon harbors.

Some of the best places to view whales from shore include: Davenport Cliffs, Asilomar Beach, Point Pinos, stretches of Pebble Beach including the Lone Cypress lookout, Point Lobos, and the highway pullouts located all along the Big Sur Coast. Gray whales can be seen close to shore at San Simeon Cove and along the Cambrian shore. Although they can be seen spouting and breaching with the naked eye, binoculars bring them closer.

The gray whale and humpback whales were the main prey of the "shore whaling" industry that had its beginnings in Monterey about 1854. They were harpooned from boats, towed ashore, rolled on the beaches, and their blubber rendered into oil in kettles over open fire pits. Whaling stations were established up and down the coast, at Pigeon Point, Davenport, Santa Cruz, Moss Landing, Monterey, Point Lobos, Big Sur, and San Simeon. These whaling stations and the slaughter of mothers and calves in the southern lagoons brought the gray whales to near extinction. The passing of the whaling industry and the tightened

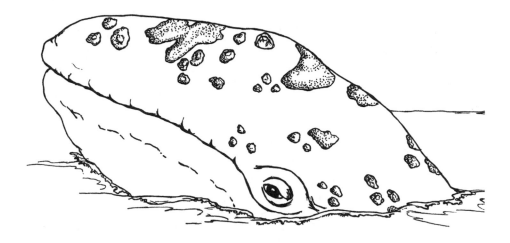

Gray Whale

government protection of the species has made the gray whale the first California species to be considered for removal from the endangered species list.

Other whales too are spotted in sanctuary waters. Blue whales, *Balaenoptera musculus,* arrive in late June or July in most years, with frequent spottings through October. The largest animal that has ever lived on earth, the blue whale is blue-gray in color, long and sleek. Reaching lengths of a hundred feet, blue whales feed in the sanctuary on a diet of several tons of krill each day. Humpback whales are often seen in the sanctuary beginning in late April and early May. These are black or gray, with some white on the throat and belly. The flippers of the humpback whale are very long, approximately one-third of the whale's body length. Humpbacks are known for their dramatic breaches above water and their songs.

Dolphins and porpoises are the smaller members of the toothed whale family. Dolphins are usually identified by their long beaks, whereas the shorter-beaked species are usually referred to as porpoises. The common dolphin, *Delphinus delphis*, and the Pacific white-sided dolphin, *Lagenorhynchus obliquidens,* are the most frequently sighted dolphins in the sanctuary. If you sail about the bay, you will probably experience dolphins leaping beside your boat. "I always feel happier when I see those fellers popping the waves alongside me," a local surfer told me. Among surfers it is felt that the presence of dolphins signals the absence of sharks.

Orcas, the largest members of the Odontoceti family, also frequent sanctuary waters. Adults grow to twenty-five feet in length, and they often hunt cooperatively in groups. Known commonly as "killer whales," the orcas are easily identified by their striking black and white markings, rounded flippers, and huge white dorsal fins.

As the Cetacea dominate ocean travelers' attention on the blue-green surface, colorful varieties of fishes and invertebrates draw divers' attention around the granite outcroppings, shale reef, and any of 1,276 known shipwrecks that jut up here and there from the soft, flat sea floor. Rockfish are common year-round. Salmon arrive in summer to feed. Anchovies, albacore, squid, and flatfishes are among the other main types found offshore. The waters of the sanctuary encompass much of the "red triangle," the section of California with the highest recorded number of white shark sightings and attacks. White sharks feed here on the seals, sea lions, and sea otters, among other sea mammals that fish the sanctuary waters.

The floating islands you see offshore are the tips of the kelp forest. Just as pyrite, "fools gold," fooled early miners into believing they had struck it rich, the bobbing bulbs of bull kelp, *Nereocystis*, fool many an otter seeker into thinking, even shouting, that they are viewing hundreds of bobbing heads offshore. The proper name indicates another comparison. Nereo means "sea nymph" or "mermaid." Wishful sailors may have seen the bulbs and surrounding leaflike blades as sea nymphs' heads with encircling hair. Otters do favor the kelp beds and often wrap themselves in the branches to keep from drifting with the currents. The bulbs of bull kelp, the most visible of the hundreds of sea plants in the sanctuary, are the "treetops" of underwater forests a hundred feet deep. The name comes from the hollow tapered stems, which resemble bull whips. Bull kelp is an annual that begins growing early in spring and reaches full size by autumn.

When conditions are right a different variety, giant kelp, *Macrocystis*, can grow up to ten inches a day—faster than any plant on earth. As you walk over kelp washed ashore in winter the sand may pop under your feet. You've found the remains of gas-filled bulbs (the size and shape of Christmas tree lights) that form the base of the long, reddish brown rippled blades that help the perennial giant kelp keep afloat. The kelp forests support a wide variety of sea life, including invertebrates and the larval and adult forms of many fishes.

Kelp wrack and varieties of sea plants wash to shore quite prolifically at Spanish Bay Beach in Pebble Beach (formerly known as Moss Beach) and along Asilomar Beach in Pacific Grove, especially by Jewell Avenue. Besides kelp, varieties include *Ulva*, or sea lettuce; *Laminaria*, shaped like a long-bladed oar; and *Egregia*, or feather boa. Around the turn of the nineteenth century the gathering of varieties of sea plants for art was a favorite pastime of tourists. If you turn over the kelp on the shore you will see that it teams with life—particularly the insects called sandhoppers and small crustations. This provides an important food source for the shorebirds. The earliest inhabitants of these coastal regions used *Nereocystis* for food. The dried blades can be eaten like potato chips or pickled. Kelp is much more a part of your life, too, than you may realize, as it is used in toothpaste, some commercial ice cream, and pharmaceuticals. Many visitors perceive the local shores to be polluted because of foamy waves and shores. The foam is not pollution but a natural by-product of decomposing kelp and other organisms.

The southern sea otter floats about the kelp forest like a jester, somersaults, and dives deep to resurface nearby. Along Point Lobos and sections of the Big Sur coast you can spot "rafts" of twenty and more floating otters. When I kayak the bay, I grab on to the kelp if my arms are tired, the current is too strong, or I just want a special view of an otter to last a while. Looking a bit like floating logs, otters are distinguished from pinnipeds by their thick dark fur. They rely on their thick coats for warmth in the cold waters; unlike pinnipeds and whales, they do not have a thick protective layer of blubber. Otter fur may be as thick as a million hairs per square inch.

While swimming on their backs with hind webbed feet waving as flags, otters use tools such as rocks to pry abalone loose from rocks beneath the surface. You might see an otter tuck its favored prying rock in the body sac under its arm, dive repeatedly, then finally float on its back to stuff a shell's soft insides in its mouth. Otters also smash enclosed shellfish, most notably urchins, against rocks that are balanced on their stomachs to get at the soft morsels inside the shells. Just as ladybugs keep my roses from being devoured by aphids, otters keep the

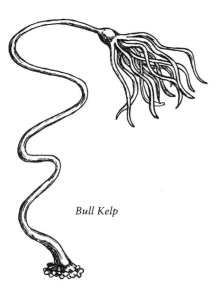

Bull Kelp

Sea Palm

Sea Otter

kelp forests from being devoured by sea urchins and abalones. When all populations are in balance, otters limit the growth of the grazing abalone and urchins, which allows for greater kelp growth, which in turn supports new abalone and urchins. When the otter population was at its lowest ebb, the abalone population bloomed explosively. Vast reserves of abalone were harvested, first for their shell value and later as food. Ironically, some abalone harvesters now complain that otters limit their catches.

To distinguish female from male otters is not always easy. An especially rambunctious juvenile is likely to be a male. Females are often identified by their bloodied or scarred noses. As part of the mating ritual the male otter pulls the female's head back with his flipper and bites her nose severely. Most pups are born between February and March or between August and September. Mothers can often be seen sculling along, each with a small furry pup resting on her stomach. Researchers at the aquarium have discovered that otter mothers pass food and tool preferences to their offspring. The grandchildren of one mother at Lover's Point in Pacific Grove are noted for their preference of beer bottle hammers. Voracious eaters,

Red Abalone

otter fathers put their stomachs first and may even hold babies hostage for a share of a mother otter's food.

Although otters were noted as shore-dwelling animals in the early 1800s, they are now radically reduced in numbers and rarely seen on shore. Counts are taken each May to trace the comeback of a species that once numbered close to twenty thousand, then was nearly wiped out by hunters who prized their thick pelts. By the midnineteenth century hunters had virtually exterminated the southern sea otter. A few scientists were aware of the otter's survival, but the newspapers didn't believe a local restaurateur who reported he had "rediscovered" the California otter in a bed of kelp near Bixby Creek on the Big Sur Coast in 1938. The range of the over two thousand endangered otters now stretches from Año Nuevo Island north of the Monterey Bay to Point Purismo in Southern California. Otters remain extremely vulnerable to the effects of a large oil spill because of their need for air insulation in their fluffy fur. Part of the reason for the length of the Marine Sanctuary is the necessity to protect otter habitat. On Saturdays from 11 p.m. to 4 p.m. during late spring and summer the volunteers from Friends of the Sea Otter in Carmel (408/625-3290) set up free viewing scopes at various locations along the bay from Cannery Row to Point Pinos.

The rugged rocky shores that surround the aquarium are hundred-million-year-old exotic-terrain granites, possibly formed in the South Pacific. When the Pacific plate dipped under the North American plate, millions of years ago, the pressure melted the underlying rocks to form granite, which cooled slowly and floated northward on the magma on top of basalts. Large feldspar crystals can be found in the rock formations from the aquarium to the southern reaches of the Big Sur Coast. The granite results in the crystalline clearness of the water. More conglomerate rock foundations around Santa Cruz cause the water to be murkier on the north end of the bay.

After the high tide recedes from rocky outcroppings by the shore, water remains in depressions in the rocks: tidepools. Waves wash blankets of food over these tidepools, homes to colorful creatures including shore crabs, flowery sea anemones, sculpins, and spiny sea urchins. Barnacles open their shells and sweep the water with feathery legs to catch food. More species of sea stars are recorded within the sanctuary than any other place on earth. Limpet and chiton populations are also some of the most diverse in the world. An abundance of tidepools are located north of Santa Cruz in San Mateo County at Fitzgerald Marine Reserve, at Natural Bridges Park in Santa Cruz, along Ocean View Boulevard in Pacific Grove, along Seventeen Mile Drive in Pebble Beach, along Carmel beaches, at several park beaches along Big Sur, and near Point Piedras Blancas in the southern reaches of the sanctuary.

The first step in tidepooling is to locate a tide table to find the time of the lowest tide. Free tide table booklets are available at the local Longs Drug stores, the concessions on Fisherman's Wharf in Monterey, and at many of the shops

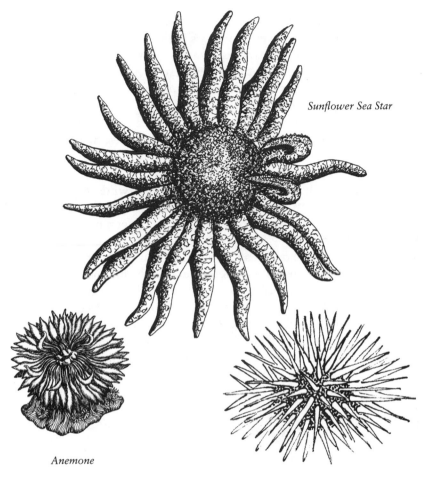

Sunflower Sea Star

Anemone

Sea Urchin

along the Big Sur Coast. Bring extra shoes—an old pair of tennis shoes is fine—to get close to the pools. Remember to be aware of the ocean; never turn your back on the waves while turning your attention to the creatures of the rocky shores. Sneaker waves can whisk tidepoolers off secure ledges. If you tug creatures off rocks just to look at them, you may tear their legs off. There is no harm in picking up creatures that release easily. They need frequent dips in water and like to return to their territory in the original tidepools.

At first tidepooling sounds like a treasure hunt. "A purple sea star! Sea anemones—hundreds of them! A crab, over there, he's under that rock!" After the initial excitement you might want to choose any tidepool and observe it at leisure. Your reward will be a greater understanding of the creatures. Tidepools are the creatures' homes, so walk lightly, and let them stay, for the good of the sanctuary.

The kelp forests and rocky shores are also home base for many seals and sea lions. Eighty percent of the marine mammals in the northern Pacific spend all or part of each year in the sanctuary waters. The land shakes when the huge elephant seals hunker heavily across their Año Nuevo reserve at the northern border of Santa Cruz County. Sea lions drape themselves on rocks along the coast. Harbor seals give birth in spring along the Cypress Point shore in Pebble Beach and the Big Sur Coast. Over the last twenty years the estimated populations in California of northern elephant seals (80,000), California sea lions (estimated at 110,000), harbor seals (20,000), and northern fur seals (4,000) have rebounded to numbers far greater than those of 1910, when the northern elephant seals numbered just 200. California sea lions are making harbor masters work overtime as they take over boat docks from Monterey to San Francisco. Conservationists and representatives of fisheries are studying the effect of rising pinniped populations on the fishing industry.

To observe these playful mammals, bring binoculars and check tide tables. In general seals and sea lions will be out feeding during the highest tides and resting between tides and diving periods. All but the northern fur seal are commonly seen year-round. Several clues help viewers tell the difference between true seals and sea lions. Check for external ear flaps; sea lions have tiny ear flaps, seals don't. "Seals sink, sea lions dive" often holds true. True seals float in the water vertically, with only their heads sticking out, and submerge by sinking back tail first instead of diving like the sea lions. Sea lions often raft and hold their flippers

Sea Lion

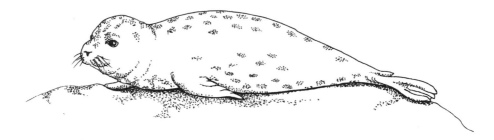

Harbor Seal

straight up in the air. Networks of tiny veins in the flippers bring the warmth of the sun or the cooling air to their bodies. When the animals haul out on beaches or rocks their colorings, vocalizations, and flippers will help you identify them. The tawny brown Stellar sea lions are the largest; bulls reach ten feet and two thousand pounds. Bulls have a leonine mane and roar. If it barks, it's the smaller and darker California sea lion that is used as the trained "seal" in circuses. Sea lions can walk on their hind legs. If it's bouncing and wriggling like an inchworm there's an excellent chance you've spotted the chunky harbor seal. Harbor seals have spotted silvery gray coats and large eyes. If you are walking along their beach they may follow you curiously from just offshore. Harbor seals groom with the long claws on their flexible fore flippers. Seals and sea lions both seek refuge on beaches during rough winter weather. On the sands of Año Nuevo the elephant seal bulls often stage bloody battles to win harems.

As the largest of the pinnipeds in this region, the male northern elephant seal is recognized for its large drooping snout and mammoth size, up to twenty-one feet long and five thousand pounds. At UC Santa Cruz's Long Marine Laboratory, Burney Le Boeuf heads the world's longest-running study of elephant seals. One of his findings is that the elephant seal can dive the deepest of any mammal studied—to over four thousand feet.

Miles and miles of sandy beaches in the sanctuary rise in places up to five hundred feet high. Waves deposit sand on beaches and in the mouths of man-made harbors, and westerly winds blow the sand inland, where it meets a drift line of coastal plants and forms a barrier of dunes. Over time the dunes themselves grow a mat of vegetation, which anchors the inland side. The dune system along the inner crescent of the Monterey Bay is one of the most extensive in the Western United States. Many volunteers, ranging from preschoolers to community elders, are replanting native vegetation along dunes that have been trampled, mined, and planted with carpets of ice-plant. Two years ago our family spent one Saturday morning planting sprigs of buckwheat and coastal daisy in the dunes along the Asilomar Beach in Pacific Grove. We had walked the ocean-view trail along Asilomar often and planted as a way to give back. Now when I walk the path I realize the gift was ultimately to us. We used to walk through stretches and stretches of quiet, monotonous ice-plant spikes and focus on the beauty of the crashing surf. Now the walk includes butterflies flitting over small purple flowers, chirping birds, and grazing deer. Healthy dunes, planted in several varieties of native vegetation, support abundant wildlife that ranges from endangered butterflies, lizards, and mice to songbirds, hawks, and deer. Many state beaches schedule nature walks to help visitors and residents become more acquainted with dune life. You might consider joining a volunteer dune restoration planting during a coastal visit. Nature will water the planting, the deer will trim it, and on your return visit you will get flowers at your feet.

The farthest inland reaches of the sanctuary habitats are the most fragile. At the center of the coast along the Monterey Bay, Elkhorn Slough flows inland for twelve miles. Rain-swollen creeks wash nutrients from inland to the coastal wetlands; from offshore, the nutrients flow inland along the same channels during high tide. Thus fed from both sides, sloughs and other wetlands are nurseries for many fish species, home to a variety of mud-dwelling animals, and the food source and nesting habitat for millions of migratory birds.

Numerous sea and shore birds roost in rocky outcroppings and dot sandy beaches along the sanctuary. Endangered brown pelicans, cormorants, snowy plovers, and common murrets are among the ninety-four different species of birds found in the region.

On land the endangered brown pelican is one of the most comical birds you can watch. It waddles along, balancing its huge scooped bill above its neck. In flight, the pelican commands the skies. Pelicans fly singly and in long gliding squadrons of up to thirty birds. When a hunting pelican spots food it tips toward the water, wings bent in a V, and dives like a jet straight down at rapid speed, then hits the water so hard the fish two yards beneath the surface are stunned. The pelican swoops up the stunned fish, drains water from the sides of its bill, and stores the fish in its stomach. Abundant air sacs in its bill protect the pelican during its high-speed dives.

In the 1960s and early 1970s high percentages of DDT in their diets caused the pelican populations to drop dramatically. Today the pelicans are endangered but recovering.

A sea gull is just a sea gull until you begin to look closely at feather patterns and feet, bill, and eye colors. Over a dozen varieties of gulls visit the sanctuary. Western gulls are large and dark with long yellow beaks. Heerman's gulls have bright scarlet bills, white heads, and gray bodies. Juvenile gulls are usually lightly spotted. One of nature's designs for gulls' grabby nature became clear at the birth of a harbor seal along Cypress Point beach, in Pebble Beach. As the mother lay exhausted after the birth, the baby lay nearby caught in a placental covering. Observers from a blind considered approaching to save the baby,

Brown Pelican

though threatening the mother could have a counter effect, when a trio of gulls swooped down, gobbled the placenta and freed the baby, and even snipped the umbilical cord—leaving mother and baby safe.

Whether you are a scientist, avid beachcomber, or occasional visitor, each moment in the sanctuary brings new discoveries. The zones and varieties of life within the sanctuary are waiting to be explored with care. The Monterey Bay Marine Sanctuary Diver's Map published by Cooper Brothers Maps (P.O. Box 148, Pacific Grove, CA 93950), offers a detailed description of sanctuary waters from Monterey to Point Sur. The map is especially valuable for divers, kayakers, surfers, and boaters.

TOUR: THE AQUARIUM

The Monterey Bay Aquarium exhibits are a living extension of the Monterey Bay Sanctuary. Visitors are encouraged to first explore a habitats trail that begins to the left of the aquarium's main entrance. One of several aquarium shops stocked with a good selection of natural history books, posters, quality nature items, and tourist treasures is located near the entrance. Before you start along the trail, check the visitor information board just inside the main entrance for times of special shows, such as Kelp Forest, Otter Feeding, Tidepool Divers, and Live Net. The shows are popular, informative, and will add to your enjoyment

Hermit Crab

of the aquarium. Plan to get to their locations fifteen minutes early for good viewing spots. Aquarists often elicit audience questions as part of the shows.

The three-story kelp forest marks the beginning of the habitats trail. The kelp forest looks so natural, many visitors believe they are looking through a window to the bay. Anchored to rocks by tangled holdfasts, the bladed strands of giant kelp grow through filtered sunlit water, spreading flat blades and bobbing bulbs. Sunlight pours through the roofless exhibit. Pumps propel up to two thousand gallons of seawater a minute through jets to create natural currents.

Julie Packard rates the Kelp Forest exhibit as the most exciting in the aquarium. "These beautiful plants exhibit remarkable adaptations. At a hundred feet they are taller than most trees, but if they remained stiff like trees they would perish; instead they are flexible, they go with the flow. Different pigments capture sunlight in the various light changes at ocean depths. The exhibit represents a challenge met. We were the first to recreate the world of the kelp forest in an aquarium."

Dark turban snails and amber kelp crabs glide along the swaying branches. Pictures at the rim of the Kelp Forest exhibit help you identify some thirty-five different species of fish circling about. You will certainly notice a flash of gold as Senoritas dart by on their way to nibble tiny creatures from rocks and the backs of other fish. Like ocean opossums, kelp rockfish hang about, upside down and motionless. Leopard sharks glide by. These sharks aren't after anyone's arm. The electroreceptors in their snouts are searching for the single foot of the sea worm.

Red algae cover the rocky bottom, which also boasts a wide variety of sea stars and sea anemones. If it weren't for volunteer divers like Patrick Malone and Gary Haas, all you would see is red algae. Brought in from the open sea by the pumps, the red algae attach to any hard surface, including windows. Patrick Malone waited for two years for his name to get to the top of a volunteer waiting list; now he drives over a hundred miles from San Francisco to Monterey every other Saturday to clean windows by scrubbing the algae with suction cups and elbow grease. Haas leads diving tours in various locations around the world, but his favorite spot is the aquarium. "It's a thrill," relates Haas. "Out in the bay the dives are spectacular, especially off Coral Beach in Pacific Grove, but you never get the opportunity to swim with so many species at one time. These fish are fed to keep them satisfied and prevent them from preying on each other. It's a fish Club Med. Out in the ocean the leopard sharks will spook at fifteen feet; here they brush against you. The best part, though, is picking a kid who is transfixed on your cleaning. You move very slowly, turning your body upside down. Suddenly the kid catches your upside-down-grin and shrieks with laughter. The people are almost as fun to watch outside as the fish are in here." Divers like Malone and Haas enjoy the Kelp Forest exhibit most when they talk with the audience through an underwater microphone, during the twice-daily feeding shows.

In the adjacent Monterey Bay Habitats exhibit, leopard sharks, a large sevengill shark, and smaller sixgill sharks cruise a ninety-foot tank designed especially for their long glides. Leopard sharks and dogfish are fed smelt and other fish twice a day. Emma, the largest sevengill in captivity, is fed pieces of salmon (at the end of a long pole) twice a week, and more, depending on her cycles of hunger. The habitats meld together here as they do in the bay. Clouds of rockfish float over rocky reefs as flatfish lie half-buried in nearby patches of sand. To accentuate the Monterey Bay Aquarium's quest for authenticity, real shale reefs were brought from the bay, with clams, mussels, and other dwellers intact. Pilings from an old Monterey wharf, encrusted with decades-old anemones, barnacles, and tubeworms, anchor the far end of the habitats. Hungry surfperches pick their meal of mollusks as they would in open water.

You may see an aquarist such as Andy Case vacuuming the bottom. When I asked Andy how he works alongside the sharks he replied, "I move slowly, just as you would in a field of cows. The important thing is to keep them from getting excited, so they don't panic and injure themselves."

Andy's favorite tank is that of the curious octopus that seems to enjoy his gentle pats. Along the same wall with the octopus, exhibits highlight the deep reefs, the sandy sea floor, the shale reefs, and the slough.

The corridor of exhibits then opens to an interactive area, which is bordered by an aviary of sandy shorebirds. Signboards help to identify the flowers of native dunes. Foraging sandpipers, avocets, plovers, and black-necked stilts probe the shore for food. My personal wish is that the aquarium double the size of this exhibit, as it is often crowded with people straining to view such treasures as the nests of ducks and marsh wrens.

Outside the aviary several bat rays flap through their shallow pool like giant birds. This is a place to roll up your sleeves. The spikes at the base of the bat rays' tails have been removed so that visitors can reach into the water to pet their silky backs as they glide by on their circular journey. Around 4 p.m. the bat rays hover near the sides of the pool and shake their wings. Lucky bystanders feed them a concoction of squid, clams, and shrimp.

A touch pool awaits visitors at the far corner of this floor. Sea stars, rock crabs, sea slugs, chitons, and various tidepool animals are available here for close tactile exploration. This is a helpful introduction to tidepooling, as you can ask the trained docents here questions.

Other highlights of the first floor include the outdoor great tidepool, a recreated coastal trout stream, and the otter exhibit. In the early days of the otter exhibit the otters were provided with live shellfish so visitors could watch them use rocks as tools to crack the shells. The playful otters used the rocks and discarded shells to pound and scrape against their see-through walls, making it necessary to feed them only the soft insides.

Upstairs, the aquarium features world-renowned special exhibits. Different views of the Kelp Forest, a machine that replicates tides, and an upper-story observation deck border the special exhibits. The observation decks offer captivating construction views of the next wing, which will open in 1996.

WHAT ELSE TO SEE AND DO

After visiting the aquarium you may be asking yourself, now what? Other tours in this book begin right outside the front door. The aquarium is built half in Monterey and half in Pacific Grove; flip a coin. We next visit Monterey, California's most historic city. If your coin says Pacific Grove, skip ahead one chapter.

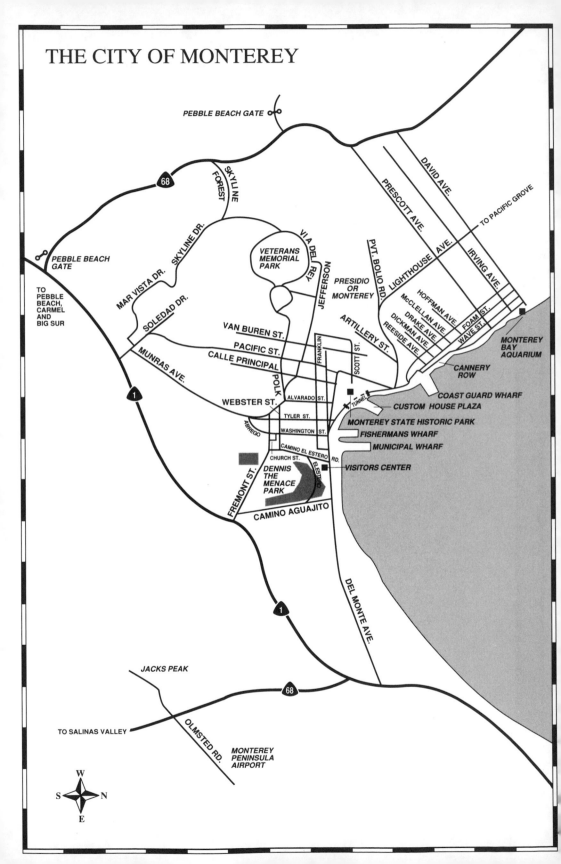

CHAPTER 2

THE CITY OF MONTEREY

SHOWCASE OF HISTORY

Monterey's vibrant downtown has clusters of the most historic buildings in California. Cannery Row, Fisherman's Wharf, and sunny beaches front the open harbor.

GETTING READY

THE BEST TIMES TO VISIT AND THE SPECIAL EVENTS

Traffic to Monterey can be quite heavy during summer weekends and three-day-holiday weekends throughout the year. However, Monterey has so many visitor destinations, spread over so wide an area, that with two exceptions the city never seems crowded. Cannery Row and Fisherman's Wharf can get shoulder to shoulder during such weekends as Memorial Day and Labor Day, but the upbeat atmosphere of both places make them feel like big parties rather than crowded spots. Traffic does get unpleasantly congested there. Walk or take the WAVE shuttle bus as often as possible.

Monterey offers many special theater and music activities during the summer. Most of these are centered near Fisherman's Wharf at the Custom House Plaza. Monterey offers a variety of ways to spend your days, from early morning to the late night hours.

John Steinbeck's birthday is celebrated on February 27, with music, play excerpts, and readings. In April, the Monterey History and Art Association presents an annual tour of historic adobes (408/372-2608), led by local guides dressed in period costumes. Plays, music, and dances of the period enliven the adobes, some of which are opened at night. Funds raised support the Monterey History and Art Association. The oldest continuous jazz festival in the United States returns to the city annually in September, bringing the biggest names on the scene and hot rising stars. Concerts are held outdoors under the fog, the stars, and the occasional jet from the nearby airport.

CLIMATE AND CLOTHING

Monterey shares the typical coastal weather pattern. Due to its location on the bay, the city gets the sun earlier on foggy days and more often than communities to the south. Artist Douglas Walker paints outside his studios in Monterey and Carmel. "Monterey's changeable light seems to alter maybe four or five times during the day. In Carmel, if the morning is foggy, the sun and fog don't travel so fast and I can usually paint in an even, consistent light."

Dress in layers for the changeable temperatures. Casual clothing is the norm for this city. Good walking shoes are a must for the many excellent walking paths.

TOUR LENGTHS

Part of the downtown is a state historic park that features over two dozen adobes, many of which are separate museums. To really appreciate Monterey and the history of California plan to spend a whole day. You can walk to Cannery Row from downtown in thirty minutes, by picking up the walking and bike path along the Custom House Plaza. Allow at least two hours for Cannery Row. Monterey is so rich in history, it really deserves at least a weekend; this is the cradle of United States' government in the West.

WILDLIFE WISDOM

Sea lions and pelicans hang out at the Municipal Wharf. In the winter young male sea lions crowd the Coast Guard Wharf. Sea lions have been known to haul out on boats anchored in the harbor, causing them to sink. Otters are commonly seen in the waters off Cannery Row. You can rent kayaks for closer views of otters and sea lions at the beach north of Fisherman's Wharf and at the Custom House Plaza. Jacks Peak, a regional park located in the pines above Monterey, is a birders' favorite. The trails in Jacks Peak offer dramatic mountain-to-sea views. Jacks Peak is a day-use-only park. To reach it travel east on Highway 68 and turn right on Olmsted Road.

VISITOR INFORMATION

The Monterey Visitor's Center, 401 Camino El Estero, is open seven days a week for walk-in traffic. The Monterey State Historic Park (408/649-7118), in the Stanton Center near the Custom House Plaza, the Monterey Peninsula Chamber of Commerce (408/649-1770), 380 Alvarado Street, and the Cannery Row Association (408/373-1902), in the green train car by the bike path near Prescott and Hawthorne streets, also provide visitor information. Pick up a copy of the free *Coast Weekly* for theater listings, music, and special events.

PARKING

To cover all possibilities, pick up the city brochure "Smart Parking in Monterey." You may want to call or write the Monterey Chamber of Commerce for a copy of it before you visit. Parking in Monterey is available in lots, on metered streets, and along unmetered streets for limited time periods. You must have a residential permit to park for longer than one hour in certain residential sections; look for the signs that designate these.

Change for meters is available at the parking attendant booth in Fisherman's Wharf, the harbor master's office, and at lot 22, located between Cannery Row and Reeside Avenue. Usually the farther you are willing to walk, the less you will pay for parking. The most expensive lots charge $1.00 for each half hour. At the preferred downtown parking garage, on Washington Street between Franklin Street and Del Monte Avenue, parking is available at $3.50 for the full day with Sundays often free. At this writing the least expensive lot is located across from the Larkin House, on Calle Principal, where you can park for up to twelve hours, $.25 each hour.

ALTERNATE TRANSPORTATION

The WAVE shuttle bus connects the downtown area with Cannery Row, for a nominal fee. The Simoneau Metro-Amtrak Plaza is located downtown across from the Cooper-Molera Complex. From here you can walk to all downtown locations, and the local bus service is convenient.

PLACES TO STAY

Monterey offers a variety of accommodations throughout the city. Cannery Row, the downtown area, and lower Munras Avenue are within walking distance of most locations of visitor interest except La Mirada Museum and Dennis the Menace Park.

CANNERY ROW

MONTEREY PLAZA HOTEL, 400 Cannery Row. This hotel offers sweeping bay views, 285 remodeled spacious rooms and eight grand suites, and full conference facilities. Floral fabrics and duvet bed coverings create a warm, homey feeling. Minibars, VCRs, computer hook-ups, and terry cloth robes. Full fitness center. Restaurant and lounge. 800/631-1339. AX, MC, V; others also accepted. For two, from $145.00 to 195.00.

SPINDRIFT INN, 652 Cannery Row. Situated along the bay, this elegant and romantic inn features canopy feather beds, woodburning fireplaces, and ocean views. Refrigerators, VCRs, and valet parking. Special packages available (lovely for honeymoons). 408/646-8900, 800/841-1879 (in California), or 800/225-2901. AX, MC,V; others also accepted. For two, from $200.00 to $300.00. Winter rates available.

DEL MONTE BEACH

MONTEREY BEACH HOTEL, (off Highway 1, Del Rey Oaks exit), 2600 Sand Dunes Drive. Your room is close to the sand and surf at this bright and airy beach-front hotel, which offers 196 newly refurbished rooms. Oceanside rooms have beautiful bay views. Restaurant, lounge, banquet rooms, pool, and spa. 408/394-3321 or 800/242-8627. AX, MC, V; others also accepted. For two, from $99.00 to $149.00.

DOWNTOWN

DOUBLETREE HOTEL, (by Fisherman's Wharf), Two Portola Plaza. A perfect plaza location for visiting historic downtown Monterey and Fisherman's Wharf. Beautiful atrium lobby. Large rooms with calming pastel decor, some with ocean views. Full service. Also the site of the Monterey Conference Center. Pool, restaurant, lounge. 408/649-4511 or 800/528-0444. AX, MC, V; others also accepted. For two, from $125.00 to $225.00.

HOTEL PACIFIC, 300 Pacific Street. In a garden setting, the feeling and adobe style of Old Monterey in newer construction. The hotel specializes in comfort, service, and amenities. Country-style decor with private decks and fireplaces. Very few rooms have a view of the city or ocean. Refrigerators, wet bars, and some whirlpools. 408/373-5700. AX, MC, V; others also accepted. For two, from $150.00 to $215.00.

MUNRAS AVENUE

MARIPOSA INN, 1386 Munras Avenue. Though Munras Avenue is a busy street of motels and hotels leading from the freeway to downtown, every effort is made by the management to secure the quietest room possible for guests. Pastel walls, fireplaces, and newer facilities make this a pleasant place to stay. Beautiful gardens surround the best pool and spa location in the area. In-room coffee; complimentary breakfast in a sunny community room or on the garden deck. Most rooms with fireplaces, some with private spas. 408/649-1414. AX, MC, V; others also accepted. For two, from $70.00 to $140.00.

EAST OF HIGHWAY 1

LONE OAK MOTEL, 2221 North Fremont Street. This reasonably priced motel offers comfortable rooms. Although Fremont is a busy street, the courtyard of the motel is set back from the noise. Some rooms have fireplaces and hot tubs.

TV, fresh brewed coffee in the rooms, and a shared spa are available for all guests. 408/372-4924. AX, MC, V; others also accepted. For two, from $38.00 to $125.00.

RESTAURANTS

ABALONETTI, 57 Fisherman's Wharf. Here enjoy casual dining in a bright dining room or outside on a private terrace. Oceanside views on the wharf. Fresh fish from the private loading dock; a dozen varieties of calamari dishes; excellent Caesar salad. Lunch and dinner. 408/373-1851. AX, MC, V. Entrees, from $14.00 to $40.00.

CAFE FINA, 47 Fisherman's Wharf. Here find Fisherman's Wharf dining for formal occasions, with linen tablecloths, flowers, and ocean views, and for casual meals, with brick-oven pizzas and homemade fettucini and ravioli. Mesquite-grilled fresh fish, meats, and chicken. Lunch and dinner. 408/372-5200. AX, MC, V; others also accepted. Entrees, from $11.00 to $25.00.

CASA GUTIERREZ, 5090 Calle Principal. This Mexican restaurant, built in 1843, is located in one of two original Mexican-style adobes remaining in Monterey. Shrimp fajitas and carne asada are two selections from a variety of Mexican dishes. Lunch and dinner. 408/375-0095. AX, MC, V; others also accepted. Entrees, mostly under $10.00.

CHARACTERS, 350 Calle Principal. A sports bar with innovative food. Inside you'll find walls covered with sports prints, twelve sports monitors, pool, live entertainment, and dancing. "Souper bowl" soups, salads, pizzas. Lunch and dinner. 408/647-4020. AX, MC, V. Selections, mostly under $10.00.

CIBO, 301 Alvarado Street. Dark wood and patterned carpets add to the European ambiance of this Italian country-style restaurant. All pastas are fresh; the swordfish spadini rolled in bread crumbs, pine nuts, and currants is very special. 408/649-8151. AX, MC, V. Entrees, from $14.00 to $21.00.

FRESH CREAM, 100 C Heritage Harbor, 99 Pacific and Scott streets. This formal restaurant features understated elegance; there are Impressionist prints, a spiral staircase to the lounge, and three private rooms for more intimate dining. French cuisine with a California flair. Impeccable service. Dinner. 408/375-9798. AX, MC, V; others also accepted. Entrees, mostly under $40.00.

SARDINE FACTORY, 701 Wave Street. The Captain's Room, with a fireplace and portraits of sea captains, is one of five rooms that each captures a mood or time in the history of Cannery Row. For small gatherings, guests can dine around a handcarved table in the wine cellar. The Baltino, fresh Monterey prawns sauteed with tomatoes, mushrooms, and garlic, glazed with vermouth, and the Monterey pasta dish, with Monterey prawns, baby lobster tail, scallops, linguini, roasted bell pepper, glazed onion, and brandy sauce, are two selections from the impressive menu featuring continental fare. Extensive "vault" of fine wines, including rare vintages. Dinner. 408/373-3775. AX, MC, V; others also accepted. Entrees from $12.00 to $30.00.

SPADARO'S, 650 Cannery Row. The waves break outside your window at this family-owned restaurant. Specialities include Italian fare, seafood, and pastas. Lunch and dinner. 408/372-8881. AX, MC, V. Entrees, from $10.00 to $18.00.

DIRECTIONS

◆

All traffic to Monterey follows Highway 1 (see the directions to the Monterey Bay Aquarium, pp.20–21). The directions below serve as general guides to the Highway 1 freeway exits.

For southbound travelers (exits are listed north to south):
The Del Rey Oaks (218) exit leads west to Del Monte State Beach and inland to the town of Del Rey Oaks.

The Del Monte Avenue / Pacific Grove exit leads to Del Monte Avenue, the main surface street that parallels the bay. It passes the Naval Postgraduate School and Fisherman's Wharf and continues to Cannery Row and Pacific Grove.

Casa Verde Way continues to the right (northwest) to Del Monte Avenue. It continues up the hill on the other side of Del Monte Avenue to Del Monte State Beach.

The Salinas Highway, 68, intersects with Olmsted Road, which leads to the airport and Jacks Peak. Highway 68 continues to Salinas.

The Central Monterey exit is one and one-half miles south of the Del Monte Avenue exit and leads to historic downtown Monterey as well as leading to Camino El Estero. Camino El Estero leads to the Monterey Visitor's Center, Dennis the Menace Park, and finally Del Monte Avenue. Brown directional signs along this route help you locate destinations.

The Soledad Drive / Munras Avenue exit leads to the downtown by way of Munras Avenue and the Del Monte Shopping Center. If you continue straight on Soledad Drive, then turn right at Pacific Avenue, brown directional signs will guide you to the downtown area and Cannery Row.

For northbound travelers (exits are listed south to north):
The Munras Avenue exit intersects with Soledad Avenue. Turn left at Soledad and right at Pacific Avenue, which leads to the downtown and, finally, to Cannery Row and the aquarium. Munras Avenue passes the Del Monte Shopping Center and a long line of motels and ends in the historic downtown of Monterey.
The Aguajito Road exit leads to Monterey Peninsula College, the fairgrounds, and Del Monte Golf Course.
The Salinas Highway, 68, Casa Verde Way, and Del Rey Oak exit directions are the same as for southbound.

INTRODUCTION TO MONTEREY WITH HISTORICAL HIGHLIGHTS

Monterey is a historical highlight, a veritable open-air museum. Monterey was the point where Vizcaino landed in 1602 and claimed "the Californias" for Spain. It was the site of the first Northern California mission and the capital of the Spanish and Mexican regimes. The state's constitution was drawn in downtown's Colton Hall.

From two-thousand-year-old Rumsen village sites to the cutting edge of modern marine technology facilities, Monterey is like a layer cake of California history. In fitting juxtaposition on any given day in the bay, the tall ship *The Californian* may sail to port over the exploration zone of the MBARI ROV submersible research vessel. Even above water several centuries of experiences intertwine. The feeling you get while holding on to the solid wood runner of the tall ship as the latest in 1990s tour vessels, the *Nautilus* semisubmersible submarine, passes by is definitely akin to a Rip Van Winkle experience. Step ashore. Most of the historic parts of Monterey can be reached by interconnecting walking paths.

The city of Monterey extends from the bay on gentle hills to surrounding upland forests. From Presidio Hill in the northwestern section of the city you see the layout of the land, facilities, and population of Monterey as well as enjoy incredible ocean views; they stretch from your vantage point across the bay, to the Gabilan Mountains. Once the site of a Rumsen village, the hill has rested under four different flags—serving as the location for gun encampments and forts of Colonial Spain, Mexico, Argentina, and the United States. The hill is now part of the Presidio of Monterey, home of the prestigious Defense Language Institute.

From Presidio Hill your gaze may focus on the ribbon of cars that flows along Lighthouse Avenue, separating the Presidio and its surrounding residential area of New Monterey from Cannery Row. You can pick out the two fiberglass faux smokestacks of the Monterey Bay Aquarium. Cannery Row, once a line of sardine factories, now hooks visitors with a selection of shops, restaurants, and motels, many of which are within original or rebuilt cannery buildings. The discerning eye finds many of the haunts John Steinbeck wrote about in *Cannery Row* and other books.

A walking and bike path, a former route of the Southern Pacific Railway, borders the Monterey waterfront, where three piers jut into the bay. The loud barking of sea lions may drift up to your vantage point from the Coast Guard Wharf, the first of these piers. Tourists and locals frequent fresh seafood restaurants and curio shops at Fisherman's Wharf, the second of them. Fishing boats unload their catch at the third, known as the Municipal Wharf.

The historic heart of Monterey lies in a confusing mishmash of downtown streets that fan out from the Fisherman's Wharf area. Unlike the East Coast, Monterey was not won from the colonial rule of the English. All of California and what are now seven adjacent states were under the rule of Spain at the time of the American Revolution. After Mexicans successfully revolted against colonial Spanish rule, these lands became part of the country of Mexico. U.S. rule of the seven-state area was first officially declared when land regiments under the command of Commodore Sloat raised the U.S. flag in a bloodless takeover at the Custom House, one of thirty-seven downtown historic adobes that now serve a multitude of uses, including as museums, a restaurant, banks, and private residences. During the summer, and at select times during the year, actors and volunteers fill the shoes of notables from the city's history and roam the historic section in period dress, engaging in lively debates, pontificating their philosophies, and reminiscing about the life that was, in Old Monterey. Where trade in hide and tallow occupied the streets a hundred years ago, coffee shops and bookstores now anchor a revitalized downtown, one that boasts the most historic buildings east of Williamsburg.

Lighthouse Drive continues south from the wharf and downtown areas to El Estero, once a marshy estuary, now a landlocked lake. Dennis the Menace Park, a circular lakeside path, and a historic cemetery surround the lower Lake Estero, while the tiny upper lake accompanies the newest part to the Monterey Peninsula Museum of Art, beautiful La Mirada.

Custom House in Monterey

As you view Monterey from Presidio Hill, the sunlit beaches and forests seem so inviting, it is clear why Charles Crocker of the Southern Pacific Railway deemed Monterey the "most elegant seaside resort in the world." Crocker directed the building of the historic Hotel Del Monte. The railroad was extended to Monterey in the late 1800s, and the Hotel Del Monte attracted trainloads of San Franciscans to the peninsula. The twice-rebuilt Hotel Del Monte, with surrounding grounds, now houses the Naval Postgraduate School.

Various residential areas fill the pine forests that surround Monterey. Highway 1 cuts through the city limits with Del Monte Golf Course, Monterey Peninsula Community College, the County Fairgrounds, and the airport lying on the highway's east side. Farther inland, on Highway 68, the newest business park is situated at Ryan Ranch. If you are driving north to the peninsula on Highway 68 you will pass the entrance for the highest mountain in the area, Jacks Peak. From Presidio Hill it can be spotted as the high peak just south of the airport.

In the late 1800s a land investor named David Jacks acquired most of the land that now comprises Monterey, Seaside, Del Rey Oaks, Pacific Grove, and Pebble Beach, plus additional acreage. In 1859 David Ashley, a partner of Jacks, was employed by the city of Monterey to investigate the title it had received to thousands of acres of Mexican rancho lands. He presented the city with a $991.00 bill for his service. When the city leaders couldn't meet his wage from the empty treasury, Ashley convinced them to pass an act to sell off the Mexican rancho lands, more than thirty thousand acres, in order to pay the debt. A notice of the sale was then placed in an obscure Santa Cruz paper. On the day of the sale, Jacks was the only one who showed up, and he placed a lone bid of three cents an acre. Even the money he bid was basically worthless scrip. Upon learning of the transaction, city leaders and citizens were furious. They took the case to the U.S. Supreme Court, but Jacks prevailed.

From either Jacks Peak or Presidio Hill, the serene environs of Monterey stretch before you, layered with the cultures and traditions of the Old West. The current Monterey is one of fifteen California cities honored to participate in the state's "Model Cities" program, with the revitalization of the downtown as the major focus.

TOURS

The first tour highlights the historic downtown. The Monterey waterfront, including Cannery Row and Fisherman's Wharf, is featured in the second tour.

HISTORIC DOWNTOWN TOUR

If you would like a historical perspective for this walk, begin at the Sloat Monument and on Presidio Hill, also known as Presidio Knoll. To reach the hill, enter the Presidio by turning inland on Artillery Street, off Pacific Street, just past Heritage Harbor. You can drive to the parking lot by the museum and then climb the hill to the Sloat Monument, or you can park at the top by the monument. Parking is presently free and unlimited in this location. The hill is a microcosm of the many layers of Monterey. As of yet it has not been discovered by many tourists, or locals, for that matter, and you may be one of the few people there or even alone.

A self-guided walking tour on the hill leads through the site of a Rumsen village, which some archaeologists pinpoint as the one called Tamotk in mission records. You'll see "rain rocks" with small mortar holes, which are believed to have been used by the Rumsen people in ceremonies for controlling rains. The Rumsen hunted and gathered their food. Larger mortar holes on the site were used for grinding acorns and other nuts.

The next layer in Monterey's history is evidenced by the cross marking the grave of Alexo Nino, a black free man who died while traveling with Vizcaino in 1602. The oak under which Vizcaino, and later Portola, claimed the land for Spain grew at a point across from Artillery Street. The oak has since died, but you can see its preserved wood at the Cathedral San Carlos (Royal Presidio Chapel) on Church Street (see What Else to See and Do, p. 67). The Spanish built their Castillo (fort) on the hill, and its superior location gradually replaced the armament of the original Presidio by the chapel.

A memorial to Father Junipero Serra is found on the bayside foot of the hill, as is a monument to Hippolyte de Bouchard. Dreaded pirate Hippolyte de

Bouchard and his crew sacked and looted Monterey in November 1818 and claimed the land for independent Buenos Aires, now Argentina—then sailed out of town a month later.

With the Presidio's sweeping views of the bay, you can see why it was used for encampments of the Spanish, Mexican, and successive U.S. armies. The Sloat Monument commemorates the taking over of California by the United States from Mexico without a shot being fired on July 7, 1846. If you look out to the ocean at the monument, then turn back in the direction of your right shoulder, you will see the earthen fortifications of Fort Mervine, named after the commander who led the ground forces directed by Commodore Sloat. One of the five cannons on Fort Mervine dates to 1846. Fort Mervine operated until 1852. The other cannons date to the 1860s and may have been in use when Fort Mervine was reactivated in 1864 for the Civil War. After the Civil War Fort Mervine was again abandoned and the Presidio was unused until 1902, when the 15th regiment moved in. The Presidio Museum displays historical items of the site as well as artifacts of the Rumsen and other indigenous groups. The museum is currently closed to visitors. The Public Affairs Office of the Defense Language Institute (408/647-5184) can inform you about a new schedule.

The first U.S. vessel to land in Monterey Bay, *The Otter*, arrived in the 1790s. The "Boston men" followed the hide and tallow trade to California and became entrepreneurs. To pick up the trail of the Boston men, and also begin the downtown tour, walk or drive to the Custom House Plaza.

You can pick up self-guided tour maps at the Monterey State Historic Park Visitor and Information Center, located in Stanton Center on the plaza across from Fisherman's Wharf. The guided walking tours led by state park personnel for a slight fee begin at this location. Three tours, each one to two hours in length, are offered daily (408/649-7118) and are heartily recommended. The park consists of eleven historic downtown buildings, which are marked with blue signs that give a short overview of the buildings' special qualities or history. Four of the eleven buildings require a $2.00 per building entrance fee: the Larkin House, Casa Soberanes, the Stevenson House, and the Cooper-Molera House. For $5.00 you can purchase a two-day pass that includes a guided tour and entrance to all the buildings.

Stanton Center is a good starting point for a walking tour of downtown. The state park's information center, the Monterey Maritime Museum, a small theater, and a gift shop are located here. The theater presents a free twenty-minute movie about the history of the Monterey Peninsula. The movie stars local residents, and great care was taken to portray the history as accurately as possible. On some weekend afternoons, especially in the summer, live performers reenact special moments or cultural contributions from the past. Some performances feature impromptu roles for volunteers from the audience.

The Monterey Maritime Museum (408/373-2469), 5 Custom House Plaza, began as the private collection of Allen Knight and was formerly open free to the public, with fewer exhibits, at an adobe on Calle Principal. In its current location the museum has been expanded and houses extensive exhibits that trace the cultural and nautical history of the Monterey area. There is an admission charge for adults and children. Rotating beams of light from the Big Sur lighthouse Fresnel lens brighten the walls of the two-story building. Upstairs you can step beyond a recreated captain's room to view mementos such as whaling harpoons and the metal helmets of Japanese abalone divers. One room features scale models of various ships, including the *Savannah,* Commodore John Sloat's flagship.

During the summer, thanks to Monterey's commitment to theater in the open air, the plaza in front of the Stanton house is a lively, friendly place. Musicians and theater groups present performances that are free and first rate. Arts and crafts shows often line the outer edges of the plaza. Frequent special events include the annual Greek celebration that features foods, music, and dancing. Along the other side of the plaza, players meet for friendly boccie ball games.

When you can tear yourself away from the plaza, cross to the Pacific House. This building was designed by Thomas Larkin, one of the enterprising Boston men who traded and built in Monterey in the 1830s. He first came to California at the request of his half-brother Capt. Roger Cooper, who had come with the China trade. Captain Cooper had sold his ship the *Rover* to Arguello, the then governor of California, and at the governor's request stayed on to captain the ship. While in port Cooper stayed at the Vallejo home. Vallejo was a wealthy member of the Mexican land-owning elite; Cooper married one of Vallejo's daughters, and became a Catholic and a Mexican citizen as well as a wealthy landowner himself. With his large cattle ranchos (one of which was located at what is now San Quentin Prison in Marin County) and shipping business Cooper wrote home for someone to come west and help manage his business affairs. Larkin sailed west to help Cooper, established his own businesses, and served as consul to the U.S. government and secret agent to the President.

Larkin worked for peaceful transmission of Mexican California to U.S. control. His buildings are examples of the "Monterey style" of architecture. Original homes in Monterey were constructed of adobe, a mixture of local mud and straw. Roofs extended over the sides to prevent the walls from melting in the rain. "Monterey style" designates two-story adobes with Yankee woodwork, such as doors, windows, hipped roofs, and second-floor balconies.

Larkin's original use of the Pacific House land was to sell its fresh well water to the ships at anchor in the bay. He later rented the building to the U.S. Quartermaster for offices and supplies. David Jacks bought the building in 1880 and it stayed in his family until it was given to the state in 1954. A museum of California history occupies the first floor, while the second floor holds a collection of artifacts from the indigenous peoples of California and some other regions of the United States.

The Custom House is the neighboring building. The Spanish government had forbidden international trade in California; the Mexican government welcomed trade as a source of revenue. Everything that came to port was taxed—sometimes at 100 percent of value. As Richard Henry Dana described the trade, in *Two Years Before the Mast,* "Our cargo was an assorted one, that is it consisted of everything under the sun, we had in fact everything that can be imagined from Chinese fireworks to English cartwheels." On July 7, 1846, the U.S. flag was raised on the little flagpole at the north end of this building and the lands of seven present states became part of the manifest destiny of the United States.

From the Custom House you can easily walk to the first brick house in Monterey and the Old Whaling Station. Visitors often wonder where at the station the whales were processed. "Old Whaling Station" is a bit of a misnomer, as the "station" was actually the headquarters and employee resident's house. The whales were boiled down into fat on the beach in front of the house. Old-time photographs show whale bones scattered throughout the roads and yards of town. Look at the ground in front of the Whaling Station; the round dark disks are one of the few remaining whale vertebrae sidewalks, which once stretched throughout Monterey. Behind the station sits a pot that was used to render the whale (and that always makes me a little sad).

As is the case with most of the public homes along this tour, the lovely gardens around the homes are open for your enjoyment. Almost every time I relax with a lunch in one of these gardens, I am visited by two companions, a squawking jay and a delicate hummingbird.

The general path of your walk leads next up Pacific Avenue, turns at Jefferson to include the old jail and Colton Hall, then crosses to the Larkin House and over to the Cooper-Molera complex. *Historic Monterey: Path of History Walking Tour,* published by the State of California and available for sale at shops along the way, offers short narratives about each of the historic adobes. The pamphlet does not replace the walking tours led by guides from the state parks department, which add detail and ambiance to the route. It is also fun to wander through the area and pick the ones that hold the most interest for you. When you see the little adobe houses remember that large families used to call these home. Some of the older children, especially those who worked as cowhands, would sleep on the front porches with their saddles for pillows.

California's First Theater is located at the corner of Pacific Avenue and Scott Street. It opened in February 1850 with performances by U.S. Army officers, who produced some plays for the grand ticket price of $5.00. This is a great place to get a cool soda or sparkling water during the day. In the evening you can watch spirited melodramas.

Farther along Pacific Avenue, the government complex has several notable buildings. The chunky adobe walls and metal doors of the jail hold many stories, including the escape of a suspected German spy in 1918. What is amazing to me is that the jail was used as recently as 1956.

Colton Hall was built in a New England style to house the city's first school and meeting hall. Rev. Walter Colton was the first American alcalde, or chief judge, of California and the hall was his brainchild. Erected from the labor of those found guilty of crimes and paid for with liquor and gambling taxes, it was completed just in time for the state's first constitutional convention. The second floor has been restored to look just the same as it did at that convention in 1850. Every year on October 13 local citizens reenact the signing of the constitution. The lower half of Colton Hall is presently used for city offices.

Although it is not a historic adobe, the Monterey Peninsula Museum of Art, across the street at 559 Pacific Avenue, traces some of the early history of the area with its collection of early California artists. Asian and Pacific Rim art, ethnic and tribal arts, photography, and graphics are also featured. You can walk through the museum's sculpture garden to connect with Calle Principal.

The Larkin House, at the corner of Jefferson Street and Calle Principal, was one of the earliest two-story houses in California. Originally part store, as well as the house of the American consul Thomas Larkin, it is presently one of the best house museums in the United States. Larkin's granddaughter willed to the state the house and a number of furnishings, many of them original, in 1957. Guided walks are given, featuring a collection of antique English, American, and some Chinese furniture.

To step from another century to the cutting edge of modern architecture, walk through the Galerie Building, which fronts both Calle Principal and Alvarado Street. The adaptive reuse of the building exposes the timber trusses and concrete walls of the old Bank of America Building. With the addition of steel beams the entire building opens to a walkway of light. The building won a gold nugget award at the Pacific Coast Builders Conference for the Best Rehabilitated Commercial Building. "I take old bank buildings and recycle them," architect Stephen Eschler described the work to me.

As you exit on Alvarado Street you can turn left to visit the revitalized downtown or right to visit the Cooper-Molera complex. Whichever you choose first, be sure to come back for the other. The Cooper-Molera adobe is the site of the original Cooper home. As you walk in the store you will catch the fresh fragrance of a flower bouquet—some rose and lavender. The source is soaps hand made from the recipe of Alice Larkin Toulmin, granddaughter of Thomas Larkin. The items sold in the store support summer workshops for children who study California history here, the hands-on way. They make adobe brick, play nineteenth-century games, and help with the livestock and garden. Behind the Cooper store, behind walls of thick adobe, an eighteenth-century garden blooms in almost every season. Chickens scratch for feed and sheep ruminate. This is a very peaceful spot for writing letters or sharing lunch. The property also includes a museum of old wagons.

Pictures of the Coopers and Larkins as well as other early California settlers are displayed in a museum in one of the adobe rooms behind the store. An otter pelt to feel and samples of period china recovered from an excavation site are also displayed.

When you are ready to leave the urban sanctuary, venture onto Alvarado Street. Old brick sidewalks, aromas of freshly brewed coffee, and a variety of shops fill this "model city" area. Second Shot Sports (408/373-7468) sells equipment from surfboards to computerized rowing machines at second-hand prices. You might be ready for a Java Jolt, the coffee drinker's equivalent of a power breakfast at Monterey Coffee House Bookshop (408/647-1822). You can also rent a listening book for your future ride down the highway; just send it back in the envelope the store provides for you. Farther down the street you can join a crowd of locals and visitors at Vivas (408/373-4430) to catch the local band scene and share stories and drinks. The Monterey Victorian Hotel at 406 Alvarado Street is a remodeled William Weeks Hotel that features an ornate facade. A treasure is located just off Alvarado: the Old Monterey Book Company (408/372-3111) at 136 Bonifacio Place, where the walls are lined with old and rare books, first editions, and prints.

WATERFRONT TOUR

"Cannery Row in Monterey in California is a poem, a stink, a grating noise, a quality of light, a tone, a habit, a nostalgia, a dream," as John Steinbeck described it in *Cannery Row*, about 1945. The only thing that really stinks about the Cannery Row of the nineties is the traffic. It is still a poem. You walk along the elegant oceanfront hotels, waterfront restaurants, and the cornucopia of shops to notice the predominate aroma as chocolate, fresh-roasted coffee beans, and fresh sea air. Steinbeck's Cannery Row has not been razed; rather its past has risen as a dream to be discovered.

Rohana LoSchiavo, who leads Historic Cannery Row Walking Tours (408/373-5571), brings some of the fascinating stories and colorful anecdotes of the past to life. "One of the first questions people ask me is, 'Where are the canneries?' The more you find out about the history of Cannery Row, the more you find out that many of the shops are housed in what were once canneries and factories."

The history of Cannery Row begins just north of the aquarium within the Pacific Grove city limits. Walk along the biking and walking path to a point just south of the building named Monterey Boat Works. All the buildings you see on the ocean side are part of the Hopkins Marine Station, a marine research school operated by Stanford University. As you look over the water you will see a grouping of white rocks. These same rocks may have been markers for groups of Chinese fishing families who, in the 1850s, loaded their belongings onto fifty-foot Chinese junks. They sailed north from their province of Canton, around the Bering Straits, down the wild West Coast, and into the Monterey Bay.

The white rocks mark the area where a Chinese fishing village flourished from the 1850s until it was burned by a fire of "mysterious origins" in 1906. The Chinese arrival in Monterey coincided with the abalone boom that was brought about by the overhunting of the southern sea otter. Abalone and later squid were dried for boat shipment to Chinese gold and railroad camps, as well as to Chinatown in San Francisco. The Chinese fished for squid by hanging lanterns over the bows of their boats in the dark of night. Attracted by the light, schools of squid would swim into the nets. If you are walking around the bay at night you might see bright lights gliding over the water. These are modern-day squid boats, the current generation of the Chinese lantern boats.

Some residents of the nearby community of Pacific Grove found the odor of dried fish and the site's shacks, as well as the accompanying opium dens, to be irksome. On a spring night the village burned, presumably set afire. Thereafter the village moved about a quarter-mile north, to the shores of McAbee Beach.

As you walk back to Cannery Row you'll see a large wooden square resting on the grassy slope. This hopper was one of many that held fish just offshore before pumps from atop the canneries would suck the fish inside through long tubes. As you look back at the Monterey Bay Aquarium note the little square recreated pumphouse atop the roof.

On the side of the aquarium you'll see the red sign "Portola Brand." Many buildings along the row have similar signs, which denote the canneries that operated at their spots. The aquarium occupies the site of the Hovden factory, the largest and longest-operating cannery on the Wharf. Although Steinbeck captured its soul, its reigning royalty, "King of the Canneries," was the Norwegian Knut Hovden. Before Hovden, the sardine cans were hand crimped; Hovden introduced the machine solderer. One of his employees, Pietro Ferrante, adapted the *lampara*, or "lightning net" from his native Sicily. Sicilian immigrants arrived to man and eventually own fleets of lampara boats. In 1926, Knut Hovden again increased the tonnage of sardine catches with the introduction of large purse seiners, vessels with nets as large as football fields. As you look north on Cannery Row you will see several "crossovers." The canneries were built at the waterfront to allow direct access to the ships. Across the street most of the buildings were storerooms, built next to the railroad (where the bike path is now) for easy shipping. Cans that started out empty would ride conveyor belts through the crossovers, be filled with sardines, which were cooked in the cans, and be shuttled back across to the warehouses for labeling and shipment. The northernmost crossover has been added for architectural integrity, but the Monterey Canning Company crossway and the Aneas crossway by the Monterey Plaza Hotel are authentic.

Cannery Row was published at the peak of the sardine fishing industry, when nineteen canneries and twenty reduction plants packed 250,000 tons of sardines a season. Sardines were canned for food and were pulverized in the reduction plants for their oil, with solids sold for fertilizer. Many of the haunts of the book's

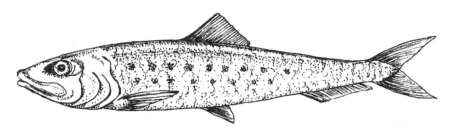

Sardine

characters Doc, Eddie, Mack, Dora, and Lee Chong are now visited by millions of visitors each year, many of whom are unaware of the stories hidden in the buildings' walls.

Kitty-corner from the aquarium, at 851 Cannery Row, a yellow stucco building houses Kalisa's "La Ida Cafe." Steinbeck's Eddie served bar here. Now children stop in to get ice cream. For thirty years the cafe has been owned by Kalisa Moore, who occasionally hosts magic shows and belly dancing on the second story, which was one of the three brothels in the Cannery Row of Steinbeck's time. Kalisa helps to organize the annual Steinbeck birthday party on February 27. During the canneries' heyday the grocery store next to Kalisa's was the Wing Chong (loosely translated as Glorious-Prosperous) Market, 835 Cannery Row. This market was owned during Steinbeck's time by Won Lee, who was identified in *Cannery Row* as Lee Chong. The Lee family still owns the real estate of the old market that has lived up to its name. If you walk back behind the displays of the present tenant, the Cannery Row Shell Company, and look in the corner, you can open the door to the little freezer where Doc would pick up five quarts of beer when he had company.

Doc Ricketts, the real scientist and the fictional one, lived and worked across the street in "Doc's Lab." The unpainted slat-board building looks much the same as when Ricketts worked in the back room, "dressed in a long rubber apron and rubber gloves." Both he and Steinbeck were avid tidepoolers. When Steinbeck was young he enjoyed beachcombing while visiting his parents' summer home in Pacific Grove. Doc and Steinbeck were good friends and traveled together by purse seiner to the Sea of Cortez, which resulted in their collaboration on the book *Sea of Cortez*. According to tour leader Rohanna LoSchiavo, "Ed Ricketts was the heart of Cannery Row in the 1940s, and even today you never hear an unkind word said about him." Ricketts worked in his lab to build one of the most comprehensive files of marine tidal animals attempted in his time. His book *Between Pacific Tides* has been widely used as a marine reference book.

Ricketts used to fry steaks and share beer with his friends at the lab. Since the late 1950s the lab has been the site of many a friendly dinner prepared by a club of local men who pooled their resources to buy it. The men sold the lab to the city in 1993 but retain use of it for some meetings over the next sixteen years.

If you want to view a special exhibit of Steinbeck memorabilia, walk to the back of the Wing Chong Market to Alisa's Antiques, a room filled with Americana. Alisa opens the Steinbeck Memorial Room to the public daily from 12 noon to 6 p.m. You can view family photos, handwritten letters, and some personal effects of Steinbeck's.

The site of Flora Wood's (in *Cannery Row*, Dora Flood's) Lone Star Cafe, 799 Cannery Row, looks nothing like the most famous of the Cannery Row houses of ill repute. Flora named her place the Lone Star after her home state of Texas. Steinbeck changed the name to the Bear Flag. After being closed in the 1940s the house burned, and its generous madam died penniless. The site's present tenant, Mackerel Jacks Trading Company, sells such items as tourist T-shirts and windsocks. If you eat up the street at Bullwacker's, 653 Cannery Row, in what is now called the Bear Flag building, you will hear the claim that the restaurant site was the Lone Star Cafe.

On the next block a temporary, six months' construction mural has been turned into an art fixture. Organized by Bruce Ariss, a resident author and artist, the mural painted by local artists depicts scenes from Monterey's culturally diverse history and holds some surprises. Longtime Monterey County resident Hank Ketchum painted one of the murals; see if you can spot Dennis the Menace. One of them depicts Chinese settlements on the bay. Since this was painted in 1989, the picture from California's past includes a camouflaged depiction of the battle in Tiananmen Square. The square painted by Bruce Ariss features Steinbeck and Ricketts talking together. Steinbeck rated only one mural picture to four of Ricketts.

A bronze bust of Steinbeck faces Cannery Row in the parking lot above McAbee Beach, which was the second site of the Chinese village. Since Monterey had an ordinance to prohibit commercial fishing from the beach, the Chinese changed their economic base from fishing to small business ownership. You can see the influence of Chinese business ownership in the pagoda-style roof across the street from McAbee Beach.

Farther up Cannery Row is an overview of the history of California, Monterey, and particularly Cannery Row at the Steinbeck's Spirit of Monterey Wax Museum (408/375-3770). This may be one of the few wax museums that features local history instead of a parade of waxed celebrities. Thirty other businesses share this building at 700 Cannery Row, the site of the Monterey Canning Company. This cannery made huge profits when World War I cut off supplies of fish from Europe and domestic sales boomed. You can still see the original wood construction and rooftop pumphouse. A chromatic essay of Monterey by journalist

Tom Webber hangs on the rustic wooden interior slats. Upstairs you can visit twelve galleries, some of them working studios, of a colony of artists who have grouped together as the American Renaissance Movement. Samples of the wines of local vineyards can be savored as you overlook the bay at the Paul Masson Wine Tasting Room (408/646-5446) or the Bargetto Winery (408/373-4053). A sweeter or younger crowd may enjoy tastes at the Old Fashioned Fudge and Candy Company (408/373-6451), the first stop in the "sweet route" woven into this tour.

Nearby, where cans to be filled used to cross Cannery Row, the aerial crossover now marks a good point at which to digress and wander the shops along and above the bay front. Behind the row of buildings that front Cannery Row you are likely to see three generations of families out for a bike ride—all on the same bike! Six-seater surrey bikes, roller bladers, and strollers pass you along a wide bike and walking path. The Del Monte Express of the Southern Pacific Railway chugged along here until the 1960s.

On the upper side of the bike trail The Edgewater Packing Company, a World War II-era venture located at Prescott and Cannery Row, shares a common wall with the brick building that was the area's first reduction plant. Nowadays inside the Packing Company, the noise at the main amusement arcade probably approaches the previous noise level of the cannery. But the whirling horses on the merry-go-round could outrace a conveyor belt any day. Popcorn, candied apples, and Oscar Hossenfellder's ice-cream parlor here add to the children's delight.

Farther along the sweet route a sidewalk fudge bear offers coupons and invitations for the Old Cannery Row Fudge Company (408/373-6672), 807 Cannery Row. Rocky Mountain Chocolate Factory of Monterey (408/372-1065), 647 Cannery Row, offers specialty chocolates and sauces as well as at least twenty varieties of candied apples and flavored truffles. You can fill up baskets and buy candy by the pound at the Candy Baron (408/372-4601), 601 Wave Street.

Wave Street offers more for adult palates. The tasting room for Monterey Peninsula Winery (408/372-4949), 786 Wave Street, offers wine tasting and stocks such other Monterey products as Gil's wine-flavored salsas. Cannery Row businesses are a mixed bag of the touristy and the elegant. One of the most unusual is a reduction plant turned redwood carving gallery: Stohan Furniture and Design, 484 Cannery Row (408/649-8086). Here wood sculptures, such as dolphins, and burl chairs are carved with chainsaws on a wood platform built right over the crashing surf. The Enterprise Packers Warehouse at 225 Cannery Row is a triple pleasure to visit: On the outside wall you can view the migration of whales in a wall mural by local marine artist John Jennings. Inside the structure retains the industrial integrity from when it was used as a warehouse, during World War II. And one of its tenants, the Bayside Trading Company (408/646-9944), features elegant imported furniture and clothing.

Before the canneries changed the waterfront from peaceful beach to full industrial center, a large mansion called the Trevis estate was located at the north end of Cannery Row. The large shingle house across the street at 417 Cannery Row was built in conjunction with the turn-of-the-century estate. If the house looks a little familiar, maybe you saw the 1951 movie *Clash by Night*. The movie featured Barbara Stanwyck and fish-cutter Marilyn Monroe in her first costarring role.

From Cannery Row you can continue a waterfront tour by a very scenic walk along the walking and bike trail. If you have parked your car on the Row, you can take the shuttle back.

The path continues to the Coast Guard Wharf. On special occasions the Coast Guard opens its boats to tours. The sea lions bask on the wharf in great numbers during the winter. The private docks just to the south of the Coast Guard Wharf have a ten-to twelve-year waiting list, so sign up now. On your walk to Fisherman's Wharf you'll pass about 180 boats on private moorings, if they are not out enjoying the bay or the daylight-savings-time Wednesday night races. On one corner of the wharf, Bradley's Restaurant (408/655-6799) specializes in fresh fish and hearty California cuisine.

When asked about her favorite part of her trip to California, Joan Hakun of Pennsylvania answered, "Eating all those delectable morsels of seafood they sell in the fresh air at the Monterey Fisherman's Wharf." Fresh-air seafood markets, casual and elegant seafood restaurants, some with their own boats, seashell shops and art galleries, ice cream cones and cotton candy make the Wharf a lively destination. At the end of the Wharf the Famous Voices Museum (408/373-5911)

Fishermans Wharf in Monterey

carries thousands of cassette recordings of voices from the past. Performers such as Enrico Caruso and historical figures such as John F. Kennedy are popular requests. The museum also carries collector editions of limited lithographs by famous portrait photographers, such as Edward Steichen, as well as reasonably priced photographs of world-renowned personalities. Nearby, the Wharf Theater (408/649-2332) presents live performances featuring local actors and actresses.

The Wharf is the pathway to adventures on the sea. The whalewatching excursions, tours of the sanctuary, and fishing expeditions you will see departing can be arranged by calling any of these: Chris's Fishing Expeditions (408/375-5951), Monterey Sport Fishing (408/372-2203), Randy's Fishing Trips (408/372-7440), or Sam's Fishing Fleet Inc. (408/372-0577). A glass-bottom boat ride (408/372-7150) around the harbor will give you an idea of how cloudy summer waters contrast with the crystal-clear waters of autumn. Cruises aboard the the forty-five-foot sailboat *Chardonnay II* (408/373-8664) and historic rides on the tall ship *The Californian* (800/432-2201) also board at Fisherman's Wharf. If you want the best view of the sanctuary try scuba diving; next to scuba diving, the semisubmersible submarine the *Nautilus VI* (408/647-1400) gives the closest look at the world underwater.

To see the local fishing industry at work visit the Municipal Wharf, just north of Fisherman's Wharf. A few processors continue to operate at the end of the Wharf but business is not at all like it was in the heyday of fishing, in the 1940s. Four hundred fifty berths share this wharf. The chances are good that the all-steel drag boats with the thick rolls of net in the back are bringing their catch to Tringali's wholesale fish market at the end of the Wharf. You might see them unloading salmon, sole, or cod. Many of the colorful fishing boats you'll see are no longer in use. When one goes up for sale it is often bought by a local sailboat owner who resells the fishing boat and retains the slip for a pleasure craft.

Your walk can continue along the walking and bike trail or along the beach, or you may want to visit some of the other Monterey highlights below. If you opt for the beach, remember that rip currents and sneaker waves are common.

WHAT ELSE TO SEE AND DO

LAKE EL ESTERO. Located along Camino El Estero. This part of the city includes the visitor's center, a lake where you can rent paddleboats, two historic cemeteries, a walking path around the inland estuary, and the children's favorite, Dennis the Menace Park. If Dennis could have built a park this would be it. In fact, the park was designed to be a place for "dos" rather than "don'ts" by its creator, Hank Ketchum. Children can climb on a real steam train engine, ride a flying sculpture, board an old fishing boat, slide down an airplane, and run through a planted maze.

La Mirada. At 720 Via Mirada (408/372-3689). This is an elegant addition to the Monterey Peninsula Museum of Art. When this museum opened the *Monterey County Herald* headline read, "Deep Pockets Make La Mirada a Reality." The historic house has been home to Gen. Jose Castro, explorer John C. Fremont, and movie couple Elizabeth Taylor and Richard Burton when they were filming *The Sandpiper* in Monterey. The museum's galleries include the Jane and Justin Dart wing, which houses the Darts' extensive collection of Armin Hansen paintings, and the Virginia Klemme gallery of Asian Art.

San Carlos de Borromeo de Monterey Cathedral / Royal Presidio Chapel. On Church Street, opposite Figueroa (408/373-2628). This is the oldest church in continuous service in California. First built in 1770 under orders of Carlos III, King of Spain, to serve the first presidio in Monterey, the chapel was the worshipping place for the Spanish governors, the king's representatives in California, and was thus designated a Royal Chapel. Coats of arms are painted on the wall behind the altar: the shield of the Kingdom of Leon and Castile in Spain marks this as a royal chapel. The doorway and facade of the entrance are part of the original chapel, which was completed under the direction of Father Lasuen in 1794. Manual Ruiz, the stonemason who directed the building of the chapel and the Carmel Mission, is credited as the carver of the statue of Our Lady of Guadalupe on the facade. The fever to bring the Christian religion to the first peoples of California was fueled by devotion to the Lady of Guadalupe that arose with her visit to an Indian on Teypeyec Hill in Mexico City, as recorded by the Catholic Church in 1531.

In 1850 this church became the first cathedral in California. The sandstone for the construction was quarried near Carmel. The exterior of the building shows a neoclassical facade and a square bell tower. Transepts were added in 1858 to increase the size of the original chapel, which is now part of the cathedral. Hidden rooms, believed to be early confessionals, have only recently been discovered between overlapping walls. Some of the whale vertebrae used for sidewalks during Monterey's days as a whaling port can still be seen behind the church. Sections of the original oak that shaded the masses said at the Viscaino Landing in 1602 and the Serra Landing in 1770 are preserved in the entrance.

The office in the cathedral has a written guide to its many pictures and statues, several of which date from the eighteenth and nineteenth centuries. They include statues brought from the Philippines at the time of Serra and a statue of Mary that features scafito work of gold under the design of the garments and that is regarded as California's finest statue of the Spanish era. The statue of Santa Rosalia, patron of Sicily, has been carried every year since 1935 in a procession through Monterey to the Wharf for the blessing of the fishing fleet.

UNITED STATES NAVAL POSTGRADUATE SCHOOL. On University Circle off of Del Monte Avenue (408/656-2441). The school's buildings and grounds are those of the lavish Hotel Del Monte. The first two hotels on this site were the acclaimed tourist destinations operated by the Pacific Improvement Company as the "most elegant seaside establishment in the world." After the first two burned, the present building was constructed by the next landholders, the Del Monte Properties Company, under the direction of Samuel F. B. Morse.

Visitors are welcome to walk the grounds and visit the main hall of the former hotel. First check in at the Quarterdeck Office at 220 Herman Hall. The view from the tower is a beautiful overlook of Monterey. Outdoor concerts are presented on spring and summer holiday weekends by the the Monterey Bay Symphony. Certain areas are restricted, but ample parking is available.

VETERANS MEMORIAL PARK. On Jefferson Street and Skyline Drive (408/646-3865). This fifty-acre park offers picnic facilities, a playground, hiking trails, and campgrounds within the city limits, in the skyline forest area of Monterey. Camping is allocated on a first-come, first-served basis.

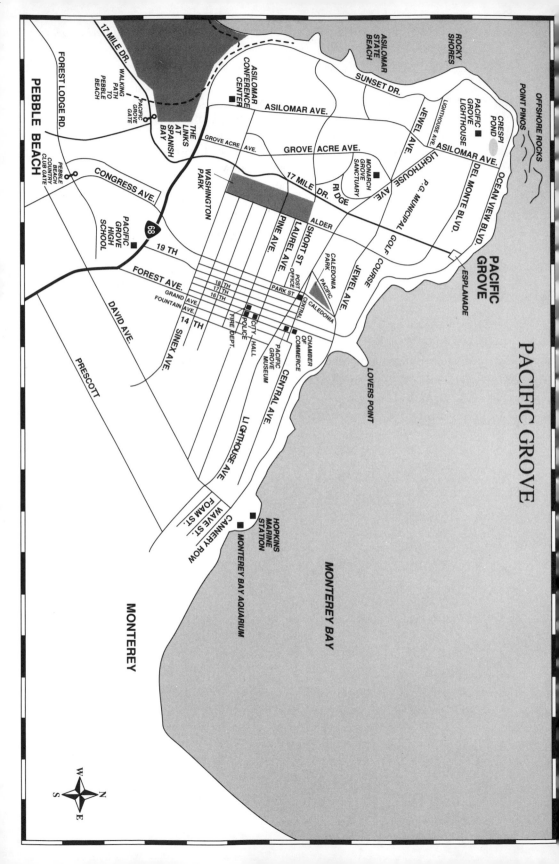

CHAPTER 3

PACIFIC GROVE

THE LAST HOMETOWN

Monterey pines and Victorian houses crown the coastal community of Pacific Grove, which includes part of the Monterey Bay Aquarium within its city limits. A rugged coastline borders this "Piney Paradise" of approximately 2.6 square miles with some sixteen thousand residents.

GETTING READY

THE BEST TIMES TO VISIT AND THE SPECIAL EVENTS

Pacific Grove is congenial at any time of the day. As of yet P.G. (as the town is known around the Monterey Peninsula) doesn't have the heavy traffic of the neighboring cities of Monterey and Carmel. Pacific Grove does not feature the lively nightclubs of Monterey, but some restaurants and coffeehouses offer late night music.

Many special events add to the already attractive scenery. In spring the town celebrates its birthday during "Good Old Days" with a parade, old-time entertainment, a wildflower show, a quilt show, and an arts and crafts festival. In mid-summer the very popular Feast of Lanterns draws crowds to the streets, ocean bluffs, and beach for an outdoor pageant and fireworks commemorating the Chinese settlements in the community. As the summer winds down, the best day to walk the coastal route is when it closes to traffic during a 10K walk-run along Ocean View Boulevard, sponsored by the nonprofit Beacon House. In early October children parade through the downtown to welcome back the monarchs, which return to winter in Pacific Grove just as local gardens and parks specially planted with the butterflies' favorite nectar plants burst into winter blooms. Victorian homes, inns, and churches open their doors to tours on the same weekend. Scores of high school bands march through town and present gala evening performances on the first weekend of November, during the Northern California High School Band Review. Many pods of gray whales spout offshore along the coastal bluffs from late December through January, lessening through March. The Natural History Museum and the Pacific Grove Art Center offer special programs throughout the year.

CLIMATE AND CLOTHING

Pacific Grove offers a year-round temperate coastal climate. Spring and autumn are usually warm and sunny. The section of the town east of Forest Avenue is the summer sunbelt.

When I think of Pacific Grove clothing I think of wheels almost as an accessory: kids (adults too) on rollerblades with bodyboards or surfboards tucked under their arms, mothers pushing baby strollers, bicyclists pedaling along Sunset Drive. Comfortable clothes with athletic shoes are the best bet. Always bring a jacket and a bathing suit, since it can be in the seventies in January and in the sixties in August and vice-versa. Patrons of downtown restaurants and businesses look stylish; they take pride in the appearance of their town and themselves. The cold ocean waters around Pacific Grove require a wet suit for anything more than a quick dip or wading at Lovers Point.

TOUR LENGTHS

The complete coastal walking tour described below could take four to five hours round trip. Plan on a couple of hours for the other tours. As this is a small town, the best-bet weekend would include a visit to the Monterey Bay Aquarium, one special event and parts of all three tours. I can remember visiting here for weekends and always thinking that I had to leave too soon. If you really want a relaxing trip, stay a week. A friend of mine from the San Francisco Bay Area comes here just to breathe the air and walk the coastal route; she swears it rejuvenates her better than health spa resorts.

WILDLIFE WISDOM

Bison that had been sold to the Pacific Improvement Company by a Wild West show, and native elk, too, roamed the streets in the 1890s. The bison were rounded up and donated to Golden Gate Park in San Francisco, where their descendants can be seen by visitors. The elk are also gone, but the tradition of wild animals roaming the streets continues. Deer walk freely through the residential streets and gardens, especially near the Asilomar area. They can often be seen in herds on the golf courses or eating the flowers placed at the city cemetery. Fawns are born in late spring and early summer. Some residents equip their cars with high-frequency deer alarms to help warn the deer, especially fawns, that roam the streets. They are especially active and difficult to see around dusk. Drive slowly and keep a lookout for leaping deer.

Butterfly-crossing signs have been installed along Grove Acre Road, near the town's Monarch Grove Sanctuary. Thousands of monarchs fly into this "Butterfly Town U.S.A." in early October, to winter here through March. The butterflies resemble golden clouds while flying around flower gardens and dry leaves while clustering in their favorite trees. The butterflies are slow flying. For their protection the city has a law that makes it unlawful "to molest or interfere in any way

Monarch Butterfly

with the peaceful occupancy of the monarch butterfly." And it's serious. The punishment for breaking the law is a $1000.00 fine or a six-month prison term.

This coastline is abundant with sea life—otters, harbor seals, seal lions, pelicans, and tidepool animals. It is truly a remarkable place for the nature lover. Please help keep it that way. Take nothing from the beach or rocks (except perhaps trash, if you are inclined to help). Also do not feed any animals—birds, squirrels, raccoons, deer or other furry or feathered friends. Some species of wild animals are having serious overpopulation problems as a result of people feeding them.

VISITOR INFORMATION

The Pacific Grove Chamber of Commerce is very helpful. Reach it at Forest and Central streets or P.O. Box 167, Pacific Grove, CA 93950; 408/373-3304. The Heritage Society of Pacific Grove at P.O. Box 1007, Pacific Grove, CA 93950; 408/372-2898 operates the Barn Museum at Laurel Avenue and Seventeenth Street. On Saturdays from 1 p.m. to 4 p.m. you can pick up back issues of their pamphlet called *The Board and Batten* which highlights the town's history. Check with the Pacific Grove Museum, at Forest and Central streets, for answers to local natural history questions and information including on the monarch butterfly migrations: 408/648-3116. The free *Coast Weekly* and the *Monterey County Herald* (especially the Thursday "Go" section) available at newsstands offer information about restaurants and special events in town. For an older history of Pacific Grove, obtain a copy of *A Piney Paradise: A Pictorial Story of Monterey Peninsula,* by Lucy Neely McLane.

ALTERNATE TRANSPORTATION

Monterey Salinas Transit (408/899-2555) serves Pacific Grove with buses from the Monterey Simoneau Metro-Amtrak Plaza every thirty minutes. The Pacific Grove Asilomar Bus #1 route stops at the Monterey Aquarium, Cannery Row, downtown Pacific Grove via Lighthouse Avenue, and Asilomar.

PARKING

To really enjoy this small town, park your car and walk around the downtown area. You can park along the street on Lighthouse Avenue if you plan a short stay. Parking is limited to two hours, so if you plan to stay longer drive up to the public parking lot on Fountain Avenue, behind the Lighthouse Cinema.

PLACES TO STAY

Pacific Grove offers some truly elegant Victorian bed and breakfast inns as well as more conventional motels. These are just a few of the lodging possibilities that show the character of Pacific Grove. You might want to contact the Pacific Grove Chamber of Commerce, P.O. Box 167, Pacific Grove, CA 93950 (408/373-3304) for more information.

COASTAL SETTING

BEACHCOMBER INN, 1996 Sunset Drive. A beach-style motel next to Asilomar Beach, the Beachcomber has a pool, sauna, complimentary bicycles, and barbecue facilities. Adjacent to The Fishwife Seafood Cafe. 408/373-4769. AX, MC, V. For two, from $75.00 to $90.00.

GREEN GABLES INN, 104 Fifth Street. This Queen Anne-style impeccably restored Victorian inn on Monterey Bay serves full breakfast and afternoon tea to guests. Most private, some shared baths. 408/375-2095. AX, MC, V; others also accepted. For two, mostly from $100.00 to $160.00.

THE MARTINE INN, 255 Ocean View Boulevard. An ocean-front mansion built in the 1890s has elegant and gracious rooms. Full breakfast. A player piano accompanies afternoon hors d'oeuvres. All with private baths. Spa available. 408/373-3388. AX, MC, V. For two, mostly from $125.00 to $230.00.

SEVEN GABLES INN, 555 Ocean View Boulevard. A Mobil-rated four-star bed and breakfast, this Victorian mansion on the bay has private baths, gardens, and patios. All rooms offer stunning views of Lovers Point and the coastline. 408/372-4341. MC, V. For two, mostly from $105.00 to $205.00.

DOWNTOWN SETTING

THE CENTRELLA, 612 Central Avenue. There are luxury accommodations here in a near-hundred-year-old Victorian inn with garden cottages. Full breakfast, afternoon tea. Private baths and wet bars. 408/372-3372. AX, MC, V; others also accepted. For two, mostly from $125.00 to $250.00.

GOSBY HOUSE INN, 643 Lighthouse Avenue. A Queen Anne Victorian inn that is listed in the National Register of Historic Buildings has antique furnishings. Full breakfast, afternoon tea. 408/375-1287. AX, MC, V. For two, mostly from $85.00 to $150.00.

WOODSY SETTING

ANDRIL FIREPLACE COTTAGES, 569 Asilomar Boulevard. Across from Asilomar Conference Center and an easy walk to the beach, these separate cottages and family houses include kitchens. The grounds include a meadow area where deer and seasonally butterflies join you. Spa. 408/375-0994. MC, V. For two, from $70.00 to $106.00.

BEST WESTERN LIGHTHOUSE LODGE AND SUITES, 1150 Lighthouse Avenue. Thirty plush suites and sixty-six standard rooms share two different settings along Lighthouse Avenue. One standard section of rooms is located near the grounds of the cemetery, which is visited by deer and raccoons. Towering pines and cypress add to the woodsy feel. Breakfast, afternoon wine, and hors d'oeuvres; jacuzzi, pool. AX, MC, V; others also accepted. 408/655-2111, 800/858-1249. For two, standard rooms from $89.00 and suites from 159.00.

BIDE-A-WEE, 221 Asilomar Boulevard. The Bide-A-Wee offers family units in a quiet setting near beach and golf. 408/372-2330. MC, V. For two, from $40.00 to $95.00.

BUTTERFLY GROVE INN, 1073 Lighthouse Avenue. This inn shares butterflies with the Monarch Sanctuary grounds behind it. Pool, spa, and some kitchenettes and fireplaces. Suites in an old Victorian home. 408/373-4921. AX, MC, V; others also accepted. For two, from $60.00 to $140.00.

ROSEDALE INN EXECUTIVE SUITES, 755 Asilomar Boulevard. These private units are nestled in the pines, across from the woods of the Asilomar Conference Center. All the suites here feature cathedral ceilings, pine log furniture, fireplaces, and over-sized jacuzzi tubs. Microwaves, VCRs, and wet bars add to the amenities. 408/655-1000. AX, MC, V; others also accepted. For two, $115.00.

ASILOMAR. You can also stay at Asilomar Conference Grounds, even if you are not attending a conference. Located at 800 Asilomar Boulevard, the conference grounds are on 105 acres of pines and dunes, with breathtaking views of the sea. Here you can stay in the historic buildings, deluxe buildings, guest inn cottages, or the forest lodge. Advance reservations are recommended. 408/372-8016. No cards. For two, rooms from $65.00 to $88.00.

RESTAURANTS

It's good there are so many great running and biking trails in this area. I would exercise four hours daily just to eat to my delight at the restaurants in Pacific Grove. The restaurants listed here are just the beginning. Those in the first list are ones we enjoy more if our young children are not with us.

EL COCODRILLO ROTISSERIE AND SEAFOOD GRILL, 701 Lighthouse Avenue. Below tropical paintings and in comfortable seating, enjoy the food of the Caribbean, Yucatan, and Central and South America. Jamaican curry crab-cakes, Bahamian chowder, smoked West Indian ribs, and on and on. Dinner. 408/655-3311. MC, V. Entrees, from $7.00 to $14.00.

FANDANGO RESTAURANT, 223 Seventeenth Street. A warm Mediterranean setting includes patio dining and accommodations for large parties. Romantic private nooks. Flavorful foods of Europe, including fresh seafood from the mesquite grill, rack of lamb, an array of paellas, and more. Full bar and extensive wine list. Lunch and dinner. 408/372-3456. AX, MC, V; others also accepted. Entrees, from $14.00 to $20.00.

GERNOT'S VICTORIAN HOUSE, 649 Lighthouse Avenue. Situated in a century-old mansion, Gernot's offers Austrian specialties including breast of duck with raspberry sauce, local wild boar, fresh seafood, pasta, and wiener schnitzel. Private parties. Dinner. 408/646-1477. AX, MC, V. Entrees, from $17.00 to $20.00.

MELAC'S, 633 Lighthouse Avenue. In a charming and intimate historic house, Janet Melac, a Cordon Bleu–trained chef, and her husband, host Jacques Melac, invite you to a superior French restaurant. Daily menus ensure only the freshest ingredients. Specialties include duck, lamb, and seafood. Lunch and dinner Tuesday through Saturday. 408/375-1743. AX, MC, V; others also accepted. Entrees, mostly under $25.00.

THE OLD BATH HOUSE, 620 Ocean View Boulevard. For its beautiful ocean views, elegant Victorian interiors, and candlelight this restaurant is consistently voted most romantic in the county. New American fare. Specials include duck Merlot, veal Frangelico with hazelnuts, and fresh mesquite-grilled seafood. Cocktails from 4 p.m., dinner from 5 p.m. 408/375-5195. AX, MC, V. Entrees, from $18.00 to $33.00.

PASTA MIA TRATTORIA, 481 Lighthouse Avenue. Light-wood decor with cafe chairs and tables creates a casual atmosphere. Italian fare combines northern and southern Italian dishes with California touches and includes grilled fish, lasagna, gnocchi, and fresh pastas such as Linguini Marini with sun-dried tomatoes, spinach, and raisins. A fine wine list features Italian wines. Dinner. 408/375-7709. AX, MC, V. Entrees, from $9.00 to $15.00.

TASTE CAFE & BISTRO, 1199 Forest Avenue. When I go to the county's freshest farmer's market I follow the chefs from this cafe around the stands; the farmers pull out boxes of their choicest produce for selection. An award-winning European restaurant, featuring the finest ingredients available. The menu features such items as herb-roasted chicken, escargots, fresh-made sausages, and daily soups. For dessert, the perfect bread pudding and crème brulée. Dinner. 408/655-0324. No cards. Entrees, from $10.00 to $14.00.

THE MORE CASUAL OPTIONS AVAILABLE

ALLEGRO GOURMET PIZZERIA, 1184 Forest Avenue. Here enjoy cozy indoor dining, with a separate room for families. Adults will savor pesto calzones, seafood pastas, risotto dishes, garlic Caesar salads (voted the best in the county), and gourmet pizzas. Recipes meet the standards of the American Heart Association, and whole wheat pizza crust is available. Kids get to watch the chefs toss dough made from scratch and take some dough to the table to sculpt. Peanut butter and jelly pizza captures the young palates for sure. Lunch, dinner, and catering and take out service. 408/373-5656. AX, MC, V. Entrees, from $7.00 to $12.00.

BECHLER PATISSERIE, 1215 Forest Avenue. Light breakfasts and lunches of tasty quiches and sandwiches are served with delectable desserts. Famous as a place to choose scrumptious wedding cakes. Breakfast, lunch. 408/375-0846. Lunch entrees, from $4.00.

CENTRAL 159, Fifteenth Street between Lighthouse Avenue and Central Avenue. The centrally located Central 159 has entrees and appetizers such as crabcakes, pumpkin ravioli, grilled fish, and more. Lunch and dinner. 408/372-2235. AX, MC, V; others also accepted. Entrees, from $7.00 to $14.00.

FIFI'S CAFE & BAKERY, 1188 Forest Avenue. In a French home atmosphere with pastry shop seating, choose French bistro or healthy spa cuisine. Seafood, pasta and chicken entrees, perfect French onion soup. Fruit tarts, chocolate chip cheesecake, and lemon mousse begin the delectable assortment of desserts to eat in or take out. Great cakes for birthdays being celebrated on the peninsula. Lunch and dinner. 408/372-5325. AX, MC, V; others also accepted. Entrees, from $9.00 to $13.00.

FIRST WATCH, at the American Tin Cannery, 125 Ocean View Boulevard. Especially for breakfast, brunch, and lunch try the comfortable indoor booths or outdoor garden setting here. Pancakes of every variety, sandwiches that match ingredients to characteristics of local places, and Mexican- and Italian-style frittatas are a slice of the menu selections. 408/372-1125. MC, V. Entrees, mostly under $10.00.

FISHWIFE SEAFOOD CAFE, (at Asilomar Beach), 1996 Sunset Drive. With fresh ocean breezes and Caribbean atmosphere, this is a heaven for fresh-fish and seafood lovers. Pastas smothered in seafood, Prawns Belize, grilled fresh catch, and delicately cornmeal-battered calamari. Sensational key lime pie for dessert. Lunch and dinner. 408/375-7107. MC, V; others also accepted. Entrees, from $8.00 to $10.00.

MICHAEL'S GRILL & TAQUERIA, 197 Country Club Gate Center. Eat in casually at comfortable booths, or take out. Grilled fare and Mexican and Cajun specialties that include blackened chicken burritos, fajitas, grilled chicken tacos, and charbroiled shrimp specialties. No animal fats. Lunch and dinner. 408/647-8654. MC, V. Entrees, mostly under $10.00.

PACIFIC GROVE COFFEE ROASTING CO., 510 Lighthouse Avenue. Coffee freshly roasted on the premises and irresistible desserts make this an indoor or outdoor resting spot to enjoy on the downtown walking tour. 408/655-5633.

PEPPERS, MEXI CALI CAFE, 170 Forest Avenue. This "hot" local favorite features innovative Mexican and Latin American cuisine. Snapper Yucatan and homemade tamales are two favorite selections. Consistently voted by locals "Monterey Peninsula's Favorite Mexican Restaurant." Lunch and dinner. 408/373-6892. AX, MC, V; others also accepted. Entrees, from $5.00 to $11.00.

ROCKY COAST ICE CREAM CO., 708 Lighthouse Avenue. They don't serve lunch or dinner, but you can enjoy cones, shakes, and sundaes inside or out on the patio. If children read five books in the summer reading program they get a free cone. Literacy at its sweetest. 408/373-0587.

ROUND TABLE PIZZA, 1116 Forest Avenue. Pacific Grove has some of California's best beach picnic areas, in Lovers Point and Asilomar Beach. This chain pizza parlor is included for its attention to customers' needs. Eat in or call for delivery. The pizza, whether it's classic pepperoni, vegetarian, barbecued chicken, or another variety, will get to you hot and on time. 408/373-0178. MC, V. Pizzas vary in price.

SIZZLER STEAK HOUSE, 1146 Forest Avenue. This chain fish, poultry, and steak house is consistently voted "Best Salad Bar" in the county by *Coast Weekly* readers. Comfortable booths. This is a hometown Sizzler—I've observed the management running out to cars with children's forgotten toys and taking out cables to jump start the cars of people who have left their lights on while dining. Sunday brunch, lunch and dinner. 408/649-0339. AX, MC, V; others also accepted. Entrees, mostly under $10.00.

THE TINNERY, 631 Ocean View Boulevard. Overlooking Lovers Point, the Tinnery has separate comfortable pub and formal dining rooms with warming fireplaces. Pasta, seafood, and steak. Breakfast, lunch, dinner; bar menu until midnight. Nightly entertainment in pub. 408/646-1040. AX, MC, V. Entrees, from $9.00 to $18.00.

TOASTIE'S CAFE, 702 Lighthouse Avenue. A cozy restaurant that feels like a country home offers indoor or outdoor dining. Popular with locals and visitors. Pancakes, huevos rancheros, and omelettes lead off all-day breakfasts. Lunch is also served alfresco. Homestyle dinners have fresh-daily ingredients. 408/373-7543. AX, MC, V. Entrees, from $8.00 to $15.00.

DIRECTIONS

◆

Downtown Pacific Grove from the Aquarium. Drive west up David Avenue to Lighthouse Avenue, just past Central Avenue or one block up from the Nob Hill Super Market. (This is a bit tricky as Lighthouse makes a jog at David Avenue. The old Lighthouse Avenue turns into Central Avenue and Hawthorne turns into Lighthouse Avenue.) Turn right on Lighthouse Avenue; this will become the main street through Pacific Grove. Travel along Lighthouse Avenue for about a half-mile and you will start to see the shops of Pacific Grove. The main town of Pacific Grove is along Lighthouse and Forest avenues. The commercial area is just a few blocks long and most of the sights are within easy walking distance.

Downtown Pacific Grove from Highway 1. Take the Pacific Grove / Highway 68 West exit. Travel down this curving pine-forested road to the city limits of Pacific Grove. Stay in the right-hand lane. Highway 68 curves left to the Asilomar / Pebble Beach area. The fork of 68 that continues straight is called Forest Avenue and leads to the heart of Pacific Grove. You can turn right on Lighthouse Avenue or Central Avenue to backtrack to the aquarium.

INTRODUCTION TO PACIFIC GROVE WITH HISTORICAL HIGHLIGHTS

Although the history books may read differently, Pacific Grove was really created one year when Father Time was ringing out the old and in the new. Cherishing some of the old, he decided that he needed some place where he could put the best of good-old hometown America. About the same time Mother Earth needed help protecting migrating butterflies, a piney paradise inhabited by deer and raccoons, and a rocky coast with hidden beaches. She offered her land to Father Time. Together they hand picked a caring community of Pagrovians to be stewards of the land and restorers of more than a thousand Victorian homes and cottages. Preservationists continue to cherish old-time values in Pacific Grove with an emphasis on preserving nature and nurturing families. They offer visitors their best: delectable restaurants, unique shops, and Victorian inns.

Throughout the year the community comes together to strengthen its home ties. In spring, on opening day of kids-league baseball, the line around the block never stops as the whole town turns out for an opening day barbecue. More community barbecues raise money to refurbish playgrounds in town. At the town's summer festival every child who enters the sand castle contest walks on stage to receive a prize, be it "Most Magical" or "Best Use of Kelp." In autumn the "Butterfly Parade" welcomes the monarchs' return; Pacific Grove is one of the most important wintering homes for the migrating butterflies. The kindergartners get the privilege of dressing as giant monarchs, the preschoolers as caterpillars. Once the butterflies are here, one of the many laws that protects them prevents the use of power tools around their clustering areas, so that the peace of their environment prevails. In election years, signs of favored candidates plaster the front lawns of homes and political discussions are rampant on the front steps of the post office. In winter sunshine the Victorian inns open their doors for holiday tours sponsored by the Pacific Grove Heritage Society. Before spring comes again chefs from local restaurants and merchants volunteer time, expertise, and goods to "The Great Taste of P.G.," a dining extravaganza to benefit local schools. Throughout the year, deer roam the streets and neighborhood gardens, otters frolic offshore, and people walk the paths above the surf. The sun even sets extra gently on Pacific Grove; dipping into the ocean, as it seems, just off the shore from this timeless community.

Located next to Monterey, Pacific Grove could have melded into the larger town, losing its character and history just as many other little towns have in California. Instead Pagrovians have, over the years, fought to retain its small town charm. Driving from Monterey into Pacific Grove produces an entirely different feel. A main street bordered by little shops, Lighthouse Avenue is reminiscent of early times when horse-drawn carriages bustled along dirt roads. Many grand old church buildings are visible, with greenbelt parks winding down to the shore. The older seaside cottages and majestic turn-of-the-century houses still provide homes for many in the downtown area.

Pacific Grove was first developed in the 1800s as a dry coastal retreat for Methodist churchgoers, who came to worship in a quiet and beautiful natural environment. In 1875, land baron David Jacks donated one hundred acres of land to the Methodist Episcopal Church for a religious resort community. Reportedly, after the first minister spent a few months in a cabin along what is now Lighthouse Avenue to test the setting for its appropriateness as a resort, he was cured of an acute respiratory ailment. The next year he brought his brother and both their wives, who suffered from the same illness; they slept in hammocks under the trees and were restored to health. With high regard for the salubrious benefits of the area, the church formed the Pacific Grove Retreat Association. The West's first chautauqua (a religious camp meeting of sermons, educational lectures, family get-togethers, and psalm singing) was held in August of 1875. For the next ten years the meeting became an annual event. Sections of the retreat acreage were subdivided into thirty-by sixty-foot lots to be used as tent sites for seasonal visitors. Hundreds of tents were set up. At the end of the summer the visitors left, with only a caretaker remaining.

A series of "blue laws" were passed that dictated strict rules of behavior in the Grove. For example, one ordinance passed in the early 1900s stated: "It shall be unlawful for every person wearing a bathing suit or portion thereof, except children under the age of ten years, to appear in or upon the beach or in any place open to public—unless attired in a bathing suit or other clothing of opaque material, which shall be worn in such a manner as to preclude form. All such bath suits shall be provided with double crotches or with skirts of ample size to cover the buttocks."

Waltzing, playing the zither, reading the great Sunday dailies, selling popcorn on the beach, and playing tenpins were similarly outlawed. A bell was rung each night to warn of curfew. A fence was put up circling the retreat area, and the gate was locked after curfew. The fence also discouraged vehicular traffic. In 1880 Judge Langford, who had forgotten his key, finally became so enraged that he axed down the gate, thus opening Pacific Grove to the dangers of civilization.

Eventually many of the summer residents decided to stay. Gradually tent frames were converted to year-round single-wall structures. The construction of "modern" family homes complete with framed walls, second stories, gas and electric fixtures, and plumbing began in the 1890s.

Today, large Victorian mansions still grace hilltops while clusters of miniature Victorian cottages fill the grid of small-scale streets between Lighthouse Avenue and Ocean View Boulevard. Many lovely seaside cottages can still be found, in an area bordered roughly by First Street, Ocean View Boulevard, Pacific Street, and Lighthouse. Examples of a variety of architectural styles can be noted while walking around in this older part of Pacific Grove: Gothic Revival, Queen Anne, Stick/Eastlake, Colonial Revival, Shingle, Spanish/Mediterranean, American Foursquare, and Tudor.

Small green plaques on some five hundred of the older buildings, placed by the Pacific Grove Heritage Society, designate the year the houses were constructed. A building qualifies for a plaque if it was built in 1910 or earlier and still retains its original character and architectural style.

For over twenty years the Heritage Society of Pacific Grove, the Pacific Grove Art Center, and the Pacific Grove Chamber of Commerce have cosponsored the Victorian Home Tour. In 1993 the tour date was changed from during the "Good Old Days" to the weekend of the Butterfly Parade in October. (See the Calendar of Events, p. 310.) Homes, inns, and churches, some of Pacific Grove's finest Victorians, open their doors to visitors and display turn-of-the-century woodwork, antique furnishings, and stained glass embellishments, as well as original art of the owners.

The result of preserving Victorians looks so fitting and elegant, the process of restoring them appears straightforward, even easy. In actuality it is, of course, hard work, and with a dilapidated Victorian, quite complex. When builder-artists Geoff and Joy Welch purchased a one-story board-and-batten house on Third Street featuring a hipped roof with gables, daylight could be seen through the walls. Ivy had made its way though the windows and into the house. Although they'd fixed up other homes, this was their first Victorian. They rebuilt the foundation to level the floors, installed new plumbing, heating, and electrical systems, and removed the suspended ceiling. They researched and incorporated "hardware from brass switch-plate covers to sash lifts, period wall paper, and reproduction plaster." Geoff milled Victorian door casings and kitchen cabinets to suit the architecture of that period. When the Welch family outgrew the little Victorian, they constructed a new home at 1033 Bay View Avenue that drew from the style of Julia Morgan's Asilomar. For their skill and care they won first place in the 1992 Heritage Society of Pacific Grove contest for "Best New Design Award," honoring construction that fits in with the historic design of the town.

In the first tour, the downtown area of Pacific Grove, there are many reminders of pleasures of the past. But if you walk slowly and ask a few questions along the way you'll also enjoy the town's true treasure, its people.

TOURS

The three tours in this chapter focus on different aspects of the town. The first is a tour of the historic main street and downtown area of Pacific Grove. This is meant to be a walking tour, with time to see some of the historic places and to do a bit of shopping along the way. The second is a tour of the coastline of Pacific Grove. This can be driven, but to really see the remarkable features I suggest walking or, if you are inclined, bike or kayak rental (see the Resource Guide for listings, pp. 300–301, 302). Finally, the third tour describes the butterfly groves, a short walk through the pine forests.

THE DOWNTOWN WALKING TOUR

This circular route through some of the downtown area is less than a mile in length, and can be done in parts. If there are young children in your group you may want to plan a play break at Caledonia Park, which also has restrooms and picnic tables. To make the tour more interesting for children, you might play such games along the way as "Who can find the smallest house?" "Who can find the house with the oldest plaque?" I've also found it helpful to make a quick stop at Sand Pebbles, a sticker and small-gift shop owned by a former teacher who loves kids, or at any of the other gift shops as an incentive for keeping up during the trip. At 545 Lighthouse (408/375-3569), toward the top of the avenue, the Scotch Bakery, a Pacific Grove tradition for over a hundred years, offers cookies, doughnuts, and milk for the trip and an assortment of baked goods for anytime.

Espresso, relaxing cups of tea, and chocolate fantasies could be sufficient incentive for me to climb the Alps. There are a number of small coffeehouses with coffee, tea, juices, and light fare. The Bookworks Bookshop & Coffee House is across from the Post Office at 677 Lighthouse Avenue (408/372-2242), Juice N' Java is at 599 Lighthouse (408/373-8652), and the Pacific Grove Coffee Roasting Company at 510 Lighthouse (408/655-5633) has indoor and outdoor seating across from the cinema.

If you have children and want a casual place to eat, Toasties on Lighthouse across the street from the Post Office is a good choice. Rocky Coast Ice Cream shares the sidewalk and patio with Toasties. More-elegant lunches can be obtained at Melac's or Fandango. There are a number of excellent restaurants in this downtown area, so walk around and choose what looks good to you.

Begin the tour at Lighthouse and Fountain avenues. Walking on the east side of Lighthouse you will pass some of the oldest stores downtown. A restaurant, a bakery, and health food, clothing, and shoe stores are nestled together on the ground floor of a common-wall building. The large square building across the street was originally Holman's store, once the largest department store in the county.

When I first moved to Pacific Grove and would ask directions or say good morning to passers-by I found myself entering into discussions with heretofore strangers about the effects of El Niño on the weather, the new grandchildren, the latest show at the Pacific Grove Art Center, or the errant puppy. I was a little too hurried for the shopkeepers who conversed with and didn't just sell to their customers. As you discover Pacific Grove, rediscover the human warmth of yesteryear. Shopkeepers do have appropriate radar; if you're in a hurry they can get you on your way extra fast. But especially if you're from another country or have shopped primarily in malls, shop in Pacific Grove for an experience of hometown Americana.

When you reach Forest Avenue turn left to proceed up the hill. Along the way the Pacific Grove Florist (408/375-9809) displays the artistic touch this community attracts. You can pick up a warm barbecued chicken or deli items for a picnic at Grove Market (408/375-9581). The butchers will probably know about the latest town event and sell you tickets for some worthy cause. In the 300 block of Forest Avenue mesmerizing eyes catch your glance at Antiques by Trotter. Unusually select antique doll collections can be seen by prior reservation. In addition to other quality antiques, the Trotter Galleries at 309 Forest Avenue (408/373-3505) specializes in early California artists.

At the corner of Laurel and Forest you will see the Pacific Grove City Hall with its tall square clock tower. Here too are the chimes that can be heard every fifteen minutes throughout the town. At Christmas they serenade with carols, and the townspeople celebrate the season with the lighting of a tree next to city hall. (If you are here at Christmas, don't miss what is referred to as "Candy

Cane Lane," which is located off Forest at Morse Avenue. The houses and the neighborhood park are ablaze with lights and decorations.)

Turn right on Laurel. Next you see the Ketchum Barn, at Laurel and Seventeenth. Long after this barn was built by H. C. Ketchum in 1891 to house animals it was left vacant and became a refuge for a variety of "lost souls." Now it houses the Heritage Society of Pacific Grove museum and administrative office. It is open to the public on Saturday from 1 to 4 p.m. all year. Inside you can ring the original chimes from city hall, wind up an old Victrola, and check out the goods and fashions of a recreated turn-of-the-century store. For a greater understanding of the town's heritage, view old photos and pick up previous copies of *The Board and Batten.*

If you like, at this point you can take a one-block side trip up Seventeenth Avenue to the fire station at Pine Avenue. In front of the fire station is the bell that was used to ring out curfew, when it was unlawful for any minor to be on public streets of Pacific Grove between 8 p.m. and daylight the following morning.

Going back down Seventeenth Street to Lighthouse Avenue you pass a number of Victorian cottages that now house shops and restaurants. Once at Lighthouse Avenue turn left and walk another four blocks, to Congress Avenue.

Here you also find the Gosby House Inn, 643 Lighthouse, a Queen Anne–style home built in 1886 and 1887 by J. F. Gosby, a shoemaker. Gosby added many more rooms over the years to accommodate overflowing guests. This house is listed on the National Register of Historic Places and among California Historical Landmarks. Hart Mansion, next door to the Gosby House, is another Queen Anne–style building, constructed in 1892. Bookworks Bookshop & Coffee House (408/372-2242), on the corner, wafts the aromas of espresso and hot chocolate. Often the location for book signings and talks by writers, the store features a display of books by local authors.

Cross Lighthouse Avenue at Congress Avenue. The Post Office is on this corner. Card tables are set up during local campaigns to introduce citizens to their candidates, and petition drives sometimes fill the sidewalks with avid debaters. A good selection of local papers and guides fills the newsstands here.

If you proceed down Congress Avenue, which becomes Caledonia Street, you will come to Caledonia Park at the corner of Caledonia Street and Central Avenue. Once a swamp, Caledonia Park now has a play area for children, and benches and picnic tables. As you walk down residential Central Avenue consider a jog along Eighteenth or Nineteenth streets, to enjoy the look of some of the cottages that were built on the tiny tent-size lots, which first sold for an average of fifty dollars each. When workers tear down interior wall coverings in these cottages while renovating they often find the old tent frames still intact inside the walls.

Back on Central Avenue you will see the grand Centrella Inn. The Centrella Cottage was built in 1886. When it opened it was described as containing fifteen rooms fitted with all the conveniences of a first-class boarding and lodging

house. It served as the headquarters for the Methodist ministers and their families in 1888. This is now a beautifully restored bed and breakfast inn.

Across the street is Chautauqua Hall, at the corner of Seventeenth Street
and Central Avenue. This building is a state historic landmark, built in 1881.
Chautauquas were the substance of a movement started in 1874 as an educational camp meeting on the shores of Lake Chautauqua in New York. The hall
is still in use today. It frequently is used for community functions, including the
schools' science fair, the quilt show, and exercise classes. Next to the hall on the
south side is Elmarie H. Dyke Park that has recently been built to offer a quiet
corner to rest in and where townspeople can congregate.

Proceed down Central (north) and you see the small cottage that houses the
Pacific Grove Chamber of Commerce. The Chamber, at the corner of Forest and
Central, is open noon to 4 p.m., Monday to Friday. The people here offer helpful
visitor information. Directional maps and event information is posted outside
(408/373-3304).

Kitty-corner from the Chamber of Commerce you'll see a lifelike gray whale
lying in the sand next to the sidewalk. Kids may be climbing all over this sculpture's back and sliding down the cement flukes. Named by the kids in town,
"Sandy the Whale" welcomes visitors to the Pacific Grove Museum of Natural
History at the corner of Forest and Central. The museum is open every day from
10 a.m. to 5 p.m., except Mondays and holidays. There is no charge, but a do-
nation is always appreciated. The museum began as adults and children made
excursions into the surrounding country and brought back specimens of flowers, shells, or anything that might be of instructive value. Prizes were awarded
to encourage interest on the part of both adults and children. Over the years the
museum has received many gifts, and today it has grown into an impressive
array of native specimens. Here you can find as well a relief map of Monterey
Canyon that shows the steep drop of the ocean floor. The museum also has a
small outside garden of native plants. In a special exhibit hall the rotating displays include the annual fungi exhibits in late winter and the wildflower show
in April.

Jewell Park, across the street from the museum, hosts the town's annual
birthday "Good Old Days" pancake breakfast. In spring, the Pacific Grove Arts
Commission presents "Sundays in the Park," a series of free concerts with music
ranging from reggae to Vivaldi. Pacific Grove High School's award-winning
high-school jazz band often performs.

The Pacific Grove City Library is across the street, on the corners of Grand,
Central, and Fountain. Bulletin boards inside post information about community events. The Pacific Grove Public Library was established in December of
1905 and first opened to the public in 1908. This library is a great source of
pride to the community.

After leaving the library you can either proceed down Central for a few more blocks and see some of the oldest churches in Pacific Grove or you might choose to head back up Fountain Avenue to your starting place. If you proceed down Central Avenue you see white, green, red, and brown spires rising above the homes. In the early days most of the sermons were preached outdoors in a quiet grove. The first building to be used solely for church services was built in 1877 near the Centrella Hotel. That building is no longer here, but others still are.

Mayflower Church was built in 1889 and a Sunday school wing added in 1908. In 1914 a fire destroyed the building, and it was rebuilt as the large brick structure it is today on Central Avenue at Thirteenth Street. Saint Mary's-by-the-Sea Episcopal Church at Twelfth and Central was built in 1887 and still has its original seventy-five-foot spire. Modeled after a British church in Bath, it was designed in the Old English Gothic style. When the congregation outgrew the tiny chapel it was sliced in two and three bays were added in the middle. Stained glass windows include two signed Tiffany lilies.

Once you decide to head back to your car, walk up one of the numbered streets for one or two blocks until you come to Lighthouse Avenue. To learn more about the history of Pacific Grove you might want to stop and see some of the old photographs of the area. Pat Hathaway has a wonderful collection in his shop at 171 Forest Avenue, just beyond Fountain and Lighthouse where you started.

THE COASTAL TOUR

Directions from the Aquarium. The aquarium sits on the border of Monterey and Pacific Grove, and the Monterey Peninsula Recreation Trail extends between the aquarium and Pacific Grove's Lovers Point. Located on the former Southern Pacific Railroad right-of-way, the trail has a separate walking and cycling path. So if you are at the aquarium you are ready to start this coastal tour route. If you decide to park your car check the signs, as most of the parking along this section of Ocean View Boulevard is limited to two hours.

Except for a few areas, all of the Pacific Grove shoreline is owned by the city or state. Hopkins Marine Station has a private section owned by Stanford University. Two parcels adjacent to Asilomar State Beach are also privately held. Otherwise all of the coastline is open to public use. In the section designated as the Pacific Grove Marine Gardens Fish Refuge from the aquarium to Point Piños, fish, invertebrate life, crustaceans, mollusks, and plants cannot be taken or disturbed without proper permits or licenses.

Concern over public access to the beach is a part of the history of Pacific Grove. At one point the owner of the bathhouse that once stood near Lovers Point erected a barrier across her property to prevent access to the point and the beach. In 1932, Dr. Julia Platt challenged the owner to throw the gate wide open. The owner retaliated by padlocking the entrance. Dr. Platt filed the padlock. Then the gate was nailed shut. Dr. Platt, wielding an axe, chopped down the gate. The beach was opened to the public and has been open to this day. Unlike many other geographic areas, Pacific Grove has virtually unobstructed access to its coast.

The coastal tour described in this section extends approximately four miles along Ocean View Boulevard, which becomes Sunset Drive and follows the ocean all the way to Pebble Beach. If you leave your car you will need to double back on the same route, walk along the town's residential streets, or catch the MST #1 bus.

There are few places to stop and eat along the way. Sandwich shops can be found in the American Tin Cannery on Ocean View Boulevard. The restaurant First Watch offers great breakfasts and lunches. Once you start your trip the next place to find bathrooms, water, and a place to eat is Lovers Point. The snack bar is open in the summer and on some weekends. The Tinnery Restaurant on Ocean View Boulevard offers comfortable family dining with views of the bay. The main town, with a bevy of restaurants, is just a couple of blocks up the path from Lovers Point. About a mile past Lovers Point at the intersection of Asilomar Boulevard and Ocean View Boulevard it is possible to walk a couple of blocks up Asilomar Boulevard to the Pacific Grove Golf Course Club House for breakfast or, at lunch, sandwiches. With so many incredible views and picnic spots along the path, consider taking water and a picnic along.

Thanksgiving in April? If you forgo food during your walk you may have added empathy afterward for the four hundred Spanish colonists who held a huge banquet of fish and fowl on the present U.S. side of the Rio Grande after a sixty-day desert journey from southern Mexico. You might want to stop and eat at The Fishwife restaurant, located just past Asilomar State Beach. Each year this restaurant and El Cocodrillo sponsor a celebration of the April 30, 1598, Thanksgiving during the last week of April. For the fish and pastas offered throughout the year this restaurant consistently wins as the best in the county. Up the road the Korean Sunset View Restaurant offers light and fluffy tempura and other authentic specialties for lunch or dinner. It also has chocolate and strawberry stick treats for any young troopers with you.

If you plan ahead, at the end of the walk on Sunset Drive you can turn left at the next street, which is the south end of Asilomar Boulevard, to reach the conference center complex. Asilomar will reserve lunches and dinners and offers snacks at the conference store.

The coastal trip follows the coastline along the furthermost tip of the Monterey Peninsula. Keep in mind that for about a mile the bike trail merges with the regular road. This occurs from Lovers Point to Asilomar Boulevard. So if you are on bikes be very careful; warn children to watch for parked cars that might open a door unexpectedly. Also, be very careful next to the ocean. The water is very cold, the rocks are slippery, and the waves can be unpredictably high. Pacific Grove is famous for its sneaker waves.

Begin at the Monterey Bay Aquarium, heading west. You soon see a building with a sign, "Monterey Boat Works." This is a part of Hopkins Marine Station of Stanford University. Farther on there is a gate, and there are many large classrooms and laboratories. Recently celebrating its 100-year birthday, Hopkins Marine Station is one of the world's foremost marine research institutes. The grounds are private and the beaches are protected in order to safeguard biological research.

The area near here was once one local Chinatown. Several Chinese fish companies established a small village on what is now Marine Station Point. The properties between Chinatown and Lighthouse Avenue were used for drying squid. Hundreds of tons of it were dried on lattices, then tossed on the ground and turned with rakes. The annual Feast of Lanterns celebration is a reminder of the cultural richness of the early settlers.

Past the Hopkins Station the trail skirts the bay, offering breathtaking views of the blue-green waters, rocky outcroppings, and sea life. Sea otters float in offshore kelp beds, dive for sea urchins, and crack shells on the rocks they have balanced on their stomachs. Harbor seals stretch on rocks in unusual positions. They lie so still it seems as if a sculptor has molded them to the rocks. When the harbor seals are active their smooth heads bob in the waves, swimming so close with their eyes staring so directly at you it's as if they are trying to communicate some secret message. As you walk along you'll notice, on calm days, multicolored kayaks gliding over the glassy surface.

Berwick Park, on the coastal side of Ocean View Boulevard between Ninth Street and Carmel Avenue, south of the recreation trail, has a large, well-manicured lawn and a natural landscape area consisting of rocky outcrops and native plants. There are benches and plenty of areas in which kids can run around. This is also a favorite setting for outdoor weddings. We counted four, one afternoon. As you travel along the path to Lovers Point you will see rows of Victorian houses on the inland side of the trail. Many of these are now used as bed and breakfast inns. Giant carved pumpkins fill their yards at Halloween and doors are opened to participants in the inn's tour at Christmas.

Lovers Point Park is the next park on the trail. The name of this park is most often attributed to its amorous history, but some accounts describe it as a derivative of "Lovers of Jesus Point." Located at the end of Seventeenth Street, this is a landscaped community park of 4.4 acres. Here windswept cypresses arch over sculpted rock. There are two sandy beaches, one on each side of a concrete pier. Each is reached by going down stairs. The main beach is one of the safest in the county for wading and swimming. Extreme care should always be taken, however, as the water is usually extremely cold. Additionally, this park has a volleyball court, a children's swimming pool (summer only), sandy beaches, a concrete pier, restrooms, water faucets, picnic tables, and a snack bar. The waves offshore are favorites of surfers. The prodigious kelp beds offshore are favorites of otters and scuba divers.

Currently an elegant restaurant, the Bath House sits high above the beach. It takes its name from the early bathhouses at this location, in 1875 a little brown frame shack that was used for saltwater bathing and in 1882 a rambling structure with twenty-two dressing rooms and eight private saltwater baths.

William Smith acquired the land at Lovers Point in 1904 when it was mainly a pile of stones and cliffs of solid rock. At the time he acquired it, Pacific Grove was still a Methodist camp meeting ground and there were objections to a beach where people could go on Sunday. Despite opposition, Smith blasted in the cove and set up a new bathhouse, bathing resort, and boathouse. He blasted clear the cove to cut away more of a beach and with the rock he blasted loose he constructed the stone wall that stands today.

Once past Lovers Point the separated bike trail ends. The walking trail continues. If you are on a bike you will need to ride on the street for about a mile until a painted bike lane reappears.

On any Sunday in April the billowing sails of rainbow catamarans race offshore behind rolling waves that build to snow-white pillowy hills. The waves crash on ancient rocks just beyond a shoreline draped in phosphorescent lavender-pink succulents. This area beyond Lovers Point is known as Perkins Park, named after Hayes Perkins, a landscaper, who laid out gardens in African and other countries. Perkins singlehandedly transformed this once poison-oak-filled area into a beautiful shoreline park.

If you travel on along Ocean View Boulevard you encounter the wilder part of the trail. The path winds on until there are fewer houses and the ocean and bay waters meet. At Ocean View Boulevard and Asilomar Avenue you come to the edge of the Municipal Golf Course. Crespi Pond is off to your left, on the inland side of Ocean View Boulevard; this is a tiny freshwater pond named for Father Crespi, chronicler of the Portola expedition, who noted it in his annals in 1770. Just beyond the pond the stone shelter offers the only bathrooms available for the next mile, until the conference grounds.

Across from Crespi Pond is Point Pinos, "the Point of Pines," named by the Spanish explorer Sebastian Vizcaino in 1602. The outreaching point marks the meeting of the southernmost tip of the Monterey Bay and the greater Pacific Ocean. The Spanish admiral Gonzales reported in 1734 that the southern headland of the Monterey Bay, which he called the Punto de Pinos, was heavily wooded to the shoreline. The one-mile stretch around Point Pinos is owned today by the U.S. Coast Guard and maintained by the city of Pacific Grove. Presently, during low tide you can climb out on the rocks and have a panoramic view both out to sea and back to the lighthouse that is perched on the grassy knoll. Because of the 1993 identification of a variety of endangered plant species, the city has requested that the state park system restrict entrance to the area, with boardwalks, fences, and trails.

Pacific Grove Lighthouse

Be very careful when close to the ocean here. The waves can be unexpectedly high, and this is not a good place to swim or even wade.

The Point Pinos Light Station can be entered from Asilomar Avenue, across from the El Carmelo Cemetery. This is the oldest continuously operating lighthouse on the West Coast. Its beacon has flashed nightly since February of 1855. The first light source was a sperm whale oil lantern. Later lard oil replaced the sperm whale oil, then kerosene, then incandescent vapor, and finally electricity (1915).

The light source is now a 1,000 watt bulb, amplified by lenses and prisms to produce a 50,000-candlepower beam, which is visible under favorable conditions up to fifteen miles out at sea. The light flashes in a simple on-off arrangement. In addition there is a horn that is used to blast warnings to fogbound travelers. On a foggy day or night you might hear the foghorn even if you are a long way away. Robert Louis Stevenson wrote of visiting keeper Allen Luce in 1879, after a walk through the woods from Monterey, and praised Luce's hospitality, piano playing, ship models, and oil paintings. The lighthouse is open to the public on Saturdays and Sundays from 1 to 4 p.m. Inside you will find some of the early records, including descriptions of ships that wrecked nearby. You can tour the ground floor of the building, but the light itself is not open to the public since it is still in use. If you take the Pebble Beach tour look back this way from Spanish Bay Beach to see the light flashing.

If you go back to Ocean View Boulevard and continue with the tour you will encounter even wilder coastline. There are benches to rest on and tidepools to explore. Be very careful here, though, as the waves have taken away the unwary who have ventured too far. Again, please don't take anything from the pools, alive or dead. This is the home of many creatures and we are lucky to be able to find tidepools with inhabitants still busy and thriving.

The Lighthouse Avenue Extension is the old line between city and county limits. Here Ocean View Boulevard changes names to become Sunset Drive. Asilomar State Beach and Conference Grounds is located on Sunset Drive between Jewell Avenue on the north and Spanish Bay, the northernmost section of Pebble Beach, on the south. Asilomar State Beach consists of rocky coastlines, tidepools, sand dunes, and a large white crescent of sand. In addition to the beach area, Asilomar Conference Grounds has pine forest and dunes that provide a natural setting for deer, raccoons, and a variety of other wildlife. In all, Asilomar covers 103 acres. Asilomar State Beach is a part of the California State Park system. The conference facilities are operated by a nonprofit corporation.

Asilomar, meaning "Haven by the Sea," was first established in 1913 as a YWCA retreat. The architect of Hearst Castle, Julia Morgan, designed the original buildings, which are listed as a State Historic Landmark, as a National Historic Landmark, and on the National Register of Historic Places. One can observe Morgan's informal wood Craftsman architecture at the entrance gates (built 1912 to 1913), the Administration Building (1913), Chapel (1915), Crocker Hall (1927), Scripps Hall (1927), and Merrill Hall (1927 to 1928).

In recent years there has been extensive restoration work on the beach to revegetate the area with native plants and preserve the dunes. You can view a native plant nursery on the Asilomar property and participate in dune planting days.

Farther on, Sunset Drive becomes Highway 68, which continues to Highway 1. You can drive back to the business center of Pacific Grove by turning left on Seventeen Mile Drive. If you are walking you might choose Asilomar Boulevard. If you walk back along Grove Acre Avenue you will get to the butterfly sanctuary in about twenty minutes.

To Connect with the Pebble Beach Tour. If you are driving or biking turn right off Sunset Drive at Seventeen Mile Drive. Drivers need to pay a fee to continue. If you would like to walk on into Pebble Beach, you can choose either of two routes. You can walk along the beach to the south end of the sand. From here a slat-board walkway continues to Spanish Bay. Or you can take the other entrance to Pebble Beach located off Sunset Drive; just past the Beachcomber Motel turn right at a dirt pathway. This leads behind a gravel yard to the outskirts of the Links at Spanish Bay. The path leads to the top of a small scenic knoll before descending to a rest area with restrooms and water. (See the Pebble Beach section, p. 105.)

Before you leave the Pacific Grove area, come back to this coastline route at sunset. The ocean often glows silver and gold beneath crimson skies as the sun melts into the horizon beyond this gentle town.

THE BUTTERFLY TOUR: THE MONARCH GROVE SANCTUARY AND WASHINGTON PARK

Pacific Grove is known as "Butterfly Town U.S.A." Each year monarch butterflies arrive in Pacific Grove in late October and stay until mid March. The numbers vary from year to year, but as you drive through town you will see many gardens covered with flittering sheets of gold. You are most assured of seeing butterflies at the Monarch Grove Sanctuary. Washington Park was a mass of color in former years, and hopefully, with the new plantings that citizens of Pacific Grove are continuing to make, the butterflies will return in greater numbers to favored pines and nectar sources in the park.

More than fifty thousand of the four-inch orange and black butterflies may congregate in a single grove. They migrate to the groves to find relief from winter's cold. In cool and foggy weather or early in the morning they can be seen hanging on branches in dense clusters, looking something like a bunch of dead leaves. When the sunshine warms the clusters, they burst apart and light up the sky with a flurry of orange and black. The cold makes them sluggish, and the warmth allows them to fly.

You may want to bring binoculars to view the clustering butterflies up close. Be sure to watch your step, since butterflies are sometimes on the ground. In January and February you can see the courtly mating ritual. The female drifts from a tree to the ground, and a male joins her, and then carries her back to the tree.

While there are no facilities at the sanctuary, bathrooms and water are available at Washington Park. There are also picnic tables and benches and a play area for children at the far south section of the park. Unless you have brought a picnic lunch, you will need to go back to downtown Pacific Grove to find food. You might want to try the Monarch Cafe, Home of the Monarch Burger, at 162 Fountain Avenue. It's open for breakfast and lunch Monday through Saturday, and for dinner Monday through Friday (408/373-7911).

DIRECTIONS

Directions to the Monarch Grove Sanctuary from the Monterey Bay Aquarium. Take David Avenue up three blocks and turn right at Forest Avenue. Continue on Forest until Lighthouse Avenue. Turn left on Lighthouse and pass through downtown Pacific Grove until you come to Grove Acre Avenue. Turn left and continue to just past the apartment buildings.

Directions to the Monarch Grove Sanctuary from Highway 1. Take Highway 68 to Pacific Grove. Highway 68 becomes Forest Avenue; continue on to Lighthouse Avenue and turn left. Take Lighthouse through downtown Pacific Grove for one-half mile. Turn left on Grove Acre Avenue and continue to just past the apartment buildings. The Monarch Grove Sanctuary will be on your left.

Washington Park is the largest of Pacific Grove's city parks, with approximately twenty acres. It is six blocks long and is bordered by Short, Alder, Sinex, and Melrose streets. The park has been left as natural acreage with large Monterey pines and oaks towering above the ground. It offers important wildlife habitat and is a wintering area of the monarch. To find the butterfly groves, follow the wood-chip trails into the center of the forest. The butterflies move around from tree to tree, so you will need to look carefully. Look for large clusters hanging from branches in the taller trees.

As mentioned, in recent years few butterflies have been found in Washington Park. To help bring back the large masses of monarchs that formerly congregated here the city of Pacific Grove is in the process of reworking it to suit them. Volunteer work forces have been laying trails and planting new Monterey pines and native understory. Though the trails are obviously for humans, the overall aim of the work is to achieve a balance of shade and wind-breaking capacity with full sun hitting the trees during the day. Butterflies need direct sun for at least thirty minutes during the late morning to early afternoon, so that they can warm up and fly to locate water and nectar sources. Of course the paths also prevent further compaction of the soil around the roots of the trees, as long as we humans stay on them.

You can plan to spend a few minutes or many hours looking at and enjoying the butterflies and relaxing in the pines. The forested park offers a glimpse at the way Pacific Grove looked before settlement. Reportedly, the pines were so thick that people were frequently lost.

WHAT ELSE TO SEE AND DO

THE PACIFIC GROVE ART CENTER. At 568 Lighthouse Avenue (408/375-2208) the Art Center has two of the largest galleries in Northern California. This is an excellent place to find the works of local artists. Rick Deragon, art scene reviewer for the *Monterey County Herald,* reported in 1993, "No other local venue provides exhibition space like the art center, and no other grassroots organization takes on theme shows with the same fearlessness and ambition."

MUNICIPAL GOLF COURSE. At 77 Asilomar Avenue (408/648-3177) the municipal course offers eighteen holes, a clubhouse, golf equipment rental, electric carts, and a driving range. This course, which backs on the ocean, is a rare golfing bargain, with relatively low nine- and eighteen-hole greens fees.

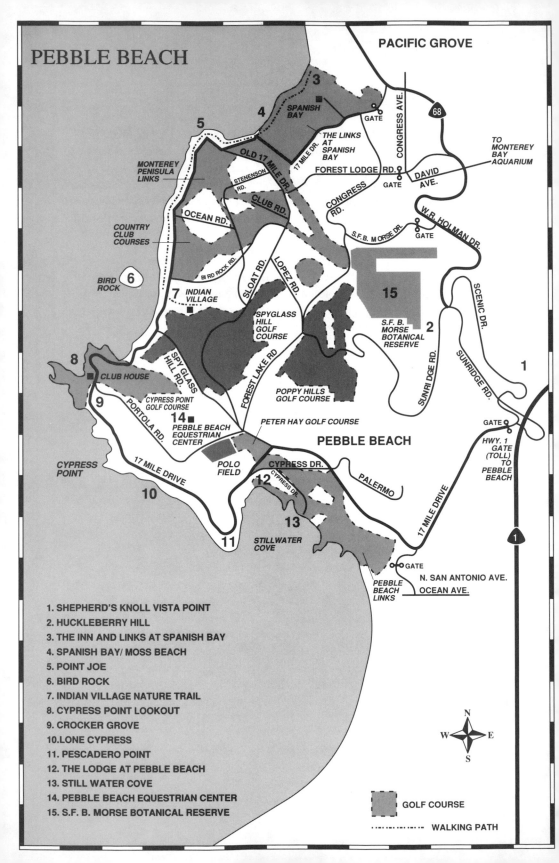

CHAPTER 4

PEBBLE BEACH

THE BEACH, THE FOREST, THE GREENS

Pebble Beach is a gated enclave of residences—some of which are true mansions—and forests and golf courses. Seventeen Mile Drive winds through the area and leads to several points of interest, the most popular of which is the Lone Cypress.

GETTING READY

THE BEST TIMES TO VISIT AND THE SPECIAL EVENTS

On a morning tour you might catch a glimpse of a wobbly fawn nuzzling its mother in the forest on one side of Seventeen Mile Drive as surfers and playful otters catch a wave together on the other. If it's the golf you have come for, according to Pebble Beach Links golf pro Soney Bae the best time to play golf is "early, early morning, about seven o'clock." At any time of the day you can enjoy a trail ride, relax with a book on the sands of a sheltered cove, tour a posh residential area, or walk among over one hundred varieties of wild flowers, some of them fragile dune dwellers found nowhere else in the world. Every evening, as the sun dips through wind-whipped skies, a bagpiper plays a farewell tune. You will find him walking the headlands between The Inn at Spanish Bay and the ocean.

Crowds vary more with events than seasons in Pebble Beach. Seventeen Mile Drive is closed to tour traffic during the AT&T Golf Tournament in early February. A favorite time to be in Pebble Beach is during the Concours d'Elegance in early August. Equestrian shows are featured in August, March, and April. In May the top-rated Del Monte Kennel Club Dog Show stars on the greens around The Lodge at Pebble Beach. Regattas in Stillwater Cove start in May and continue through September. Golf tournaments tee off almost every month.

Wildlife-viewing times are another consideration for trip planning. Pods of whales blasting geysers and breaching offshore can be seen best in late December and January. Dappled fawns are born in spring and summer and can often be observed at close range. Wildflowers bloom year-round and most profusely in spring.

CLIMATE AND CLOTHING

The best time to play golf is September to November. In the usually mild winter months it's not unusual to see golfers dressed in short sleeves running through rain with golf clubs bouncing on their backs. Winds and fog are common but below-freezing temperatures are extremely rare.

What you wear at Pebble Beach will mirror how you choose to spend your time. Since the area combines fine resorts, forests, beaches, casual horseback trail riding, and fashionable golf, your wardrobe may vary from dinner jackets and evening wear to tennis shoes and hiking clothes depending on your choice of activities. Bring binoculars for wildlife viewing and for golf viewing, which also may be wild if Bill Murray is on the course.

TOUR LENGTHS

The Seventeen Mile Drive from Pacific Grove to Carmel through Pebble Beach takes twenty minutes. With light sightseeing at major attractions, set aside at least two hours. Pebble Beach offers a full day, weekend, week, and lifetime of possibilities for relaxing and learning. If you do not choose an extended stay you can still experience the many moods of Pebble Beach by traveling through it early, on the way to Carmel, and again later, on the return drive.

WILDLIFE WISDOM

The number of visitors to this area increases each year. The treasured environment of this area appears rugged but is actually quite fragile, dependent in its natural balance on responsible tourism. No plant or animal life should be disturbed or removed. The deer in this area have very little fear of people. Drivers need to pay special attention to speed limits and keep watch for deer darting onto roadways, especially at dusk.

The temptation to feed animals such as cute ground squirrels and calling gulls is easier to resist if you are aware that overpopulation of one species endangers others, and that food from people spreads disease. Animals catching their own food provide great moments for human spectators.

VISITOR INFORMATION

You can enter Pebble Beach through any of the five fee gates. The Highway 1 Gate and the Pacific Grove Gate lead to the most scenic drives. The cost for tourists is $6.00 per car at this writing. Gatekeepers clear those who are guests of residents, and resorts refund the entrance fee to diners and lodgers. To help drivers from any entrance locate and remain on Seventeen Mile Drive, the center lines of the entire route have been painted red. A walking path leads into Pebble Beach by way of a slat-board walkway at the south end of Asilomar Beach, and another walking path begins at the Pacific Grove Gate. Bicyclists can enter at any gate, for free. On holidays and weekends bicyclists may enter only through the Pacific Grove Gate. Bicycle rentals are available in Pacific Grove, Monterey, and Carmel (see the Resource Guide, pp. 300–301).

A visitor-use pamphlet will be handed to you at the gate. No overnight camping or fires are permitted. Fire danger is usually extreme. Swimming in the rough water anywhere along Seventeen Mile Drive is hazardous; the undertows and sneaker waves are powerful, even at the wading level. Keep your eye on the ocean while wading or playing near the surf.

Courtesy for golfers is expected. Maintain quiet on the backswings. Hiking isn't allowed on golf cart paths or on courses. For information about events or gates or to ask questions call the Pebble Beach information line at 408/647-7493.

PARKING

Parking is provided in pullout areas along Seventeen Mile Drive. Parking at Stillwater Cove is behind The Lodge. Parking for events is in designated areas, with shuttle-bus service.

ALTERNATE TRANSPORTATION

County transit buses do not serve Pebble Beach. Private tour buses include Pebble Beach in coastal tours. If you have all day and love exercise use my favorite way to see Pebble Beach, with a combination of walking or biking and horseback riding. You can rent bikes, pp. 300–301, and reserve trail rides, (408/624-2756). A leisurely walk from Asilomar Beach to a point parallel to Bird and Scal rocks (two-and-a-half miles) and then, crossing the street, along the Indian Village nature walk takes about three hours (at an athletic pace, one-and-a-half hours). Trails from here connect with the equestrian center. A one- or two-hour trail ride leads along miles of incredible vistas. You can hike back or call a cab. Pack drinks, snacks, and a backpack picnic. You can also stop at a restaurant at Spanish Bay along the way and choose from such selections as a giant, pan-fried chocolate chip cookie or a crispy salad.

RESTROOMS

Since this is primarily a forest, golf, resort, and residential area, finding a restroom is not always easy. Public restrooms are located a couple of miles south of the Pacific Grove Gate at the Bird Rock turnoff and, closer to the Carmel Gate, at Stillwater Cove.

WHERE TO STAY

A tradition of elegance and the highest standards prevails in the only two lodgings available in Pebble Beach. For golf and room reservations at the resorts call 800/654-9300. AX, MC, V, and other cards are accepted at all resort facilities.

THE INN AT SPANISH BAY. In an architectural blending of Spanish and Old Monterey styles, four stories of rooms feature elegant oversized furniture and sweeping ocean views of the wild coast and the Spanish Bay golf course. Amenities include tennis, pools, spa, and restaurants. 408/647-7500. For two, from $245.00 to $350.00.

THE LODGE AT PEBBLE BEACH. Located in the heart of Pebble Beach, surrounded by the famous Pebble Beach Links, and opening to beautiful ocean vistas, this grand resort has kept pace with the times. Warm interior pastels compliment architecture of Spanish and Italian influence. Four fine restaurants. Access to golf courses, tennis, swimming, and fitness facilities. 408/624-3811. For two, from $295.00 to 450.00.

RESTAURANTS

FORMAL

CLUB XIX (at The Lodge at Pebble Beach). Here have first-class French cuisine with views of the links and ocean. Lunch is served at a French bistro with patio dining. Romantic downstairs setting for dinner (jackets are required at dinner only). 408/624-3811. AX, MC, V; others also accepted. Entrees, mostly under $30.00.

SEMIFORMAL

THE BAY CLUB (at The Inn at Spanish Bay). Fresh orchids, elegant seating, and marble counters inside set off spectacular ocean views. Truly gracious service. Contemporary and classical Northern Italian cuisine and desserts show off chef Drew Prevetti's attention to detail and quality. Dinner. 408/647-7500. AX, MC, V; others also accepted. Entrees, mostly under $25.00.

CASUAL

CLUBHOUSE BAR & GRILL (at The Inn at Spanish Bay). In a pro-shop atmosphere, dine outside or in. Breakfast, lunch, and dessert. Skillet-baked chocolate chip cookie smothered with a hot fudge sundae. You can indulge yourself and get a gate-fee refund. Open 6 a.m. to 3 p.m. 408/647-7500. AX, MC, V; others also accepted.

THE CYPRESS ROOM (at The Lodge at Pebble Beach). In elegant surroundings, view the eighteenth fairway, Carmel Bay, and the coastal mountains. Fresh seafood specialties include fresh abalone and almond-crusted softshell crabs. Ice carvings and weekly specialties highlight the exquisite Sunday brunch. Breakfast, lunch, dinner. 408/624-3811. AX, MC, V; others also accepted. Entrees, mostly under $25.00.

THE DUNES (at The Inn at Spanish Bay). A garden-room setting has beautiful ocean views. Romantic candlelit dinners feature classic California cuisine and exceptional service. Friday clambake features a buffet of lobster, shrimp, oyster bar, sushi, and more. Deep down you'll know you truly are the descendant of royalty. Breakfast, lunch, dinner. 408/647-7500. AX, MC, V; others also accepted. Entrees, mostly under $20.00.

THE TAP ROOM (at The Lodge at Pebble Beach). An English pub with an eclectic collection of golf memorabilia, this is where golfers relax and share great stories. Prime rib, vegetarian platter, and lighter fare. Voted "Best Late Night Restaurant." Lunch, dinner, late-night service; full bar with thirty-six varieties of beer. 408/624-3811. AX, MC, V; others also accepted. Entrees, mostly under $15.00.

DIRECTIONS

◆

Pebble Beach is accessible from fee gates near Ocean Avenue in Carmel, Highway 1 at the Highway 68 intersection, on Highway 68 into Pacific Grove (the S. F. B. Morse Gate), and in Pacific Grove (the Country Club Gate and the Seventeen Mile Drive Gate).

For more spectacular views include Pacific Grove's section of the drive in your Pebble Beach–entry route. Drive around Ocean View Boulevard in Pacific Grove, pass Asilomar State Beach, then connect with Seventeen Mile Drive at Sunset Drive (call 408/624-3811 for gate information); or continue on Sunset to Highway 68, driving to the top of Highway 68 to enter Seventeen Mile Drive at the Highway 1 Gate for spectacular summit views.

Direct Route from the Monterey Bay Aquarium. *From the aquarium drive up David Avenue to Forest Avenue (on the Pacific Grove map). Turn right at Forest Avenue and immediately move into the left turn lane; turn at the first street, which is Sunset Drive / Highway 68. Drive west on Sunset until you come to the second stop sign. This is the intersection of Sunset and Seventeen Mile Drive. Turn left on Seventeen Mile Drive; you soon see the gated entrance.*

From Highway 1. *Take the exit for Highway 68, Pacific Grove / Pebble Beach. This leads directly to the Highway 1 Gate; enter Pebble Beach and follow the scenic route around the summit.*

INTRODUCTION TO PEBBLE BEACH
WITH HISTORICAL HIGHLIGHTS

Serene one moment, wild the next, the route of panoramic Seventeen Mile Drive through exclusive Pebble Beach is world renowned. Five different gated entrances invite the traveler to nine miles of spectacular coast, towering pine forests, rare wildflowers, cypress groves, and seven world-class golf courses. Exquisite residences and luxury resorts are interspersed in this Edenlike atmosphere, cradled between Pacific Grove and Carmel.

The area known as Pebble Beach lies within the Del Monte Forest, thick with tall, closed-coned Monterey pine and a rare grove of indigenous Monterey cypress. A century ago thick, impenetrable forests grew from inland through to the dunes and highlands above the ocean's edge, on lands now shared with world-famous golf courses and estates. Archaeological studies of the area, including an important discovery in Pebble Beach in 1991, reveal that Del Monte Forest was inhabited by people for five thousand years before the first Spanish explorers landed. These earlier inhabitants, often described as the Ohlone people, may have been the distinct dialect and family group called the Rumsen people. They were probably predated here by the Esselen, who later moved down the Big Sur Coast. Tools such as bone awls and arrowheads, still found at Pebble Beach, show the importance of the area as a food-gathering territory. Today there are archaeological sites with findings that have been proved to date to these times at Spanish Bay, Cypress Point, Fanshell Beach, Pescadero Point, Stillwater Cove, and on the oceanside stretch of Pebble Beach Golf Links, including the famous seventh hole at Arrowhead Point.

Pounding in winter, lapping gently on calm days, the relentless ocean waves meet the rocky promontories and scenic beaches along the six-mile ocean frontage of Pebble Beach. The forest and dunes provided shelter from strong ocean winds for Juan Gaspar de Portola, who camped at Spanish Bay, just south of Asilomar Beach, during his 1769 expedition for Spain. During this first expedition he explored the areas around the Monterey Bay but missed his landmarks and lost his bearings. He returned to his post as governor of Baja California with the misunderstanding that he had not found Monterey Bay. The following year cannons roared when a land expedition led by Portola and Father Crespi met the companion ship the *San Antonio,* with Father Serra aboard. Ground was broken the next day for the presidio and mission.

After Rumsen inhabitants were driven away from Spanish, Mexican, and early California settlements, Pebble Beach remained as primitive forest, sharing some lands with grazing cattle and sheep. Two Mexican land grants, El Pescadero (the Fishing Place) and Punta de Piños (Point of Pines) Rancho, encompassed a major part of present-day Pebble Beach, from 1835 to 1860. In 1840 El Pescadero was owned by Doña Maria del Carmen Barreto, who sold it for an adobe in

Monterey. The Lodge at Pebble Beach stands at about the center of the old ranch, and the Doña's ghost is said to roam the cypress trees (probably losing sleep over her selling price of five hundred dollars for the whole four thousand acres).

Eventually the land was acquired at a sheriff's trustee sale by the famous land wheeler and dealer David Jacks of Monterey, who in turn sold it in 1879 to the Pacific Improvement Company, holding company for the Southern Pacific Railroad. Jacks leased back some of the land to graze cattle and sheep. Charles Crocker of the "Big Four" railroad empire proposed the old Del Monte Hotel in Monterey, which was built as a magnet to draw the very rich to the Monterey Peninsula. Pebble Beach became the recreation destination for visitors to the hotel. The original Seventeen Mile Drive, several miles longer than today, circled the peninsula from the old hotel and back.

The road was described by J. R. Fitch, a travel writer of the late 1800s, as being at first "a waste of sand through which horses plodded laboriously." By 1887 a "fine graveled highway permitted rapid trotting" as hotel guests traversed in grand tally-hos pulled by three matched pairs of lively horses. The brisk ride took several hours and then some. An elaborate picnic near where The Lodge stands today was the highlight of a stay at the Del Monte. Fifty wagon coaches completed the Seventeen Mile loop trip each day. President Theodore Roosevelt rode the loop on horseback, roughrider style.

The name Pebble Beach was garnered, according to Fitch and later others, from a section of especially "pebbly" beach by the then-soon-to-be-built first lodge. "One bit of this bay is worth passing notice. It is known as Pebble Beach, because of the myriads of pebbles that take the place of ordinary sand. The waves come in with a peculiar swish on these loose pebbles, and their constant action results in beautifully rounded specimens of all kinds and of every shade of color. The Beach is a favorite resort for collectors of pebbles, but the search usually proves disastrous to clothes and shoes, since the waves come up with great rapidity, and yet so noiselessly that the incautious seeker after pebbles, finding too late that he cannot escape in this yielding mass, is overcome by the water and receives a thorough drenching." The beach by Stillwater Cove still swishes with pebbles, though many fewer in number than in the 1880s as reported by Fitch.

The mansions of Pebble Beach were mere dreams in those days. The only settlement was a Chinese fishing village at Stillwater Cove, which along with Jacks's dairy barn occupied the seventeenth green of the present-day Pebble Beach Golf Course. The Chinese, prohibited by law from owning land, originally leased the land from Jacks for six dollars and two dozen abalones each month. In 1888 the village had over thirty inhabitants. After the drive opened for tourists the villagers offered what may have been Monterey County's first commercial souvenirs—polished abalone shells, sold at a stand. Jung San Choy, the last Chinese villager, left in 1912 following the demise of the village from age, changes in the fishing industry, immigration laws, and development of surrounding land.

The "Duke of Del Monte," Samuel F. B. Morse, nephew of the inventor of the telegraph, served as a successful manager of the Del Monte Properties. In 1919 Morse and partner Herbert Fleishhacker, president of Anglo Bank in San Francisco, bought the Del Monte holdings for $1.3 million. It was through the vision of Morse that Pebble Beach developed as a golf resort with exclusive residences.

The original lodge burned the day after Christmas, 1917. A reconstructed lodge and a golf course designed by amateur golfer and real estate salesman Jack Neville, now famous as the "Links at Pebble Beach," opened the same year Morse began his new company. Golf had a new mecca.

The oldest and most grandiose estates stretch over the land south of The Lodge to the border of Carmel. Most of these opulent mansions were built before the Depression of the 1930s. The style imposed on all construction was Spanish or Mediterranean. Between the mansions and Highway 1 and in a few other parts of Pebble Beach primeval forests grow thick with lush undergrowth. Highway 1 to the east climbs Carmel Hill. In summer tourist traffic the cars slow to the pace of horse-drawn wagons.

From numerous horseback surveys Morse divided Pebble Beach into four areas: (1) The Lodge area; (2) Cypress Point, which was to welcome one of the most privately exclusive golf clubs in the United States, still owned primarily by the 100 founding families; (3) the Country Club area, which extended into present Pacific Grove; and (4) the highlands sports area, which now includes the S.F.B. Morse Botanical Reserve. Through the leadership of Morse, lots were plotted away from major vistas, to protect the open ocean views.

From the opening of the links, the intent of Morse was to attract the rich and famous both as residents and visitors. Some of the memorable visits have been Douglas Fairbanks in the 1920s, Prince George in 1928, Bing Crosby in 1947 at his first pro-am tournament, John F. Kennedy, a senator when he posed on the lawn in front of The Lodge, Ringo Starr of the Beatles, riding incognito at the height of their popularity in 1966, and Pavarotti, singing at a fund raiser in 1991.

Nothing has brought more fame and celebrities to Pebble Beach than the Crosby Golf Tournament, which first opened in 1947. Pros, amateurs, and celebrities come together for a week of golf and the famous clambake dinner that accompanies the tournament. Bob Hope described the Crosby as "a place for the elite, where ocean and golf ball meet."

Today the Crosby lives on in the AT&T Pebble Beach National Pro-Am. The initial purse was $10,000; in 1992 it was $1,100,000. The original venues were Pebble Beach Links, Cypress Point, and the Monterey Peninsula Country Club. Spyglass Hill replaced Monterey in 1967 and Poppy Hills replaced Cypress Point in 1991. In 1993 Bill Murray took golf into theater on the links with comic skits at each tee. In his final hi-jinks he carried a woman into the sand pit on the eighteenth and then sunk a twenty-foot birdie for the best finishing shot. The bleachers of normally sedate golf fans went wild.

The present owner of the Pebble Beach Company is the Lone Cypress Corporation. Its holdings include 2,300 of the 5,300 acres in Pebble Beach. Included in these acres are the two resorts and three golf courses: Spyglass Hill Golf Course, The Links at Spanish Bay, and the Pebble Beach Course. The corporation also owns the equestrian center, other acreage, a realty company, artistic rights, and the famous Lone Cypress logo. This new ownership polished the "Jewel of California" to gain a return invitation for the U.S. Open in the year 2000. Morse, who died in 1969, referred to Pebble Beach as "a garden for generations to enjoy."

TOUR: THE PEBBLE BEACH SEVENTEEN MILE DRIVE

If your pleasure is golf, you probably intend to take an intimate tour of a very special set of eighteen holes. To take full advantage of the variety of activities that Pebble Beach offers you might also include a visit to the beach, Point Joe, a resort, the cypress grove and the Lone Cypress, Bird and Seal Rock lookout, and a slow drive by an enormous mansion or two. Also explore other areas of Pebble Beach that are less known but included in this guide; consider this tour of Seventeen Mile Drive an invitation to all the offerings highlighted along it.

Wildlife is especially abundant here. Enthralled drivers have been known to leave their Mercedes in the middle of the road with doors wide open as they rush to take a picture. More than a hundred varieties of plants and two hundred different birds, a forest of trees, and a constant parade of sea, tidal, and land animals will bring you so close to nature you may wish you could grow roots.

If you enter Pebble Beach at the Highway 1 Gate you then wind back under Highway 68 to the turnouts for the Shepherd's Knoll and Huckleberry Hill vista points. In 1989 a fire burned the forest and several residences at Huckleberry Hill. The thousands of small pines you see are the natural seedlings of the burned pines—a forest renewing itself. Winding down the wooded hills you intersect Seventeen Mile Drive where it enters Pebble Beach from Pacific Grove.

If you enter Pebble Beach from Pacific Grove you can park your car and walk or jog along a dirt path that wanders through pines and skirts The Links at Spanish Bay. Refer to the Resource Guide for bike rental locations if you left yours at home and want to pedal through (pp. 300–301). The path will continue to The Inn at Spanish Bay, then to a boardwalk that winds through dunes and bunkers to the beach. A path behind the parking lot connects with Sunset Drive.

Gaspar de Portola camped in the forest surrounding Spanish Bay in 1769 while trying to locate Monterey Bay. Frustrated after mistaking the Pajaro River for the "River Carmelo," he unknowingly did choose a Carmel River site for emplacement of a cross as his return marker. When he returned the next year he realized his oversight.

Gardens grace the next right turn from Seventeen Mile Drive. If it is close to sunset roll your windows down as you turn and you may hear a bagpiper welcoming you to The Inn at Spanish Bay, the newest and largest resort of the area. You can park in the main parking lot and wander through shops, enjoy a meal, or walk to Spanish Bay.

A gated driveway leads to the Residences at Spanish Bay. The Inn and Residences are operated by the Pebble Beach Company, which describes their style as "new traditionalist." They are the largest structures on the coast: a 270-room luxury hotel, several fine shops, and restaurants. Rolling sand dunes covered with native grasses and wildflowers are over twenty feet tall and encapsulate the look of the eighteen-hole golf course here.

Back on Seventeen Mile Drive take the next right and the beautiful breakers off Moss Beach, which fronts Spanish Bay, roll into view. Due to its variety of undersea habitats this area has the greatest diversity of marine algae on the Monterey Peninsula. It was already famous in *Picturesque California* in 1887: "This is Moss Beach, famous for the delicate specimens of sea moss washed up every day at high tide. These are as infinite and as graceful in design as the coral, and one of the favorite pastimes of the dwellers at Pacific Grove is the floating out and preserving of these mosses." One of our family's favorite pastimes is to get pizza and calzones from Allegro Gourmet Pizzeria in Pacific Grove and picnic at tables here, then stroll the boardwalk through the dunes. Allegro's will deliver to the beach for large groups.

Point Joe is an easy walk to the southwest of Moss Beach and is the next natural stop if you're driving or biking. The offshore area here has been dubbed "The Restless Sea" for the wave action caused by its underwater topography and meeting of ocean swells. Turbulent waves smash from different directions, then clash and crisscross for some of the most unusual and wildest surf in California.

Waves crash over rocky Point Joe, conjuring ghosts of shipwrecks, but by the 1890s a small Chinese wooden fishing village had been built along the rocky point. During the abalone rush of the 1850s hundreds of Chinese had arrived in the Monterey area to harvest the shellfish, which had multiplied in numbers since the overkilling of its natural enemy, the sea otter. The abalone harvesting took place at two places along the Pebble Beach shore, Point Joe and Stillwater Cove. The rocks claimed many ships, including the coastal steamer the *Saint Paul*, which wrecked off the rocks in 1896. The Chinese salvaged the lumber for future buildings. Today experienced surfers ride the waves with abandon.

After the turn of the century only a solitary Chinese man named Joe fished, tended a herd of goats, and sold trinkets at this point. He was a familiar sight as he walked from the point to Monterey with a cat on his shoulder. It is not known whether the point was named for Joe or whether Joe was named for the place he lived, but the two are linked and no other reason for the name Point Joe remains.

As you leave Point Joe to meander down Seventeen Mile Drive, exclusive residences dot the forest side. Further south huge mansions hug the cliffs above the ocean and guard their own private beaches. Movie and TV stars, old and new rich, and corporations have estates here. Architectural styles vary from the early Spanish Colonial preferred by Morse to old southern mansion to Cape Cod to modern.

Some of the names on gated entrances disclose or hint at the identity of occupants. Past The Lodge on Seventeen Mile Drive, "Wit's End" still identifies the home of late cartoonist Jimmy Hatlo.

One of the most memorable homes awaits you just before you reach the Carmel Gate. Built as a marble Byzantine castle for one of the Crockers, this mansion contains many rooms and has indoor and outdoor arches made of thirty-two different kinds of marble. The private beachfront is heated by underground pipes.

Who needs a mansion when you can carry a roomy, comfortable house on your back as you enjoy beachfront property with a solar-heated pool? You might not be caused to ogle by his domicile, but you can enjoy the little hermit crab's antics as you investigate the many tidepools along the walking path connecting Point Joe with Bird and Seal Rock.

In late December and January, then lessening through March, this path and the picnic tables at the bottom of Ocean Road are perfect vantage points to watch the migration of gray whales. Pods of geysers line the horizon. Occasionally they get close enough for you to see the massive hulks breach and flukes slap the water.

One Christmas as I was making breakfast a puff of white caught my eye in our ocean-view window. I blinked my eyes, not sure if late-night wrapping had made me weary. Three more white steamy fountains and....Whale ahoy! We actually packed our Christmas dinner, tablecloths, and fine china and celebrated the day at the beach. It's a widespread enthusiasm here; if you need a conversation piece to break the ice with locals just mention whales.

The greens of the Monterey Peninsula Country Club's Shore Course extend to both sides of Seventeen Mile Drive below Point Joe. Membership in this private club was used to entice the home buyers of this area. Some deeds still come with membership.

As two offshore islands come into your view just south of Ocean Road, you hear barking sea lions challenging each other for offshore lounging rocks. At first you think there are just a few. Then as your eyes focus you see hundreds of pinnipeds, the majority of which are California sea lions, resting on Bird and Seal Rock (which actually is several rocks). Their barks can be heard for miles through the calm air of evening and morning. For close-up viewing, telescopes line the shore.

One day as friends of mine were walking at the beach, a young sea lion dodged up and down in the water and became so caught up in its game of pitch and roll that a wave washed it onto the shore. It paused for a moment, looked them in the eyes as if asking, "What are you doing here?," then waddled back into the frothy surf.

The birds used to share the larger island until Morse came up with the industrious plan to scrape the bird guano off of it to use as fertilizer for the golf courses and appease the surrounding residents, who didn't like the rocks' appearance or odor. The pinnipeds apparently liked the rocks guanoless and moved there, displacing the birds. However, the larger rock is still marked on maps as Bird Rock and the smaller one as Seal Rock.

You might think a sea gull is a sea gull, period. Check out the beaks, feet, wings, feathers, and colorings to distinguish the many different varieties that share the smaller rock roost with cormorants, sandpipers, kingfishers, and the rare blackfooted albatross. Brown pelicans glide by on their way to better fishing at Stillwater Cove.

Each year from late January through spring, wintering Canadian geese give free manicures to surrounding golf courses. Throughout the year jack rabbits race golf carts and raccoons' eyes shine bright from the brush at night.

Herds of deer graze freely on the greens. In early summer the air is heavy with expectation as fawns are born in surrounding brush. Around September bucks sprout majestic antlers. One of the unusual deer you might see, an albino buck, is known as the "Ghost of Pebble Beach."

Across the road from Bird and Seal Rock a nature trail winds through the dunes, past a pond, and into a forest oasis. A picturesque private residence called the Gingerbread House borders the trail.

The trail is an easy loop hike. Sand verbena, Menzies wallflower, and lupine hold the fragile dunes. Up the hill beneath the pines, globe lilies, California iris, and ceanothus are guarded by poison oak and milk thistle. If you stay on the wide path you and the plants will be happier. The trail loops at a large grassy clearing known as Indian Village.

Although historians are not clear on the authenticity of an actual Indian village located here, Morse related, "The legend of the place is that the Indians had used it as a sort of a cure; that when they were sick they came there to camp and that after they had stayed here a few days and taken of the waters of the spring they frequently felt better....It is an interesting thing that they should have a spa comparable with Saratoga and Baden-Baden."

Back on Seventeen Mile Drive you soon see a sign on the left for the Spyglass Hill Golf Course. Robert Louis Stevenson reportedly found the places for his book Treasure Island along the Monterey Coast. Each hole at this course is named after a place or character in the book. Hole one, an island in the sand, is aptly named "Treasure Island." "Long John Silver," "Bad Dog," and friends are all represented. The demanding course combines dunes and forest. A cafe here offers burgers and refreshments.

About a half-mile south of Spyglass Hill Road, Fan Shell Beach, a moon on earth, lies along the turn of the road. This white sand beach is perfectly crescent shaped. Is that why the sands sing? Truly, they do. If you walk along the sand and drag your feet, high-pitched tones will follow your movements. A midden of piled abalone shells was found nearby from early tribal days. Apparently this has been a favorite picnic spot for centuries. Pink sand verbena and Menzies wallflower grow here too on the dunes, which also provide a home for the black legless lizard.

The drive now passes through the exclusive and very private Cypress Point Club. Morse engaged the well-known Santa Barbara architect George Washington Smith to design the Cypress Point Clubhouse. The exclusive club was started in 1928. More recently its exclusivity caused it to be dropped from AT&T tournament play. The course was designed by Scottish architect Alister Mackenzie. The famous par-three sixteenth hole is separated from the back tee by an ocean gorge.

As you drive by the Cypress Point Course take the turnoff for the Cypress Point Lookout. On a clear day, from this spectacular lookout you can see twenty miles south. Black oystercatchers, western gulls, and cormorants nest on rocks offshore. In the spring, a dark canvas covering with holes cut for peeping naturalists covers the fence that separates the lookout area from the beach, which is the birthing place for Pacific harbor seals. The Pebble Beach Company participates in the Harbor Seal Protection Program along parts of the coastline in Del Monte Forest. The Pacific harbor seal is a true, or earless seal, which spends equal amounts of time on land and in the ocean. The female seal is a devoted parent, but noise from tourists can cause the adults to stampede, crushing the young ones. Docents lead very quiet tours to educational groups. Viewing by the public, with the exception of organized groups, is not allowed every year. Call the Pebble Beach Office for information (408/647-7493).

Across the drive, in Crocker Grove, thirteen acres of cypress grow in a protected reserve. The Monterey cypress grows wild in indigenous groves only in this stretch of roadway and at Point Lobos. The oldest and largest single Monterey cypress grows in this protected grove. The distinctive greenery of these trees masses at the top, forming a dark canopy. The lower branches die but remain as twisted, gnarly arms.

At the midway point on your tour a turnout and slat-board walkway provide the opportunity to view and photograph the Lone Cypress. Access beyond the lookout has been restricted due to extreme soil compacting and danger to the tree. The gnarled tree, hugging its rugged precipice above the waves, is portrayed on the Pebble Beach logo. Twisted and alone, it is the sentinel of its precarious perch. Yes, it's definitely camera time.

The Lone Cypress

"Ghosts fleeing before the wind" welcome you to Pescadero Point. That's how Robert Louis Stevenson described the cypresses at this point with their wind-whipped and salt-spray-bleached white trunks. The white sand beaches of Carmel and Point Lobos are glimpsed from the best benches on the drive at this point. This is where major developer Frank Devendorf first envisioned the future Carmel. Legend has it that this outlook is where the ghost of Doña Maria del Carmen Barreto, owner of this land in the days of Ranch El Pescadero, roams at night.

Continuing south, the drive curves inland to The Lodge, the village, and the famous Pebble Beach. The stately lodge blends Old World elegance with comfort. The public is invited; dine and shop, play golf, and of course stay as long as you like. You'll enjoy the walk through the outer lobby, down the steps, and into the Terrace lounge. Through tall French windows you'll see the green of Pebble Beach's eighteenth fairway. This was the finishing hole for the 1972, 1982, and 1992 U. S. Open Golf Tournaments.

You may be seated on the lawn in front of The Lodge some day in May to watch the finals of another event, the "Classic of the Pacific"—the most respected dog show of its kind.

In August, the need for homes that have garages with a three-car minimum becomes apparent. Garage doors that have remained closed all year open and large car-carrier semis twist through Pebble Beach: destination, the eighteenth green. You'll rub your eyes and wonder if you're dreaming another era as classic cars traverse the roads, heading for the Pebble Beach Concours d'Elegance. This epitome of classic car shows is the anchor event of a summer automotive weekend in Monterey County.

You won't need a classic car to enjoy the vicinity of The Lodge. A Post Office, bank, service station, and deli market serve residents and visitors. Relax and enjoy people watching, as well as a deli sandwich on picnic tables near the Post Office.

The village offers an array of shops. You might really need the bank after viewing the mesmerizing art at the Coast Gallery, especially the marine and wildlife sculptures.

Behind The Lodge, you can walk between the links to beautiful Stillwater Cove. Public parking is also available at the cove. On any day you'll likely see pelicans speed diving for food and golfers power swinging to hit wayward balls back to the greens from the beach. The water here is relatively calm. Public boat launching is permitted, with certain restrictions. You'll get a unique view of the coast and resort if you kayak over the glassy surface of the cove.

Continuing on Seventeen Mile Drive after your sojourn in The Lodge area, you can enter Carmel by staying to the right. The Crocker Castle appears to your right as you leave Pebble Beach. George Washington Smith designed the marble-encrusted mansion for Mrs. Templeton Crocker of the banking and railroad fortune. If you bypass Carmel and continue on the original drive you'll climb through a canyon and be treated to sweeping views at Shepherd's Knoll and Huckleberry Hill. Seventeen Mile Drive ends at Highway 1.

WHAT ELSE TO SEE AND DO

The Golf Courses. The private Cypress Point and the public Pebble Beach golf links rank number three and number five in *Golf Digest*'s ratings of the top 100 courses in America. The public Spyglass Hill and the Links at Spanish Bay also receive high ratings. Three other courses in Pebble Beach, the public Poppy Hills and the private The Shore and The Dunes of the Monterey Peninsula Country Club, share the wondrous surroundings. The Peter Hay, a reasonably priced public nine-hole par-three practice course, lies inland from Seventeen Mile Drive.

PUBLIC GOLF COURSES

PEBBLE BEACH GOLF LINKS, adjacent to The Lodge at Pebble Beach. 408/624-3811, 408/624-6611. Site of the annual AT&T National Pro-Am Golf Tournament. Eighteen holes, 6,806 yards, par 72.

PETER HAY PAR 3 GOLF COURSE, near The Lodge at Pebble Beach. 408/624-3811. Nine-hole golf course; very reasonable greens fees; gate pass refunded.

SPYGLASS HILL GOLF COURSE, Stevenson Drive and Spyglass Hill Road, Pebble Beach. 408/624-6611. Eighteen holes, 6,810 yards, par 72.

THE LINKS AT SPANISH BAY, at The Inn at Spanish Bay, Pebble Beach. 408/624-3811, 800/654-9300. Eighteen holes, 6,357 yards, par 72.

OTHER RECREATIONAL FACILITIES

PEBBLE BEACH EQUESTRIAN CENTER, Portola Road., Pebble Beach. 408/624-2756. This Currier & Ives-lookalike facility with green lawns, rail fences, and white-painted board-and-batten buildings offers trail rides and private lessons. Thirty miles of riding trails weave through Pebble Beach. The finest horse trainers and showriders of the West Coast gather here each summer for annual horse and dressage shows.

S. F. B. MORSE BOTANICAL RESERVE, in the northeast area of Pebble Beach. Turn left at Bird Rock Road from Seventeen Mile Drive. Hiking trails begin in the Bird Rock–Congress Road area. In the spring, wildflowers bedeck the thirty miles of trails that loop through Pebble Beach. Naturalists associated with the Pacific Grove Natural History Museum sometimes lead nature walks of the S. F. B. Morse Botanical Reserve. This eighty-six-acre reserve is the only place in the world where Monterey pines and Bishop pines grow together. Huckleberry Hill is the highest point of the area. After the area was submerged by ocean, millions of years ago, the wave-cut marine terraces of Huckleberry Hill were left with Pleistocene deposits of poor-draining claypan soil and acidic podzol, having only enough nutrients and support for the usually towering Bishop pines and the endangered endemic Gowen cypress to grow as a stunted "pygmy forest." The Gowen cypress is known to occur only at this location and at Point Lobos State Reserve. Many other rare and endangered varieties of plants also are found here. Harvest mice, jack rabbits, deer, and an occasional mountain lion (yes, in Pebble Beach) find homes in or pass through this area.

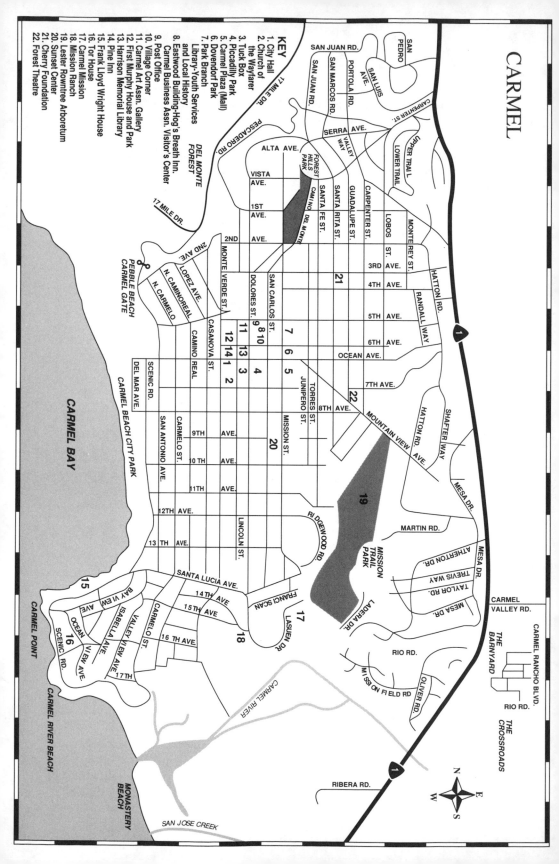

CARMEL

KEY

1. City Hall
2. Church of the Wayfarer
3. Tuck Box
4. Piccadilly Park
5. Carmel Plaza (Mall)
6. Dovendorf Park
7. Park Branch Library-Youth Services and Local History
8. Eastwood Building-Hog's Breath Inn. Carmel Business Assn. Visitor's Center
9. Post Office
10. Village Corner
11. Carmel Art Assn. Gallery
12. First Murphy House and Park
13. Harrison Memorial Library
14. Pine Inn
15. Frank Lloyd Wright House
16. Tor House
17. Carmel Mission
18. Mission Ranch
19. Lester Rowntree Arboretum
20. Sunset Center
21. Cherry Foundation
22. Forest Theatre

CHAPTER 5

CARMEL

THE VILLAGE AND ENVIRONS

Snowy white beaches, shady lanes, and meadow trails grace the one-mile-square village of Carmel-by-the-Sea. As a historic haven for professors, artists, and writers, Carmel-by-the-Sea retains a commitment to the arts, a strong community identity, and respect for individualism, while busloads of visitors are charmed by its storybook architecture, unique shops, and galleries. Woodland and meadow trails lead from the downtown area and the surround, known as Carmel, to the historic Mission San Carlos Borromeo De Rio Carmelo, which was the headquarters for Spanish colonial growth in California.

GETTING READY

THE BEST TIMES TO VISIT AND THE SPECIAL EVENTS

On weekdays in October and November you might be one of a handful of visitors wandering through the sunny village. During Christmas season, the absence of neon lights here and the presence of carolers heralds a scene similar to a Norman Rockwell painting. If it does chance to rain, this is one of the best getaways-turned-stormy imaginable. Carmel has a plethora of warming fireplaces. There's even one in the stationery store and in the library. Spring wildflowers along the coastal and woodlands trails are an added plus March through June.

If you are visiting just for the day plan to arrive before 9 a.m. during the summer—especially on weekends—and also on holiday weekends throughout the year. Have breakfast or enjoy one of the coastal or woodland walks. This way you'll be able to find a parking place and see the village before the crowds. Later in the day traffic can be bumper to bumper for one mile up Ocean Avenue and on to Highway 1. The best entrance route in high season is from Pebble Beach through the Carmel Gate or from the Carpenter Street or Rio Road exit from Highway 1.

Most shops open at 10 a.m., although more and more are opening at 9 a.m. on weekends. The shops begin to close around 5 p.m. The Plaza (downtown shopping center) stores stay open later seasonally, and some shops stay open later on particular nights. On Friday evenings during the summer artists open their studios for art walks.

City ordinances prohibit music in eating establishments. Nightlife is conversation in pubs (some are open until 1 a.m.) and walks on the beach. Some of the restaurants serve until 10 p.m and have wonderful outdoor firepits. The Mission Ranch, just outside the city limits, and the Rancho Carmel restaurants across Highway 1 offer livelier nightlife possibilities.

Special events to plan for include: the Rio Resolution Run (call The Treadmill, 408/624-4112) on January 1; this is a cross-country run on trails, beaches, and roads. The Tor House Garden Party is held in late spring. The local Surf About Competition fills the waves and beach in May. The Bach Festival (408/624-1521), three weeks of concerts, is usually scheduled during July and August. The autumn Arts and Crafts show takes place in September.

CLIMATE AND CLOTHING

Bring a sweater or jacket for the cooling fog. Locals and visitors dress stylishly casual. Bring a comfortable pair of walking shoes and pack binoculars for bird watching at the lagoon.

TOUR LENGTHS

If you asked most regular visitors how to see Carmel in an hour you'd get disbelieving looks. However, one afternoon I asked various Australian tourists how they had spent the one hour in Carmel that had been allotted to them by their bus guide. The sweatiest had chosen to jog down the mission trail. Those with packages had shopped. Some had wandered the galleries. All were glowing.

Can you spare a week or long weekend for just Carmel? Check into a historic inn and, if you have to, misplace your car keys. If your visit must be shorter, try for at least a half-day. Schedule a minimum of two hours for the village walking tour, one hour for the mission, and two hours for the coastal and woodland trails.

WILDLIFE WISDOM

The presence of kelp beds at the north end of Ocean Beach toward Pescadero Point almost guarantees otter sightings. Tidepools dot the shoreline there and south of Carmel Point. Gaze over the horizon from December though February for the spouting of gray whales. Bring binoculars for the abundance and variety of birds at the River Beach lagoon.

VISITOR INFORMATION

Since there are no street numbers in the village, if you ask about a certain location you'll receive instructions such as "the third house up from the northwest corner" of a given street. Residents and businesspeople have a warmth and patience uncommon in a fast-paced world.

Mediterranean Market in Carmel

Pick up a copy of the free *Carmel Pine Cone,* the *Sun, Coast Weekly, The Review,* or the *Monterey County Herald*'s "Go!" section at newsstands for the latest village news and information about events and gallery showings. The Carmel Business Association Visitor's Center, open 9 a.m. to 5 p.m. Mondays through Fridays with extended summer hours, is located on the second floor of the Eastwood Building, San Carlos Street between Fifth and Sixth avenues, 408/624-2522.

PARKING

At the western beach end of Carmel Village free all-day parking is available in the Ocean Beach lot and on lower Ocean Avenue. Around the village you might get lucky and find a free all-day parking spot on Junipero Avenue, south of Ocean Avenue. Free parking is also available in the city lot located about three blocks from the center of the village at the corner of Junipero Avenue and Third Avenue. The maximum parking available on most streets near the center of the village is two hours.

You can pay to park at Carmel Plaza's underground garage (from Junipero Avenue, turn right at Seventh Avenue and right on Mission Street) or at the lot next to Sunset School on Eighth Avenue and Mission Street. Rates for the Sunset lot are $1.00 per half hour with a $14.00 maximum.

ALTERNATE TRANSPORTATION

Monterey Transit, 408/899-2555, serves Carmel with hourly service. Buses leave and return to the Monterey transit center.

RESTROOMS

Public restrooms are located at the base of Ocean Avenue at Carmel Beach and also five blocks up from the beach just north of Ocean Avenue on Lincoln, at First Murphy Park (behind the Pine Inn). At the top of the business district restrooms are located in the Carmel Plaza and across the street at Devendorf Park.

PLACES TO STAY

IN CARMEL, WITHIN WALKING DISTANCE OF THE VILLAGE AND BEACHES

Carmel has truly wonderful lodging opportunities. These are some of the places that offer the flavor of Carmel. Many more await you.

COBBLESTONE INN (on Junipero Avenue between Seventh and Eighth streets). Cobblestones from the Salinas River cover the exterior of this inn. Teddy bears, country pine furniture, floral wallpaper, and fireplaces in every room create the warm feeling of a country home. Full breakfasts, afternoon wine and hors d'oeuvres, and late-night cookies are served in a cheery lobby and parlor filled with early American antiques, an original carousel horse, and handmade crafts. Each room has a refrigerator stocked with complimentary soft drinks. All private baths. Special-occasion packages. Friendly, thoughtful service. 408/625-5222. MC, V; others also accepted. For two, mostly from $95.00 to $175.00. Special suites available.

CYPRESS INN (Lincoln Street and Seventh Avenue). A grand hotel, the Cypress Inn has a Moorish Mediterranean facade. Warm-toned interiors with floral fabrics. Many ocean-view rooms. The unique tower room with European bath offers views to Point Lobos. A decanter of sherry and full breakfast are complimentary with each room. Movie posters in the cozy cocktail lounge feature Doris Day, one of the owners, whose love of animals is extended to guests; this hotel is pet friendly. Locals out for a walk with their dogs often stop by the lounge. 408/624-3871, 800/443-7443. AX, MC, V. For two, $78.00 to $198.00. Off-season rates available.

EDGEMERE COTTAGES (San Antonio between Thirteenth Avenue and Santa Lucia Avenue). Sequestered in a quiet neighborhood, these older French Normandy cottages were part of an early Carmel estate. Very private: just three separate cottages with vaulted ceilings and kitchens and one French room over the proprietors' house. Bright floral decor in the rooms matches the surrounding English gardens. Very near the beach trail, the site is six easily walked blocks from town. Two cottages have fireplaces. All rooms have private baths. 408/624-4501. AX, MC, V. Cottages for two, from $60.00 to $100.00. Cottages have extra rooms and beds to accommodate more people.

GREEN LANTERN INN (Seventh Avenue and Casanova Street). Carmel-stone walkways lead through gardens to a variety of rooms, ranging from very cozy to spacious with lofts. Both European feeling and Old Carmel ambiance. Some individual cottages. Many rooms have special features. The Teak Room was designed especially for writers. Hobbit ceilings lead to a private attic retreat with an antique desk lighted by an ocean-view dormer window. The inn is just a few blocks to town or the beach. All rooms have private baths; some, fireplaces. Homemade bread, muffins, cereals, fresh fruit, and beverages are served for breakfast in a French-country dining area or outside in the courtyard. Afternoon tea and wine. 408/624-4392. AX, MC, V; others also accepted. For two, from $80.00 to $160.00.

HAPPY LANDING INN (Monte Verde between Fifth and Sixth avenues). Built in 1925 as a family retreat, this early Comstock-designed inn offers quintessential bed and breakfast lodging at moderate rates. Carmel-stone paths lead through a country garden with gazebo and pond to pink cottages with wood cathedral ceilings and antiques. Set back from a quiet wooded street, the inn is an easy walk to beaches and the village. All rooms have private baths; some, fireplaces. Breakfast served to your room. Early room reservations suggested. 408/624-7917. MC, V. For two, from $90.00 to $110.00. Suites, $145.00.

LA PLAYA HOTEL (Eighth Avenue and Camino Real). The Mediterranean-style historic hotel, which began as a large private estate, has grounds voted by locals as the loveliest garden walk in Monterey County. Seventy-five units on three levels, many with ocean views. Private patio rooms available. Full-service hotel. Pool, spa. Terrace Grill Restaurant with courtyard dining, and a convivial pub. Seasonal Thursday-night performances in a small theater room often feature Taelen Thomas, a local actor who portrays Jack London and other famous local celebrities from the past. Walk through Carmel's history in extensive display areas of photographs. 408/624-6476, 800/582-8900. AX, MC, V; others also accepted. Rooms for two, from $110.00 to $210.00.

MISSION RANCH (26270 Dolores Street, just outside the city limits by the mission). Clint Eastwood saved this former ranch and resort from razing. Award-winning attention to detail preserves the charming exteriors of the former century-old farmhouse, creamery, and barn, and the 1930s cottages. Handmade quilts, trademark oversized furniture, and Carmel-stone fireplaces add special touches to renovated and newly built rooms. Tennis courts. Twenty-one acres to enjoy, complete with grazing lambs! Lively full piano bar and a restaurant that serves brunch, lunch, and dinner. Pastoral views opening to panoramic ocean vistas. It's an easy walk to Carmel River Beach, a twenty minute walk to the village. 408/624-6436, 800/538-8221. Fax: 408/626-4163. AX, MC, V. For two, from $95.00 to $225.00.

OUTSIDE OF CARMEL: CARMEL HIGHLANDS

See the next chapter (p. 151), on points south, for information about the Highlands area, a two-mile stretch of coastline that begins four miles south of Carmel. I mention it here because the Highlands Inn (408/624-3801), with the California Market casual restaurant and ultradeluxe Pacific's Edge Restaurant (408/624-3801), caters to Carmel visitors. I have often been stopped on Ocean Avenue by disoriented people trying to find the Highlands. Go south, my friends.

OUTSIDE OF CARMEL: CARMEL VALLEY

A popular lodging place for visitors to Carmel-by-the-Sea, Carmel Valley has tennis, golf, and sunny summer weather. Various lodges attract many to this area. For a tour of it see the Carmel Valley section (p. 196).

RESTAURANTS

If you move to Carmel don't bother to pack your kitchen. One couple I know dines out five days a week. These are some favorites. There are over sixty restaurants in Carmel. More are noted under "The Village Tour" (p. 132).

The first five restaurants are ones we enjoy more if our young children are not with us.

IN CARMEL-BY-THE-SEA

CASANOVA (Fifth Avenue and Mission Street) Nooks, fireplaces, and open-air dining create a romantic setting in this Spanish-style historic home. Italian and French country-style three-course dinners melt any palate and heart. The grilled rack of lamb is a house specialty. The owner or maitre d' will lead your personal tour of an extensive hand-excavated wine cellar under the restaurant. American-style breakfasts and Italian and French lunches are also served (408/625-0501). MC, V. Three-course dinners, from $24.00 to $29.00.

CREME CARMEL (Carmel Square on San Carlos Street, between Ocean Avenue and Seventh Avenue). Fourteen tables share an intimate dining area. French and continental specialties include rack of lamb and roast breast of duck with a wild mushroom sauce. Sauces meet diners' personal requests. A tasting menu varies weekly. The chocolate souffle is heavenly. Award-winning wine list. Dinner. All nonsmoking. 408/624-0444. AX, MC, V. Entrees, mostly under $25.00.

FRENCH POODLE (Fifth Avenue and Junipero Avenue). In this elegant French restaurant the chef-owner prepares delicate, complex sauces. Specialties include abalone, duck, lamb, and fresh-daily fish. 408/624-8643. AX, MC, V. Entrees, from $14.00 to $24.00.

GIULIANO'S (Mission Street and Fifth Avenue). A local favorite for romantic dining and fine Italian fare. Penne pasta and pan-seared venison tantalize. Watch for lunches going out the door to local shopkeepers. Lunch and dinner everyday. 408/625-5231. AX, MC, V. A la carte menu. Entrees, from $15.00 to $25.00.

Q POINT (on the north side of Ocean Avenue between Lincoln Street and Dolores Street). A Carmel-stone fireplace warms intimate tables set back from arched windows. A private collection of vibrant prints by Hiro Yamagata decorates the walls. French-Japanese-California fare prepared by Chef Max Muramatsu features selections such as duck ravioli in an orange buerre blanc sauce and oak-grilled calamari. Extensive wine list. Dinner. 408/624-2569. AX, MC, V; others also accepted. Entrees, from $13.00 to $18.00.

BULLY III (in the Adobe Inn, Dolores Street and Eighth Avenue). In your choice of a lively pub or casual English lodge dining room, a variety of American dishes featuring prime rib is served. Pub fare featuring tasty prime rib reuben is available in the lodge dining room on weekdays. Lunch and dinner. 408/625-1750. AX, MC, V; others also accepted. Pub selections, mostly under $10.00. Dining room entrees, mostly under $20.00.

CAFE BERLIN (on the west side of Junipero Avenue between Fifth Avenue and Sixth Avenue). A Bavarian eatery, the cafe is popular with diners who enjoy authentic German food. Sauerbraten and goulash are among favorites. 408/626-8181. Lunch and dinner. AX, MC, V. Entrees, from $7.00 to $14.00.

CHEZ CHRISTIAN (in the Court of the Golden Bough on Ocean Avenue at Monte Verde Street). This bistro with a cozy home feeling serves fine French cuisine, featuring pastas, seafood, and duck. Great burgers highlight indoor and outdoor lunches. A favorite place for cappuccino. Tuesday through Sunday. Lunch and dinner. 408/625-4331. MC, V. Dinner entrees, from $10.00 to $16.00.

CHINA GOURMET (Fifth Avenue between Dolores Street and San Carlos Street). Casual surroundings and friendly, gracious service highlight Mandarin Chinese fare. Tasty kung pao chicken. Lunch, dinner, or take-out service. 408/624-3941. AX, MC, V; others also accepted. Entrees, from $6.00 to $10.00.

CLAM BOX (Mission Street between Fifth and Sixth avenues). You can dine casually here, by a warm Carmel-stone fireplace. Family owned and operated since 1962. Seafood and chicken for the whole family. California wines and full bar. Dinner. 408/624-8597. AX, MC, V. Entrees, from $10.00 to $20.00.

FORGE IN THE FOREST AND THE GENERAL STORE (Fifth Avenue and Junipero Avenue). Years ago this really was the general store, with a telegraph office in front. Metal sculptures were welded in the forge. Cheery gardens make a delightful spot for an outdoor casual lunch. Original board-and-batten walls frame the wine-cellar-style dining room. A fire pit and hand-carved bar warm the inviting pub for foggy days and late nights. Great hamburgers, quesadillas, and Chinese chicken salad for lunch. Grilled prawns are a favorite for dinner. The special wine cellar room for private parties (eight to twelve) and the assortment of Bavarian baked goods at the The Bakerei add to the ambiance at the Forge. Lunch, dinner, Saturday and Sunday brunch. (408/624-2233. MC, V. Dinner entrees, from $9.00 to $16.00.

KATY'S COTTAGE (Lincoln Street between Ocean and and Seventh). Hand-painted arches lead to fireplace-warmed rooms with wonderful food. Quintessential cottage atmosphere. Beveled lead glass enhances the Snug Room and Stone Room, which can be reserved for groups. Heavenly hollandaise sauce, panettone French toast, great omelettes, and more. Breakfast and lunch only. Very reasonable. No cards. 408/625-6260.

OUTSIDE CARMEL-BY-THE-SEA

The next three restaurants are samples of the many eating places located across Highway 1 from Carmel Village, in the Crossroads Center and Barnyard shopping areas. Take the Rio Road exit east. Turn at the first right for the Crossroads. For the Barnyard turn left at the next street, Carmel Rancho Boulevard. Look left for the large groupings of Western wood buildings, lit with garlands of white lights at night.

RIO GRILL (in the Crossroads Center, 101 Crossroads Boulevard). A local favorite, the Rio Grill has a lively atmosphere. Paper table coverings for the artists or kids with you. Nouveau Southwestern-Californian decor. Baby-back ribs and salmon tacos are samples on a menu that features regional ingredients and innovative dishes such as grilled emu. Lunch, dinner, lounge with full bar. 408/625-5436. AX, MC, V. Dinner entrees, from $13.00 to $20.00.

ROBATA (3658 the Barnyard). A traditional setting with a Japanese garden, Robata has been voted the best Japanese restaurant in Monterey County. Sushi; tempura and fried oysters; mesquite grill cooking to perfection. Dinner only. 408/624-2643. AX, MC, V. Entrees, from $11.00 to $21.00.

SILVER JONES (3690 the Barnyard). "Good to see you, Jack." Jack Silver is often here to return guests' greetings with the warmth of a proprietor who cares. Tapestries add warmth to the walls. Fireplaces make for comfortable solo, couple, or group dining, outdoors or in. Menus are printed daily to ensure that the Californian and European dishes are prepared with the freshest local ingredients. Top-rated Sunday brunch, lunch, and dinner. 408/624-520. AX, MC, V; others also accepted. Entrees, from $7.00 to $15.00.

DIRECTIONS

From the Pebble Beach Tour. If you are continuing from the Pebble Beach tour (p. 105) follow the signs on Seventeen Mile Drive that direct you to the right to Carmel. You will exit Pebble Beach through the Carmel Gate. After the first stop sign follow the curve of the road. The eucalyptus trees on your right were a windbreak for an original rancho. The oldest house in Carmel, built in 1864, is hidden from street view behind shrub fences. You will now be traveling south on San Antonio Avenue, which at the next stop sign intersects Ocean Avenue. Turn right and you will enter the beach parking lot. This is one of the lots where you can park all day. From here it is a delight-ful tree-shaded five-minute uphill walk to the first shops and galleries.

If you are in a hurry to shop or dine, and you want to skip the uphill walk and save the beach until later, then at Ocean Avenue instead turn left. Drive up the hill nine blocks. Turn right at Junipero Avenue. You will drive by the Carmel Plaza (and pass tour bus park-ing); the village tour connects at the Plaza, on the north side of Ocean Avenue. You can also begin the tours at any point in the descriptions, as they are loop tours.

Ocean Avenue can be very congested. It is better to drive on a par-allel street such as Seventh Avenue during busy days.

From the Monterey Bay Aquarium. Follow David Avenue up the hill to its intersection with Route 68 / Forest Avenue, and turn left. Travel east to Highway 1, staying in the right lane to enter Highway 1 south. Continue below.

To Carmel, for Highway 1 Travelers. Carmel is one and one-half miles south of Pacific Grove and four miles north of Point Lobos. From Highway 1 take the Ocean Avenue exit. Travel west, downhill, past one stop sign. For Carmel Plaza turn left at the next stop sign, onto Junipero Avenue. Or continue on Ocean Avenue down the hill to park at the beach or start a tour there.

From Highway 1 southbound an alternate entrance to Carmel is via Carpenter Street. Travel south on Highway 1 past the Highway 68 / Pacific Grove exit for one-half mile. Turn right at the first light, which is the Carpenter Street exit. Follow truck route signs. Turn right on Third Avenue (city parking is available at the corner of Third Avenue and Junipero Avenue), then left at Junipero Avenue, and continue four more blocks to the village.

To Mission Carmel, and Mission Trail Park. From Highway 1 take the Rio Road exit (one mile south of the Ocean Avenue exit). Travel one-half mile west. Look for Mission Carmel on the left. Parking is available at and around the mission, and Mission Trail Park is across the street. For the Carmel River Beach follow River Road to Santa Lucia Street and turn left. After about five blocks turn left on Carmelo Street, which leads to the large parking lot near the lagoon at the beach.

INTRODUCTION TO CARMEL WITH HISTORICAL HIGHLIGHTS

"I wandered out to the point and looked across to the deserted beach and sloping forests, and thought it was one of the most beautiful resort sites ever conceived." A hundred-some years after developer Charles Devendorf thus envisioned Carmel, hundreds of thousands of visitors each year agree. The wonder is that this one-mile-square "storybook hamlet in the forest" also maintains a strong residential community with ecologically important coastal, forest, and wetlands habitats. Carmel's future depends on the delicate balance struck by developers, artists, preservationists, families, and merchants who live side by side but are often worlds apart in their ideas of what Carmel is to be.

Many businesses, including the neighborhood drugstore and bakery, serve residents' needs as they have for decades. Home delivery of prescriptions and the tradition of a free cookie for the neighborhood youngster continue on the same streets with what is probably the greatest number of galleries and specialty shops per capita of any city in the United States. Through the years, numerous forest, ocean bluff, and village walking trails—some centuries old—have served as quiet passageways for the first inhabitants, the missionaries, a throng of famous writers and artists, and locals. In summer one pair of sidewalks running the length of the Ocean Avenue business district stays packed with visitors.

The pure white sands that first caught Devendorf's eye in the 1890s still rise in sixty-foot dunes from foaming waves at Ocean Beach to sculpt Carmel's western boundary. Dark cypresses frame crimson sunset skies over dunes and the expansive beach, which is hemmed by emerald Pescadero Point to the north and the rugged Abalone Point to the south. These two headlands block the intrusion of river and ocean sediment, which tan so many California beaches.

The dazzling sands of Ocean Beach are the result of sixty million years of earthquake and volcanic action. Colliding plates of the earth's crusts caused molten magma to form deep under the earth's surface. Earthquakes and collisions thrust the magma, which had cooled to form granite, upward. Ground smaller and smaller by relentless waves, the pure quartz crystals and feldspar of the exposed granite whitewash the shores at Ocean Beach.

A cypress-canopied walking path winds above the dunes and melds with the narrow and windy Scenic Drive, which curves with the city limits along the ocean's shoreline south to the Carmel River. In January 1603 the Spanish explorer Sebastian Vizcaino explored "a copious river descending from high snow covered mountains." During rainy season, this river is like a liquid chainsaw artist, carving new patterns in its banks daily as it flows under Highway 1 to its outlet at Carmel River Beach, on the southern outskirts of the city limits.

In honor of the Carmelite fathers who were his chaplains Vizcaino named this river "El Rio Carmelo." The name "Carmel" refers to the order of monks who founded their monastery at Mount Carmel in the Holy Land in the thirteenth century. From 1603, "El Rio Carmelo" is one of the oldest Eurocentric place names in the United States. Beats Plymouth Rock.

When the Spanish landed they were met by the first inhabitants of this land, a peaceful tribe of people who were later identified in mission records as the Rumsen. The Rumsen settled in at least two places in Carmel, one close to this river and the other one by San Jose Creek, to the south. In 1993 rushing storm-swollen waters of the Carmel River washed away sand dunes from an ancestral site at Carmel River Beach that may date back four thousand years. Twenty-some mortars for acorn grinding were uncovered. Most archaeologists place the Esselen tribal group as present here prior to the Rumsen.

The beautifully restored Mission San Carlos Borromeo Del Rio Carmelo, known as Mission Carmel, lies near the southeastern border of Carmel. Father Junipero Serra, founding father of the California missions, was dissatisfied with the first, 1770 mission location in Monterey. In 1771 he moved the mission to Carmel, which he described as "a locality indeed most delightful and suitable because of the excellent quality of the land and the water supply necessary for abundant harvests." It also exemplified Serra's desire for a division between church and military, especially to keep the Rumsen and Esselen, as well as

Mission San Carlos Borromeo Del Rio Carmelo

women of other groups, separated from the often raucous soldiers. The military remained at the Presidio in Monterey. Father Serra went on to found nine more missions. He envisioned a great stone church, but a wooden chapel and adobe outbuildings were his headquarters until his death in 1784. He was buried in the sanctuary of his beloved mission at Carmel. The stone church was not completed until 1797; later yet, when the mission was restored, he was buried under its altar. Two centuries after Serra's death Pope John Paul II attended beatification ceremonies in Carmel as part of the steps to sainthood for Serra.

The missions were funded by an endowment fund set up by the Jesuits, transferred to the Franciscans, and then held in trust by first the Spanish and subsequently the Mexican government. They served a dual purpose, to expand the teaching of Christianity to aboriginal peoples and to serve the Spanish government as the means to subjugate the tribal populations of California lands. During the Carmel mission period the Rumsen and neighboring Esselen people were both enticed from and forced to leave their native villages and to relocate onto mission land. The natives who were Christianized were called neophytes. They were put to work, often against their interest, building the mission, planting and tending the surrounding orchards, and caring for the mission cattle.

The mission system had been abandoned by 1836. The Mexican government had divided the mission land among settlers, with some neophytes receiving land shares. The dwindled numbers of Rumsen and Esselen who had survived disease and relocation were scattered. Although both the Rumsen and Esselen tribes are declared extinct by the U.S. government, a number of direct Esselen and Rumsen descendants continue their ceremonial traditions and those of other tribes. The Ventana Wilderness Camp near Carmel Valley is one center for tribal information.

At the mission site by the 1860s "Cattle had free access, broken columns were strewn around, thousands of birds lived in nooks," according to the written captions under historic drawings that hang on interior mission walls. Once a year a mass was held among the ruins to commemorate the feast day of its patron saint, San Carlos Borromeo, a leading Catholic reformer of the Counter-Reformation. Robert Louis Stevenson attended the event in 1879 and suggested that the Monterey newspaper start a fund drive for restoration of the buildings. Private donations were then collected from visitors, who were brought by horse-drawn tally-hos to the abandoned mission as part of the Seventeen Mile Drive tours offered by Hotel Del Monte. A roof was raised, but authentic restoration did not begin until a half-century later under the direction of Harry Downie.

In the late 1800s the presence of the mission and the Methodist community of Pacific Grove were the inspiration for a "Catholic resort" to be known as Carmel-by-the-Sea. Abbie Jane Hunter from San Francisco, founder of the Women's Real Estate Investment Company in San Francisco, joined investor Santiago Duckworth in the venture. Her cottage at the corner of Guadalupe Street and Fourth Avenue is beautifully preserved and includes Carmel's only woman mayor, Jean Grace, in its long succession of owners. The majority of early lots were bought by San Francisco school teachers and administrators.

The railroad was not extended to Carmel, Duckworth developed other interests, and the dream of a Catholic resort folded. By 1901, three-quarters of what is now Carmel-by-the-Sea was owned by San Francisco attorney Frank Powers and his wife, artist Jane Gallatin Powers, whose father was president of one of the largest hardware, steel, and iron companies on the Pacific coast. Eschewing a fancy mansion, the couple chose to live in a rustic log cabin with a dirt floor. The cabin can still be seen on the dunes at the northern border of the town. In 1902, financier Frank Powers teamed up with Charles Devendorf to form the Carmel Land Development Company. Devendorf's first marketing brochure was addressed to "School Teachers of California and other Brain Workers of Indoor Employment." Prospective buyers and resort guests were met at the Monterey train station, then transported for the half-day trip by buckboard stage. Some of the male passengers would walk part way when the straining horses couldn't make it up the steep hill to Carmel.

Stanford University professors had homes built along Camino Real, soon to be known as "Professor's Row." Word of Carmel spread and was caught by

George Sterling, a San Francisco poet and fellow member of the San Francisco Bohemian Club with Frank Powers. Devendorf and Frank and Jane Powers encouraged artists and writers, and they came—some to visit, some to stay. One of the first, writer Mary Austin, wrote in a "wik-i-up" tree house. Obscured from view, her first home is maintained as a private residence. The Mary Austin minipark honors her contributions to the literary and Carmel world.

Xavier Martinez, like many other San Francisco artists, had his studio and much of his work destroyed in the earthquake of 1906. San Franciscans fleeing their devastated city swelled the population of Carmel. The arty group, known as the "Seacoast Bohemians," grew in numbers and local recognition. Names associated with this group and Carmel either as visitors or residents included Jack London, Sinclair Lewis, Upton Sinclair, William Rose Benet, and Xavier Martinez. Their community was headlined in a 1910 *Los Angeles Times* as a "Hotbed Of Soulful Culture, Vortex Of Erotic Erudition."

The unbohemian side of Carmel in those days boasted a dozen stores, two stables, a school, and a library. The community was close to what Devendorf actually described, an "all round healthy little town."

The natural beauty and freedom of the area attracted photographers. Edward Weston moved to Carmel in 1929 and set up a small portrait studio. Through his close-ups of rocks and details of trees and other natural objects Weston brought nature's own designs into the area of the abstract in art. His four sons joined him in Carmel. Brett Weston and Cole Weston shared exclusive printing of their father's work after he was stricken with Parkinson's disease in his later life. Cole Weston managed the Carmel Sunset Cultural Center in the late 1960s and, together with Ansel Adams and others, formed "The Friends of Photography." Although moved from Carmel to San Francisco, the nonprofit organization continues to play a lead role in fostering creative photography.

When I talked with the energetic Cole Weston, now famous in his own right as a color photographer and director of local plays, about his childhood memories of Carmel, he told of being able to run from the top of Ocean Avenue to the beach through a natural pathway of vacant lots. Nowadays one still hears more rustling of leaves than rumbling of car engines on pine-scented residential streets. The windy roads that lead to residential areas have neither sidewalks, streetlights, nor numbers. One story goes that early bohemian artists and writers kept the numbers off to make it almost impossible for Internal Revenue agents to find their houses. In 1953 a bill was introduced in the California State Legislature that would withhold state gas tax funds from cities without house numbers. Rather than change the numbering system Carmel's city attorney called for a movement to secede from the state. The state bill failed, and Carmel remained in California.

Distinctive architecture helps with directions and highlights Carmel's respect for individualism. Poet Robinson Jeffers commissioned a house of stones carted up from the beach and added rooms and a three-story adaptation of an Irish tower with his own hands. With this Tor House as a base and inspiration, Jeffers wrote and published several volumes of poetry seemingly endemic to this area. His long narrative poems welded his own individual spirit with that of soaring hawks and granite and tapped the raw sensuous beauty of the coast southward though the Big Sur area.

Throughout the village, hand-carved and hand-forged gates lead to log cabins, redwood board-and-battens, thick-walled Colonial Revival homes, Spanish villas, subterranean modern structures, and the only Frank Lloyd Wright home on the Monterey Peninsula. Cottages in the storybook style that was developed by Hugh Comstock and emulated by others dot the residential and business sections. Several of the residences and homes in Carmel have entrances or exteriors that are covered with a soft, irregularly shaped stone with creamy golden coloring. Known as Carmel stone, these sedimentary rocks are quarried at the base of the Santa Lucias in Carmel Valley. Some of them might be from the quarry presently owned by Clint Eastwood—look for the telltale stars in his.

Ocean Avenue descends from Highway 1 through the upper residential section to the village core. At the east end of the business section Junipero Avenue intersects Ocean Avenue. To your left a sign points uphill to the Mountain Theater, where patrons are warmed by fireplaces on cool nights as they continue a tradition begun in 1910 of enjoying plays under the stars. Dame Judith Anderson starred here in Jeffers's first successful play, *The Tower Beyond Tragedy*.

The relatively steep Ocean Avenue, known as the "Devil's Staircase" in its dirt road days, remained unpaved for years with consent of the majority of citizens as a deterrent to the village's development for tourism. A cartoon lampooning the present road shows the driver of a car turning into a skeleton as he waits for a chance to cross Ocean Avenue, packed with cars and tourists, on a typical summer weekend. This main artery is lined with an array of historic businesses, intriguing shops, and the usual sweatshirt and cup collectibles stores.

Historic inns were built as buffers between business and the surrounding residential section. Businesses are also zoned as resident serving and tourist serving. Attempts by city councils to enlarge the tourist-serving section of the city are met with referendums and full-page ads to "Save Carmel."

The Post Office is the heartbeat of the village core for residents. Since their houses have no numbers, residents collect their mail here every day. Outside the front door and around their boxes they share personal tidbits and discuss the latest hot political topic—whether it be the rerouting of the freeway or the permit denial for a tree's removal.

Some of the best-kept secrets in Carmel are found on side streets and along narrow walkways. Tucked in Spanish-style courtyards and English garden alcoves, specialty shops and museum-quality galleries offer anything from Gucci fashionware to keepsake hand-quilted vests, from Remington sculptures to canvases being created in the moment by artists outside their front doors, from Guatemalan rainmakers to antique violins, from hand-carved carousel horses to Eastwood-signature oversized leather chairs.

Romantic cottages and luxury inns with ocean views share wooded nooks with bistros, patisseries, and elegant restaurants. From the historic Pine Inn you can view the forest of Pebble Beach, which grows into the northern border of Carmel. From bay-view rooms you can see Carmel Beach. The snowy sands extend north to rocky outcroppings and the emerald links of Pebble Beach.

Along with your favorite shop and place to view a sunset, Carmel offers plenty of benches for people watching. Many tourists are watching for Carmel's most famous present citizen, actor and Academy Award-winning director Clint Eastwood, who served one term as mayor beginning in 1986. Eastwood fans flooded the town during the duration of his term, seeking him and settling for Eastwood posters, cups, and a meal or drink at his co-owned restaurant, Hog's Breath Inn. The-most asked questions from tourists are still about his where-abouts.

Since its beginning Carmel has been a spirited community with an independent spirit. On each Halloween, children and dignitaries still parade down Ocean Avenue to mark the day and commemorate the town's founding. Through years of community action the beaches remain bare of commercial development. Issues are passionately discussed in town meetings.

Knowing where to find the best of Carmel while avoiding the throngs of tourists that swarm the village on high-season weekends is an insider's art. When tree-lined Ocean Avenue, the main thoroughfare, is packed you can feel like a sequestered guest as you explore hidden passageways to one-of-a-kind shops and wander peaceful forest trails described in this chapter. Then relax on beaches shared only with gentle breezes, perhaps an artist with easel perched on a rocky outcrop, and the glances of a bobbing sea otter.

TOURS

How should you see Carmel? Slowly. One suggestion would be to complete the village tour first. It features the shops, galleries, and history of the village core—one of the most charming and popular shopping areas in America. To complete the day or to fill another one choose portions or all of the coastal and woodland walks, especially at Carmel Mission, to experience the beautiful natural environment. As you plan your day first consider phoning the cultural and historic destinations of interest to you for special programs and schedule changes.

THE VILLAGE TOUR

This tour can be completed in one hour but it would be better to allot at least three, and it could last three weeks. In Carmel you are either "north of Ocean" or "south of Ocean." Let's begin with the south side of Ocean Avenue. This would be on your right as you walk uphill from the Carmel Beach. (If you are starting at the Plaza at the top of Ocean, skip ahead in this text to Devendorf Park, p. 137. All tour buses park at the Plaza.)

From its beginning Carmel has been known as a village in a forest. Native Monterey pines fill the upper slopes while gray-foliaged oaks hug the lower lands. Trees help decipher the history of the location. Before you cross Ocean Avenue at the northwest corner is the largest tree in the village, a blue-gum eucalyptus that measures twenty-two feet, eight inches around at the trunk. The most popular theory about this tree, a native of Australia, is that its seed was probably brought here by early Spanish explorers or mission padres. The tree possibly marked old rancho boundaries. A walking-tour map to sixty-one of the city's heritage trees is available at the visitor's center.

As you walk uphill on Ocean, as throughout Carmel, twisted cypress, spreading oaks, tall eucalyptus, and native Monterey pine shade your walk. Devendorf sold many lots with the condition that the buyers agree to plant trees. One of Carmel's first laws prohibited the cutting of trees without city approval.

A drawing by Bill Bates, a well-known Carmel cartoonist, shows a house on fire as the owner yells to the firemen: "To hell with the house; save the trees." In 1993, the decision of the city council to overrule the city forestry commission and allow the cutting of a pine that was lifting a house from its foundation made TV and front-page news in the local *Pinecone* and *Monterey County Herald*. The trees proponents argued, "Without our trees Carmel would be an expensive slum."

The first business on your right as you walk up Ocean Avenue is the Lamplighters Inn—located at Ocean Avenue and Camino Real. These storybook cottages with picturesque lanterns are one of Carmel's oldest (since 1916) and quaintest tourist courts. If you have children with you they will enjoy visiting the elves in the front courtyard.

A couple of blocks north at Monte Verde Street, the Laurel Burch Gallery (408/626-2822) features the work of California jewelry and design artist extraordinaire Laurel Burch. Chinese officials taught her their cloisonne techniques in 1971. Her passion in the nineties is to create images of "symbols that bridge the distance between ages and races, cultures and beliefs, and even spiritual and physical worlds." Laurel owns a home in Carmel Valley. A retrospective of her work is upstairs.

Brick stairs lead down from the Laurel Burch store to Candlesticks of Carmel (408/626-4305). Hand-dipped candles, candles pressed with grape leaves or real flowers and then dipped in beeswax, and sculpted candles fill a cozy room. The metal folk art pieces of artist and owner Shelley Risko are among the selection of candleholders. Risko draws her designs on sheets of steel and hand pounds copper plates. These are welded, then bathed and brushed in acid solutions. The candleholder sculptures are then laid out in her backyard in Carmel Highlands to receive finishing touches of the corrosive ocean air, on artwork not possible in Iowa.

While many of their garrets have disappeared in Carmel, there are many local artists, and like Shelley Risko they display their work in Carmel's galleries and shops. In the local tradition some artists still create by gallery windows, or doors, or on the street, as well as in back rooms. Over sixty galleries crowd Carmel. They often offer special shows and feature particular artists along with museum-quality collections. You will walk by some of the especially memorable galleries on this tour. On Dolores Street, between Fifth and Sixth avenues, about a dozen are grouped in what is sometimes called "Gallery Row."

Carmel doesn't as yet have too many in-your-face galleries that address the world's revolting situations. Some galleries are mass production print and art dealers. There is no more pressure to buy art in stores of reputable dealers than in a museum. A Carmel gallery guide is available at the visitor's center and at many galleries.

From the corner of Monte Verde and Ocean, city hall is located half a block south on Monte Verde Street. (On another outing you might choose to hike directly up the parking lot and steps adjacent to city hall to see the gardens of Wayfarer Church, with their outlet to Lincoln Street, described p. 134.) City hall is memorable mainly for some of the mayors that Carmel has voted in. Perry Newberry posted ads that admonished, "If you truly want Carmel to become a boosting, hustling, wide-awake, lively metropolis, DON'T VOTE FOR PERRY NEWBERRY." Mayor Barney Laiolo took law into his own hands and dressed undercover to help stop drug deals in a local park. Clint Eastwood, by being Clint Eastwood, increased world recognition of the hamlet, but many cite the children's library as an endearing accomplishment in his mayoral term.

For this sojourn continue on Ocean Avenue. A few doors up, the aromas of chocolate and candies will sweeten your walk at the Cottage of Sweets (408/624-5170), outlet for the Carmel Candy and Confections Company. California Wine Truffles and old-fashioned favorites await you. The Cottage of Sweets is cited as the original ticket booth area of the Golden Bough Theater, which opened in 1924 to accolades as the "crown jewel of small American theaters," but burned twice during separate productions of *By Candlelight*. Four entrances invite visitors through what remains, the rebuilt Court of the Golden Bough. The founder, Edward "Ted" Kuster, had been a successful lawyer in Los Angeles with a yen for theater and a continuing relationship with his former wife Una and her later husband, the poet laureate of the Central Coast, Robinson "Robin" Jeffers.

The present court retains the original architecture, which has influenced many of Carmel's buildings. Fouratt-Simmons Real Estate is located in what was the lobby of the Golden Bough. A delightful miniatures shop, coffee and tea specialty shop, Spencer's Stationery with its cozy fireplace, and more are tucked inside. You'll next pass Sade's Cocktail Lounge, the city's oldest bar, serving at the same quaint building on Ocean Avenue since 1926. Locals enjoy telling stories here of their Pebble Beach sightings of Frank Sinatra in past years of the Crosby tournament.

Continue on Ocean. The Talbott Tie Shop (408/624-1747) is a success story born in Carmel. In 1950 banker Robert Talbott and his wife Audrey left New York with young son Robb for Carmel. Audrey began making ties as gifts for friends and hand sewed the first ties she sold. What began as a cottage industry with attention to detail and selection of the finest silks, cottons, wools, and linens has grown to a staff of two hundred. Production studios and offices are located on the Monterey Peninsula. The first shop was opened in Carmel in 1958. Another store is here on Ocean Avenue at Dolores, a third is at The Lodge at Pebble Beach, and a fourth opened recently in New York.

The Seven Arts building at the corner of Lincoln and Ocean has launched many artistic Carmel highlights. You can view the lighting of the old studio at the Carmel Bay Company (408/624-3868), which replicates the tradition of an old mercantile. It carries a fine selection of California furnishings, including hand-crafted Shaker-style furniture by local craftsman Jeff Hildreth. Another frequented tenant in the building is the original Monterey Baking Company (408/625-3998), with a deli and fresh breads and pastries.

Walk upstairs to bathe in the light of Edward Weston's former studio, now part of a shop. With the exception of the stairway entry the building and studio room remain the same as they were sixty years ago. Weston made a number of portraits here, including his famous one of Steinbeck and those of his second wife, Charis.

Halfway up the block on Lincoln is the Spanish Colonial–style La Rambla, which was built in 1929. Typical of this style are its thick whitewashed walls with irregularly placed windows, tile roofs, and decorative ironwork. Through the center of this building is an arcade leading to the Garden Shop (408/624-6047), where you'll find the metal artists Flo and Milton Williams soldering artistic sculptures and whimsical fountains. Over thirty-five years ago they bought this little backyard garden, then basically dirt with one fruit tree. Now their creations of countless waterfalls, copper and brass garden creatures, and lanterns share the courtyard with trees and lush greenery.

Find resting benches in the peaceful, Biblical gardens of the Church of the Wayfarer (408/624-3550) at the corner of Lincoln Street and Seventh Avenue. Planted in 1941, all the plants in this mature garden, such as aloe, tamarisk, rosemary, and olive, are labeled with their Biblical reference in either the New or Old Testament. Established in 1904, this Methodist Church is the oldest continuously operated church in Carmel. Its picturesque setting is a favorite for weddings. Eighteenth-century hand-carved Italian paneling graces the inside. Services as well as seasonal concerts are offered, with a new, thirty-two rank Soenstein pipe organ.

As you explore the shops and galleries on the walk back to Ocean Avenue, Hero, the town parrot, may welcome you from his perch outside a fashionable shop. Although usually generous with hellos, Hero was squawking up such a racket when I walked by him one day in 1992 I thought the neighbors would have him evicted. Then I felt the rolling. A California earthquake rumbled through Carmel. No damage, just a few ruffled feathers.

Back on Ocean Avenue enjoy the aromas and tastes of the Carmel Bakery—Carmel's oldest (408/626-8885), established in 1923. You'll soon be walking by a hidden-away park that has benches for relaxing, and for enjoying bakery treats. Another bakery, Wishart's (408/624-3870), at the top of Ocean on the north side, will entice you again midway through your walk. There, if a local child walks in with mom or dad, the kid will probably get a pat on the head, the daily joke, and a free cookie from the person behind the counter.

Dolores Street, the next right turn from Ocean, is a study in Spanish Colonial Revival architecture. Note outside staircases and upper porches. Halfway down the first block a semicircle of benches, a stone drinking fountain, and a wooden gate frame the entrance of peaceful little Piccadilly Park. Before 1981 the hanging plants and overflowing flowering pots of the Piccadilly nursery occupied this space. Threatened with development of the space into more shops, after the nursery closed, the city purchased the lot. A moss-lined lane winds back from the gate to a fish pond, tiny waterfall, and shaded English-armchair-style benches.

Just beyond Piccadilly Park at the New Masters Gallery (408/625-1511) amid a selection of contemporary and historic art, you might view an "Audience with the Cardinal"—not in a church but among the illustrated one-liners on the animal kingdom found in the fine pun art of local Will Bullas. "A strong reality on this planet is a smile," is the Bullas perspective. "It disarms better than the threat of guns...I enjoy making people laugh...it's good medicine."

Across the street the gingerbread-style Tuck Box (408/624-6365) is a local favorite for afternoon tea. Lunch and dinner are also served. Built by Hugh Comstock in 1926 the Tuck Box followed in style his Hansel and Gretel Cottages that you can see on the east side of Torres Street between Third and Fourth streets. He built the original fairy-tale house for his wife's doll collection and business, and each cottage cost $100 to build. In 1993 the Hansel and Gretel Cottages were listed together for sale at $450,000. At least eighteen Carmel buildings are Comstock constructed.

Walk a few doors south to the El Paseo building. In this courtyard with its brick flagstones you'll see two Spanish figures that were sculpted by Joe Mora in 1928. The real estate office here has early Carmel photos and maps and warm fireplaces for cool days. If you are interested in real estate many long-time residents who now sell real estate will share their stories of the town, for example about Charles Devendorf. In the early 1900s he was the genial real estate sales and land management end of the Carmel Land Development Company; until the city was incorporated he also was the leading town official, and did everything from helping deliver babies to settling builders' disputes. Perry Newberry, a writer, actor, and later preservationist mayor of Carmel, bought his Carmel lot for five dollars down and five dollars a month in 1910. In 1924 Devendorf reported he had traded some Stockton land he owned for Carmel acreage. Today, if you could trade your five-acre Stockton ranch with pool for a tiny-plotted Carmel board-and-batten fixer-upper you'd be getting a good deal.

On the same side of the street toward Ocean Avenue, Photography West Gallery (408/625-1587) features works by Monterey photographers such as Morley Baer and John Wimberley in addition to Ansel Adams and Edward and Brett Weston and Steve Crouch.

As you again walk north on Ocean look for the entrance to the Doud Arcade. Remodeled in the 1980s, the arcade now houses a variety of shops including Sun Country (408/625-5907) which specializes in kaleidoscopes and the glass creations of owner Ray Anderson, and Paolina's (408/624-5599), an indoor bistro. Exit on San Carlos.

At the next corner Nielsen Market keeps you in those apples a day. The wine shop stocks a selection of fine and vintage wines, including a Yquem priced at over eight hundred dollars. A mural of sights in Carmel painted by Bill Bates covers a wall outside the market

For a few minutes' rest or a meal stop, take the insider's passageway that begins across from Doud's; pass through the Carmel Square Shops (the Owl's Nest has over five hundred teddy bears) to find a narrow walkway at the back left. Walk around and downstairs to emerge at the Court of Fountains. The glassed-in gazebo shops reflect the sparkles of the shooting fountains, and garden benches invite you to stay awhile. Write a letter on handmade paper with an antique pen from Bittner's Fine Stationery & Writing Accessories (408/626-3510). Enjoy watching an artist at his easel. Anton & Michel Restaurant (408/624-2406) at the entrance to the fountains and Patisserie Boissiere (408/624-5008) across the street (Mission) both serve moderately priced lunches and dinners with deluxe food and service.

On Ocean Avenue at the corner of San Carlos Street a World War I arched monument designed by Carmel architect Charles Green fills the center divider. The monument replaced a horse trough; though it was made obsolete by the automobile the road was still unpaved when the monument was completed, since paving of the roads might bring progress.

The Carmel Plaza, a three-level shopping center with Saks Fifth Avenue and I. Magnin as anchor stores, fills the block at Ocean Avenue and Junipero Avenue. Gardens, fountains, and an outdoor fire pit are flanked by fifty stores and restaurants. Construction of this block-sized shopping center was stalled for two decades in the 1950s and 1960s as townspeople debated its size and needs in proportion to the town's. The intersection of business interests and residents' desires often stirs community debate.

As you enter the Plaza from Ocean Avenue you pass the Plaza Restaurant, on your right, which has a varied menu to fit the preferences of almost everyone in your party. Desserts here are scrumptious, even to just look at.

The Carmel Plaza Dollhouse is a short walk in from this Plaza entrance. The custom-made revolving doll house was built to one-inch scale in 1984 at a cost of $25,395. Its draperies and soft goods are handmade, and many furnishings are signed by their artists.

Tour bus parking is at the Plaza exit to Junipero Avenue. This is the midway point of the tour, where the loop back to the beach parking lot begins.

Cross Ocean Avenue at Mission Street. A beaded entranceway ushers you into the Mediterranean Market (408/624-2022). Hanging dry sausages and gourmet cheeses clue you that this is a great place to get sandwiches and deli fare for a picnic at the beach or just across the street at Devendorf Park. Artists, children at play, old timers, and picnickers share the park's green lawns and manicured gardens and sometimes a concert. "The Patriarch," a coast live oak recognized as the largest one in the village, shades the southwest corner. This tract too was once within Devendorf's holdings. He lowered the price on ocean frontage and threw in the park as an incentive to get residents to vote for a resident-launched city deal to save ocean dunelands. It worked. Voters approved the deal in 1922. Devendorf's daughter, Edwina, sculpted the bust of her father that now looks over the park.

After enjoying the park walk down Ocean Avenue toward Dolores Street. Between Mission and San Carlos streets you'll find Books Inc. (408/625-2550) one of the oldest bookstores in the area, offering an outstanding selection of books on Monterey, Carmel, and the central coast. Also on Ocean Avenue is the Dansk II shop, an outlet store. In the next block, between San Carlos and Dolores streets, the Carmel Drug Store stands as a town landmark: it's been in business since 1910.

Turn right at Dolores Street, doubling back to enjoy the side streets. Several galleries dot this area. Wander Dolores Street until you come to the Em Le's Restaurant (408/625-6780). The french toast here is memorable but young eyes will remember the fantasy world created here during Halloween and Christmas. Near Em Le's a tiny gate leads to the Secret Garden and on to San Carlos Street. This whimsical garden shop lane is the backyard of a home that used to front Ocean Avenue. The Garden Gate is open 10 a.m. to 5 p.m.

The lane emerges near the Hog's Breath Inn (408-625-1044) and the Eastwood Building. Owned in a partnership by Clint Eastwood, the restaurant features a courtyard with a flagstone dining patio. As five fireplaces warm outdoor diners, the rural Salinas hills seem to come to life on a large patio wall mural by local artist G.H. Rothe. Several stuffed boar's heads peer out from the interior restaurant and pub walls. Among offerings on the menu are the Dirty Harry Burger, Sudden Impact, Mysterious Misty, and Eiger Sandwich. The pub is open until 1:30 a.m.

In the Eastwood Building, next door on San Carlos Street, take the elevator or walk upstairs to the visitor's center operated by the Carmel Business Association (408/624-2522). You can continue your courtyard tour across the street at the Jack London Mall, really a pleasant courtyard of galleries, a rock and crystal shop, and The Jack London Pub. In the Siner Gallery (408/625-9628) you'll find quality etchings of California landscapes, particularly the Central Coast. At the John Mason Gallery (408/625-3868) the visionary art of John Mason and Andrew Jackson captivate many an open mind. You might catch a special showing of Mason's computer images.

After wandering along San Carlos Street take one of the several pathways back to Dolores Street. At the corner of Sixth Avenue and Dolores Street you'll spot the Village Corner. This Spanish-style one-story building with outdoor dining is a cherished gathering spot and nostalgic heart-place for locals. In the late 1970s plans for a two-story building at the site surfaced and a citizens group called "Old Carmel" led a Save-the-Village-Corner campaign. When a loss of electricity blacked out Carmel during the quake in 1990 a gas generator kept coffee warm here, where locals gathered.

Across Dolores on Sixth Street the Weston Gallery (408/624-4453) features prints by the finest masters of nineteenth- and twentieth-century photographers. Prints by Ansel Adams, Edward Weston, and the Weston sons Brett and Cole are focal points of the gallery, which is the exclusive representative for work directly from Karsh. Gallery shows change frequently. One of the most popular is of eighteenth- and early-nineteenth-century prints. The gallery includes a prime selection of photography art books, as well as boxed notecards of the artists' prints of local sights.

The sculpture garden on Dolores Avenue between Fifth and Sixth Avenues leads to the Carmel Art Association Galleries (408/624-6176), which display the works of seventy-five local painters and sculptors. Originally situated in the Seven Arts Building, the Carmel Art Association was formed in 1927 by local artists in order to organize to display their talents and protect their place in Carmel. Membership in this cooperative included locals Salvador Dali, Armin Hansen, and seascape painter William Ritschell.

Only originals are offered for sale in the gallery. For nine months special one-person shows fill one of the five display floors. At the show's opening reception the public is invited to mingle with local artists and association patrons. Special retrospective shows offered in autumn trace important influences on California Art by such early association members as Mary De Neale Morgan, Donald Teague, and Armin Hansen. Some of these shows are so popular that lines form in the sculpture garden.

On some days artists who belong to the association stop by the gallery, in part to visit. One day I talked to artist Keith Lindberg, who displays colorful, warm, impressionistic paintings. "I came here with a friend in the sixties. Artist studios were common. Not all these galleries like today....The coffee shops were meeting places, get-together spots with other artists....Very expensive for new painters to come here now." A bench in the outdoor courtyard invites you to rest before your next discovery.

The courtyard, El Prado de Su Vecino, translated as the passageway of your neighbor, leads from Dolores Street through a variety of shops to Lincoln Street. Marking the entrance is the clock shop, Timepeace.

You'll emerge through the Cortille San Remo onto Lincoln. Across the street is the M. J. Murphy house (tour hours vary: 408/624-2781). The family home of one of the major builders and designers in Carmel, this house was lifted by crane over the tops of businesses and homes from its original location up Ocean Avenue. During the week it serves as a community center. A small park with restrooms is adjacent to the Murphy House.

The Harrison Memorial Library, at the corner of Lincoln Street and Ocean Avenue, was one of the most famous buildings that Murphy designed, this one in consultation with San Francisco Bay Area architect Bernard Maybeck, who designed the Palace of Fine Arts. The library was a gift to the city from Ella Reed Harrison in memory of her husband, Ralph Chandler Harrison, who had served as a California Supreme Court justice from 1890 to 1903. Light and airy, and with over eighty-two thousand volumes to be enjoyed by a huge fireplace, this adult library could be your perfect gift to yourself on a foggy afternoon. Ninety-five percent of the town's residents hold library cards. A walking-tour guide to the library's paintings and sculptures is available at the reference desk.

The children's library and local history room annex, earlier mentioned for being acquired when Clint Eastwood was mayor, is at Mission and Sixth streets. The story goes that during his tenure he took a holiday ski trip with an executive of Wells Fargo Bank, the corporation that owned the property. Eastwood was reportedly so persuasive about the need for the annex that Wells Fargo dropped its asking price half a million dollars. In addition to children's library services the building also houses the Carmel History Library.

The courtyard of the Pine Inn connects across Lincoln Street and also to Murphy Park. Before you leave Ocean Avenue look up the street and imagine it as the bumpy dirt road of 1904.

Recycling isn't new. Original sections of the Pine Inn were formerly the Hotel Carmelo, which was built from the old Tivoli Opera House in San Francisco. Devendorf had the hotel moved down the hill on "thundering" pine logs to greet guests at its present closer-to-the-beach location. M. J. Murphy refitted and enlarged the hotel, which has since seen many additions.

Brick walkways edged with hedges and gardens weave through sections of the Pine Inn. Walk through an original beveled-glass door to the lobby. The same antique clock that timed Devendorf's early sales and kept time at gala dances keeps the pulse of the present lobby, which is furnished with antiques from his Carmel Development days.

The Lobos Lodge (408/624-3874) at Monte Verde and Ocean Avenue was built as a buffer between residences and the business district and as such is the last commercial location at the foot of Ocean Avenue. Traditional and antique quilts and quilted apparel warm your last glance at Carmel shops in Quilts LTD. (408/625-2314), which is tucked into the hotel's first courtyard.

THE COASTAL AND WOODLAND WALKS TOUR

Scenic walking trails traverse the areas west of Highway 1. They connect to almost anywhere you want to go in the village.

THE BEACHES AND TOR HOUSE. Ocean Beach is the wide expanse of snowy white sands that grow into the dunes hugging the parking lot at the bottom of Ocean Avenue. Parking also can sometimes be found along Scenic Drive. Stairways lead down to the beach from several points along Scenic. The only public restrooms for this beach are located near the parking lot.

The waves here are beautiful but dangerous. No swimming or wading is advised on any Carmel-area beach. News clippings back to the city's founding tell of heroic saves and tragedies. The people you see surfing or skim boarding have been taught to swim here; they understand the currents and undertows.

You will get a feel for Carmel's international reputation as you watch a mosaic of people from all over the world descend the dune from the Ocean Avenue parking area to the beach flats. Some people begin elegant arm in arm strolls and soon are laughing sand waders in the soft dunes. Some race their dogs in downhill dashes. Some roll down, in a celebration of childhood.

Once at the ocean's edge, walk toward the northern end of the beach, scrambling over granite rocks as you walk along. If the tide is low peek into tidepools. Sea otters especially enjoy the feeding grounds of these northern beach waters. In early spring this is an excellent spot from which to view mother otters with babies riding on upturned chests. A path climbs to a rocky outcropping and an expansive view.

After enjoying the rocky area head back down the beach. Probing the wet sands for tasty crustations, shorebirds like willets and sanderlings might scurry along the tide line with you.

In the spring, usually on Memorial Day weekend, a tent fills the beach midway south of Ocean Avenue. A horn blows. A row of surfers run to the water, land flat on their boards, and paddle frantically out to the waves. One catches a wave. He's up! Now he crouches. A wall of water blocks him from view. He pops out! The crowd on the shore erupts with whooping and thunderous applause. For two days local surfers join with boards and waves in a fluid dance to perform with the greatest skills for the longest distance. The annual Surf About continues from sunrise to sundown until finally, in categories ranging from youngsters to grandmasters, the local surf champions claim their prizes and applause.

The same sands are filled again, usually on the lowest-tide weekend in early fall, for the annual Sand Castle Contest. To discourage mobs of people the exact date of the event is not announced until one week before the contest. A general theme embraces entries ranging from whimsical to political. Three-foot-tall sand mice guard a detailed Cinderella's castle for one entry while a lifelike whale collapses an oil platform as another. Each year a local architects' group replicates a notable Carmel building in the sand. In the afternoon the judges, usually a group of local architects and civic notables, award seashells and the coveted golden shovel for "the Grand Sand Award."

Return to the bluffs by way of one of the staircases or back through the dunes—especially, return to the bluffs at sunset. You may be joined by many local shopkeepers and artists who walk her for the evening event. The sky bursts with colors reflected on the shimmering beach. Dark headlands and silhouettes of cypress trees frame a sun dipping through an erubescent sky that may be on fire one night and softly blushing through the fog on the next.

Scenic Drive and a walking path parallel the beach and offer spectacular views for one and a half miles. The shady walking path along Scenic resounds with the crashing of waves and meanders into sunlit patches of beautifully planted scenic bluffs. Benches along the way invite you to view breakers, gliding pelicans skimming the waves in summer and, in the winter, the geysers of migrating whales. Close by you a hummingbird may be feasting on native plants.

To extol the twelfth-night winter celebration a group of residents continues a Carmel tradition along this route. Old Christmas trees are dragged to the beach, usually at the bottom of Thirteenth Avenue. Toasts to the New Year are raised as a bonfire of the branches lights the evening sky. The pathway ends at the Frank Lloyd Wright–designed house at the point just past Martin Way. Completed in 1954, the house was declared by the architect to be "durable as rocks, transparent as a wave." The exterior is thin-layered stone with a porcelain enamel roof.

The road becomes a narrow cliff-hanger after it passes the Frank Lloyd Wright house. As you walk or slowly drive past Ocean View Avenue, look up to your left. For a moment you will feel transported to Ireland as the stone Tor House and Keats-inspired tower fill the grassy knoll above you. Writer Robinson Jeffers (1887-1962) arrived in Carmel in 1914.

Jeffers commissioned M. J. Murphy to build a house of ocean stone on the cliff. With his own hands and later those of his twin sons, Jeffers added to the home, which he named Tor House. Charlie Chaplin, Carl Sandburg, Charles Lindburg, and Edna St. Vincent Millay were among those who visited and shared his guest room. For his wife, Una, he built a three-story adaptation of an Irish tower with thousands of granite rocks that he wheelbarrowed up from the beach below his house. Each day he built, a hawk would circle around him and sometimes light on the structure, which Jeffers later named Hawk Tower. Unicorn statues and wall moldings beloved by Una, artifacts and rocks from throughout the world, personal mementos, and the Jeffers' furnishings are on view during hourly tours of the unique home and tower, Fridays and Saturdays. Call (408/624-1813) for reservations; the location is Stewart Way, off Scenic Avenue.

To reach Carmel River Beach follow the panoramic but hair-raising Scenic Drive to the end at Carmel River Beach, or travel back to Junipero Avenue and loop around to Rio Road. The Carmel River meanders through the wetlands areas and bird sanctuary before it flows to the sea during rainy seasons. When the lagoon is filled and threatens to flood, bulldozers arrive to push the summer buildup of sands aside and let the river rush free. Crowds gather on the shore to toast and cheer the annual event.

The lagoon is a birders paradise. On the hillside hovering marsh hawks, sparrow hawks, and red-tailed hawks glide and dive. Great blue herons and egrets stand and elegantly turn at the marsh's edge. Mallards and coots paddle by, and dip and dive.

After the river is dammed, usually sometime in spring, you can walk over and up an easy slope to a smooth service-road trail. In spring and early summer lupines and paintbrush flowers highlight mixed bouquets of surrounding wildflowers. Along this trail you'll see various paths leading down to picturesque coves. Artists often set up easels here and on the rocky crags.

Numerous benches dot the hillsides and pathways along your walk. At a major fork one of the inland paths leads to a large wooden hillside cross, which marks the site of the Portola-Crespi Spanish explorers party of 1769. The party, searching for Monterey Bay, left a message at the foot of a cross they erected here. "[We have] made every effort to find the Port of Monte-Rey; penetrating well into the mountains, skirting it along the shore, in spite of its ruggedness, but all in vain," (This is the party that retreated to San Diego and returned to recognize Monterey Bay the next year.) At the cross there is a panoramic view of the bay and Point Lobos and the river's route from the mountains.

Follow the road again to a gnarled rocky promontory. Climb the wooden steps up to the outlook. Breathe deep: this view is a sweep. You'll see the pristine bay at beautiful Monastery Beach, which extends in a sandy crescent north to San Jose Creek. When rushing river water prevents your crossing from Carmel River Beach, or if you want to begin at Monastery Beach, you will need to drive on Highway 1. Turn west off 1 onto Ribera Road just south of Rio Road or turn right after you pass the little red Bay School. You can also park at Monastery Beach.

Many people mean Monastery Beach, also known as San Jose Creek Beach, when they talk about the Carmel Beach. Busy with locals and scuba divers on weekends, the post-card beach offers many private stretches of sand.

THE MISSION. Mission San Carlos Borromeo Del Rio Carmelo (408/624-3600), located one-half mile west off Highway 1 on Rio Road, is opened for visitors every day. From Carmel River Beach drive or walk along Carmelo Street, then turn right at Fifteenth Avenue, which becomes Lasuen and leads to the mission. The walk takes fifteen to twenty minutes.

In the summer and on weekends busloads of visitors view the authentically restored Mexican Baroque church, its two museums, and the flowering gardens. Off season it is so deserted you can almost hear footsteps from the past as you walk in the old mission cemetery and view relics. Masses are offered year-round, and special concerts fill the basilica, one of only two basilicas in the western United States.

The exterior of the outbuildings that now surround the "cells" of Father Serra and Father Lasuen has been left unplastered in sections to reveal the original adobe brickwork. A landmark Moorish star tower and vaulted ceiling cover the basilica, which displays historic oil paintings and religious statues. Father Serra's private room is found in the interior hallway between the gift shop and the first restored room.

Inside the first restored room the *Serra Cenotaph* by sculptor Joe Mora may well be the definitive California sculpture. Look into the eyes of the kneeling figures and the small grizzly for the melding of dreams, reality, and stone. Originally built as a sarcophagus for Serra, the sculpture grew too large in scope and is now a freestanding monument.

Two museums on the grounds depict early California life and the story of the loving restoration of the mission that was directed by cabinetmaker Harry Downie, who scoured records to restore the mission in exacting detail. Flanking the mission are gardens and a cemetery dating back to its origins. An estimated three thousand Esselen and Ohlone tribespeople are buried on the mission grounds. A self-guided tour leads through the church, museums, and grounds.

WOODLAND AND MEADOW TRAILS. Before there was pavement, before there were the wide, dusty, buggy roads, Father Serra and mission workers would journey from the Carmel Mission to Monterey and back along a web of narrow walking trails. Today you can follow the footsteps of Father Serra, beat the traffic and parking of modern times, and enjoy wooded glens and carpets of wildflowers along these same trails, which are preserved in Mission Trail Park. There is a loop trail within the park that leads though the Lester Rowntree Memorial Arboretum. The loop trail is a leisurely hour-and-a-half walk.

You can pick up the trails at any of several locations. On Mountain View Avenue walk to the top of the avenue, where it ends. (Only limited parking is available). From the bridge there, walk to your right to enter the park. The main entrance is located at Rio Road, just across from the Carmel Mission. A gateway entrance at Junipero and Eleventh Avenue is about a half-hour walk from the mission and three easy blocks to shops. Few cars can be accommodated at the entrance marked by a small sign near the Flanders estate section of the park, located off a narrow residential stretch of Hatton Road.

If you travel up to the Mountain View Avenue bridge, a few steps up from the Serra trail leads to the Flanders trail stairway. The Doolittle nature trail connects to this trail and winds back to the Rio Road starting point. Picnickers will not find tables in the glens along the way, but the Rowntree Arboretum has many benches.

From the Rio Road entrance across from the mission, the Serra trail and Willow trail lead to Eleventh Avenue. Highlights of the Serra trail include a redwood glen and serene canyon. Clusters of benches invite you to sit and listen to bird symphonies and the rainy-season murmur of a nearby stream. Surrounding houses are obscured behind forest groves. A generation ago the trail up to Mountain View Avenue would sparkle some nights with a parade of candles in coffee cans as neighborhood groups made their way up the hillside, past the Eleventh Avenue bridge, to the Mountain Theater.

WHAT ELSE TO SEE AND DO

SUNSET CENTER. At the corner of San Carlos and Eighth Avenue (408/624-3996) the center is host location to several events in Carmel. Sunset Center is a former school that now houses a theater with excellent acoustics plus meeting rooms and studios where instruction is offered. The annual Bach festival brings artists of renown for two summer weeks. The city also sponsors a playwriters' contest, with the winning play presented here in summer.

CHERRY FOUNDATION. At Guadalupe Street and Fourth Avenue (408/624-7491) the Cherry Foundation combines an art gallery, instructional center, and performing arts center. Peaceful gardens surround the former home of inventor Carl Cherry and his artist wife, Jeanne D'Orge.

Lester Rowntree Memorial Arboretum. There is very limited parking at this easy-to-miss location off Hatton Road. It's best to use the Rio Road entrance from Mission Trail Park. Walk up Doolittle nature trail, which is the main entrance to the park. It is located to your right as you stand with your back to Rio Road. California native plants, many of which the garden's founder collected on her trips through California's wilderness, are labeled and grouped in discrete environments, such as desert, woodland, and chaparral. Redwood benches offer good views throughout the garden.

The Barnyard and Crossroads. East of Highway 1, off Rio Road, two shopping centers have unusual offerings among the shops and restaurants. A large windmill marks the redwood buildings of the Barnyard, where the gardens are a palate of flowers during every season. Local watercolor artists set up their easels or paint flat on the walkways. At the Barnyard Sea Otter Center (408/625-3290) the volunteers who are the Friends of the Sea Otter provide information about sea otters and schedules of free observation tours. They also offer such items to purchase as otter ties made by Talbott Ties of Carmel, sea otter watches, hand-carved otters, sweatshirts, and more. The Thunderbird Bookshop and Restaurant (408/624-1803) offer wide selections of books, an informative lecture series, and weekend concerts for children. You can browse through books and enjoy garden and mountain views while savoring menu items from the restaurant. At the northern end of the Barnyard steel, iron, and bronze are pounded and shaped over a pit of hot coals in the working forge of award-winning metalsmith Chris Axelsson (408/624-3909). Hundreds of tools used to handle and form the metal and control the fire hang on the barnlike walls. Hand-forged sculptures, lighting bases, gates, and furniture are displayed and sold in a room adjacent to the forge.

More shops and top-rated restaurants can be found at the Crossroads. The Treadmill (408/624-2210) is the local information center for runners' events. If you've been on the run, the Power Juice Company (408/626-6577) will squeeze you fresh organic juices of any combination you desire. Gepetto's Collectibles (408/ 625-6162) offers thousands of hand-created stuffed animals by ninety different artists, handcrafted porcelain dolls, handcrafted chess sets, and an array of collectibles to appeal to a wide variety of interests.

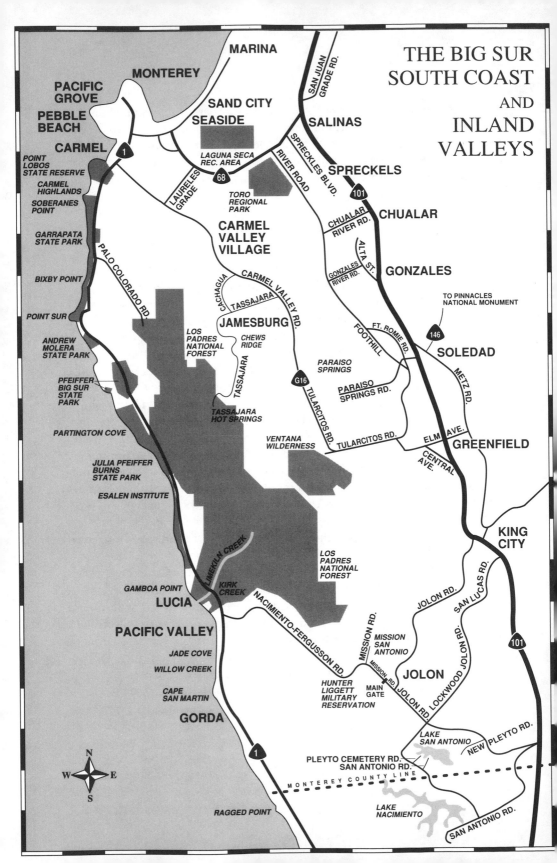

CHAPTER 6

HIGHWAY 1 SOUTH COAST ROUTE

POINT LOBOS, BIG SUR,
HEARST CASTLE,
AND ON TO CAMBRIA

Ninety miles of spectacular coast stretches south from Carmel to the southern border of the Monterey Bay National Marine Sanctuary. San Simeon, home to Hearst Castle, and Cambria are included as natural extensions of the route.

GETTING READY

THE BEST TIMES TO VISIT AND THE SPECIAL EVENTS

The scenery and curves of Highway 1, the coast route, are best suited for daylight traveling. Plan to enjoy a sunset over the ocean. Traffic is heaviest in summer, the traditional vacation season: sun warms the inland valleys, rivers and creeks offer refreshing dips, and rangers lead hikes and campfire programs. In autumn and spring the route is less crowded and the fog lifts sooner for clear views. As the number of visitors drops, so do the rates for lodging. Ask about winter rates and room specials. The California Transportation Department describes Highway 1 as a safe road in winter. However, travelers need to be advised that minor slides and some major ones do occur. Drought years have the fewest. Most of these slides are cleared within an hour by maintenance crews that live along the highway. Motorists are urged to use common sense. As on any mountainous road, hazardous conditions are going to occur along Highway 1 in stormy weather.

When I asked for information about special events at Point Lobos the ranger answered, "We open every day." Agreed, every day along this route is special. Check "Wildlife Wisdom," below, for nature's parade of events. Gatherings include: In February, as Masters of Food and Wine gather at the Highlands Inn (408/624-3801), international star chefs and vintners present cooking classes, tours, wine tastings and gourmet meals. Call to get on the mailing list. Tickets sell out as soon as offered. In April, the Big Sur International Marathon (408/625-6226) also offers a 5K walk/run, when Highway 1 is closed to morning traffic. In late September or early October the River Inn Resort sponsors an Octoberfest (408/625-5255) to benefit the Big Sur Volunteer Fire Brigade. In late October runners fill Julia Pfeiffer Burns State Park during the beautiful Big Sur River Run (408/667-2797). Also in October, artists display the largest collection of Big Sur and Monterey jade (nephrite) ever assembled in one spot, at Gorda's Jade Festival (805/927-5574).

CLIMATE AND CLOTHING

There are fifty or so microclimates between Highway 1 and the eastern reaches of the Santa Lucia Mountains. It is said that every thousand feet you climb vertically represents an inland climate span of 150 miles. People grow macadamia nuts and small bananas on sheltered headlands and inland valleys, as though this were the tropics. In summer you can hike from thick fog to a heat wave in a few hours. The average high temperature for January is 60 degrees; average low, 41 degrees. In July the average high temperature is 68 degrees; average low, 52 degrees. Pfeiffer State Beach is beautiful, but the wind-blown sands can sting your face any day of the year. The rainy season lasts from November through early April and the rain produced ranges widely, from twenty inches annually along the coast to over sixty inches at higher elevations.

You can dress fancy for the Highlands, and you don't have to dress at all for some of the beaches. Casual, layered clothing is the norm for travel along Highway 1. Good hiking shoes, sunscreen, a canteen, a camera, and binoculars are advised. Once you've started hiking some of these trails you won't want to quit. Bring a swimming suit for dips in the rivers and at protected China Beach at Point Lobos. The water is, however, freezing at the beaches, and the surf is dangerous at most. The surfers you see along the coast are experienced ocean swimmers.

TOUR LENGTHS

Highway 1 can certainly offer a week's worth of views and pleasures. For Mickey Muenning, the architect of Post Ranch, a two-week vacation has lasted twenty years. If your schedule will allow only one day to drive Highway 1 you can have an enjoyable day, with time for a few walks and a few stops at galleries or restaurants. It would be best to explore Point Lobos on a separate day, but don't miss it if this is your only chance; allow at least three hours. Point Lobos is one of the best places to bike in the area. For the one-day drive, the easily accessed half-hour hike to the McWay Waterfall at Julia Pfeiffer Burns State Park and the hour creek-trail hike in Pfeiffer Big Sur State Park are suggested walks. The gallery at Ventana Resort displays works by local artists and is well worth a part of your day. For the day drive, plan an hour driving time for thirty miles. Although the maximum speed limit in California is fifty-five miles per hour, few stretches of curvy Highway 1 warrant this speed. The prima facie speed limit in California is the speed at which a vehicle can travel a given roadway safely. There are numerous signs, yellow with black lettering, at the beginnings of curves. Their speed limits are the suggested safe speeds for the curves only, and drivers should resume a normal safe speed after leaving them. Two types of drivers cause difficulties on Highway 1; the driver who speeds and the driver who drives too slow rather than pull over at any of the numerous turnouts, to view the magnificent vistas.

WILDLIFE WISDOM

Marine and inland wildlife abound year-round. In the summer the birds are the first to catch my eye. Legions of pelicans fly along the coast. At some cliffs along Highway 1 golden eagles soar alongside your car windows. Sometimes it feels as if you are flying with them. Migratory marine birds, most notably Brandt's cormorants, nest at the bird-rock island at Point Lobos from spring through summer.

Of the marine mammals, sea otters and harbor seals are the ones seen year-round. Otters are best observed in the kelp beds at Point Lobos, Soberanes Point, Julia Pfeiffer Burns State Park, Big Creek, Limekiln Beach, Kirk Creek, and Alder Creek. Seals give birth on the beaches of Point Lobos, especially Whalers Cove, in the spring. Sea lions are most often seen from August to March.

Deer, raccoons, squirrels, and an occasional bobcat are among the animals that inhabit the mountains. Mountain lions, wild boar, and rattlesnakes rarely cross your path but do inhabit this region. When we first camped at Pfeiffer Big Sur some twenty years ago we didn't take the wild boar reports seriously. During the night the pounding of many hooves in our campsite awakened us and our tent was jiggled by rooting boars. Stay calm if you come upon a herd of these fellers. Noise can provoke them. Backing away easy is advised; if charged, rangers say, climb the nearest tree. Damage to possessions, let alone people is quite rare. Herds of boar can be seen in the daytime from the high ridges. Mountain lions usually avoid human trails. None of the hundreds of hikers I have talked to has ever seen one. Rangers do report sightings. If you are in the backcountry, it is advisable to carry a stick just in case. Rattlesnakes may show up in Big Sur; be careful before putting hands on rocky ledges or sitting on rocks or logs.

When the crowds leave at the end of summer Big Sur seems almost reborn. In the warm sunny autumn weather the leaves of maples, sycamores, and cottonwoods wave in yellow and orange. Poison oak, which is prolific off the trails, turns fiery red. In October the first monarch butterflies begin arriving for the winter months. The eucalyptus grove by the historic Cooper cabin in Andrew Molera State Park is a good viewing location.

Mid-November marks the opening of the steelhead and rainbow trout fishing season. In the Big Sur River anglers catch steelhead weighing up to twelve pounds. From mid-December through February gray whales begin to be spotted with regularity offshore as they migrate to and from the warm lagoons in Baja California. Some of them come within fifty feet of the shore. If you pull off the road at any turnout with a good ocean view and keep a good watch on the water, you will probably be rewarded with a white geyser and perhaps a full body breach. Prime whalewatching spots are found at Point Lobos, Garrapata State Park, Point Sur Lighthouse (access is by guided tour only), and Julia Pfeiffer Burns State Park. During the peak five weeks of the season you can join a ranger-led whale watch. The rangers will provide binoculars and share displays of whale bones and baleen, and informational handouts. Call Pfeiffer Big Sur State Park at 408/667-2315 for specifics.

Wildflowers bloom on hillsides and meadows in March and April, tapering off in May. The Garrapata hike offers some beautiful varieties. Picked wildflowers wilt quickly and their seeds are lost for the coming years. Fire danger is extreme during dry summer and autumn months. Campfires need to be legal and tended.

VISITOR INFORMATION

Most of the land adjacent to Highway 1 is private property. Hike and enjoy posted trails and parkland. These numbers serve public lands: Point Lobos State Reserve information, 408/624-4909; USDA-Forest Service Big Sur Station, 408/667-2423; Pacific Valley Station, 805/927-4211; California Department of Parks and Recreation, Monterey District, 408/649-2836; Big Sur District, 408/667-2315. For more visitor's information call the Big Sur Chamber of Commerce, 408/667-2100. For road conditions call the CALTRANS state-wide road information line, 800/427-7623.

Point Lobos, An Illustrated Walker's Handbook, by Florence Thompson, from Inkstone Books, is a good reference for the natural history of Point Lobos. *Hiking the Big Sur Country*, the 1992 edition by Jeffrey Schaffer, from Wilderness Press, is an excellent guide for the coast and Santa Lucia Mountains from Carmel River Beach to Lucia. Pick this book if you want a good source for extended backpacking trips.

Pick up a tide table before you begin your journey. They are usually available free at chain drugstores and sporting goods stores. Along Highway 1 almost every market has them. Plan your visits to tidepool locations to coincide with low tide.

ALTERNATE TRANSPORTATION

From April to October, Monterey-Salinas Transit line 22 serves Carmel, Point Lobos, Carmel Highlands, Yankee Point, Garrapata Beach, Bixby Creek Bridge, Point Sur Light Station, the River Inn, Pfeiffer Big Sur Park, Pfeiffer Beach, Ventana Inn, and Nepenthe. Buses depart from the Monterey transit center and offer a relaxing ride. Call 408/899-2555 for complete information.

PARKING

There are over three hundred turnouts on the west side of the highway. Take advantage of the great views. If you find yourself with a line of five vehicles behind you, pull over. If you are leaving your car by the roadside and embarking on a hike, secure your vehicle before leaving it. Take valuables with you.

PLACES TO STAY

CARMEL HIGHLANDS

HIGHLANDS INN (four miles south of Carmel at signs, above Highway 1). This is a romantic destination for newlyweds. Even Brian Whitmer, the renowned chef of the resort's Pacific's Edge Restaurant, honeymooned here. One hundred forty-two units, set on cliffs above crashing surf and twisted cypress. All suites with whirlpool baths and fireplaces. 408/624-3801. AX, MC, V; others also accepted. For two, from $240.00 to $300.00.

NORTHERN BIG SUR COAST

BIG SUR LODGE (within Pfeiffer Big Sur State Park). Sixty-one garden court cottages with redwood decks, in the midst of Big Sur Park. Close to hiking trails. Some rooms include fireplaces and full kitchens. Restaurant and grocery store on premises. Conference facilities. Swimming pool. 408/667-2171. MC, V. Three different rate seasons. In summer, for two, from $100.00 to 120.00.

DEETJEN'S BIG SUR INN (just off Highway 1, approximately four miles south of the entrance to Pfeiffer Big Sur State Park). This inn is registered as a national historic site. Rustic cabins under the redwoods, near the babbling Castro Creek, have dark woods, antiques, oriental and country throw rugs, and hand-hewn doors in rooms each with its own name and history. Some rooms feature Deetjen's handcrafted furniture. Cabins range from tiny to two-family size. Walls are planks of locally milled or scavenged redwood. As walls are thin, guests with children must rent two adjacent rooms. TV? Never. Favorite pastimes here are renewing relationships, cozy honeymoons, walking in the forest, and writing and reading journals that are passed on from guest to guest. Some fireplaces, some full kitchens. Most rooms have private baths. Reserve at least two months in advance. 408/667-2377. No cards. For two, from $70 to $140.

POST RANCH INN (west of Highway 1, approximately thirty miles south of Monterey, across the highway from the Ventana Inn entrance). The newest inn on the Big Sur Coast has spectacular ocean views and also redwood, oak, and madrone forests, fern grottos, and meadows. Located on ninety-eight acres of coastal ridge, set well back from Highway 1, the thirty deluxe rooms meld with their surroundings. Wildflowers grow on the sod roofs of five ocean houses that are recessed into the ridge. Seven tree houses are built on stilts to protect the roots of surrounding redwoods. Rooms offer the ultimate in privacy while preserving ocean and starlit views through expansive use of glass. Intricate wood interiors, slate floors, and marble baths. Sierra Mar restaurant offers regional cuisine for guests and reserved seating for visitors. Complimentary morning yoga. Two pools, fireplaces, state-of-the-art music systems, and minibars. A spa offers exercise equipment and massages. Drivers escort guests from parking areas to the secluded ridge. 408/667-2200, 800/527-2200. AX, MC, V; others also accepted. For two, from $290 to $450.

VENTANA INN (inland from Highway 1, a little over two miles south of Pfeiffer Big Sur State Park). Everytime I visit here deer are grazing nearby. The secluded mountaintop adult resort of sixty-three accommodations is set within meadows framed by forests and spectacular ocean view points. Rooms have light-cedar walls and high ceilings; many rooms have fireplaces. Some have private Japanese hot baths; some townhomes have whirlpools; two pools and Japanese hot baths are shared. Walk along nature trails or through meadows to Ventana's quintessential California-cuisine restaurant. TV, pay movies. Complimentary evening beverages. 408/667-2331, 800/628-6500. AX, MC, V; others also accepted. For two, from $190 to $480, summer season.

SOUTHERN BIG SUR COAST

ESALEN INSTITUTE (on the ocean side of Highway 1, fifteen miles south of Peiffer Big Sur State Park). Most people stay here while attending workshops in a variety of disciplines over a weekend or during the week. Spaces do open for people who just want lodging, board, and baths. Rooms have two single beds, dressers, and desks. Some have spectacular ocean views. No TVs, radios, or telephones. Clothing is optional around pool and bath areas. Rooms include three meals with primarily vegetarian cuisine. "Animal is served about three times a week." Reservations are taken as early as seven days in advance for nonworkshop participants. Drop in vacancies do occur; call prior to arriving. Also, cliffside mineral baths are open to anyone from 1 a.m. to 3:30 a.m., with reservations and fee. All lodging includes three meals. 408/667-3000, 408/667-3023. AX, MC, V. For two, $230.00.

LUCIA LODGE (twenty miles south of Pfeiffer Big Sur State Park). Nestled in cabins, a group of ten very rustic rooms sits on the edge of an oceanside ridge. Dark slat-wood walls and beamed ceilings. Fine-quality beds and showers. Units seven through ten offer incredible views of Lucia Bay and the southern Big Sur coastline. Outside your room, ocean watching and a reading bench offer the only recreation on this isolated headland. The Lucia store and restaurant is a short walk around the bend. 408/667-2391. MC, V. For two, from $82 to $165. The more expensive rooms offer the better views.

RAGGED POINT INN (off Highway 1, fifteen miles north of San Simeon). Panoramic southern Big Sur views from rooms set on a cliff above the ocean. A pathway for an invigorating walk is cut across a rugged cliff to the beach below. Nineteen large, modern rooms with high sloping, textured ceilings. A restaurant is planned. TV, coffee, and full baths. 805/927-4502. MC, V. For two, mostly under $100.

CAMBRIA AND SAN SIMEON

In Town

OLALLIEBERRY INN, 2476 Main Street, Cambria. The town's first "chemist" lived in this fully restored historic bed and breakfast inn with six guest rooms. A century-old redwood tree, cottage gardens, and caring proprietors welcome guests. Each room has special touches. The Olallieberry Room features blue, lavender, and white wall coverings, a ceiling canopy, and an antique chaise lounge. All rooms feature Victorian-era or companion-style furnishings, linens, and wall coverings oozing with warmth and romance. Sunken tubs or antique ball-and-club tubs and showers. There is a creekside setting, with town just a half-block away. Full breakfast and afternoon hors d'oeuvres with wine and sparkling water are included. 805/927-3222. MC, V. For two, most rooms from $85.00 to $115.00.

Along Moonstone Beach Road

FOG CATCHER INN, 6400 Moonstone Beach Drive, Cambria. This new inn is across the road from Moonstone Beach. The thatched roof and gardens are complemented by floral linens in the rooms, for an English-botanical ambiance. Pine walls, vaulted ceilings, rattan chairs, and special touches such as carved ivy lamps add to this inn's charm. Fireplaces in each room. Some rooms have sweeping shore views. Locally crafted garden benches invite you to relax in ocean-view gardens. Full breakfast included with room. Mini-microwaves, VCRs, and honor bars. 800/445-6868, 805/927-1400. AX, MC, V; others also accepted. For two, from $80.00 to $135.00.

SAN SIMEON PINES (five miles south of San Simeon, near Cambria, at Moonstone Beach). Set in the pines and cypress, with an easy stroll to Moonstone Beach, this is a casual resort for families or adults. Large rooms with high sloping ceilings, some with fireplaces. Mementos of the area's past accent the lobby and tree-shaded lawns—brands from Hearst Ranch, whale bones set along a pathway, an old quicksilver-mining cart, and a climb-aboard tractor. Clubs are loaned for the practice par-three golf course; solar-heated pool, complimentary coffee. Although some rooms are by the freeway, they are virtually soundproof and are landscaped for privacy. 805/927-4648. AX, MC, V. For two, most rooms from $70.00 to $90.00.

In the Pines

CAMBRIA PINES LODGE, 2905 Burton Drive, Cambria. The grand redwood Warren Leopold–designed and hand-carved doors offer a fitting welcome to the main lobby of the rebuilt historic Cambria Pines Lodge. The rustic lodge burned in 1991. Reconstruction in light-pine wood has stayed faithful to the historic architecture and ambiance. There is a lively lounge, and indoor or deck dining. Karaoke has replaced the famed avocado skin musician of the 1930s. When we stayed here fifteen years ago peacocks pecked on the dining room doors. This time I didn't see any, but the front desk said they were still about. A hundred twenty rooms range from rustic cabins to comfortable suites with pine-wooden views. Conference facilities. Indoor pool, spa, volleyball. Fireplaces, refrigerators, and microwaves in some rooms. 805/927-4200, 800/445-6868. MC, V; others also accepted. Suites available. For two, from $60.00 to $100.00.

CAMPING

To really feel the beat of Big Sur's heart, you might choose to camp in the fresh air at wooded canyons or on oceanside cliffs. Advance reservations are advised at the very popular Pfeiffer Big Sur State Park. All national forest campgrounds and Andrew Molera State Park are available on a first-come-first-served basis. Summer weekends are popular camping times; try to get to your destination early in the day on Friday to get a campsite. Tent camping is advised, as weather is unpredictable and many animals and small critters visit during the night.

CAMPING ON THE NORTHERN BIG SUR COAST

ANDREW MOLERA STATE PARK (twenty miles south of Carmel). Twenty walk-in camp sites on an open field, often windy. An easy hike to the ocean. First come, first served. 800/950-PARK. $5.00 each night.

BOTTCHER'S GAP NATIONAL FOREST CAMPGROUND (at the top of Palo Colorado Road). Oak and madrone campground with views of Pico Blanco and Ventana Double-cone Mountains. 408/385-5435, 800/283-2267. No drinking water. $5.00 to $15.00 each night.

PFEIFFER BIG SUR STATE PARK (near the Big Sur River, twenty-five miles south of Carmel). Two-hundred eighteen sites, many under the redwoods, some along the banks of the Big Sur River. Campgrounds are spaced for some privacy. Trailheads for many hiking trails begin here. Warm showers, convenience market. Mistix reservations, 800/444-7275. AX, MC, V. $16.00 each night.

VENTANA CAMPGROUND (the turnoff from Highway 1 is near Ventana Resort). Sixty-two secluded privately owned campsites under the redwoods next to Post Creek, which trickles slowly in the summer. Warm showers. Trails lead to Ventana Restaurant for the wilderness gourmand and to some of the best views in Big Sur. RVs are not recommended. 408/667-2688. $20.00 each night.

Four other Big Sur Valley private resorts offer cabins and campgrounds: Big Sur Campground and Cabins, 408/667-2322. Fernwood Resort, 408/667-2422. Ripplewood Resort, 408/667-2242. Riverside Campgrounds and Cabins, 408/667-2414.

CAMPING ON THE SOUTHERN BIG SUR COAST

KIRK CREEK NATIONAL FOREST CAMPGROUND (twenty-eight miles south of Pfeiffer Big Sur State Park, just north of Nacimiento-Fergusson Road). Thirty-three sites in an incredible ocean ridge setting. Painters are here with their easels, writers have their journals on their knees, naturalists scan the waters with binoculars. Campers here are radiant; they probably have the best camping views on the West Coast. 408/385-5435. $10.00 each night.

PLASKETT CREEK NATIONAL FOREST CAMPGROUND (thirty-six miles south of Pfeiffer Big Sur). Forty-five campsites, close together in an open field and among trees. Sand Dollar Beach and picnic area is a half-mile away. 408/385-5433. $10.00 each night.

RESTAURANTS

CARMEL HIGHLANDS

HIGHLANDS INN, THE CALIFORNIA MARKET (five miles south of Carmel). Of the two well-favored dining locations for visitors and locals here, this is the more casual. Sweeping ocean views, from indoor or deck seating. Salads, sandwiches, fresh fish, and California cuisine. Breakfast, lunch, and dinner. 408/624-3801. Entrees, mostly under $15.00.

HIGHLANDS INN, THE PACIFIC'S EDGE RESTAURANT. This is the home of the Masters of Food and Wine. It also has stunning architecture and walls of glass. The waves crash seemingly beneath your window table. California and other versions of American cuisine are featured. Braised Monterey salmon and filet of beef atop black pepper ravioli with Roquefort cheese are among entrees that inspired locals to vote this the best restaurant to which to take someone you would like to impress. Grande Spectator Wine Award for an outstanding wine selection. Jackets suggested for men. 408/624-0472. Entrees, mostly under $30.00. Prix fixe menu, $40.00.

NORTHERN BIG SUR COAST

BIG SUR RIVER INN (two miles north of Pfeiffer Big Sur State Park). This casual roadside lodge with redwood beams and a stone fireplace has a creekside deck; after lunch you can relax on outdoor rockers or cool your toes in the creek while sitting on rustic wooden river chairs. The local Abalone Stompers liven up the deck with music on the weekends. Delightful lunches feature the "River Inn Burger," salads, sandwiches, pasta, and fresh fish. Dinners offer grill, seafood, and pasta selections. Friendly service. 408/625-5255. AX, MC, V. Dinner entrees, mostly under $15.00.

DEETJEN'S BIG SUR INN RESTAURANT at Deetjen's Big Sur Inn, just off Highway 1 approximately four miles south of the entrance to Pfeiffer Big Sur State Park). There is a warm homestead feeling here, with redwood walls, fireplaces, candlelight, and classical music. Rack of lamb with herbal crust, roasted duck, and fresh pasta and coastal fish are specials nightly. Beer and wine are served; the wine list features wines from Monterey County. Hearty breakfast menu. Try blueberry pancakes for your day on the road. Dinner reservations advised; sittings every fifteen minutes. Breakfast, lunch, dinner. 408/667-2378. No cards. Dinner entrees, mostly under $20.00.

NEPENTHE (three miles south of Pfeiffer Big Sur State Park on Highway 1). Open redwood beams blend with the cliffside environs of trees and ocean. Nepenthe is derived from a Greek word meaning "no sorrow." For many it is a tradition to stop at Nepenthe, a special place on the coast. Steve has been serving us the famous ambrosiaburger here for over fifteen years. Also at Nepenthe, the Amphora Cafe for breakfast, lunch, or espresso offers wonderful views.

Behind the cafe, the Nepenthe gallery features crafts from throughout the world. Lunch, dinner, full bar. 408/667-2345. AX, MC, V. Dinner entrees, mostly under $20.00.

SIERRA MAR (at the Post Ranch Inn, west of Highway 1, approximately thirty miles south of Monterey, across the highway from the Ventana Inn entrance). Located on a magnificent ridge with endless miles of ocean views, constructed with expansive use of glass, slate, and exotic woods, and devoting attention to the smallest detail, this restaurant sets otherworldly standards. Four-course prix fixe menus offer the freshest vegetables and seafood and the highest quality meats, all prepared to impeccable standards. Each course is served on its own style of plate, ranging from hand-blown glass to hand-thrown terra cotta. Menu items are available a la carte. Lunches include salads, sandwiches, and main courses that are consistent with Big Sur–area prices. Reservations are required for lunch and dinner. Fine French and California wines. 408/986-7080. AX, MC, V. Prix fixe menu, $50.00.

VENTANA INN RESTAURANT (at Ventana Inn, inland from Highway 1, a little over two miles south of Pfeiffer Big Sur State Park). Rough cedar beams, eye-level ocean views, wood tiles, bistro chairs, and a large outdoor hearth fireplace combine to provide a relaxing atmosphere. Executive chef Kurt Grasling defines California cuisine. Grilled salmon with artichokes and pasta with rock shrimp and basil may be on the menu, which varies to feature the freshest of ingredients. Lunch and dinner. Reservations advised. 408/667-2331. AX, MC, V. Entrees, mostly under $25.00. Prix fixe menu, $45.00.

SOUTHERN BIG SUR COAST

LUCIA LODGE twenty-four miles south of Pfeiffer Big Sur State Park). Here enjoy the best outdoor oceanview seating on the entire coast. Your cliffside seat overhangs the ocean and, in a suggestion of a tropical Big Sur, a small grove of banana trees. Views span a series of jade coves south to Cape San Martin. Fresh fish selections, and a heaping fish and chips basket. Meat and pasta also served. Lunch only. 408/667-2391. MC, V. Lunch entrees, mostly under $15.00.

PACIFIC VALLEY CAFE (thirty-two miles south of Pfeiffer Big Sur State Park). In a meadow setting, deck and outdoor seating across the road from the ocean shore. Indoor seating in a rustic cafe. Burgers, pizza, and fresh fish, and scrumptious pies made with organic flours. Breakfast, lunch, and dinner. 408/927-8655. AX, MC, V. Entrees, mostly under $10.00.

CAMBRIA AND SAN SIMEON

BRAMBLES DINNER HOUSE, 4005 Burton Drive, Cambria. Built in 1874 as a family home, this quaint cottage offers gracious American dining. Dark wood accents, candlelight, red-cloth-draped tables, and deep-hued carpeting create the ambiance for imbibing blackstrap molasses bread, baby-back pork ribs, seafood brochette, and oakwood broiled steaks. Victorian ornaments decorate trees in the restaurant during the Christmas season. Dinner. 805/927-4716. AX, MC, V. Entrees, mostly under $15.00.

IAN'S, 2150 Center Street, Cambria. Soft lighting and romantic booth and alcove seating underscore a relaxed elegance. The owner and chef, Ian McPhee, is a master at combining seemingly discordant tastes and decor into sensational environs. The menu changes often, as Ian likes creating new choices. The California cuisine—fresh local vegetables daily—comes in ample portions. Try the chocolate cake with lime and caramel sauce for dessert. When Ian is on break he mingles with guests on the steps of the renovated and enlarged Victorian restaurant. Sunday brunch, weekend lunches, nightly dinners. 805/927-8649. AX, MC, V. Entrees, mostly under $15.00.

ROBIN'S, 4095 Burton Drive, Cambria. Batiks, oak furnishings, and a stone-hearth fireplace enliven this wood-beamed home. A columbine and bougainvillea trellis surrounds the outdoor patio. Eclectic international selections include tandori prawns, hot Sri Lanka chicken curry, pasta, and quesadillas. Take-out orders for incredible picnics. Lunch and dinner. 805/927-5007. MC, V. Entrees, mostly under $10.00.

DIRECTIONS

◆

Travel to Highway 1. From the Monterey Bay area drive south on 1 passing the exits for Pacific Grove and Carmel. Big Sur country begins just south of Carmel.

INTRODUCTION TO THE HIGHWAY 1 SOUTH COAST ROUTE, WITH HISTORICAL HIGHLIGHTS

Highway 1 snakes along ninety miles of legendary raw and rugged coast from Carmel to the Carpoforo Creek, just north of San Simeon. The road cuts across the young Santa Lucia Mountains, which rise from relentless waves to heights of five thousand feet and are still growing. Miles of mountain and sea vistas remain virtually wild and free. Early Spanish explorers called parts of these lands "Ventana," meaning window. Anthropologists and geologists are not sure whether this name refers to an eroded natural ocean bridge or the canyons that open with windowlike views. Many people feel the window is of a deeper sort, an opening of the spirit, emotions, and creativity.

The spirit frees itself quickly at Point Lobos, just three miles south of Carmel. Countless artists, photographers, and writers have walked its paths. Landscape artist Francis McComas called Point Lobos "The greatest meeting of land and water in the world." Its ragged, isolated coves and churning waters are said to have inspired Robert Louis Stevenson to write *Treasure Island*. Edward Weston and Ansel Adams photographed the area and Robinson Jeffers drew from its power for his epic poems. Protected now for its rare and indigenous gnarled cypress trees, used formerly for shore whaling and abalone fisheries, and inhabited continually by a variety of marine and land animals, this 404-acre reserve features otherworldly rock formations and both meadow and forest walks, as well as wave-sculpted coves where the ocean seems to boil and "Los Lobos" (the sea lions, called sea wolves by Spanish explorers) roar into the wind. In the early 1900s Point Lobos was a favorite picnic spot for many locals. In 1933 it was saved from being divided into hundreds of parcels, to become a state reserve. Point Lobos lovers rejoiced in 1993 when the Big Sur Land Trust announced it had secured an extra 1,700 acres, formerly slated for a resort, to be added to the reserve.

Rock mortars of previous civilizations can be found at the end of the Point Lobos Moss Cove trail. Rumsen tribelets and earlier the Esselen gathered and hunted food in this area. The Esselen inhabited the lands between the Big Sur River, Lopez Point, and the upper portions of the Arroyo Seco and Carmel rivers. South of the Esselen, the Salinans lived in the coastal areas around what is now Lucia. The largest group of the first tribes, the Chumashan, lived from south of the Salinan to what is now San Luis Obispo. Descendants of the Monterey and northern Big Sur coastal tribes often refer to themselves as Ohlone. According to Ohlone legends, Pico Blanco, a high marble peak often visible from the road and on inland hikes, is the embryo of all civilization. It was here, according to the stories, that Coyote brought civilization to people.

Most locals refer to the lands five miles south of Point Lobos as the northern tip of Big Sur. Carmel Highlands lies between the two meccas of wilderness. Originally developed by Charles Devendorf and Frank Powers of the Carmel Land Development Company, the Highlands features a collage of homes that blend with land and sea.

When Cabrillo sailed up the coast in 1542 he noted, "There are mountains which seem to reach the heavens and the sea beats on them." As they stood on mountain vantage points in Monterey the early Spanish settlers in the area described the mountainous region to the south as "El Pais Grande del Sur," the great land to the south, now translated as Big Sur. Henry Miller described the area in the book *Big Sur and the Oranges of Hieronymus Bosch*: "At Dawn, 'Big Sur's' majesty is almost painful to behold. That same prehistoric look, the look of always. Nature smiling at herself in the mirror of eternity. . . ."

For some Monterey County stalwarts, Big Sur ends at the Monterey and San Louis Obispo county line. The contours of the Santa Lucia Mountains suggest that the natural boundary of Big Sur lies farther south, where sheer mountain cliffs meet the valley owned by the Hearst Corporation at the Carpoforo Creek. Hairpin curves, jagged cliffs dropping off to boiling surf and the brilliant blue water beyond, redwood forests, lush creeksides settings, and thirty bridges punctuate the eighty-some miles from the northern to southern boundaries. Capes, streams, and beaches bear the names of early settlers: Mount Manuel, Pfeiffer Ridge, Post Summit, Cooper Point, Dani Ridge, Partington Cove, and others. Some of their descendants still live in Big Sur. The main community along the route also bears the name "Big Sur." For this history and the tours that follow, "Big Sur" refers to the eighty-mile stretch of land along the coast.

About twelve hundred people live along this stretch. More than five hundred live in the six-mile stretch known as the Big Sur Valley, where numerous resorts and businesses and Pfeiffer Big Sur State Park line the highway. People here are bound by a respect for their environment. Many are here to lead a remote and private life. Long dirt driveways lead to unique homes, many hand built by the owners. For early settlers, the Big Sur experience was surely fearful. They were visited by grizzly bears, forest fires, and nature's storms, and the nearest stores were at least a two-day pack trip away. The oldest surviving structure along the Big Sur coast was built in 1861 on the 8,949-acre Rancho El Sur, owned and cattle ranched by Capt. John Roger Cooper. You can still peek into the cabin at Andrew Molera State Park. After the secularization of the missions the Mexican government formed two land grants in "El Sur Grande." Cooper had acquired Rancho El Sur from his nephew, Juan Bautista Alvarado, the then provisional governor of California. When Cooper died the land grant was divided among his five children. His granddaughter Frances Molera sold the land at a reduced price to the Nature Conservancy in 1968 with the condition that it remain undeveloped and be named for her brother Andrew, who had died in 1931.

More than any other settler's name, Pfeiffer (pronounced by the family as "pie-fur") is most synonymous with Big Sur. In 1869, during the years when the government offered 160 acres of government land free to families who would homestead parcels for five years, Michael and Barbara Pfeiffer along with four children and a small stock of horses and cattle set sail from San Francisco on the old sidewheeler *Sierra Nevada* for a two-day journey to Monterey. The trek overland to the unknown southern lands was even longer. They built their first cabin on the beach south of the Big Sur River. Later John Pfeiffer, one of their sons, homesteaded what is now Pfeiffer Big Sur State Park.

From the 1880s until the early 1900s Big Sur was an industrial center of the county, and boom settlements brought greater populations to the area than in present days. Throughout the area tanbark oak trees were lumbered for tannic acid, used in tanning, inks, and astringents; mules pulled tons of bark along narrow mountain paths on wheeled carts named "go devils" to boat landings along the coast. Limestone was smelted in giant redwood-fed lime kilns in Bixby Canyon and Limekiln Canyon; an aerial tram transported the lime from the settlement at Bixby Canyon to the company boat waiting at Bixby Landing. Thousands of redwood trees were lumbered or cut to fire the kilns. On the Big Sur River, the Ventana Power Company generated electricity.

As the redwoods were cut to bare numbers the lumber and lime industries faltered. The population dropped, and the tourist industry took on new importance for those who stayed on. The John Pfeiffer home was opened to lodgers at $3.00 a night.

Dr. John Roberts, founder of Seaside, a physician who rode the twisted coastal trails for days at a time to care for patients, proposed that Highway 1 be built as a scenic highway. Funds became available for highways that were necessary for the nation's defense, and the word "scenic" was dropped; in 1919 the state legislature appropriated $15 million for the construction of this road for the defense. Chinese laborers and convict labor provided much of the labor to build it. Highway 1 was finally opened in 1937, though traffic was limited—during World War II it was outright restricted, by gas rationing and periodic closing of the road by the military.

After the war, artists, photographers, and writers settled the area. Headlines such as "Sex and Anarchy in Big Sur," a Harper's expose about Partington Ridge resident Henry Miller, author of *Tropic of Cancer*, brought the area new attention. Later the Esalen Institute opened, a center for personal growth. Crowds began to seek out Big Sur for its beauty.

That the beauty has remained, mostly undeveloped and preserved for future generations, is to the credit of people like John Pfeiffer, who donated a large portion of his land for Pfeiffer Big Sur State Park, and the Lathrop Browns, who donated landed for Julia Pfeiffer Burns State Park. Great credit is due Margaret Owings, who founded the Friends of the Sea Otter and together with her late husband, Nathaniel, and Nick Roosevelt led communities to write master plans that preserve the coast from lines of houses, hotels, and golf courses. "It was natural, I never looked for anything, it just fell into my lap. Thirty years ago on late evenings a mountain lion howled in the canyon behind our house and we could follow its tracks in the morning. Then one day a neighbor shot it for a bounty. I just couldn't let that animal die in vain." Owings was instrumental in obtaining legislation to end the bounty payments. If you are a Californian who voted for Proposition 70 in 1988 and 117 in 1990, you can thank yourself for preserving much of this land for wildlife habitat and viewshed protection. With additional funds, the nonprofit Big Sur Land Trust continues to add acreage to the ten thousand acres it has already shielded from development.

TOURS

THE POINT LOBOS TOUR

The Point Lobos State Reserve entrance is 2.2 miles south of the Highway 1 and Rio Road intersection and 1.2 miles north of the Highlands Inn entrance. The park opens at 7:30 a.m. and closes at 8:00 p.m. during the summer; earlier in winter. All walking and picnicking must be done in designated areas.

On any day, only 110 cars are allowed in the park. The park fills to its limit of cars early on weekends. You can park along Highway 1 and walk in if the park is full. Cars are charged a state park day use fee; walkers and bikers are admitted free. Monterey transit bus 22 is a good alternative to cars. Volunteer-docent tours are very informative, presenting introductions to the history, geology, and flora and fauna of the park, though they are not operated on a given schedule. (Call before you arrive in the park for the days, times, and focus of tours.)

All fishing and collecting of marine life or natural objects is prohibited. Scuba diving at Whalers Cove is often spectacular. You must reserve in advance, as only a limited number of dive teams are allowed each day.

The west side of Highway 1 covers 525 acres above ground and 712 underwater acres. The newest addition to Point Lobos, encompassing 1,700 acres, is on the east side of Highway 1. (At the time of this writing it had not yet been opened to the public.)

The twisted formations, giant boulders, eroded hollows, and strange conglomerates here have been the thrill of many a photographer and the awakening of many a latent geologist. Some treasures are hidden except to the most trained eyes. On the tour that Todd Bliss of Bio-Tours (408/375-5089) gives of the area he points out one of the rare phenomena of Point Lobos known as the K-T line. This line contains traces of iridium brought by the theorized impact of a giant meteor, which is to have collided with the earth 65,000 years ago and is credited with the changing of conditions on land that caused the abrupt disappearance of the dinosaurs.

For your own discoveries, get a map of the reserve at the entrance or the Information Station at the Sea Lion Point parking lot. Plan to spend two to three hours if you are going to just walk the trails. Also at the Sea Lion Point Information Stand docents are available to answer questions and sell you a book or poster.

Point Lobos State Reserve has about ten different trails that are short and relatively flat. (Still, it is a good idea to wear sturdy shoes.) This tour covers two of the main trails.

THE BIRD ISLAND TRAIL. This trail leads to China and Gibson beaches, the only two beaches in the reserve where swimming is allowed. The water is very cold, but you may enjoy a refreshing dip. This .7-mile trail offers a variety of animal life and scenery with good views of Bird Island. The trail takes about twenty minutes to walk.

Walking from the entrance, just past the Ranger Station, follow the South Plateau trail left 1 kilometer to the Bird Island trail. If you drive in, follow the main road around the Information Station at Sea Lion Rock and turn south past Weston Beach and then Hidden Beach to dead end at the Bird Island trail. You will find parking spaces, a picnic area, and restrooms

The Bird Island trail first leads up a set of stairs to a knoll, a favorite from which to spot migrating whales. You can also spot the large, rounded Bird Island from this point. The trail enters the edge of a Monterey pine forest. These pine trees are host to several species of birds, such as the pigmy nuthatch (a small bird with a blue-gray and white throat). It chips out nesting cavities thirty or more feet high in the trees. Here you may also encounter the ground squirrels that eat the seeds, plants, and insects abundant in this forest. Next the trail crosses the hillside facing the sheltered emerald green baylet of China Cove. A long, steep set of stairs descends to the white sands of China Beach. If the tide is out you can look into the small cave at the base of the cliff. In the water you can see floating brown kelp. Both giant kelp and bull kelp are found here. Egrets can often be seen in this sheltered cove, walking on the kelp blades.

Back up the steps, continue on the path to a second spur. Here a second set of stairs leads down to Gibson Beach. Large boulders strewn about on the beach look like giants' marbles.

From above Gibson Beach the trail heads west to an ending loop. The larger of the two rocks you see is Bird Island, a refuge for Brandt's cormorants, western gulls, and pigeon guillemots. Although brown pelicans no longer nest here, they can still be found roosting in the summer and fall.

CYPRESS GROVE TRAIL. This .8-mile trail is one of the most popular in the park. It passes through the Allen Memorial Grove of Monterey cypresses and comes out along the clifftop to provide views of the ocean. The trail begins at the Cypress Cove parking area. This is a loop trail that takes about forty-five minutes to walk.

The path splits a short distance from the Information Station. During spring the native wild lilac, ceanothus, blossoms pink and blue along the first stretch to ocean vistas. You will probably hear the barking of sea lions before you see them. The Spaniards called his area "Punto de los Lobos Marinos": Point of the Sea Lions (literally of the sea "wolves"). One short side trail leads to North Point and a good view of Cypress Cove. Another features spectacular vistas of the ocean and the waves crashing on the ragged outcroppings. From here you can look across Carmel Bay and see the brilliant white sands of Carmel Beach.

After leaving the vista point the trail heads through a Monterey Cypress Grove named in honor of A. M. Allen, who in the early 1900s bought the land to keep it from being subdivided by developers into "Point Lobos City." Allen set up a toll gate in later years when autos and picnickers flocked to the area. Allen's family donated the cypress grove to the state when Point Lobos became a reserve in 1933. This is one of two last remaining indigenous Monterey cypress groves anywhere. The oldest trees here are probably two hundred years old. As you look coastward to the Pinnacle, the northernmost point in the reserve, you will see the gnarled, twisted trunks of trees sculpted by battering winds. To survive in the strong winds, the trees adapt with a response called "buttressing": a thin part of the trunk faces the wind while the trunk grows thicker on the opposite side to brace the tree.

Scientists theorize that the cypress formerly grew in huge forests along the coast. The conifer is easily grown from seed and since discovering the native groves here and across Carmel Bay in Pebble Beach, people have planted cypress trees extensively. The tree is so adaptable and easily reproduced, it is a puzzle why this tree's natural range is limited to the two tiny groves.

The trail turns past South Point, with a descent back to the trailhead. Close by you can join the sea lion trail for good wildlife viewing.

THE BIG SUR TOUR

It is best to allow a full day for the Big Sur drive if you are planning to complete the entire route. Highway 1 through Big Sur is slow, twisting, and scenic. Allow time to stretch your legs. I strongly suggest this as a one-way trip for the day with an overnight along the way or at a southern destination. The largest community along this section of the coast is in Big Sur. A six-mile-long stretch along the Big Sur River is the home for approximately five hundred people. The community of Big Sur consists of a collection rustic homes as well as restaurants, resorts, general stores, and specialty shops. It is well known as a rural retreat and artists' colony.

There are no other towns between Carmel and Cambria, so you should plan to take most of your supplies with you. There are small rural communities consisting of a gas station, deli, artist galleries, and small shops, so you can pick up small items if needed. It is always a good idea to take water and wear good walking shoes.

After leaving Point Lobos you drive through Carmel Highlands, an area of architecturally stunning homes perched on rocky cliffs. Homes here compliment the rugged coast and sometimes appear much smaller than their actual size. For the turnoff to Highlands Inn (408/624-3801), watch the left side of the road.

Just past Carmel Highlands, the steep canyon walls of Malpaso Creek mark the beginning of Big Sur country. At Malpaso, meaning "bad crossing" in Spanish, let your mind wander back to the times when no bridges crossed the steep ravines, and imagine the hardships of early travelers.

For the purpose of this tour I have included mileage markers. "S" marks the numbers of miles south from the Carmel River Bridge and "N" marks the number of miles north from the turnoff to Hearst Castle.

Garrapata State Park's northern boundary is 2.0 miles south of Carmel Highlands Drive. Rugged coastline and sweeping ocean views especially from Rocky Ridge trail make this a representational slice of the Big Sur Coast. As the park has been open to the public only since 1983, it is still relatively untraveled. Within it along Highway 1 are sixteen numbered (unless signs are vandalized) state highway turnouts that lead to a variety of scenic overlooks. The only safe waterfront access is at the highly visible Garrapata Beach at the southern border of the 3,067-acre park. For day use only, the park has as facilities only outhouses, between turnouts 13 and 14 and between 15 and 16. Turnout 10's trail leads to a good example of the war of land and sea; waves are wresting a large shoulder of granite from the shore.

Seventy-yard-long turnout 13 marks the beginning of the oceanside Whale Peak trail system, Rocky Ridge trail, and the Soberanes Canyon trail. Clusters of cypresses that were probably planted as windbreaks by the Soberanes family, early settlers of the area, now hide an outhouse. These cypress also mark the rocky promontory of Soberanes Point. Around the back side of a small headlands, a bench offers a great spot to sit and watch the ocean at this good whale sighting area.

To hike to a creek setting and memorable views, cross Highway 1 from turnout 13 to reach the beginning of the Soberanes Canyon trail and the Rocky Ridge trail. "Garrapata" means wood tick in Spanish, so tuck in your pant legs and stay on trails in this area. A main trail begins behind an old barn. After crossing Soberanes Creek you will come to the sign for the beginning of Soberanes Creek trail. Rocky Ridge trail and Soberanes Creek trail form a loop back to your starting point. I recommend ascending the first trail that veers right, Soberanes Creek trail, which is a little steep for a while as it winds through a bushy ridge, then enters a small redwood forest. You will need to cross the creek a few times before you climb to a grassy path. Sometimes in the very early spring multitudes of ladybugs hatch here. You will be treated to panoramic ocean views as you descend a path dotted with golden yarrow, bush lupine, and sage.

Rocky Creek Bridge

11 S, 80 N. Rocky Point Restaurant (408/624-2933), "excellent food on the edge of forever," serves lunch and dinner on a point rumored to have been used by pirates and later bootleggers. Sweeping views of the unfolding coastline, including Rocky Creek Bridge, are some of the best on the coast. The picturesque bridge span is often mistaken for the famous Bixby Bridge. Downhill from the restaurant, waves have carved a natural arch out of a cliff on the shoreline.

11.1 S, 79.9 N. Palo Colorado Canyon Road, carved along the Palo Colorado fault, winds four miles as a very narrow one-and-a-half-lane twisty road before widening and eventually ending at Bottcher's Gap National Forest Campground. Drive slow for the curves and extra slow to watch for children and animals along the way. Lower Palo Colorado Canyon Road is darkly shaded by tall, closely set redwoods, and dotted with a surprising number of homes and cabins. "Palo Colorado" roughly translates from Spanish as "tall redwood."

At Bottcher's Canyon a number of trails lead to the Ventana Wilderness. There are stories but no evidence or pictures that a land bridge once spanned Bottcher's gap, forming a natural window: the "ventana" of the wilderness. At

3,709 feet Pico Blanco, meaning "white peak," towers over the southern section of the gap. The tons of white-gray marble that form the peak are the largest chunk of the oldest metamorphic rock in the parks. Geologists theorize the peak was formed millions of years ago when river sediments in Mexico or even farther south were pressed, heated, and folded by an underriding of the earth's crust. Pico Blanco rode north by movement of the San Andreas fault.

13.4 S, 77.6 N. Along your drive and various sojourns you have probably been catching great views of the stunning 260-foot-span Bixby Bridge. You can travel the Old Coast Road by turning left just before you cross the bridge from the north; from the south take an immediate right after crossing the bridge. Before the bridge was opened in 1932, Old Coast Road was the only route available for traversing the coast. For veteran Big Sur travelers who want a change of pace or photographers in search of sweeping coastal views this ten-mile-long, graded dirt road is a pleasant, but very curvy, backroad route. It requires up to an hour to travel. If you want to hike here look for the trailhead along the way; you can walk by the Little Sur River, bounded by redwoods, ferns, and in spring, shade-loving flowers. Stay on the trail. The "no trespassing" signs here are strictly enforced. Backpackers and long-day hikers, note this trail connects with the Pico Blanco camp trail. The Old Coast Road winds along hillsides, into dark stands of redwoods, along the river, and up through more redwood groves to top-of-the-world views. Hawks and eagles may be soaring in the skies around you. The road ends at the Highway 1 entrance to Andrew Molera State Park.

14 S, 77 N. Bixby Bridge, one of the world's highest single-span concrete bridges, stretches 700 feet, rises over 260 feet high, and features a 320-foot arch over the V-shaped Bixby Creek Canyon. The bridge took over a year to build. Its continued existence symbolizes the successful fight by Big Sur residents to stop the widening of Highway 1 into a four-lane freeway. Before you leave try to imagine the tram here in the early part of the century, carrying limestone from the lime kilns up in the canyons to ships waiting at Bixby Landing in the cove below.

14.3 S, 76.7 N. Just be happy you aren't running the Big Sur Marathon as you climb this steep grade to Hurricane Point, probably the most wind-blown point on the highway. From the turnout, an eight-hundred-foot overhang, you can view Point Sur Rock to the south and the symmetrical beauty of the Bixby Bridge to the north. If you look down you will see an ancient marine terrace, littered with the rusted hulls of several cars that didn't make it. Take care.

16.6 S, 74.4 N. The Little Sur River flows through a horseshoe valley carving new channels at whim as, during wet winters and springs, it flows to the ocean. In the dry season the river collects in a lagoon behind a sand bar built by wind. Pico Blanco is easily spotted from the turnoff here. The beach is on private land. Even from your lookout you can see that the waves are too treacherous for swimming or even wading here, as along most of the coast.

18.7 S, 72.3 N. Atop the 370-foot-tall block of lava that resembles a large pillow, facing cold mists and sweeping winds, is the Big Sur Lightstation, the only lightstation on the West Coast with all its nineteenth-century buildings intact. A hundred feet below the cluster of keepers' buildings a working lighthouse hugs the side of the mound. The lightstation as a whole is connected to the shore by a tombolo (sand bar). Early Big Sur residents sometimes benefitted from the cargos of wrecked ships, such as the linens and wagons on the *Ventura,* which wrecked in 1875.

The first light was a large multiwick kerosene lamp surrounded by an approximately six-thousand-pound Fresnel lens that projected a beam visible for fourteen nautical miles. The lighthouse was controlled automatically after 1972. Today the light and radio beacon are computer-directed and project a beam for twenty-four nautical miles. The original lens can be seen at the Monterey Maritime Museum.

The collection of intact buildings and architectural features and workmanship of the unique rough-cut sandstone, including rock keystones and arched doorways, prompted the reclassification of the lighthouse as Point Sur State Historic Park. Volunteer-led guided tours include the lighthouse, the keeper's houses, the blacksmith shop, and the barn, where livestock was kept for food and transportation. Cormorants and seagulls fly eye to eye with tour groups alongside a cliffside walk to the lighthouse. On sunny days the view is spectacular. On foggy days rocks offshore are swallowed from view. The Central Coast Lighthouse Keepers, a group of California State Park volunteers, is presently working to preserve the lightstation for future generations.

Tours are currently offered every Saturday at 10 a.m. and 2 p.m. and Sunday at 10 a.m., weather permitting. Visitors who wish to go on tours should arrive one-half hour before the scheduled times. Meet along the west side of Highway 1 at the locked gate, a quarter mile north of the Point Sur Naval facility. Depending on the number of volunteer guides available, tour size may be limited. Tours last two-and-a-half to three hours and include a walk of approximately one-half mile up an access road with a 360-foot rise in elevation. There are two flights of stairs; the longest has sixty-five steps. Admission is $5.00 per adult, $3.00 for ages thirteen to seventeen, and $2.00 for ages five to twelve. The weather is unpredictable. Wear comfortable walking shoes, bring coats, and dress in layers, even if Highway 1 is sunny. Since the tour includes steep cliffs without barriers it is not recommended for small children, and strollers are not permitted. No pets, food, or drink are allowed. Call prior to your trip. A weather and tour information recording may be reached at 408/625-4419. For more details about Point Sur State Historic Park and lighthouse tours, contact the Big Sur State Park Office: 408/667-2315.

21.5 S, 69.5 N. Andrew Molera State Park and Big Sur Trail Rides (408/625-8664) share the same entrance on the west side of the highway. We like to cook a pancake and Corralitos sausage breakfast at the riverside barbecue area in the park, then spend the rest of the day in riding or hiking and biking the numerous trails within this 7.4 square miles. The Camp trail, which merges with the Headlands trail, is the only year-round coastal access route because it doesn't cross the river. However it does not access the main beach, which is cut off by the river. The trail begins as a river bordering road to an open-field walk-in-only campground, which has a few special wooded spots. Beyond the campground you'll pass a eucalyptus grove favored by migrating monarchs from November through March. When it is cold or foggy the orange and black butterflies fold their wings to resemble dry leaves hanging from trees. The historic Cooper cabin is nestled in this grove—where the road narrows to a trail. If you want beach access continue ahead. If you take the Headlands trail spur you'll climb to where some thoughtful person has set some of the best-located benches along the coast. Look up and you may see a red-tailed hawk soaring or an American kestrel hovering. Nature planted a hedge of ceanothus around the bench, and in spring the sweet blossoms add another layer to the expansive ocean view.

Take someone you love along if you climb higher, to the tip of Molera Point, to view the little cliff-shrouded hidden beach to the north. This overlook is my pick for the most romantic place on the coast. The Big Sur River flows free to the ocean below. The golden sands, the rocky headlands, and the aquamarine waters intertwine, as the wind whispers secrets in your ear....Another love affair unfolds offshore as surfers glide with the waves. Sometimes when my feet are feeling a little weary with the mile walk to the beach, I'm humbled by a surfer running the distance, with board hefted underarm. Remember, the waves here are dangerous for those of us who aren't experienced surfers.

Bicycles are allowed only on the Camp trail, Creamery Meadow trail, and Ridge trail. To walk along Molera Beach you'll first need to cross the Big Sur River. During summer months there is a footbridge a short distance from the entrance parking lot that leads to the beach and Creamery Meadow trails. More trails are mapped in a brochure you can pick up from the ranger. Big Sur Trail Rides (800/303-8664) offers a selection of two- and three-hour rides, which lead through redwood groves, along ocean bluffs, and over beaches in the park. Luncheon and sunset rides are available.

24.5 S, 66.5 N. Bud's In A Bus Ice Cream, adjacent to the River Inn, welcomes travelers to the community of Big Sur. Ice Cream, shakes, and floats are signals that this sunny inland valley can get pleasantly warm. Parking is found alongside of Bud's, in front of the River Inn and behind the village shops. If you are here on a weekend afternoon, check whether the local Abalone Stompers are jazzing it up on the River Inn deck. The inn offers a grassy expanse to a river beach. Patrons pull their chairs into the water and dangle toes or soak hike-weary feet. This is a fun place to stretch and wander galleries and shops. The Heartbeat Gift Shop (408/667-2557) offers a selection of wood drums, other musical instruments, and jewelry. You might want to check out the resorts with private campgrounds and cabins along the next couple of highway miles: Big Sur Campgrounds and Cabins, Riverside Campground and Cabins, Ripplewood Resort, and Fernwood. Four gas stations, several delis, and a small grocery line this route. Across the street from the clean and comfortable Glen Oaks Motel, the Glen Oaks Restaurant (408/667-2623), owned by long-time residents, serves an elegant meal and special Sunday brunch. Just a half-mile south of Glen Oaks, Saint Francis of the Redwoods Catholic Church (408/624-1271) holds mass in the open air.

26 S, 65 N. When most people say they're going to Big Sur they are headed for Pfeiffer ("Pie-fur") Big Sur State Park, which offers day use and over two hundred campsites with facilities. It is located thirty minutes north of Julia Pfeiffer Burns State Park, which offers day hikes and four walk-in campsites. Favorite activities at Pfeiffer Big Sur include wading in the river and participating in the park's many interpretive programs. You can spot deer during the day. You might lose anything that is not locked and secured to the bandits of the night, those wide-eyed raccoons. The Big Sur River meanders through the park's 810 acres.

Redwoods, ferns, a babbling creek, and a small waterfall await day visitors on the half-mile mostly level Pfeiffer Falls trail. This is a gentle leg stretcher for the whole family. The best swimming holes I've heard about in the area are some boulder hops away, up the River Gorge trail. This trail is not an official, maintained trail but is one of the two most popular in the park. The gorge should never be entered alone, during rainy weather, or when a strong current exists in the river. It is ideal for hot summer days and can get quite crowded then. The trail begins at the north tip of the campground as the east-bank trail. By early summer, campers have usually built a steppingstone crossing on the river about three hundred yards up the trail. Once across you need to scoot over some large boulders to the edge of a large rock-lined pool. The water temperature is warmer than the ocean but still brisk and refreshing. On the oak grove trail you will pass a homesteader's cabin. A ring of rocks surround the graves of the children of the Innocentis, the first family to settle in Big Sur.

27.6 S, 63.4 N. Pfeiffer Beach is located at the end of Sycamore Canyon Road—from the north, the second right turn you can make south of Big Sur State Park. After the movie *The Sandpipers,* with Elizabeth Taylor and Richard Burton, the area attracted many tourists in search of idyllic life-with-beach. Pfeiffer Beach is one of the most beautiful beaches I have ever seen. Immense wind-and-wave-sculpted rocks, ocean-powered blowholes, and eroding rock arches beckon. However, the winds here can be outrageous and the sand stings even the most ardent seeker.

28.1 S, 62.9 N. The Ventana Inn and Post Ranch Inn are opposite in the side of Highway 1 they occupy, but both appeal with casual elegance in the wilderness. Even if you eat and lodge elsewhere on this trip, consider taking the daily

2 p.m. tour of the ecologically and architecturally stunning Post Ranch Inn (408/667-2800). The relationship between perception, talent, and the Big Sur locale is on display at the Gallery of Ventana. This is a showcase for artists who live or have a long history of residence on the Big Sur Coast. The strong lines of the sculptures in the gallery corner may remind you of the "Black Monarch" at Lovers Point in Pacific Grove—they are, in fact, the work of noted sculptor Gordon Newell, who created that definitive black monarch. The layered wood sculptures by the door, so alive I could almost feel them breathe, are the works of Edmund Kara—the carver of the large phoenix at Nepenthe.

28.8 S, 62.2 N. Nepenthe's corner of the world used to be owned by Orson Welles, purportedly as a planned but never materialized hideaway for Rita Hayworth, his wife of a short time. Lolly Fassett, granddaughter of Frank Powers, developer of Carmel, and her husband, William, bought the property from Welles and developed Nepenthe, a Big Sur landmark. From a Greek word meaning "no sorrow," the name refers to a mythical Egyptian drug given to induce forgetfulness. Stairs and paths lead huffing visitors to the main restaurant, to the Phoenix Shop, with crafts, jewelry, and clothing from around the world, and to the Cafe Amphora, where guests are treated to exceptional views. Designed by Rowan Maiden, a former apprentice to Frank Lloyd Wright, the building was probably the first commercial destination on the coast to assimilate the lines of sky and coast. The "Dark Angel," a stunning redwood and mosaic sculpture by Big Sur artist and forty-year resident Cyril (Bus) Brown, stands tall to transport souls above the Phoenix Shop. Although Nepenthe has expanded and mellowed through the years, it still offers visitors an artsy, airy, in-step-with-Big-Sur aura, heightened by treetop coastal views and occasional glimpses of famous visitors.

29.7 S, 61.3 N. The Henry Miller Memorial Library (408/667-2574) is just a half-mile south of Nepenthe, one of the writer's favorite haunts. For seventeen years, *Tropic of Cancer* author Miller lived and wrote south of here atop Partington Ridge. His friend Emil White started a collection of Henry Miller materials and entertained the many visitors who flocked to the coast hoping to catch a glimpse of the author with a satyr's reputation. Today visitors enter through large wooden gates and a sometimes serene, sometimes lively sculpture garden. The library is really a light and airy gallery, which features first and out-of-print editions of Miller's books, some of the artist's paintings, and memorabilia. Some of the treasures are under glass, some are available to purchase, but none are available for library loan. Drumming classes on the lawn, life drawing classes, art retrospectives, and ongoing presentations by local artists and writers sometimes share the space.

30.2 S, 60.8 N. Slow down or you will miss the inland dirt road to Deetjen's Big Sur Inn. This collection of rustic cabins and a memorable lodge, built by Norwegian carpenter Helmut Deetjen from old wharf timbers and driftwood, nestles under redwoods by Castro Creek. A nonprofit foundation operates Deetjen's, now a national historic monument. Summer rooms are often booked months in advance. Breakfasts and lunches are casual. Candlelit dinners are served on Staffordshire china to a background of classical music. Helmut used to tell guests that music, nature, and art were the only important things in life.

33 S, 58 N. After traversing some sheer cliffs visible from the Castro Canyon Bridge and Grimes Point turnoff you'll see the Coast Gallery, tucked into the inland side of Lafler Canyon. The gardens and driveway of this gallery were washed away in a slide, but the gallery remains stalwart at the edge. The canyon is named for a former editor and friend of Jack London's. Legend has it that Lafler slept in the hollowed-out trunk of a redwood tree before moving to a ridge-hugging stone house. The legend makes the Coast Gallery, housed in two round antique redwood water tanks, all the more fitting. Handmade candles have been dipped at a studio here since 1958. A summer artists-in-action program sometimes provides the opportunity to talk with the local artists and craftspeople who display their work at the gallery.

36.1 N, 54.9 S. To hear ocean waves crack like no other place on the coast, walk through a hundred-foot tunnel, view a grove of stunted redwoods that defy scientific knowledge, and enjoy reflective waters by sparkling deep blue surf, take a hike through Partington Canyon and Cove, which mark the north-ernmost boundaries of Julia Pfeiffer Burns State Park. The trail begins at an iron gate on the west end of Partington Creek Bridge, then descends rather steeply for a quarter of a mile to Partington Creek. Upstream, the trail leads to an out-house. Downstream the route continues a short way to a junction. Straight ahead the trail leads though redwoods to a tiny beach. Supposedly, redwoods can't live this close to the ocean because of intolerance to salt air. Well, you're here and so are they! Retrace your steps to the junction and turn right, cross a footbridge, then picture sleds of tanbark oak as they are pulled through the tunnel. John Partington built the tunnel for his tanoak cutting and shipping operation at Partington Landing. As you walk through the six-foot-wide, eight-foot-high tunnel to the beach, the waves crash against cliffs pitted with caverns. You can still see the rusted remains of the landing. Experienced scuba divers explore the kelp beds here. Clearance is given through Pfeiffer Big Sur State Park.

38 S, 53 N. A short, level walk to McWay Falls punctuates the beauty at this main entrance to Julia Pfeiffer Burns State Park. The quarter-mile trail takes about twenty minutes. From the parking lot descend the first set of stairs to your left to see the tiny McWay Creek ripple over rocks shaded by redwoods. Then, accompanied by waters rushing ever faster, turn right and walk along a path decorated by orange sticky monkeyflower, spring-blossoming pink ceanothus, and in the autumn, the beautiful scarlet of poison oak (far from your reach if you stay on the path). The path leads through a tunnel under the coast highway

to an overlook where you can watch the creek plummet fifty feet to foamy ocean waters, in high tide, or to a sandy beach, in low. Across from the falls, isolated cypress trees pull nutrients from a rock that is being torn from the main headland by constant pounding of surf. To the best of my knowledge, this is the only place on the California coast where a creek forms a waterfall directly into the ocean.

In addition to the waterfall Julia Pfeiffer Burns State Park offers trails through the redwoods and along the creek. Usually-sunny weather here makes this a favorite picnic location.

41 S, 50 N. A wooden sign on the west side of the road marks an entrance to the reservations-required Esalen Institute (408/647-3005), which has offered seminars emphasizing human potential and values for over thirty years. Seminars range from weekend-participant to three-month-resident and internship programs. For a catalog, send five dollars to the Esalen Institute, Big Sur, California 93920. A special program is arranged for children ages one to six for $200.00 on weekends and $400.00 during the week, with some additional classes for older children. Since January 1980 Esalen's human potential movement has also focused on global needs. Esalen's Soviet-American exchange center, now called the Russian-American Exchange Center, has conducted several hundred exchanges between Soviet and American individuals and groups. Esalen hosted Boris Yeltsin during his first visit to the United States.

Esalen was frequented by Esselen tribespeople and perhaps Salinans for the soothing hotsprings in the cliffs above the ocean here. Shell mounds and in some places mortars are found on the grounds. September 1993 marked the first time a workshop given by local Esselen descendants teaching the ways of indigenous peoples has been offered at Esalen. In 1860 Thomas Slate, reportedly crippled with arthritis, lost all symptoms after soaking in the springs repeatedly for several weeks. Slate bought the springs, and in the Esselen way, opened them to any and all who needed or wanted soaks. Slate's Hot Springs were bought by Dr. and Mrs. H. C. Murphy from Salinas. Their son Michael cofounded the Esalen Institute here in the 1960s. Today, with millions of cars traveling Highway 1 annually, the public soaking hours are limited to 1 a.m. to 3:30 a.m. and only by reservation (408/667-3047). Overnight accommodations are sometimes available, depending on attendance at seminars.

45.5 S, 45.5 N. Even though it has double arches, Big Creek Bridge is often mistaken for Bixby Bridge. The four-thousand-acre Big Creek Ranch lands around the bridge were purchased in 1977 by the Nature Conservancy. The University of California operates a large portion of the former ranch as the Landels Hill-Big Creek Reserve. The Nature Conservancy has retained ten acres for educational purposes, and special groups are allowed in by contacting the Nature Conservancy (415/777-0541).

51 S, 37 N. In 1895, Wilbur Harlan hiked down the coast from Santa Cruz to land around the present community of Lucia. The Lucia Restaurant, convenience market, and rustic cabins are set on land the Harlan family homesteaded.

51.6 S, 36.3 N. Camaldolese Monks, whose order was established in the Apennine Mountains of Italy in the year 1012, bought part of the Harland land for the Immaculate Heart Hermitage, New Camaldoli. Visitors are welcome to attend daily masses and are reminded by a mildly worded sign to observe the quiet contemplation of the order. Retreat facilities are open to men and women for a usual stay of three days. For reservation information you can write Immaculate Heart Hermitage, New Camaldoli, Big Sur, CA 93920, or call 408/ 667-2456.

53 S, 38 N. A trail that rock-hops up Limekiln Creek leads to large rusted metal cylinders and massive brick ovens, where limestone from the surrounding canyon was smelted into lime. Limekiln Creek flows to a sandy cove beach shared by campers and fee day users of this private campground, presently run by the Esalen Institute. In 1993 the front page of the *Monterey County Herald* often carried the latest news of the tug of war between a Walton Drug Store heir and the state of California for purchase rights to the land here. When I visited, sixty-six camping sites were crowded under redwoods in the inland canyon and out on the open beach. Kayaks were skimming the cove; but check with the helpful staff for surf information.

55 S, 36 N. The trailhead for the Kirk Creek trail, also known as the Vicente Flat trail, begins across from the Kirk Creek Campground. Here climb steep switchbacks as Highway 1 shrinks to a hairline S below. All along the trail mountains and seashore form expansive views. The trail takes about one hour to walk, to the crest. It then continues to Vicente Flat Camp.

55.4 S, 35.6 N. Many tour books and some motel personnel recommend scenic Nacimiento-Fergusson Road to the Salinas Valley and Highway 101, for the ultimate in ocean views. The road is a narrow, twisty cliffhanger. In some places where rocks have slid from sheer cliffs the road isn't wide enough for one car, much less two. For a complete description, see the Inland Excursions chapter (p.216). The views are great but I'll choose hiking Kirk Creek any day.

55.9 S, 35.1 N. Mill Creek flows to the Pacific Ocean just south of Nacimiento-Furgusson Road. Picnic tables with a small accessible beach nearby make this a good place for snacks or lunch.

60 S, 31 N. Your attention may be diverted from the ocean as hang gliders and parasailers take to the skies by Pacific Valley Center. This area has become a very popular launching and landing area for these sports, for which permits may be reserved in advance by calling the Pacific Valley Station (805/927-4211). The center includes a restaurant, gift gallery, general store, mailbox, gas, and restrooms. The Pacific Valley Station Restaurant serves exceptional pie and offers a good view of the surf, just across the street. The Wildflower Gift and Gallery features

turquoise and silver jewelry. Cassette tapes include music by locals, such as Alisa Fineman. Also, there are books and local expertise available on the area. Samples of local jade in the store will help you know what you are looking for if you decide to jade-hound on the southern beaches. *Jade Beneath the Sea: A Diving Adventure,* available in the store, tells the story of a Pacific Grove sculptor's retrieval of a nine-thousand-pound boulder from offshore.

60.7 N, 30.3 S The Pacific Valley Station of Los Padres National Forest issues permits for backpackers entering the Ventana Wilderness on trails leading from this area. Topographical maps are sold here, and rangers provide information about the area and brochures, free of charge.

61 S, 30 N. At Sand Dollar Beach you'll find a clean and pleasant picnic area with fire pits and a restroom. To reach the crescent-shaped beach, where you can sometimes find sand dollars among the rocks, cross a meadow and walk down the stairs.

61.5 S, 29.5 N. Plaskett Creek Campground is set in an open clearing alongside a creek. Plaskett Cove marks the northernmost boundary of jade coves.

62.2 S, 28.8 N. A Los Padres National Forest sign that marks Jade Cove designates the series of coves that stretch from Plaskett Creek on the north to Willow Creek on the south. With the exception of Willow Creek the coves are only accessible by descents of steep cliffs subject to crashing waves.

Local jade, nephrite, is most readily found at low tides following winter storms. The jade along the cliffs has been picked over for years, and most pieces that are found near cliffs now have been freed from immersed reefs of serpentine and washed onto shore by high waves, which leave them lodged between rocks. Most local jade is a darkish blue-green color. The jade you find may have a dull appearance until you rub it against your cheek or dip it in water. Jade has a soapy feel and is stronger than steel, so a nail or knife won't scratch it.

63.8 S, 27.2 N. A road on the ocean side leads down to Willow Creek Beach, where there are a picnic area and restrooms. Plan to be here at low tide if possible, particularly for the tidepooling, which is sometimes more rewarding than the jade hunting. Kids love to do both. Watch for sneaker waves along the shore.

64.3 S, 26.7 N. Willow Creek Road, on the east side, is a very precarious road with little to recommend—no ghost town remains of the historic Los Burros mining district. The gold rush boom town in these hills burned to the ground. A few diehard prospectors work private claims, which are not open to the public. If you are going this way, stay on the road. Four-wheel drive is required.

65.3 S, 25.7 N. Gorda, population three, was once owned by some children entrepreneurs who ultimately went bankrupt. Many old-time travelers will be pleasantly surprised by its new renovations and beautiful gardens. Breakfasts, lunches, and dinners are served in the ocean-view Sorta Gorda restaurant. Kids will enjoy popcorn from the general store, which also serves as the city hall. Up the road, three cabins provide a special place to stay on the coast (805/927-3918). You might meet some artists who frequent the jade gallery a few steps up from the center. Blocks of jade, crafted items, jades from around the world, and a special boulder with million-year-old anemone holes are on exhibit. Local artists work behind the store.

There is a prime location for viewing marine mammals on a bluff across the highway from the center, where a Los Padres National Forest picnic area is being considered.

73.5 S, 17.5 N. Keep your eyes on the road but, once into the turnoff, view the Salmon Creek waterfall. Many trails, including one that leads behind the waterfall, begin here at an abandoned ranger station.

76.5 S, 14.5 N. Ragged Point is the last southern destination point in Big Sur and, northbound, the first turnoff for this stretch of coast. Walk behind the restaurant to view the dark green Santa Lucia Mountains plunging to the sea.

78.2 S, 12.8 N. The San Carpojo Creek flows at the dramatic base of the southerly Santa Lucias. Rangelands belonging to the Hearst Corporation extend from the banks of this river.

SAN SIMEON AND CAMBRIA

Points of interest along this stretch include Hearst Castle, San Simeon State Beach and Sebastian General Store, and the town of Cambria. Fifteen miles of coastal plains and rolling foothills stretch south to the little business center of San Simeon and further south to Cambria. The open lands you drive through are the private property of the Hearst Corporation. At one time the Hearst family owned forty-five thousand acres of Central Coast property. If you glance from time to time to the south you will see the outline of Hearst Castle. Thirteen miles south of the Carpojo Creek you will come to the turnoff for San Simeon Landing and, a little farther south, the entrance road to the tour staging area for Hearst Castle. If you are interested in taking a tour of the castle it is a good idea to make advance reservations, especially in the summer. If you have not made reservations or want to look around before doing so you should go directly to the center for tour information.

HEARST CASTLE

Although it is often referred to as a castle, William Randolph Hearst never used that description for the large estate on the hill; to him it was always "La Cuesta Encantada," the enchanted hill, or La Casa Grande. His guests were invited to come to "the ranch." Many visitors are surprised when they come looking for a European castle. Hearst employed Julia Morgan to design not a castle but a Spanish Plaza of the 1500s. Julia Morgan's adaptation of Hearst's wishes and the surrounding landscape in fact combines a Spanish church and plaza on the hill.

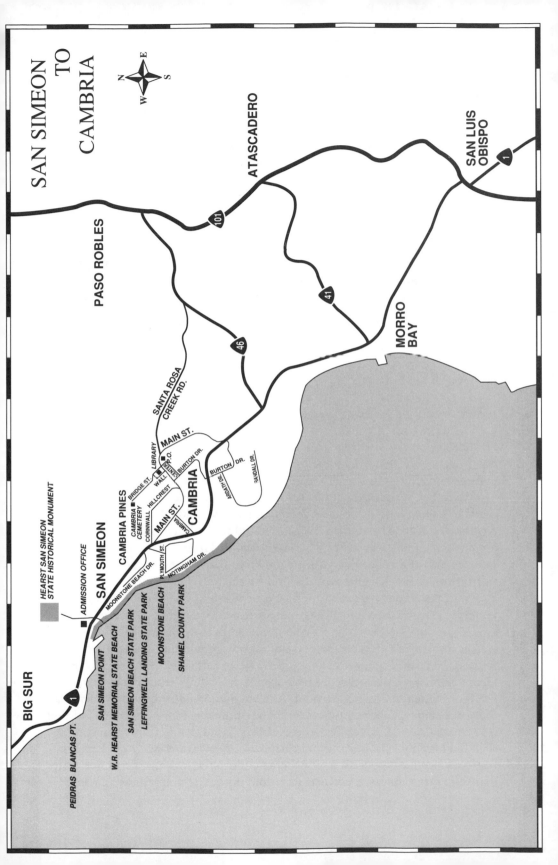

William Randolph Hearst was the only child of millionaire miner, senator, and rancher George Hearst and of Phoebe Apperson Hearst, who was herself known for her philanthropic contributions that included the founding of the P.T.A. While a senator, George Hearst acquired his major coastal land holdings. William enjoyed summers at the San Simeon site, which was originally used by the family for lavish camping expeditions. In 1887, when he was twenty-three, William convinced his at-first-reticent father to give him ownership of the financially failing *San Francisco Examiner.* William Hearst turned the fortunes of the paper around and began building a publishing empire. Between 1890 and 1920 William Randolph Hearst acquired thirty newspapers, over a dozen magazines, eight radio stations, and several film studios. He married Millicent Murray in 1903, and together they had five sons. The couple had separated by the 1920s. After the death of his mother, Phoebe Hearst, in 1919, William Hearst began a building fantasy with her good friend Julia Morgan, California's first woman architect, who had designed buildings in Berkeley and Pacific Grove for the family. In later years actress Marion Davies was his companion and hostess at the "Ranch on the Hill."

In order to furnish the lavish estate, Hearst, with Julia Morgan as advisor, began an antique-collecting spree. The rooms are museums, and the state of California, which now has ownership of the ranch, presents them as such. Hearst Corporation-owned warehouses still stocked full of unused antiques line the shore at San Simeon Landing. In addition to accumulating antiques Hearst collected, in effect, the largest zoo in the West at the time.

Five different tours of the estate are offered. Advance reservations can be made by calling the Mistix ticket reservation agency (800/444-4445). At this writing, tours are $14.00 for adults and $8.00 for children. The daytime tours are about an hour in duration. They are scheduled from 8 a.m. to 3 p.m. All vehicles park at a visitor staging area, and buses take visitors to the hill. As you ride up you may catch glimpses of zebras on the hillside.

Tour I is the tour suggested for first-time visitors. The guide greets you like you are a guest of the "Ranch." Guide positions are sought competitively. The guides take an extensive training course and seem to really enjoy their topic as well as the people they serve. Several landings of steps lead to the hundred-foot outdoor Neptune Pool, with panoramic view of the San Simeon coast through a Greco-Roman temple facade. Marble figures, including Venus rising from the foam of the sea, surround the pool. Although you might love to just bask by that pool all day, Tour I continues with one of three guest rooms, a ground-floor tour of the "castle," which Hearst called "La Casa Grande," and a look at the tiled indoor pool. The Casa Grande features rooms layered with silk Persian rugs and Flemish tapestries. Everywhere you look, furnishings are of fine craftsmanship: Etruscan vases, cabinets with gold inlay, and precision-cut crystal.

Hearst's only requirement for his guests was that they attend dinner. It was served on a three-hundred-year-old refectory table surrounded by a decorative display of silver. Diners joined a privileged list, including world leaders such as Winston Churchill, President Coolidge, and the king and queen of Greece. Hollywood celebrities included Charlie Chaplin, Greta Garbo, and Cary Grant. Guests were then invited to watch "home movies" in the private theater, the lobby of which featured "wonderous"—for that time—light bulbs in full view. Before you take another tour or continue to other treasures along the coast, see the tiled indoor pool that took eight men three-and-a-half years to finish. Not just any tiles, these have thin sheets of gold fused in Venetian pressed glass. Hearst wanted the tiles to resemble the lapis lazuli tiles of a fifth-century mausoleum.

Although five tours are available, you may find that one or two make a comfortable experience. Tour II features the upper floors of the Casa Grande, including the Gothic Suite, which was used as Hearst's private quarters; the library, with its collection of ancient Greek vases; and the kitchen and pantry areas, which were similar to those of a grand hotel. Tour III visits the smallest of the three guest rooms and the last, uncompleted guest room. Tour IV is especially recommended for photographers, as it offers the garden areas, rooms of the large guest house, and the wine cellars. Tour V is the newest. At this writing it has a ticket price of $50.00 and is available autumn through spring. It features a twilight visit to highlights of all the other tours. Docents are dressed in fashions of the 1930s and wander the rooms and gardens as though at a garden party.

When you descend from the hill, the cove at San Simeon waits for you with natural treasures. Although regarded by locals as the sunniest and most gentle of nearby beaches, the cove is still posted for rip currents.

SAN SIMEON LANDING

The building-construction foreman at Hearst Ranch and the present-day cattle workers got the beachfront property at San Simeon Landing. People on first visits to the landing often ask if their Spanish-style residences and the adjoining warehouses are California missions.

San Simeon Landing prospered in the 1850s as a whaling station and later as the center of a ranching and mining district. Sebastian's General Store was one of forty-five buildings that formed the community. A long pier and visiting ships were the community's link with the outside world, as no roads served the area. By the late 1870s the population had declined. Hearst brought new prosperity to the area when he brought his personal building industry to the hill.

Sebastian's General Store (805/927-4217) is now the only separately owned piece of property, surrounded by Hearst land. An outdoor takeout window serves fish, burgers, sandwiches, and fries for patio dining. Inside the store you can find a multitude of items including Italian fishermen's hats, hand-painted Victorian birdhouses, chocolate dolphins, and picnic supplies.

A small San Simeon commercial development begins about two miles south of the landing, at the edge of Hearst-owned land. Several restaurants, motels, residential apartments, and galleries are located here. The California Carvers Guild (805/927-4718) showcases sculptures.

Cambria

Two miles down the road the little but growing town of Cambria is the gentle grand finale of this tour. Moonstone Beach hugs the northern border of the town, which was a boom whaling and mining settlement and now draws many artists. You can hunt for opalescent moonstones at the beach. The whales slip in very close to the shore during late winter and early spring. Cambria invites you to stroll its downtowns—both of them. Take the first downtown Cambria entrance. Newer West Main Street offers pickle tasting, book browsing, a toy soldier factory, an old-fashioned bowling green, and a one-room schoolhouse now converted to a community art studio. The "Pinedorado Grounds" are a mix of fair buildings and some historical structures that include the old town jail and a historic lighthouse.

Old downtown features a mix of galleries, shops, and restaurants in hundred-year-old Victorians and well-designed replicas of such. The people strolling along with you are scattered about rather than packed. The athletic-looking couple may be heading for Cambria Bicycles (805/927-5510), known throughout the world as one of the best assemblers of parts from the best manufacturers, for bikes that cost $2,500.00 and up. Galleries attract a variety of tastes; customers range from those looking for museum-quality glass at the Seekers Collection & Gallery (805/927-4352) to those questioning the very essence of life and art at the What Iz Art gallery, where walls are painted with faces and slogans. Cue balls click at Old Camozzi's saloon and local musicians pick tunes at Molly's, a coffeehouse. You can pick up some fresh fruit at Soto's family-run market, savor some sweet low-sugar pie or jam at Linn's (800/676-1670), and find a serene bench behind the picket fence at Heart's Ease garden and herb shop (805/927-5224). There, consider: "Wear heartsease from day to day: Its simple balm doth greatly bless; and with it twine, I humbly pray, Rosemary for Remembrance."

WHAT ELSE TO SEE AND DO

"Tell them to get out of their cars and walk around, touch the ground, smell the mix of pine and sea, redwood and river glen, just don't walk on private property or land that is not marked with paths": this is the advice given by Big Sur residents. A multitude of great day hikes abounds in this area; several day hikes are highlighted along this section's tour. For a two- or three-day backpacking trip many hikers recommend Bottcher's Gap to Ventana Doublecone, for the spectacular scenery and varieties of habitats. For campsites, see under "Places to Stay," page 154.

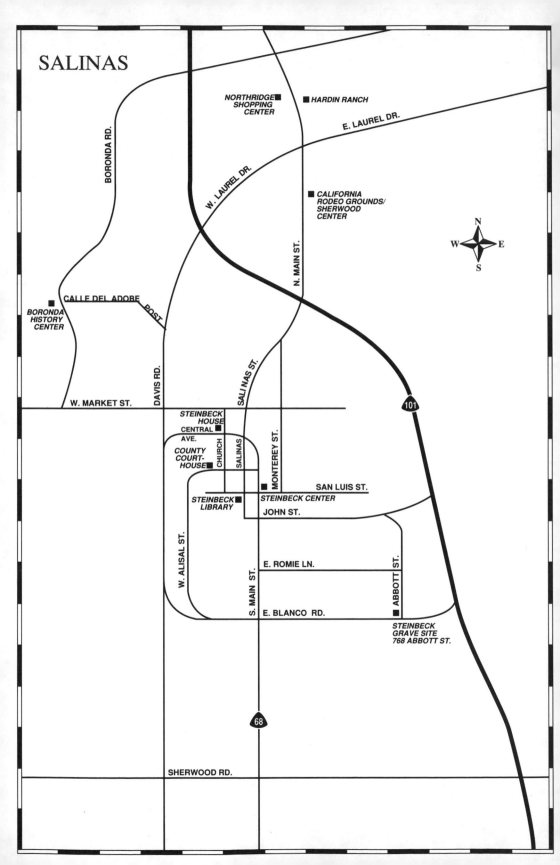

CHAPTER 7

INLAND EXCURSIONS

CARMEL VALLEY, SALINAS VALLEY,
THE PINNACLES,
SAN JUAN BAUTISTA

Carmel Valley and Salinas Valley are the interior heart of the Central Coast region. Carmel Valley Road and River Road are connecting links to farms, wineries, ranches, and resorts. Lake San Antonio and Lake Nacimiento are southern valley destinations.

GETTING READY

THE BEST TIMES TO VISIT AND THE SPECIAL EVENTS

Carmel Valley Road and Highway 68 to Salinas are busy during weekday mornings 7 a.m. to 9 a.m. and afternoons 5 p.m. to 6 p.m. Highway 1 south from Monterey to Carmel Valley Road can be thick with cars on three-day weekends and summer weekends.

February winds bring the "Hot Air Affair" balloon race and festival to Highway 68 between Monterey and Salinas. In April the Monterey-Salinas County Fair focuses on agriculture at the fairgrounds in King City. Also in April, the Bellas Artes del Valle with the Festival de Mariachi de Alta California as its centerpiece highlights Hispanic arts, music, and dance. The Mariachi Festival, featuring full-costumed Mexican bands from throughout the Western United States and also folklorico dancers, fills the Western Stage at Hartnell College in Salinas (408/755-6980). The California Rodeo rides into Salinas in mid July; advance ticket sales are suggested (408/757-2951 until the beginning of June, then 408/424-7355). Motels throughout the area fill up early. The more intimate Carmel Valley Fiesta enlivens Carmel Valley in midsummer (408/659-4000). Also in summer, usually in July, the Steinbeck Festival features tours, movies, and speakers highlighting the life and writings of native son and Pulitzer and Nobel winner John Steinbeck. The festival is offered by the Steinbeck Center Foundation (408/753-6411). The Soledad Mission Grape Stampede in September offers a showplace for vintners, great barbecue, and the unusual bare-footed grape-stompers competition.

Nature offers special events too. Plan for eagle-watch tours at Lake San Antonio from December to March. Wildflowers burst into bloom along back roads and on hillsides from April through June. In May, Lake San Antonio sponsors a wildflower show and triathlon.

The southern lakes, San Antonio and Nacimiento, are crowded during summer when the air is hot and the water is warm. Camping is usually available at Lake San Antonio. Summer gets hot! Plan sightseeing for morning hours.

CLIMATE AND CLOTHING

Spring is balmy, an average 70 degrees with occasional rains. In summer, coastal locals trade the fog for bathing suits by heading up the closer Carmel valley, for resort pools or river swimming; Carmel Valley is a very pleasant average 80 degrees, Salinas Valley about 10 degrees hotter. The southern lakes regions are much hotter, with 100-degree temperatures common. The wilderness areas and Carmel River areas do flood occasionally. Call ahead about Los Padres National Forest road conditions. Snow blankets the hills once or a few times a year.

Shorts and short sleeves greet the heat in summer and autumn. Bring sweaters for afternoon and evening breezes. Some winter days in the valleys can be in the eighties, so bring some light clothes in any season. Bring umbrellas and coats in the winter just in case a cold front moves in. Many fine restaurants, especially in Carmel Valley, request that men wear dinner jackets.

Scenic roads and incredible photo opportunities await you on this tour. Camera and binoculars are advised.

TOUR LENGTHS

Carmel Valley village and Salinas are both about thirty minutes from Monterey and the aquarium and twenty minutes from Highway 1 exits. Carmel Valley offers many choices of places to stay on an extended visit to the Central Coast area or for the week or weekend. The Carmel Valley-River Road loop is a two-hour drive with no stops. Take a full day to enjoy it.

Lake San Antonio or San Antonio Mission can be reached in two hours from Monterey by River Road or Highway 101. A leisurely drive to an afternoon eagle-watch tour or back from a morning tour makes a pleasant full day trip. Lake San Antonio campgrounds or the resort condos at Lake Nacimiento are good overnight destinations after a day tour of valley roads. Some pleasant creekside, first-come, first-served campgrounds are located at the Salinas Valley side of the Nacimiento-Fergusson Road. King City and Soledad offer lodging possibilities midway—especially well positioned if you are considering a following day trip to the Pinnacles.

WILDLIFE WISDOM

Deer, squirrels, jack rabbits, and coveys of quail are plentiful. Rattlesnakes inhabit the rolling hills and mountain areas; be careful before putting hands on rocky ledges or sitting on rocks or logs. Some of this tour borders land preserved by the taxpayers of California with Mountain Lion Habitat Preservation Funds. No attacks on humans by mountain lions in this tour area have been reported. During drought years the big cats come to lower elevations and attacks on family pets are reported. As a precaution, if you go hiking in Garland Park and the Los Padres National Forest lands with children, keep them close and carry a stick.

In 1919 Russian wild boars were brought to a hunting preserve in South Carolina from the Ukranian Mountains. Five years later, thirteen boars were shipped to the Los Padres forest region; they mated with wild domestic swine, and hundreds of bristled, tusked wild boar now roam the Santa Lucia Mountains. If you encounter a wild boar stay calm and back away quietly; noise can provoke a charge. If one were to charge, rangers advise, climb the nearest tree. Damage to possessions, let alone people is quite rare.

Bald eagles and golden eagles winter at Lake San Antonio. In the Pinnacles, raptors such as falcons, kestrels, and golden eagles can be spotted at the peaks from January to July. A dozen varieties of lizards, deer, and gray foxes can be viewed there year-round. Thousands of slow-moving tarantulas search for mates on the east-side roads and dirt paths in the fall.

Bald Eagle

VISITOR INFORMATION

The street map of Carmel Valley that is published by the local Kiwanis Club is available free at gas stations at the mouth of the valley and some businesses throughout the Carmel Valley (Kiwanis Club of Carmel Valley, P.O. Box 485, Carmel Valley 93924-0485). Fort Hunter Liggett Range Control needs to be called for information about whether Nacimiento-Fergusson Road is open, if you plan to drive it as part of your trip. The number to call is the same number as for information about visiting the Painted Salinan Cave, which are listed in the National Historic Registry and offer examples of cave painting by the area's earliest inhabitants (408/385-2503).

Monterey County Parks (408/755-4899) offers information about popular eagle-watch boat tours and reservations for camping in area county parks. The three county park campgrounds in this tour area are at Laguna Seca, San Lorenzo Park in King City, and Lake San Antonio.

The Monterey County Tourism Center has extensive information about the area and the entire Monterey County (San Lorenzo Park, 1160 Broadway, King City 93930; 408/385-1484). The National Forest Service district headquarters for the Los Padres National Forest is in King City (406 South Mildred Avenue, 408/385-5434). The National Forest Service Station is located on Cachagua Road off Carmel Valley Road (408/674-5726).

The Californian, the daily Salinas paper, lists events in its Thursday "What's Fun" section, and the *Monterey County Herald* carries event information in the Thursday "Event" and "Go" sections. "Go" is also available free at paper stands. *The Carmel Valley Sun* offers local and event news for Carmel Valley, Carmel, and the south coast. Locals keep informed at information boards that are posted outside many of the small community shopping or Post Office areas.

ALTERNATE TRANSPORTATION

Monterey-Salinas Transit serves Carmel Valley with hourly buses from the Monterey transit center (408/899-2555). Several buses travel to Salinas. Bus service does not extend to southern Monterey County.

PARKING

If you park your car along the road or in parks secure your valuables or take them with you. Parking is free and available at most locations.

PLACES TO STAY

CARMEL VALLEY ROAD

CARMEL VALLEY INN (Carmel Valley Road and Laureles Grade). A restful resort on ten acres, The Inn offers tennis, an Olympic-size solar-heated pool, the full-service Fox Hills Restaurant, and a wood-paneled lounge with fireplace. 408/659-3131, 800/541-3113. MC, V. For two, from $100.00 to $120.00.

Los Laureles Lodge (10.5 miles east of Highway 1, just past the Laureles Grade turn off). This historic country inn was owned by the Hotel Del Monte and the Vanderbilts. White picket fences, a large library, knotty pine patio rooms, country rooms, and premier suites; beamed ceilings in a comfortable lodge-type lobby with a crackling fire. Conference center in the former equestrian center. The restaurant is in the restored front porch of the original lodge, built in 1890. A mahogany-paneled bar has entertainment by local musicians. 408/659-2233; in California, 800/533-4404. MC, V. For two, from $100.00 to $450.00; $100.00 to $130.00 average.

Quail Lodge, 8205 Valley Greens Drive (off Carmel Valley Road, a little over three miles from Highway 1). A Mobil Travel Guide five-star-rated resort. Guest rooms overlook 245 acres of pastoral golf course dotted with ten lakes and with mountain vistas. The more deluxe accommodations feature patio rooms and suites and terrace rooms; the Executive Villa has private hot tubs and luxurious appointments. Guests of the lodge receive full privileges at the private Quail Lodge Golf and Tennis Resort. Conference, entertainment, and banquet facilities available. Country elegance prevails at the Covey Restaurant. 408/624-1581. AX, MC, V; others also accepted. For two, from $175.00 to $345.00.

Robles Del Rio Lodge, 200 Punta Del Monte (above Carmel Village). This oldest of the operating inland resorts is fully restored to last another century. French country decor, peaceful setting, panoramic views of the valley and mountains. Lodge rooms and cabins. Breakfast included. Complete meeting and banquet facilities. Outdoor tiled pool, spa, and full-service restaurant. 408/659-3705, 800/833-0843. MC, V. For two, from $90.00 to $190.00.

Stonepine, 150 East Carmel Valley Road (in upper Carmel Valley just past Carmel Village; on the right opposite Las Tulares Road). A Relais Chateau Gold Star-rated resort. Eight lavish suites, some with secret rooms, in the Chateau Noel, which was the private estate owned by Helen Crocker Russell. Helen and Henry Russell were famous in the 1930s, 1940s, and 1950s as the most prestigious thoroughbred breeders west of the Mississippi. The equestrian center offers a quality riding program. Fantasy, elegance, and gracious service. The butler will pick you up at the airport in a Rolls Royce. 408/659-2245. AX, MC, V. For two, from 225.00 to $750.00.

SALINAS VALLEY

KEEFER'S INN, Canal Street, King City (from U.S. 101, exit at Canal Street). Built like a Dutch village, this inn has forty-eight units, a putting green, and a family restaurant. 408/385-4843. AX, MC, V; others also accepted. For two, $50.00.

LAUREL INN, 801 West Laurel Drive, Salinas (from U.S. 101, exit at Laurel Drive). Air-conditioned rooms, pool, hot tubs, sauna, some fireplaces. 408/449-2474. In California, 800/354-9831. AX, MC, V; others also accepted. For two, $60.00.

SOUTHERN EXTENSION

NACIMIENTO LAKESHORE LODGES (at the resort, on the shores of Lake Nacimiento). Lakeview townhomes on a quiet rise, all with lake views. High ceilings, fireplaces, and modern kitchens. Romantic for just two. Large units accommodate eight to ten people per lodge; with adjoining units, up to sixteen. 800/323-3839. $130.00 to 210.00.

Lodging is also available for the southern extension of this inland excursion in Paso Robles, farther south along Highway 101.

RESTAURANTS

CARMEL VALLEY ROAD VICINITY

THE COVEY, at Quail Lodge, 8205 Valley Greens Drive, Carmel Valley (on Carmel Valley Road, 3.4 miles beyond Highway 1). Here find country elegance, with polished pewter, fresh flowers, Audubon prints, and a warming fireplace. Views of fountains and lakes. Nooks for quiet conversation. The European cuisine includes beef, lamb, poultry, seafood, and locally grown produce. Extensive wine selection. Piano bar. Men are requested to wear jackets. Dinner. 408/624-1581. AX, MC, V. Entrees, from $20.00 to $30.00.

THE IRON KETTLE, Carmel Valley Village (in White Oaks Plaza). The oldest building in the village was formerly a creamery for the Hotel Del Monte. It now has the at-home comfort of British and Australian tea rooms. Eggs Aussie features eggs benedict on a scone. Old-fashioned but salt-free, sugar-free scones are heavenly. A garden patio has outdoor service. Breakfast and lunch and afternoon tea. 408/659-5472. No cards. Selections, mostly under $5.00.

THE RIDGE RESTAURANT, 200 Punta Del Monte, Carmel Valley (above the village at Robles Del Rio Lodge). At a historic resort, the Ridge has spectacular views of Carmel Valley. California and French cuisine; menus change often to accommodate use of the freshest local ingredients. Extensive wine list. Thursday through Saturday only, for the public; reserved other days for private events and groups. Pool and courtyard dining. Dinner nightly, lunch daily except Mondays. 408/659-0107. AX, MC, V. Entrees mostly under $30.00.

THE RUNNING IRON RESTAURANT AND SALOON, East Carmel Valley Road and Via Contenta, Carmel Valley Village. A stuffed mountain lion and a boar's head watch over the passage from the lively bar to the restaurant. Hundreds of pairs of boots hang from the ceilings. Barn-burning chile and barbecued baby-back pork ribs. 408/659-4633. AX, MC, V. Entrees, mostly under $10.00.

TAQUERIA DEL VALLEY, 19 East Carmel Valley Road, Carmel Valley Village. Bright and cozy, this cantina has authentic Mexican food, Jalisco style. Chile rellenos, massive vegetarian burrito. Lunch and dinner, Tuesday through Saturday. Eat in or take out. 408/659-1473. No cards. Selections, mostly under $5.00.

THAI BISTRO, 55 West Carmel Valley Road, Carmel Valley Village (Thai Bistro II is at 159 Central Avenue in Pacific Grove). At this local favorite, patrons enjoy valley views and outdoor dining. "Laub-gai" (chicken simmered in lime juice, with shallots, mint, and chiles) is especially recommended. Vegetarian fare is available. Lunch and dinner. 408/659-5900. MC, V. Entrees, mostly under $10.00.

WAGON WHEEL COFFEE SHOP (on Carmel Valley Road in the Valley Hills Shopping Center just past the Quail Lodge turnoff). A breakfast and lunch favorite with locals, this coffee shop has old Western saddles and bridles hung outside the front door. Inside branding irons, saddles, spurs, and chaps decorate wood-paneled walls. Hearty and tasty Western breakfasts, including butter pecan waffles; later, calamari burgers. Open 7 a.m. until 2 p.m. every day. 408/624-8878. No cards. Selections, mostly under $8.00.

WILL'S FARGO, Carmel Valley Road, Carmel Valley Village (in the village center). In a turn-of-the-century Victorian setting you can select your own steak, cut to your specifications, from the attractive display case. Fresh seafood, lamb, and chicken are also offered. Tuesday through Sunday. 408/659-2774. AX, MC, V. Entrees, mostly under $20.00.

HIGHWAY 68 VICINITY

The following restaurants are located off Highway 68 between Highway 1 and River Road.

RYAN RANCH ROTISSERIE & MARKET, One Harris Court (off 68 in Ryan Ranch Industrial Park). In an exhibition kitchen with flavorful aromas, the spotlight is on rotisserie cooking. Bistro-style seating. Roasted duck, lemon chicken, and wild fowl are some favorites. Fine selection of California wines. Lunch and dinner. 408/655-5590. AX, MC, V. Entrees, mostly under $20.00.

TARPY'S ROADHOUSE, Highway 68 and Canyon Del Rey. Dine al fresco in a sunny, European-style courtyard surrounded by trellised gardens or, indoors, in the stone room and warm side dining rooms of this old stone roadhouse. The stonework varies from room to room and includes fossils as well as a shell-lined fireplace. American country favorites with innovative touches include Indiana duck served on sweet corn succotash with an apricot mint glaze and molasses bourbon porkchops. Full-service bar. Lunch, dinner. 408/647-1444. AX, MC, V; others also accepted. Entrees, mostly under $20.00.

SALINAS VALLEY

CASA TERESA, 185 Kidder Street, Soledad. The super burritos and chile verde at this family-owned restaurant with the atmosphere of a town reunion are often prepared by Teresa, who teaches the art of better Mexican cooking to chefs on the Monterey Peninsula. Lunch, dinner. 408/678-2480. MC, V. Entrees, mostly from $3.00 to $10.00.

GUTIERREZ AND RICO DRIVE-IN, 61 Sherwood Drive (corner of East Ross), Salinas. At this beach-look restaurant the Mexican seafood items are area favorites. Other menu items are also authentic and tasty. 408/424-8382. No cards. Entrees, mostly under $10.00.

KEEFER'S, Canal and Highway 101, King City. Melt into the comfortable booths here after a day's drive. A lighthearted Swedish mural gives counter seating a warm feeling. Hearty American and continental selections. Friendly service for the whole family. Breakfast (open 6:30 a.m.), lunch, dinner. 408/385-3543. MC, V. Entrees, mostly under $10.00.

THE PUB, 227 Monterey Street, Salinas. With oversized, comfortable booths and wood paneling, this is a classic steak and rib house. Open-flame-grilled barbecued chicken, huge slabs of prime rib. Lunch, dinner. 408/424-4261. AX, MC, V. Entrees, mostly under $15.00.

STEINBECK HOUSE,132 Central Avenue, Salinas. In a Victorian family home containing memorabilia, photos, and original furnishings of John Steinbeck's family, weekday lunch only is served, in two sittings. Gourmet fare features seasonal vegetables of the area. Set daily entree, menu changes monthly. Call ahead for reservations and entree selection. Local wines available by the glass. 408/424-2735. Lunch entrees, under $10.00.

DIRECTIONS

For the Carmel Valley loop, to the loop's beginning point in Carmel Valley. *From the Monterey Bay Aquarium* follow Lighthouse Avenue to Pacific Avenue. Continue on Pacific Avenue to Sherman Street. Follow entrance signs to Highway 1 and head south.

From Highway 1 take the turnoff marked Carmel Valley Road, at the signal light that is one mile south of the Ocean Avenue exit for Carmel-by-the-Sea and is seven miles north of Point Lobos.

For the Northern Salinas Valley tour of River Road and its cut-offs, and the southern extension from the Highway 68 beginning points. *From the Monterey Bay Aquarium,* follow Lighthouse Avenue to the city of Monterey. Move to the right-hand lane after you go through the tunnel. Turn right at Camino Aguajito. Follow Camino Aguajito to the end, and follow the signs to Highway 1 north. From 1, take the Highway 68 east exit.

From Highway 1 heading either direction, take the Highway 68 east exit, which is on the northern border of Monterey at Del Rey Oaks.

INTRODUCTION TO THE INLAND AREA
WITH HISTORICAL HIGHLIGHTS

When local artist Marie-Louise Rouff compares the Carmel Valley to other Central Coast landscapes, her words reflect her pictures. "The colors are less diffuse, the shadows cast are darker. Mountains lie there like breathing human forms."

John Steinbeck was a native son of Salinas, and many of his novels drew on the surrounding landscape. In *East of Eden* he called the Salinas Valley "a long narrow swale." The Gabilan range on the east he described as "light gay mountains full of sun and loveliness and a kind of invitation, so that you wanted to climb into their warm foothills almost as you want to climb into the lap of a beloved mother." In contrast he described the Santa Lucias, on the west, as "dark and brooding."

The Carmel Valley and the Salinas Valley share agricultural and historical roots as they stretch inland and southward from the Monterey Bay Area. Each has a rhythm that complements the other, each its own chamber of California's heartland. The tours in this chapter of each valley begin with turns east off Highway 1 near Monterey, but the two tours take different routes inland. They intersect, forming an inland excursion loop, near Greenfield.

Cutting through the Santa Lucias, the Carmel Valley is the narrower, more intimate, more westerly of the two—the valley of sun to the people fogbound along the coast in the summer. The dark backdrop is the verdant redwood and pine forests of the Los Padres National Forest. Carved by the Carmel River, which can run swift in winter and only trickle through shaded pools in summer or drought years, the Carmel Valley begins at Highway 1 almost as a sister to Carmel. Not to be claimed by it, this valley has its own form and beauty.

The Santa Lucias' high peaks on the Carmel Valley Road's southern side melt to gentle hills on the northern side. The road passes the Crossroads, Rancho Carmel, and Barnyard shopping centers at its Highway 1 entrance. Rolling hills separate the road from Monterey and, farther inland, Salinas and the Salinas Valley area. Due to its prime location, availability of land, and balmy weather, the Carmel Valley has faced intense and increasing pressures to develop. Resorts, many of which serve golf or equestrian enthusiasts, and residences share the valley with agricultural and wilderness land.

Miles broader than the Carmel Valley and anchored by the largest submerged river in California, the Salinas Valley is the agricultural heartland of the Central Coast region, the "Salad Bowl of the Nation." The Salinas River, one of the longest rivers in the state, is unusual both in running north and in being one of the largest submerged rivers in the United States. Just as the river flows peacefully (it surfaces at shallow levels), the Salinas Valley has a restful quality, in its spreading farmlands and open vistas. As the current building boom moves south from the Santa Clara Valley the fresh air and open views are cherished with the knowledge that they may be ephemeral, the makings of tomorrow's postcard collections. For the many Californians who grew up in now-urbanized areas, such as the orchards of San Jose, groves of Orange County, or once-discrete, now suburbia-absorbed small agricultural towns, stretches of the Salinas Valley remain like the places they remember. For readers of Steinbeck, the fields and open grasslands are yet the "Pastures of Heaven."

Highway 101 cuts through the center of the Salinas Valley. River Road, on the western side, offers a more intimate view of it. During celery-harvesting season on the western side of the valley the spicy fragrances are heady along River Road, clearing the mind and rousing the imagination.

Footsteps of the early inhabitants can be traced in both valleys. On the north side of Carmel Valley Road, about three miles from Highway 1, the gnarled El Encino del Descanso (the "Oak of Repose") holds a small religious shrine. The Rumsen and Esselen peoples who had been converted to Christianity used to stop here on the way to the Carmel Mission for burials. The Esselen territory extended east to what is now Soledad. Today, farther up the Carmel Valley in a section known as the Ventana Wilderness, the descendants of the Esselen tribe are rebuilding Esselen ceremonial grounds as they petition the government for official tribal recognition. South of the Esselen the Salinas Valley was first inhabited by the "Salinan," the name the Spanish gave to the people who lived along what the Spanish called the Salinas or, translated, "salty" river. The Salinans' name for themselves has not survived, although some descendants live throughout the county.

Two missions were founded in the Monterey County stretch of the Salinas Valley. Although other missions in California have been restored, the fragrant rose garden, small chapel, and crumbled ruins of Mission Soledad lie in quiet repose. A nearby ranch was the setting Steinbeck used for *Of Mice and Men.*

Farther south the western boundary of the Salinas Valley rolls into the Fort Hunter Liggett Military Reservation. The reservation surrounds the painted cave of the Salinan people and the restored Mission San Antonio de Padua, which stands on the edge of pine and oak wilderness. A little over two hundred years ago the missions were all outposts in wilderness, but they were not isolated from people. When Mission San Antonio was established in 1771, about twenty Salinan villages lay in a twenty-some-mile radius around the mission.

Nearest to Mission San Antonio, the typical Salinan village of Chacomex hosted several quadrangular houses averaging ten square feet in size. The roof consisted of a lattice of poles thatched with tules, which were lashed with strips of bark.

The missionaries recognized the temperate climate and gravel-laden soils of the alluvial fans at the base of the mountain ranges to be highly compatible with their European viticulture. A mission-period winery can be viewed at Mission

San Antonio. Today, the Salinas and Carmel valleys are prime wine-grape areas. Several wineries and tasting rooms welcome visitors; tons more grapes are shipped throughout the state for processing.

By the 1830s Mexican and Spanish land grants had divided the valleys of the Rumsen, Esselen, and Salinan into enormous ranchos: Don Jose Manuel Boronda and his wife Maria Juana Boronda were among the first grantees to live on the land.

Many of the large ranchos that divided the Salinas and Carmel valleys after the mission period passed from the original Mexican owners after the Mexican-American War, because of the bureaucratic difficulties to keeping the land that were built into the treaty ending the war, in 1848. Starving cattle and the parched grasslands of the drought of the 1860s sent many ranchos into foreclosure. A hundred thousand cattle grazed Monterey County in 1860, but by 1864, after the dry years, the number had dropped to thirteen thousand. David Jacks, land baron of Monterey County, became a prime landowner.

Doña Boronda sold the golden "queso del pais" (cheese of the country) made on her rancho to Santa Lucia goldminers and Monterey markets. In the 1880s more dairies came to the valleys, among them those of David Jacks. Several local stories, including the Boronda version, lay claim to the origins of Monterey jack cheese. It is not clear whether this name came from David Jacks's marketing of it or from the heavy wooden "jacks" that pressed down on the cheese while it aged.

After the livestock tragedies of the drought years, landowners turned miles of rangeland into wheat fields. Labor contractors spread groups of dispirited tribal peoples through the valley each summer to harvest grain, but according to writings by historian Sandy Lydon their numbers dropped sharply because of disease. Chinese laborers were brought in by labor contractors from San Francisco. Many of the Chinese had worked the gold fields or had been released from railroad work when lines were completed.

Claus Spreckels brought the sugar beet to the Salinas Valley in the late 1880s and built a seven-story sugar factory near Salinas. Yearly "campaigns," as the harvests were called, saw wagons, train cars, and later trucks haul out the yields of thousands of acres of sugar beets. Parts of Steinbeck's novel *Tortilla Flat* and both movie versions of *East of Eden* were filmed in the "Sugar King's" company town of Spreckels.

The Southern Pacific Railway whistled through the valley, shipping first the grain and then the beets and cheese, and made or broke the towns along the central Salinas Valley. Towns such as Chualar, Soledad, and Gonzales were built on the freight train routes; Highway 101 connects many of these shipping towns today. Salinas, at the northern end of the valley, is the governmental, agricultural, and business center for Monterey County. People of Hispanic descent are the majority of the population and contribute leadership and their traditional celebrations. In the surrounding valleys Hispanic workers are today's prime tenders of the agricultural fields.

Now it is "King Lettuce" that surrounds Salinas and stretches eastward toward the Gabilan Mountains. New shopping malls are also spreading northeast of Salinas, along the 101 corridor. Directly across from the Northridge Shopping Center travelers can pick up the San Juan Grade Road and travel northeast through the Gabilans to the old mission town of San Juan Bautista. From vantage spots along the narrow rutted road the grand vista of the Salinas Valley stretches to the sea.

The interior of narrow Carmel Valley is void of major shopping centers. Sugar beets were planted to entice the railroad to extend to Carmel but didn't succeed as a crop. Some of the original creamery buildings for Monterey jack cheese house businesses in Carmel Valley Village, the diminutive population center of this valley. The pickup trucks and cowpunchers are for real in this village: this is a ranching area. Also in the eclectic Carmel Valley Village, the Hidden Valley Music Center presents baroque, opera, and chamber music as well as theater and dance performances year-round. Local artisans exhibit at local festivals and shops.

When asked what changes he'd seen in the last twenty years the assistant fire chief of Cachagua, a relatively isolated community along Carmel Valley Road, smiled. "Everyone says the newcomers are going to change the valley. I've noticed more how it changes them."

Undaunted by change, within the southern Gabilan Mountains in the Pinnacles National Monument golden eagles soar above the wild rugged peaks of a remnant ancient volcano, gliding and circling. The trees that shade the rolling grasslands around Lake San Antonio and the digger pines by Lake Nacimiento, farther to the south, are winter homes to migrating bald and golden eagles. From their vantage point especially there is wilderness here still, wilderness prowled by the mountain lion and respected by the Rumsen, the Salinan, the Esselen, cut through with dusty mission trails—now cut much more by the fields of farmers from many lands, the resorts that cater to seekers of sunlit quietude, and the residences of the present generations.

TOURS

The Carmel Valley tour follows the Carmel River, then turns inland to Carmel Valley Village. Beyond the village the road becomes curvy and serves as the gateway to many locations in the Los Padres National Forest. Once you have completed the Carmel Valley Road tour you can loop back to the Monterey area on the Northern Salinas Valley tour, which from the Monterey end leads along Highway 68 to turnoffs for Salinas and Spreckels and then continues along pastoral G-17, which is alternately named River Road, Fort Romie Road, and Arroyo Seco Road. From Greenfield, the terminus of both the Carmel Valley tour and Northern Salinas Valley tour, you can also connect to the southern lakes tour. Visitors bound for San Juan Bautista can reach it via Highway

101 from Salinas. The Pinnacles National Monument can be reached from San Juan Bautista or Soledad.

THE CARMEL VALLEY TOUR

The tour begins at the intersection of Highway 1 with Carmel Valley Road. Heading inland from the intersection, the first right turn is Carmel Rancho Boulevard, which leads to three shopping centers: The Crossroads, Carmel Rancho, and the Barnyard. The restaurants and some shops here are featured in the Carmel chapter (p. 145).

Just past the boulevard turnoff a wooden sign on Carmel Valley Road welcomes you to Carmel Valley. Behind the sign a fence straddles the Carmel Rancho parking lot and fields of furrows dug in the rich Carmel River basinland. The fence is the first of many to separate disparate uses of the landscape in this valley. Golf ball drivers and cattle drivers share a common scenery. Christmas tree farms, fresh-egg ranches, winery tasting rooms, cattle ranches, golf courses, and hybrid begonia nurseries occupy this bucolic valley once known for pear orchards and creameries.

The valley is wide at this point, and the Carmel River flows far from your sight, nearer the base of the mountains. Along the route the river will weave closer and entice you to leave your car and listen to its swift wet-season rumbling and gentle summer babbles, very much the same as Steinbeck described it in the book *Cannery Row*.

"The Carmel is a lovely little river. It isn't very long but in its course it has everything a river should have. It rises in the mountains, and tumbles down a while, runs through shallows, is dammed to make a lake, spills over the dam, crackles among round boulders, wanders lazily under sycamores, spills into pools where trout live, drops in against banks where crayfish live. In the winter it becomes a torrent, a mean little fierce river, and in the summer it is a place for children to wade in and for fisherman to wander in. Frogs blink from its banks and the deep ferns grow beside it. Deer and foxes come to drink from it, secretly in the morning and evening and now and then a mountain lion crouched flat laps its water. The farms of the rich little valley back up to the river and take its water for the orchards and the vegetables. The quail call beside it and the wild doves come whistling in at dusk. Raccoons pace its edges looking for frogs. It's everything a river should be."

Traffic often moves quickly and turns are easy to miss on this scenic road. From Highway 1 to Carmel Valley Village nonstop takes about twenty-five minutes.

The first greens you see are on the two eighteen-hole championship courses of the Rancho Cañada Golf Course, The public courses crisscross the Carmel River. Reservations are recommended (408/624-0111).

After the road narrows to one lane, greens again carpet the valley floor, around the rooms of the Mobil-rated five-star Quail Lodge Golf Resort, "a place of serenity." Eleven lakes that dot the landscape provide refuge to migratory birds. The resort land previously housed the Carmel Valley Dairy, which was owned by the Dwight Morrow and Charles Lindbergh families. The famous aviator used it as a getaway. A new luxury home development is being built on the adjoining six hundred acres of Quail Meadows, where the understanding is, "If you can see it from the road you can't build it." Maseratis, Lamborghinis, Ferraris, and other automotive jewels take over the practice greens at the Concours Italiana, which is held at the resort in late August of each year.

At the next sharp right on Carmel Valley Road past Quail Lodge, the Valley Hills Shopping Center welcomes you to country living. Check the bulletin board for the latest livestock and community concerns. Egg-laying guinea hens cackle on top of antique stores within close proximity to Quail Lodge.

Roosters strut and rabbits scurry around pickup trucks being filled with hay at the next driveway. The Hacienda Hay and Feed store is a must stop if you have children or want a western barnyard experience. In October the hay bales are piled high and filled with Halloween surprises at the store's haunted hay house, for kids and brave adults.

October is also pumpkin-picking time at the farms along Carmel Valley Road. Some fruit and vegetable stands are open year-round, some just for the summer-autumn harvest.

A right turn on Schulte Road leads to Saddle Mountain Recreation Park. This hundred-acre park is open year-round for camping. Teepee tents are an option but are not the style of dwellings used by the Rumsen/Ohlone, who slept under the open skies during warm months and also lived in round willow and tule covered ruks. A three-and-one-half-mile hiking trail leads to an elevation of a thousand feet for a panoramic view. On clear days you can see across the bay to the Santa Cruz Mountains.

At Chateau Julien, 8940 Carmel Valley Road, wine tasting and tours offer the feeling of joining old friends at the boutique winery situated on seven country acres. In a California adaptation, the use of French-Swiss chateau architecture with high interior beam ceilings and stained glass parallels Chateau Julien's use of the French traditional methods for aging wines in new French oak. The winery crushes approximately a thousand tons of grapes each year, hand picked from growers throughout Monterey County. Tours are scheduled, with reservations suggested, at 10:30 a.m. and 2:30 p.m. weekdays. The tasting table is open daily from 8 a.m to 5 p.m. From June through September the tours begin with a circuit of the small vineyard around the chateau, with its five varieties of grapes. The winery offers several events during the year, including a summer jazz, wine, and food extravaganza (408/624-2600; fax, 408/624-6138). Many other wineries are located along the Salinas tour and in the Santa Cruz Mountains.

In June and July greenhouses full of some of the largest begonias in the world bring international visitors to the Carmel Valley Begonia Gardens, 9220 Carmel Valley Road. After determining the Carmel Valley climate to be optimal for begonias, Noel Hanssens from Belgium began the gardens in the 1950s. His mother-stock plants are displayed, but are not for sale. They are guarded as family jewels by the trio of present owners, who took over after his death. A good portion of the nursery's plants are grown from its own stock. Originally exclusively begonias, the nursery is full service at present. In May thousands of roses bloom along the walkways connecting greenhouses. Visitors may wander freely in the over four acres of gardens.

Your next stop may be Mid Valley Shopping Center, which has restaurants, a grocery store, a deli, and a movie theater. You might want to get foodstuffs here and take them to Garland Ranch Regional Park, an excellent hiking and picnic spot, three miles up the road. The five-thousand-acre Garland Park, located eight and one-half miles from Highway 1, includes picnic areas by the Carmel River, a field of old farm equipment, and miles of hiking trails.

Two bridges lead across the river to the visitor's center in the dry months. The wider year-round green bridge is located on a trail that begins about a hundred yards west of the parking lot by the mail box at 700 W. Carmel Road. If you pause at the bridge and look north you will see a dense cottonwood grove, one of the best examples of riparian woodland that remains along the Carmel River. Beyond the bridge veer left for the visitor's center, which is open 10 a.m. to 2 p.m. on weekends. In the field of old farm equipment from ranch days the picnic tables alongside old hay wagons are inviting places to have snacks or lunch. So are small coves at the river near the other entrance from the parking lot.

Three of the scenic trails include the lupine loop, the buckeye nature trail and the waterfall trail to the mesa. The lupine loop is a sea of blue flowers from April through June. A Rumsen grinding rock site and large midden lie at the terminus of the buckeye trail. Every season here has its highlights, but the spring wildflowers bedazzle more than the bees.

Garland Park is one part of the Monterey Peninsula Regional Park District (408/659-4488), all parks of which feature free admission. The new Cooper Ranch addition to Garland Park, one-half mile west of the green bridge on Cooper trail, is the only area of Garland Park open to mountain bikes. Equestrians have open access to the park trails, with the exception of the terrace trail, buckeye trail, Siesta Point trail, and portions of the waterfall trail.

Back on Carmel Valley Road you intersect Laureles Grade, which connects to Highway 68 about midway between Monterey and Salinas. The views over the mountaintops and the descent from the Santa Lucia Mountains make this road a good return route or side trip.

Los Laureles Lodge is to the left on Carmel Valley Road, just past Boronda Road. The Los Laureles Rancho was sold in the 1880s to the Pacific Improvement

Company for the Central Pacific Railroad, which needed a source of water for the newly opened Hotel Del Monte. Some seven hundred Chinese laborers built the original San Clemente Dam on the Carmel River and laid twenty-three miles of pipe to the Hotel Del Monte. The Los Laureles ranch house was enlarged and a number of cabins added to create an inland destination for guests of the Del Monte, who rode up Carmel Valley Road on horse-pulled tally-hos to take the air or to stay and hunt or fish. During prohibition this was the place where Hotel Del Monte guests imbibed in bootlegged liquor.

After the property changed hands again Muriel Vanderbilt Phelps Adams acquired it to raise racehorses. The present Los Laureles Lodge is restored as a historic country inn.

After driving through pastoral hills you come to Carmel Valley Village, the first shops of which were designed to resemble a Mexican village. Spread along Carmel Valley Road, the village has businesses that are set back from the road. A community park with picnic areas, public pool, barbecue pits, and children's play area complete with one of the first fire engines in the valley is located in the eastern end of the village.

The village is an eclectic arrangement of shops, galleries, bakeries, and markets. The Talbott Tie Factory Outlet offers neckware, fabric, shirts, and accessories at reduced, outlet prices (408/659-4540). Across the street studios offer fine hand-carved furniture and wood sculptures. The Carmel Valley Market and Monroe's Meats offer groceries, choice meats, and collector bottles of fine wines (408/659-2472).

The White Oak Properties Complex on Carmel Valley Road between Paso Hondo and Esqualine Road is the historic heart of the village. The white clapboard building with the cupola was built in 1890 to process milk from the Los Laureles Dairy Ranch, for the old Hotel Del Monte in Monterey. A rod-controlled lever opened the sides of the tower to take advantage of afternoon breezes, cooling the milk. The round trip to Monterey for a four-horse wagon loaded with milk or cheese took at least eight hours in the dry season, and longer when the roads were muddy from seasonal rains. William Hatton managed this dairy and others so successfully that he was able to purchase the Rancho Cañada de la Segunda at the entrance to the valley. The Hatton Canyon, which parallels Highway 1, was part of his landholdings.

When you are ready to continue past Carmel Valley Village travel north on Carmel Valley Road, which becomes Tularcitos Road and is best identified as G-16. It leads through hills and meadows with some sharp curves for thirty miles to Greenfield and the Highway 101 connection.

About 4.5 miles past the village you'll come to the turnoff for the very narrow Cachagua Road, which winds through very sharp turns to Los Padres Dam, Los

Padres National Forest, and the AT&T Jamesburg Earth Station, then connects with Tassajara Road to loop back to G-16. The entire loop from the village is about 29 miles. If you want a more relaxing and less winding drive to the same locations wait for Tassajara Road, which branches off Carmel Valley Road 7.5 miles farther (11.5 miles from Carmel Valley Village).

Between Cachagua Road and Tassajara Road on G-16 keep a look out for the 21.8 milepost and a dirt road on the north side. This is the right of way to the Blomquist Open Space. Before you visit the area you need to pick up a permit in Garland Park (at its visitor's center or the district office in the Cooper Ranch addition; see page 198). It's a four-mile hike down the dirt road to the open space, which features open woodlands, an old cabin site, and serenity—a lovely place to enjoy Central Coast wildflowers in the spring.

G-16 cuts through a hill just before a road marker identifies your next right turn as Tassajara Road. About 1.5 miles past the Carmel Valley Road intersection, Tassajara Road forms a Y with Cachagua Road. John James founded the small unincorporated settlement in the area in 1867. From 1904 to the end of the stagecoach era James Ranch was a stagecoach stop for visitors bound for the hot springs resort at Tassajara. Miss-it-if-you-blink "Jamesburg" is another 1.5 miles down Tassajara Road. In former days, some settlers here trapped live grizzly bears, supplementing incomes by ox-carting them to Monterey for bull and bear fights. Ladybugs were gathered in the springtime and sold to Salinas farmers, to protect their crops from pests.

To visit the Jamesburg Earth Station turn right, on Cachagua Road, at this Y junction. If you want to visit Tassajara Zen Center or Ventana Wilderness Station keep to your left, on Tassajara Road.

The turnoff for the Jamesburg Earth Station is plainly marked on the right-hand side of Cachagua Road, 3.5 miles past the Y junction. A large-dish antenna at the AT&T facility stretches a hundred feet across and stands more than ten stories high. This is the major U.S. station for international satellite telecommunications in the Pacific Ocean region. The station operates twenty-four hours a day, seven days a week. Walk-in tours are available. To ensure having a guide call ahead (408/659-2293) anytime. A front lobby shows where the transmitting satellite is in relationship to earth. You can view news broadcasts in the equipment room and see the generator that powers this immense station. A videotape relates how satellites work.

For more hiking, past the Jamesburg Earth Station and a small store turn left at Nason Road. A narrow, rutted road will lead to the San Clemente Dam and backcountry trails.

On Tassajara Road from the Y junction the route is rugged and cut with sharp curves. About 1.5 miles beyond the Y an older home is the site of the Jamesburg refreshment stand and the staging area for Tassajara. For those staying overnight at Tassajara, a four-wheel-drive stage, which costs $30.00, leaves here at 11 a.m. daily during the summer season. The staging area and the Tassajara Zen Center are closed to visitors from September to May. Just past this staging area the paving ends. The final portion of Tassajara Road will climb to the high Chews Ridge and the turnoff for the "MIRA" astronomy station and then drop to the Tassajara Zen Center, as next described. Note that it is best suited for standard transmission and preferably four-wheel-drive vehicles.

Ventana Wilderness Expeditions (408/659-0433), which offers daily two-and three-hour trail rides as well as overnight trail rides into the Ventana Wilderness, is located on Tassajara Road, 6.5 miles from Carmel Valley Road (including three-and-a-half miles of dirt road). It is owned and operated by the Nason family, which has pioneer and Esselen-tribal roots. A recreated Esselen village is opened to visitors and school groups. Trail rides meander by small streams and through oaks and pines to Chews Ridge, the highest peaks of the Santa Lucia mountain range. Incredible views of the Ventana Wilderness, the Monterey Bay, and the valleys greet ridge-top visitors. Reservations are strongly recommended for all rides.

Continue on Tassajara Road to Chews Ridge, which offers an eagle's view of the Carmel and Salinas valleys and, west, over the Los Padres National Forest to the Pacific Ocean. Snow sometimes blankets the ridge in winter, inviting young-sters to try out their sleds. The sign to the left for "MIRA" marks the ten-mile rutted dirt road to the Monterey Institute for Research in Astronomy. It is an observation and research facility, the centerpiece of which is a thirty-six-inch reflecting telescope that weighs six tons. "Stellar evolution is our specialty—T-Tauri stars. That means they are new, only a couple of million years old, like the Pleiades, for example," explains MIRA administrator Tom Logan. Open houses are held throughout summer and fall (408/375-3220).

No water is available at the U.S. Forest Service campgrounds of White Oaks Camp and China Camp located along Tassajara Road. It is beyond China Camp that a standard transmission is suggested. The fourteen-mile trip from Jamesburg to Tassajara Zen Center takes about an hour and fifteen minutes. Full tanks of gas and adequate car cooling systems also are advised.

Seventeen hot mineral springs flow out of the Tassajara mountainside. Tassajara is a monastic community established by the San Francisco Zen Center at the Tassajara hot springs. During the winter it is closed to visitors for intensive Zen training sessions. April is a transition month, with visitors invited to work at the resort in preparation for the summer months. In the summer visitors have the opportunity to stay in rustic cabins and share in Zen instruction and medi-tation. Families and individuals may also share day use of the hot springs, scenic hiking trails, smooth rock water slides, and swimming pool without join-ing the instruction. In 1993 the famous bathhouse and baths were relocated upstream due to danger of rock slides from the surrounding hillside, which was weakened by the earthquake of 1989. The vegetarian meals are offered for overnight guests only, so pack in picnics for day use. Some areas are clothing optional. All visitors should make reservations (415/431-3771).

Back on G-16 (which is also signed Carmel Valley Road and Tularcitos Road) the route leads through forested and grassy meadow areas. The white cattle you might see on the grassland are the Saint Gertrudis breed that is popular locally and not seen in many other places in California.

Hastings Natural History Reservation, a two-thousand-acre living laboratory operated by the University of California at Berkeley's Zoology Museum, lies to the east of G-16, a few miles beyond the Tassajara and Carmel Valley Road intersection. The reservation is an ecological reserve and is opened only to students and groups who are cleared through the university. You may notice that a few of the surrounding hills have dark green patches that persist while neighboring hillsides are dried brown and yellow. By the reintroduction of native grasses that covered the hills here two hundred years ago the Hastings Reserve is working to increase biodiversity, keep the hills greener longer, and provide a grassland that doesn't crowd out sprouting oak trees. Only two percent of the grasses you see on the hillsides of California are native. During the rancho days the cowhide was the "Monterey Dollar." Cattle preferred the native perennial grass and overgrazing led to its demise. Annual grass and weed seed, brought with livestock or bags of barley from Europe, took over. As reported to the *Monterey County Herald* by the Hastings lead researcher, "plots of native grasses seem to attract more native insects, more bees, butterflies, beetles, maybe mice, owls, and hawks—all kinds of things cascade from putting the base of this ecological pyramid back in order."

About seventeen miles south of the Tassajara Road intersection, G16 intersects Arroyo Seco Road. Turn right on Arroyo Seco, which leads past Miller's Resort with private swimming and camping along the Arroyo Seco River (408/674-5795) and, as well, past the day-use area, campground, and office of the Los Padres National Forest Service. Two small lakes here are stocked with bass. The gorge, a favorite swimming area here rimmed with boulders, has been often vandalized by graffiti sprayers in recent years.

To connect with River Road or with Highway 101 continue east on G-16, which is now the eastern stretch of Arroyo Seco Road. After six miles Arroyo Seco Road intersects Elm Avenue, leading to Greenfield and Highway 101. (You can take 101 south for the southern lakes and mission tour, p. 212.) Alternately, you can follow Arroyo Seco / G-17 as it turns left and loops north to Highway 68, which leads west to the Monterey Peninsula and northeast to Salinas and Spreckels. To follow the loop north keep your eyes open for the G-17 markers, as road names change; Arroyo Seco Road veers right to connect with Highway 101 at Soledad. To join River Road, leave Arroyo Seco Road and jog left at Fort Romie Road, which, farther north, becomes River Road. This backroads route parallels Highway 101 and takes nearly the same time as 101 to approach the Monterey Peninsula, but it is much longer on scenery (reverse the Northern Salinas Valley tour, below.

Greenfield is one of the most productive agricultural areas of the Salinas Valley and one of the fastest growing communities in the state. As the Highway 101 population corridor reaches farther and farther south, the pressures faced by farmers to sell their land for development increases. Miles and miles of open land in the Salinas Valley has been protected by the California Williamson Act, an agricultural preservation program, which has given farmland owners incentives for keeping their property in agricultural use. Owners have been eligible for substantial tax breaks in exchange for agreeing not to develop their property. The act has kept farming and ranching in Monterey County feasible.

Known as the "Broccoli Capital," Greenfield gained national fame when locals sent a truckload of broccoli to Washington, D.C., after then-President Bush announced he hated broccoli. The summer broccoli festival features parades and tasty and unusual broccoli dishes such as deep-fried broccoli and broccoli ice cream. Music, entertainment, and arts and crafts booths anchor the festival, which is surrounded by agricultural fields.

The Jekel Vineyards (408/674-5522) winery is located at 40155 Walnut Avenue. Visitors walk under a spreading arbor before entering the farmhouse-style tasting room. An enlarged display poster of the 1993 Presidential Inaugural Luncheon includes selections of Jekel Estate Chardonnay and Cabernet Sauvignon. Jekel Vineyards produces Johannisberg Reisling, Chardonnay, Cabernet Sauvignon, Pinot Blanc, and Pinot Noir. In years of the noble rot, *Botrytis cinerea*, which sweetens grapes, a late harvest dessert wine is offered. Tasting hours are 10 a.m. to 5 p.m. daily.

A proposed aircraft museum may change the face of Greenfield. Charles Nichols, who owns the world's largest private collection of World War II-era aircraft, has chosen land near Greenfield as the site of a museum, theater, and conference center.

THE NORTHERN SALINAS VALLEY TOUR

From Monterey, Highway 68 east, also known as the Monterey Salinas Highway, leads to Salinas and delightful backroads connections that parallel Highway 101 south to Greenfield. The tour begins on Highway 68 at its intersection with Olmsted Road (which leads north to the Monterey Peninsula Airport and south to Jacks Peak; for particulars about the park at Jacks Peak and directions see the Monterey chapter, p. 48). Leaving Olmsted Road behind, as you drive east along Highway 68, longhorn cattle graze on the grassy meadows to your right that weave through oak woodland and chaparral. Just one mile north of Olmsted Road on 68, turn left to visit the Tarpy's Stonehouse. Here Ventana Vineyards Tasting Room offers wine tasting and Tarpy's Roadhouse offers lunches and dinners, hearty American fare with innovative touches. A wall covered with gold and blue ribbons greets visitors at the stone-wall tasting room of Ventana Vineyards (800/237-8846), which deserves special recognition as the most award-winning single vineyard property in the United States.

The Ventana is the first of several tasting rooms and wineries you can visit along this tour. Monterey County has the largest number of acres planted in premium-varietal wine-producing grapes of any county in California. Growers match wine grape varieties to the climate regions and soil types. In Europe, for example, the German Riesling region is relatively cool and the French Bordeaux regions are warmer. Monterey County's cool weather is especially suited for cooler grape varieties such as Riesling, Gewurztraminer, Pinot Noir, and Chardonnay. Cabernet Sauvignon, Cabernet Franc, and Merlot thrive in the warmer areas south of Soledad and on alluvial fans west of Soledad. Gourmet Food and Wine Tours of Monterey Bay (408/655-TOUR) specializes in winery and agricultural tours of the Salinas Valley.

In February some forty brightly colored hot-air balloons race across the rolling hills along Highway 68 about three miles east of Tarpy's Stonehouse at Laguna Seca Recreation Area, in the annual "Hot Air Affair." To see the balloons fill and rise in the air for the "Hare and Hounds" competition, festival goers get to the recreation area by 6 a.m. on a Saturday and Sunday. Late arrivals driving on Highway 68 are treated to large flying balloons gliding over the gentle hills. The forty or so competing balloons (hounds) chase after one designated balloonist (the hare), who rises early and sets the course for the race. The hare lands and marks the final target with a large X. Since balloonists can't outright steer their craft they depend in the chase on the winds and on their own skills in maneuvering the balloons. When the hounds find the X they drop weighted bags. Points are awarded for the accuracy of the hit and then averaged over the two days' chases. Balloon rides, helicopter rides, and parachuting exhibitions are part of the days' festivities. A Saturday pancake breakfast, Sunday champagne brunch, crafts booths, food booths, and kiddie attractions add to the weekend. Early risers bring picnics and thermos bottles filled with warm coffee. The day usually warms up and shirt-sleeves replace jackets (408/649-6544).

Laguna Seca is most famous for its many auto racing and motorcycle racing events, and recently famous also for in-line skating and mountain bike racing. The Grand Prix of classic car races comes to Laguna Seca in mid August. These prestigious races feature two-hundred varieties of classic cars, including Maseratis and Ferraris. In October you'll see Mario Andretti, Nigel Mansell, and other top names in racing compete in the PPG Indy Cars World Series. A good spot from which to view the races is the top of the hill looking down at the racecourse. The famous corkscrew section also is an exciting view, from the other side of the hill. (For information and tickets to auto and motorcycle races call 800/327-SECA.)

In March quieter but highly competitive groups of racers whizz down the hill and around the curves. In-line skaters, road racers, and mountain bikers compete in separate events at Laguna Seca at the Sea Otter Classics. (For information, call 415/367-7797.)

Just beyond Laguna Seca, Highway 68 intersects Laureles Grade, which is a scenic fifteen- to twenty-minute drive over the rolling Santa Lucias to mid Carmel Valley Road. At the summit of Laureles Grade Road, views extend over Carmel Valley to the ocean. If the time and weather are opportune, the fog rolling in from the ocean can be caught in sunlit shimmers in the valley.

About two miles past the Laureles Grade intersection a gas station and mini-mart mark the Corral de Tierra intersection on Highway 68. George Vancouver, the English naval captain who explored the Pacific Coast in the period 1792 to 1794, viewed a fascinating sandstone formation in the area of what is now known as Corral de Tierra Road. "I was . . . there gratified with the sight of the most extraordinary mountain I had ever beheld....The whole summit of the mountain appeared to be wholly supported by these columns rising perpendicularly with the most minute mathematical exactness." This sandstone formation, known as The Castle, is located on the private lands of the Markham Ranch and looks like a sand sculpture more reminiscent of Utah or Arizona. You can view it, at a distance, from Corral de Tierra Road by looking to your left when you are 1.3 miles past the intersection. For viewing, a pull-out to accommodate two or three cars is located just before the road enters the oak groves. People who have hiked to The Castle claim it is more memorable from the road than from close range. The Castle, or "Castle Rock," as Steinbeck called it, is featured in the beginning of his short story "The Murder." Beyond the view of The Castle, Corral de Tierra Road enters the canopy of a towering oak grove. Although the buildings were located elsewhere, the setting of Steinbeck's *The Red Pony* depicts the Corral de Tierra area. Roads throughout the area are laden with curves and dotted with small ranches.

Blanchard's Wood Sculptures is located .8 mile up Highway 68 from the Corral de Tierra Road intersection. Mammoth bears, redwood seals, and an old prospector with a hopeful face are among the forty wood sculptures that surround Steve Blanchard as he carves the chainsaw masterpieces. His art is deafening but he'll take off the earmuffs and talk awhile. "When you're writing a story you have a general idea of what you're going to say but you don't know the exact words you'll be using. It's the same with carving. I can see the statue in the wood, then as I get going I cut here and cut there. It evolves." Most of his huge statues won't fit in your trunk, but he'll ship them to you (408/484-9963). Toro Place Restaurant is located next door. This local favorite serves ample and tasty country breakfasts and lunches (408/484-1333).

The entrance to Toro Regional Park is on Highway 68, about four miles north of Laureles Grade, which places it thirteen miles from Monterey and six miles from Salinas. This 4,700-acre park includes a nature center, picnic grounds, playgrounds, and miles of walking and horseback riding trails that wind through the wooded hillsides.

After Highway 68 becomes a divided road the first exit leads to River Road, which is the bucolic alternative to Highway 101. To take it south, skip to page 210. To visit Spreckels and Salinas continue on Highway 68.

SPRECKELS AND SALINAS. Spreckels Boulevard, which intersects Highway 68 just beyond River Road, leads south into the town. Just as you enter Spreckels a canopy of white-trunked black-walnut trees extends over the road. After Claus Spreckels was expelled from the sugar fields in Hawaii by its king and his supporters, in 1886, he started a sugar beet factory in Watsonville. When the focus of sugar beet planting moved to the Salinas Valley, "King Sugar" Spreckels chose it as the location for the largest sugar factory in the United States. This factory town grew nearby. After shutting down in 1982 the factory was laid waste by the wrecking ball, but the sugar storage bins, a warehouse, and the company town remain as if frozen in the past. Parking is easy on the block-long downtown section of Spreckels Boulevard. The successful new figure around the area is Billy Broccoflower, a muscular green superhero with a head of broccoflower, the combination of broccoli and cauliflower that offers more vitamins then either. He entertains at local festivals and around schools, inspiring people to eat five vegetable servings a day. His namesake seed was developed at Tanimura and Antle (T&A), one of California's largest growers and shippers of vegetables. The corporate headquarters are set in a palm-tree-covered oasis just outside of town.

Back on Highway 68 your ride to Salinas may be punctuated by motorists in a hurry. This is a major commute route. The hurrying along this route isn't new. Back in the mid 1800s stagecoaches rushed to a tavern on land that would become Salinas. Elias Howe owned the tavern, which was at the intersection of the routes for stages from Monterey to San Juan Bautista and from San Francisco to Los Angeles, and he placed bets on which ones would arrive there first. Business prospered so much that the neighboring stop, at Natividad, had to shut down.

Today Salinas is the population center, the industrial hub, and the governmental center of Monterey County. As is the case in many growing cities Salinas faces crime problems. These tour areas are in parts of the city commonly visited.

As you drive into Salinas, Highway 68 becomes South Main Street. A walking tour of the 100 block of Main Street shows many refurbished old town buildings, dating from the 1890s through the 1930s. The Steinbeck Center Foundation is temporarily located in the historic Forrester Building at 371 Main Street. Displays include some of Steinbeck's handwritten letters and sections of manuscripts, boyhood photos, and books. Film posters and copies of etchings and drawings by Monterey artist Bruce Ariss, who was a friend of the writer, decorate the walls.

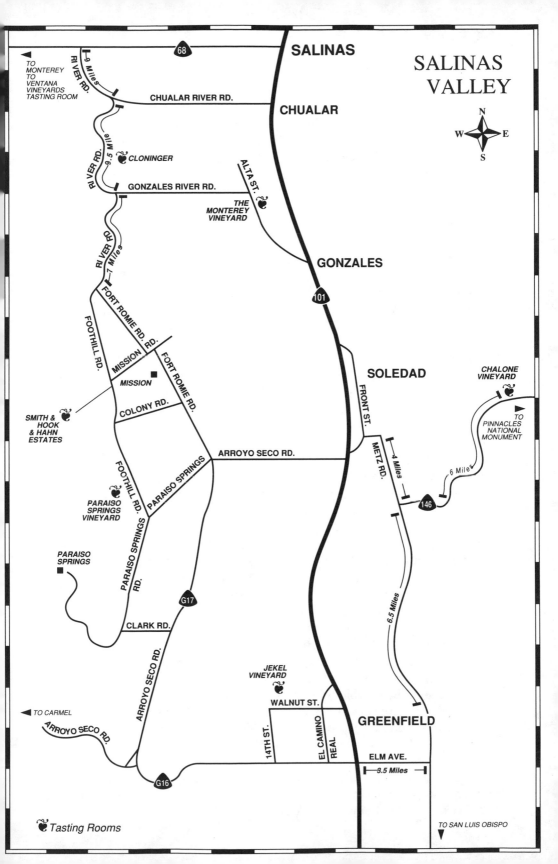

Visitors can view a model of the future Steinbeck Center to be built on the 100 block of Main Street. The present center is open 9 a.m. to 5 p.m. weekdays, with extended days in summer. Several Steinbeck events are coordinated throughout the year from the Steinbeck Center Foundation office. During the first two weeks of August the town honors Nobel-and Pulitzer prize–winning author John Steinbeck during the annual Steinbeck Festival. Each year one of Steinbeck's books is the focus for events, which include plays, films, barbecues, walking tours, and special lectures. The main location for events is the Salinas Community Center, by the rodeo grounds. Festival highlights include bus tours to private locales that played parts in Steinbeck's life and books. For information about Steinbeck and events call the Steinbeck Center Foundation (408/753-6411).

Turning left from Main on West Alisal leads to the courthouse, the oldest section of which dates to the mid 1930s. Joe Mora's sculpted heads of the pioneers of Monterey County history watch modern events from the outer walls and inside the courtyard.

From the courthouse turn right on Church Street to Central Avenue. The stately Victorian at 132 Central was John Steinbeck's family home and contains family photos, memorabilia, and Victorian furnishings. The restored home was rescued by the nonprofit Valley Guild, which bought it when the diocese of Monterey put it up for sale in 1972. The home is open weekdays, when the volunteers staff a luncheon tea room and book and memorabilia store. Gourmet weekday lunches that feature produce fresh from the local fields and local wines are served in the original living room, parlor, and dining room. The room Steinbeck was born in, his bedroom until his sister was born, is the reception area of the house. Reservations are necessary for lunch or for group tours of the house (408/424-2735).

Follow Church Street south to 110 West San Luis Street. A nearly lifesize statue of the author stands in front of the John Steinbeck Library. In addition to serving as the city's main public library the building houses over thirty thousand Steinbeck items: manuscripts, letters, autographed first editions, gallery proofs, posters, photographs of Steinbeck, and more. Research facilities are available for scholars and others who want to learn more about this native son.

The Boronda Adobe, a new cultural museum under construction, and the beginnings of a "Street of History Museum" are reached by driving west on Central with a right turn on Davis, following well-marked signs. The Boronda Adobe was built by Eusebio Boronda, son of the Borondas who were the first permanent rancheros in Carmel Valley, and it is the oldest structure at the site. Partially furnished as it was in the mid 1800s, the adobe also includes the genealogy of the Boronda family and early photographs.

Nearby is the original red one-room Lagunitas Schoolhouse, moved here from San Juan Grade Road. Rows of old wooden desks and old maps greet twentieth-century visitors inside this 1896 schoolhouse, which was made famous in Steinbeck's *The Red Pony*. An old Victorian home designed by William Weeks is being restored on the property and will feature furnishings of 1898. A new twelve-thousand-square-foot cultural museum will feature a panorama of the various cultures that have contributed to Monterey County. For information on when the buildings are open call the Monterey County Historical Society (408/757-8083).

The Bellas Artes del Valle, highlighted by the Festival de Mariachi de Alta California, presents Hispanic arts of the area each April. Lively Mariachi bands from throughout California, the Southwest, and Mexico fill the Western Stage at Hartnell College with music and colorful folkloric vestments. Mariachi bands hail from the Mexican cowboy and rodeo tradition. Band members wear velvet sombreros, black or colored pants with intricate designs, and beautifully embroidered shirts. Also typical are spurs, gunbelts, and colorful neckerchiefs. Mariachi music swells from a multitude of stringed instruments, including the vihuela (a five-string acoustic instrument) and the guitarron (a double-string bass guitar), other guitars, and harps, violins, trumpets, and an occasional accordion. Folkloric dancers, art shows, movies, ethnic foods, and lectures round out the two-week festival (408/755-6980).

Steinbeck used to be a controversial figure in Salinas, as his descriptions of the agricultural fields often were raw and they exposed wretched conditions. Now another major event in Salinas—the California Rodeo, usually held the third week in July—provokes a different kind of showdown in the new West. The event brings to town opposing forces in the best of the rodeo stars from throughout the Western United States and the most concerned of the animal rights activists. The cowboys and cowgirls and adoring fans are definitely in the majority, with tickets for seating at the rodeo necessary in advance of events. Standing room only is available at events for which ticket sales are not closed.

Everyone seems to love the preparation and camaraderie. For two weeks prior to the event in the shopping centers throughout Salinas, windows are painted with Western scenes, store clerks wear Western clothes, and even the models in a local fashion show ride horseback. Parades and barbecues add to the festivities. The rodeo grounds are located at Sherwood Park, a ninety-nine-acre recreational facility on North Main Street.

In addition to the rodeo in July, concerts are held at Sherwood Park throughout the year. In May monster trucks race around the track at the rodeo grounds. Not to be missed at Sherwood Park are three gigantic hat sculptures by Klaes Oldenburg.

Hats, trucks, and anything else you need can probably be found in the major shopping centers along Highway 101 at Northridge and Harden Ranch. Major department stores as well as local shops populate the malls here. For specialty shopping you might want to take the John Street exit off Highway 101 (north or south) and turn left at Work Street to visit the Dinnerware Outlet (408/422-4962) of Franmara, Inc. It claims to be the only factory in the United States that designs porcelain with "in-glaze" techniques practiced in Europe. The company imports hard paste (high-fired) Pillivuyt French culinary and Czech Spirito porcelains, and artisans decorate them according to individual or business requests, then fire them in a Limoges-type kiln. Tours are given depending on the production schedule or can be arranged by Gourmet Food and Wine Tours of Monterey Bay.

RIVER ROAD. If you turned south from Highway 68 onto River Road before reaching Highway 101 and Salinas, continue south. For the next twenty-three miles River Road winds through acres and acres of rows and rows of lettuce, stumpy broccoli bushes, carrots, celery, asparagus fronds—just about anything you need for a soup or salad. Roll down your windows for a mixture of vegetable fragrances forgotten by city dwellers. Weathered redwood barns, horse ranches and turning wooden windmills dot the landscape. Depending on the season, a wide slow-moving track of water or the swirled dry weeds of the Salinas River bed drift in and out of view. Farther south rows of vineyards stretch along the road and many wineries open their doors for wine tastings and tours. You may also have miles of views of slow-moving farm equipment, if you get behind a tractor or truck loaded with harvest. They usually don't pull over; this is their road. Approach curves with the understanding that tons of tomatoes may weigh down a truck just around the bend, since you don't want to be smashed into sauce. Cars and trucks also pull out of blind driveways.

In your south-facing view the Santa Lucia and Gabilan mountains seem to merge at the point of a V. In reality the ranges never meet. I love to follow this changing illusion while driving River Road.

About nine miles south of the Highway 68 intersection River Road merges with Chualar River Road to cross the Salinas river over the Chualar River bridge and eventually connect with Highway 101. Before merging and crossing the bridge, veer right to continue on River Road. Limekiln Road intersects River Road three miles south of Chualar River Road. Barlocker's Rustling Oaks Ranch (408/675-9121) at 25252 Limekiln Road offers trail rides to the Santa Lucia ridge. One last limekiln can be sighted from the ranch, kids can pet animals at farm pens, and picnics can be enjoyed on the grass under spreading oaks. Weekend horse camps for kids here offer options for parents who want to enjoy adult wine-tasting excursions. For even the adult weekend cowhand, the owners will teach cattle cutting and other ranch skills.

A few miles farther on River Road the first acres of grapevines spread their arms along the roadside. At 1645 River Road a sign on the left-hand side of the road will direct you to the Cloninger Cellar Winery (408/675-WINE), located in the buildings of an old dairy farm and a newly constructed farmhouse tasting room. Call in advance for hours of tours and tastings especially of Chardonnay, Cabernet, and Pinot Noir wines.

Splintering off River Road, Gonzales River Road leads to the town of Gonzales, where you can tour the Monterey Vineyards (408/675-2316) set in nouveau mission-style facilities at 800 South Alta Street. Through the lens of Ansel Adams a man ploughing vineyards behind a draft horse and a woman carefully examining a bunch of grapes for hand cutting bring the human saga of the vineyards to the guests of the Monterey Vineyards Gallery. The one-of-a-kind exhibit entitled Story of a Winery is a collection of photographs about the vineyards and the wine process commissioned in the 1950s. Tours of the winemaking process from crush to final bottling are offered at 11 a.m., 1 p.m., and 3 p.m. daily. The tasting room is open from 10:00 a.m. to 5:00 p.m.

Back on River Road, seven miles south of the Gonzales River Road intersection, you will come to a fork in the road. At this point River Road becomes Fort Romie Road, the left fork. If you are on a wine-tasting excursion, take the right fork Foothill Road, to Smith & Hook winery, which is known for its Cabernet Sauvignon. To reach the tasting room you will drive for 1.5 miles along a dirt road within arm's reach of Cabernet Sauvignon grapevines interspersed with chaparral. Fog may cover the trellised vines at the base of the road while sun warms those on the higher alluvial slopes. Variances in amounts of sun exposure affect the flavor of the harvest and also the choice of bottling. The sweeter, sun-drenched grapes strengthen the heavier Smith & Hook wines, which are made for longer aging, and the lighter-flavored grapes blend well with the softer Hahn Estate wines that are bottled at the same winery. The winery is set on an alluvial fan overlooking the site where the first vineyards were planted for the Soledad Mission in the 1770s. The gravel-laden soil of the sedimentary slopes make this prime grape-growing country. A four-hundred-twenty-gallon redwood barrel, which was used by the Almaden winery as an aging barrel, now serves as a tasting room. Picnics under the oaks or on the decks of the meeting room treat visitors to grand vistas of the Salinas Valley. Views from a nearby lookout are worth the hike. Estate-bottled Cabernet Sauvignon, Merlot, and Hahn Estate tastings are offered. Wine can be tasted daily from 10 a.m. until 4 p.m.; tours are by appointment only (408/678-2132).

You won't find an actual fort on Fort Romie Road. In the depression of the 1890s the Salvation Army in collaboration with other groups set up a moderately successful colony or, utilizing the military terms of the Salvation Army, "a fort" of unemployed workers and their families here. Several of the farmers in the area are their descendants. At a little over a mile up Fort Romie Road you can take a right turn for a side trip to Mission Soledad. The mission was built as the thirteenth member of the chain, in 1791, and has not received the facelifts and complete restorations of others in the area. Crumbling ruins of the old mission lie beside a restored chapel and museum of mission and ranch artifacts. In July and September lively barbecues and fiestas fill the mission grounds (408/678-2386). For the rest of the year the mission is quiet; a stroll through the patio rose garden and a picnic on benches invite quiet reflection on the past.

Fort Romie Road next intersects with Arroyo Seco Road. You can turn left at this intersection for a two-mile side trip to Soledad, one gateway to the Pinnacles National Monument. Soledad has roots as an Italian-Swiss dairy community and currently, with an approximately 85 percent Hispanic population, is the first community in Monterey County to have an all-Hispanic City Council. Several taquerias here sell piñatas and household items along with handmade tortillas. You will feel comfortable speaking either English or Spanish.

Radio stations in the valley mirror the shift of ranch land to vineyards. Although a poll of valley residents showed a strong preference for country and western music, Soledad's KQKE FM, 99.9 —"The Quake"—country Western music station converted to classical music in 1993.

If you turn right at the Arroyo Seco intersection you can travel six miles to Paraiso Hot Springs Resort. You will first intersect with Foothill Road. Across from the fork, a road leads up the alluvial fan to the family-owned Paraiso Springs Vineyard (408/678-0300), which offers Chardonnay, Pinot Noir, Pinot Blanc, and Johannisberg Reisling. The spacious tasting room, gift shop, and entertainment facilities open to a deck with sweeping views of the valley, across to the Gabilans and rugged outlines of the Pinnacles.

Paraiso Springs Road cuts through open fields to the foothills of the Santa Lucia Mountains. Palm trees sway over the green lawns surrounding two pools and the Victorian cottages that once served turn-of-the-century guests at Paraiso Springs Resort (408/678-2882). The Victorians are now long-term rentals, and overnight guests stay at a campground or at small, rustic cabins on the hillside. The day-use fee for the heated mineral pools and older enclosed paint-peeled hot pool room is $10.00 per person. Guests I spoke with chose this retreat for the mineral pools and to get away from urban life. Overnight guests and drivers who just drop in for a sandwich and refreshing drink can enjoy the panoramic view from the dining area, and also the early-times news articles and pictures posted in the lodge.

Beyond the intersection with Paraiso Springs Road, Fort Romie Road continues as Arroyo Seco Road. The Highway 101 connection at Soledad offers a more direct route to Greenfield. If you continue on Arroyo Seco Road south, turn left at Elm Avenue (G-16), which leads to Greenfield and Highway 101.

THE SOUTHERN LAKES AND SAN ANTONIO MISSION TOUR

The area south of Greenfield is vintage California. Eagles soar above their nests at Lake San Antonio, over the remnants of an old stage stop at Jolon and near the remote San Antonio Mission. Reach Greenfield by traveling south either on Highway 101 or on the Highway 68 and River Road route, or take the longer Carmel Valley Road route. Before King City exit the freeway at Jolon Road to travel directly to Jolon, the lakes, or Mission San Antonio. Sometimes sections of the military reservation in this area are closed due to training maneuvers (though Jolon Road, G-14, is not affected by the closures). Remember to call Fort Hunter Liggett Military Range Control (408/385-2503) if you plan to travel the Nacimiento-Fergusson Road (which connects to Big Sur) or to fish in the reservation reservoirs. Also call if you plan to visit the Salinan Painted Cave; in 1993, due to vandalism problems, it became necessary to arrange for a guide to accompany visits. Advance phone notice is imperative, and access is not always permitted, unless you arrange for an archaeologist who has been approved by the military.

King City is about ten miles south of Greenfield. To visit the Monterey County Agricultural and Rural Life Museum in the southern Salinas Valley marketing hub of King City, before picking up Jolon Road take the Broadway / King City exit from Highway 101, turn right, and follow the signs to San Lorenzo Regional Park.

KING CITY. Central King City is forty-five miles south of Salinas and about one mile south of the G-14 or Jolon Road exit from Highway 101. A fertile valley surrounds San Lorenzo Regional Park, where several buildings at the Monterey County Agricultural and Rural Life Museum bring the old Salinas Valley to present-day visitors. A barn structure displays the parade of inhabitants in the valley from Salinan times, through the early mission settlers, the pioneer farmers, and those of recent times. Mortars and pestles, horse-drawn plows and reapers, hand-operated drills, hand-cranked household appliances, and wine-making tools are displayed against backdrops of their eras. In the main barn a tourism center provides comprehensive information about all areas of Monterey County. The latest museum under construction explores what may be the number one issue in Monterey County today, water supply and irrigation. Through past overuse, water tables have dropped, allowing saltwater intrusion into the most northern Salinas Valley. This intrusion has resulted in strict water monitoring of farmers and strong disagreements at county supervisors' meetings.

The museum barn is open year-round seven days a week, from 10 a.m. to 5 p.m. The other buildings are open from April to November, Saturdays and Sundays, 1 p.m. to 4 p.m. As they are staffed by volunteers not all buildings are open every weekend; call for museum information (408/385-1484). RV and tent camping is available through the Monterey County Parks Department (408/755-4899).

WEST TO JOLON. To proceed with the southern extension tour, once you have exited Highway 101 at Jolon Road (G-14), follow it to the settlement of Jolon. At Jolon, as described below, you can either continue via Mission Road, which leads north to the Fort Hunter Liggett entrance gate, Mission San Antonio, the

Salinan Cave, and the Nacimiento-Fergusson Road cut-over to Big Sur, or you can continue on Jolon Road, south, which leads to Lakes San Antonio and Nacimiento.

Acres of flat farmland that extend to gentle hills covered with rows of grapes, isolated collections of farm buildings, and old corrals frame the beginning miles of Jolon Road. Oil wells and modern metallic windmills dot the midsection before it winds along rugged slopes of oak forests interspersed with chaparral. Then the road heads straight through a thick forest of ancient California oaks. Majestic valley oaks and blue oaks, many over two hundred years old, tower and weep. The blue oak is the most familiar variety in this area. Viewed from a distance it has a bluish cast, thus the name.

At close range the acorns of the blue oak can be recognized as shorter and fatter than those of the valley oak. Of all the deciduous oaks, the tribal inhabitants of California picked the valley oak as their first choice for acorns, the one main food source that the Salinans, Yokuts, Esselen, and other tribes could depend upon. Acorns were also a highly traded item among tribes, as different acorns were utilized for their different tastes. A single family might gather as many as five hundred pounds for a year's supply. The acorns needed to be dried, then peeled and pounded. Since they contain bitter tannic acid they were also leached until the brown juice from them ran clear. Bedrock mortars in the Lake San Antonio area and around the Salinan Cave remain as the remnants of this laborious process.

The miles of oaks resemble panoramas of oaks in the South that are covered with Spanish moss. The long grayish green tassels hanging from the trees are actually lichens called granny's nets. Salinan mothers used lichens for a type of baby diaper, as they are soft and absorbent.

About seventeen miles inland from Highway 101 old structures from the village of Jolon and a thriving general store hug the curve of the road. Originally called Holamma or "Valley of the Dead Oaks" by Salinans who settled the area, Jolon was first visited by the Spanish when Gaspar de Portola trudged through the area in 1769 on an expedition to find Monterey Bay.

Prospectors traveling the Santa Fe Trail in search of gold following its 1848 discovery in California passed through the present town of Jolon on their way to Pacheco Pass. To provide a place for them to eat and rest Antonio Ramirez built a small adobe inn, the ruins of which are located on the right side of Jolon Road just before you enter the town. Later the inn became an important stage stop on the Camino Real, the main route between San Francisco and Los Angeles.

In 1871 the inn property was purchased by Lt. George Dutton and Capt. Thomas Tidball of the U.S. Cavalry. They ran the inn as a Post Office, saloon, and stage stop. Tidball later moved down the road to establish his own hotel and store. Placer mining brought settlers to the area in the 1870s. The ranch-lands around the town were eventually acquired by William Randolph Hearst. Today ruins of the hotel are sheltered from devastation by a wooden roof, and the Hearst property is part of Hunter Liggett Fort.

Near the entrance to Jolon the Tidball store remains in well preserved condition. Across the road the quaint 1884 Saint Luke's Episcopal Church, built in Prairie Gothic style, holds regular services. Early Jolon settlers are buried in the old cemetery behind the church.

To continue to the San Antonio Mission, Salinan Painted Cave, and Nacimiento-Fergusson Road, turn right on Mission Road. Shortly after, stop at the access gate staffed by the Fort Hunter Liggett military police. Mission San Antonio de Padua is 4.5 miles farther on Mission Road. The officers at the gate will give you directions to the Salinan Painted Cave only if you have made prior reservations for an escort.

THE SALINAN PAINTED CAVE. The cave is located at the top of the eastern foothills of the San Antonio River Valley. The painted cave is about twenty feet long and thirty feet wide. Some of the pictographs on the walls resemble humans and others are geometric: circles, lines, and crosses. The crosses are a focal point, as they are arranged at angles and have circles at different points. It is not known whether the inhabitants of various Salinan villages in the area used the caves for hunting maneuvers, for shelter, or for religious or spiritual ceremonies. The pictographs may also have been recreated by the Salinan people from drawings left by a more prehistoric people. The red in the pictographs is from the iron oxide rock hematite. The white could be from limonite or gypsum. The black is from charcoal or manganese ore. The roofs of the caves are blackened with the soot of many fires.

Some descendants of the tribe remain, but the tribe itself is considered ethnologically extinct. The Spanish explorers and missionaries noted this to be a peaceful tribe that had no history of war but would partake in long discussions to end differences. The simplicity of their lifestyle served the tribespeople for over a hundred generations, but it could not compete with the strange diseases and the treatment they received from Spanish, Mexican, and American settlers on the land.

MISSION SAN ANTONIO DE PADUA. Local tradition has it that the original site of the 1771 San Antonio Mission, the third in the string of missions founded by Father Serra, is at or near the old military cemetery by the Nacimiento-Fergusson Road and Jolon Road intersection. By 1773 the mission complex had been moved to the confluence of the San Miguel and San Antonio rivers. The mission was named for the Franciscan Saint Anthony. After the secularization period the mission deteriorated; it was near ruins by 1949, when the Hearst Foundation funded a restoration directed by Harry Downie, who had restored the Carmel

Mission. The inside walls and the front facade of the church are part of the original building. The museum is the old *convento* with many artifacts of mission life. The mission's original eighteenth-century wine press sits under walls decorated with Spanish paintings from the eighteenth and nineteenth centuries. A painted "guidonian hand," a mnemonic device for the musical instruction of the Salinan choirs, covers one wall. Artifacts of the Chumas nation, those of the first inhabitants of areas to the south, and of the Salinan are displayed in an entrance room, as is an extensive collection and description of native plants and their uses. Frescos of the old mission and ecclesiastical items decorate the inside of the church, where a statue of Saint Anthony that dates back to the mission's beginning stands behind the altar. A mural on one of the outside walls honors the site of the first marriage in California.

Mission San Antonio is isolated from population centers and is off the usual tourist routes. The walk to the old grist mill is so quiet grasshoppers can be heard flittering in the wild oats along the dirt path. The Franciscan friars who live at the mission are friendly. The grounds, church, and museum (408/385-4478) are open daily from 9 a.m. to 4:30 p.m.

The newish barracks of the U.S. Army across the road are juxtaposed between the mission and quiet isolated grasslands. The most memorable of the military's buildings is white, in Spanish style—designed by Julia Morgan, architect of the Hearst Castle at San Simeon. This was William Hearst's hunting lodge.

Retrace your way back three-quarters of a mile from the mission to the intersection of Mission Road and the Nacimiento-Fergusson Road. Along the way you'll pass the the road to Santa Lucia Memorial Park, which is located about twelve miles north in the Los Padres National Forest. Eight primitive campsites are available to tent campers and RV users.

Nacimiento-Fergusson Road is an extremely curvy road that connects the Salinas Valley with Big Sur. Los Padres National Forest Campgrounds at Ponderosa and Nacimiento Creekside, situated next to a pleasant creek on the inland lower elevations of the road, are worth a side trip, but I do not recommend the entire trip along the narrow road.

If you do continue, the Los Padres National Forest ranger facility, near the summit on Nacimiento-Fergusson Road, offers information, maps, camping permits, registration for wilderness backpacking, restrooms, and water. Just past the summit, Cone Peak Road, an ungraded mountainous road, leads north and upward from Nacimiento-Fergusson Road seven miles to the Cone Peak Lookout, which offers a commanding view of the ocean and the Santa Lucia Mountains. Cone Peak Road is often closed to vehicular traffic due to fire danger. Nacimiento-Fergusson Road intersects Highway 1 at Kirk Creek, three miles south of the Limekiln Creek Campgrounds on the Big Sur tour (p. 174).

LAKE SAN ANTONIO AND LAKE NACIMIENTO. Both lakes are set back from dams and serve as reservoirs for county water. The blue waters of Lake Nacimiento contrast with its surrounding verdant pine-covered mountains. Lake San Antonio is situated in a vale of rolling hills, studded with oaks and some pine.

Back at Jolon, arriving from Highway 101 or backtracking from Mission San Antonio, turn south on Jolon Road (G-14) to continue to both lakes. First, to reach the south shore of Lake San Antonio, turn south (right) at the intersection of Jolon road with Lockwood Jolon Road. This road becomes Interlake Road (G-14). Pass the turnoff to the old Pleyto Cemetery Road and continue to the south shore for the nature center, ranger office, a self-guided nature walk, eagle tours, camping, mobile home (cabin) rentals, the Spring Wildflower Festival, and a large marina with store and playground.

The northern end of Lake San Antonio, which offers scenic camping, ranger information, and a second marina, is not always open. To reach the northern section of the lake from the intersection of Jolon Road and Lockwood Jolon Road, continue east on Jolon Road (now G-18). Turn right at New Pleyto Road.

In spring the hills are awash in delicate and vibrant wildflowers. Bountiful lupines, wild lilac, and chamise set the hills ablaze with color from March to mid May. When the fleeting wildflowers have gone, spring has turned to summer.

A nature center at the lake offers a look at wildlife of the area and offers written guides and maps, local artwork, and historical displays. One display includes information about Pleyto, an abandoned homesteader's town now covered by the reservoir. By some accounts the name "Pleyto" was derived from the Spanish word for "lawsuit." The Spanish who observed the Salinans in this area engage in intensive conversations to settle disputes referred to the place as "Pleito." The Pleyto cemetery was moved to a knoll off Cemetery Road before the lake was filled.

At the lake, a marina rents motorboats and pontoon boats primarily for fishing. Groceries, sundries, and prepared food are available. A population of America's most famous symbol, the bald eagle, winters at Lake San Antonio, one of the largest eagle winter habitats in Central California. Beginning around the middle of December hundreds of eagles fly south from Alaska, Canada, and Oregon to winter at warmer inland water locations. Two types of eagles nest at San Antonio. The bald eagle, so named because from a distance its white head feathers make it look bald, constructs enormous nests, some weighing a thousand pounds, in the tall trees around the lake. The regal birds feed on carrion, waterfowl, and fish. Viewers sometimes see the large birds plunge down and grab a fish from the placid waters. Golden eagles, dark brown with a pale golden neck, also nest at the lake. The birds soar above and sweep down to catch rabbits, squirrels, and other small ground animals.

A sixty-person tour boat glides over the quiet waters of Lake San Antonio, close to the nesting sites of the eagles. Eagles often hover above the boat. Tours are held on Fridays and often tandem tours are held on weekends from the December arrival through March, when most of the eagles leave to nest in northern locations. (Some of the golden eagles stay to nest along the Big Sur Coast.) On Sundays there's an added morning brunch tour. Enjoy French toast, sausages, and hot chocolate as eagles nab the catch of the day around you. Tours last about two hours and depart on time, rain or shine. A slide lecture, half an hour before the boat sails, offers an overview of the eagles, their migratory patterns, their habitat, and the causes for their threatened status on the endangered species list.

The eagle's success at Lake San Antonio is a tribute to its clean waters and safe environment. The eagle has been on the endangered species list for several decades mainly due to pesticides that enter the its system when it feeds on fish in polluted waters. The toxic substances in the pesticides interfere with the bird's calcium metabolism, causing its eggs to be thin shelled and often infertile.

Each year the number of eagles that winter at Lake San Antonio increases. At the same time more and more people are discovering the tours. Early reservations, through the Monterey County Parks Department, are advised (408/755-4899).

National and International premier triathletes swim, run, and mountain bike at the annual Wildflower Triathlons and Festival, held at the beginning of May. One of the triathlon events is designed for novice and beginner triathletes, from eleven years old to eighty-plus, who swim a quarter mile, hike ten miles, and run two miles, just for the thrill of it. Long Course triathletes here are qualifiers for national collegiate championships and international events. When you're not watching the tests of the iron-muscled people, take part in the festival; it offers music, entertainment, sports-expo exhibits, regional foods, photography competitions, and arts and crafts booths. Through it all the wildflowers reign supreme. This is often touted as the best wildflower show in the western United States (408/755-4899).

Whether you drive, bike, or run along Interlake Road, it connects you with Lake Nacimiento, 12 miles south of Lake San Antonio. After the final turn of rolling grasslands and chaparral you cross the Nacimiento Dam. Towering digger pine forests of the southern Santa Lucia range frame the glassy blue dragon-shaped lake-of-many-inlets below you. The verdant digger-pine forests that surround Lake Nacimiento are a contrast to the summer-tanned rolling hills and woodland of Lake San Antonio. Nacimiento is 16 miles long and offers 165 miles of coves and inlets to explore from rented boats. In the winter the waters near the stream inlets at the western reaches of the lake run clear. Golden eagles soar overhead, and fish fill the buckets of line casters.

Ski boats and fishing boats are rented at the marina. In the summer the main section of the lake is filled with zooming power boats. In autumn through spring, especially mid week, four hours on a pontoon boat makes for a restful afternoon and allows time to explore the lake and catch a stringful. The resort staff are very helpful to beginners and the fish are plentiful, to the smiles of little ones and ageless kids. As at Lake San Antonio the crappie is the popular favorite among eating fish. Nacimiento is the only lake in California stocked with the line-thrilling white bass. The white bass is the center of a controversy because it creates problems for trout if stocked in the same areas—and white-bass lovers sometimes sneak live white bass out of the lake to plant at other fishing holes. Because of this practice the white-bass experiment at Lake Nacimiento is being monitored.

Lake Nacimiento's open, grassy-knoll campsites (for tents to RVs) are full California service, with a nearby country store, restaurant in the summer months, playground, picnic areas, pool, and hot tubs—now that's roughing it. Summer is very crowded at Lake Nacimiento, as it is a favorite getaway from Los Angeles. Make reservations early (805/238-3256). Winter at the lake is peaceful. The rental townhomes overlooking the lake and forest catch beautiful sunsets and little noise.

DIRECTIONS

◆

To return to Highway 101 north, from the stop sign at the Lake Nacimiento Dam turn left, across the dam, and stay on the highway (G-19) for fifteen miles to the 101 junction at Bradley.

To return to Highway 101 south, from the stop sign at the Lake Nacimiento Dam turn right. Stay on the highway (G-14), following signs to Paso Robles. It is approximately seventeen miles to the 101 junction.

For Cambria, San Simeon, and the southern Big Sur Coast follow the directions above to Highway 101 south, and travel south on it for two miles. Take the exit for Highway 46 west (also marked Hearst Castle) and follow the signs to the coast (and Hearst Castle), about fifty miles.

WHAT ELSE TO SEE AND DO

THE PINNACLES NATIONAL MONUMENT. Take Highway 101 to Soledad, exit on Route 146, and drive eleven miles to West Pinnacles and the Chaparral Visitor's Center. Along the way you can visit the Chalone vineyard, the oldest winery in Monterey County (408/678-1717). Two different routes lead to separate sides of the Pinnacles National Monument. You can hike between the two sides but not drive. East Pinnacles is located south of Hollister via Route 25.

This craggy, rugged area is a spectacular but incomplete formation of volcanic rhyolite that thrusts through the nonvolcanic Gabilan Mountains. The peaks and underlying caves are the remnant of an ancient volcano fifteen miles long, five miles across, and eight thousand feet high that spewed lava some twenty-three million years ago. As evidence of the shifting San Andreas fault and of the shifting plates beneath the earth's surface, the rest of the original volcano is about two hundred miles to the south around Lancaster, California. Constant grinding along the North American and Pacific plates caused a break along the North American stress line. For more than twenty million years the Pinnacles have been hitching a very slow ride astride this northward rift line of the North American plate, which constitutes the San Andreas fault. Wind and water have ground the volcano down to a third of its original size and carved caves within its interior. In spring the peaks and spires of the West Pinnacles rise above fields awash in wildflowers: poppies, wild mustard, lupines, and Indian paintbrush. Every summer and autumn slow-moving tarantulas crawl along roads and open spaces searching for a mate in this arid, desertlike environment. They are mostly harmless but should never be touched, for their own protection and yours.

Three walks including a cave trek wind through the park. A small stream crosses the West Pinnacles, and tributaries trickle through the caves. The Balconies Flat trail is a four-mile walk to the East Pinnacles. The steep Junipero Canyon walk passes ravines painted with wildflowers in spring and leads to "Top of the Pinnacles" views. Pack at least a quart of water per person and also a flashlight for the caves. The hike to the east side and back takes about five hours.

Junipero Canyon meanders easily through mountain mahogany and juniper before it seduces you to climb higher and higher, past poppies and stone ravines, finally to the breathtaking peaks and spires. Golden eagles and falcons soar above you. You swig your water as turkey vultures circle. The trail descends two miles through chaparral into the interior of the ancient volcano, the Bear Gulch Caves. You can return to the west side by retracing your steps or along the Balconies Flat trail.

Two campgrounds serve the Pinnacles, both on a first-come, first-served basis. A small campground of eighteen sites is available on the west side. Fee is ten dollars per night. Camping is restricted at various times during the year. Picnic tables, barbecues, and the small Chaparral Visitor's Center are available.

The larger Pinnacles Campground Inc. near the east entrance is six dollars per person per night. A larger visitor's center serves the east entrance. During summer parking close in is taken early, and a shuttle bus transports monument guests from parking farther away. No bike riding or pets are allowed in the park. For information call the West Pinnacles ranger (408/389-4526) or East Pinnacles main station (408/389-4485).

SAN JUAN BAUTISTA. This town of Old California has as its center a mission plaza where visitors can view influences of Spanish, Mexican, and Early American California. Mission San Juan Bautista is the only one in California that has been in continuous use from its beginning. It centers a twelve block area where some three dozen historic structures can be visited. When the missions were secularized the priest here was allowed to stay. The other missions in California were built very narrow; Mission San Juan Bautista is the largest, with high arched roofs and side aisles. In summer the Cabrillo Music Festival presents concerts in the church because its acoustics are so balanced. Known as the "Mission of Music," its museum features some antique violins and cellos. A statue of the mission's patron, Saint John the Baptist, is the principal piece of a set of five statues and artwork that date to the mission's origin. Of the millions of visitors, the most memorable may be the bear and a coyote that apparently entered the empty edifice while the floor tiles were still drying and left their tracks in the main aisle.

The San Juan Bautista State Historic Park surrounds the mission. One of the focal buildings, the Castro-Breen adobe, contrasts the differing lifestyles of its two previous owners. Two rooms are furnished in the basic wood furniture of the Mexican period, when this served as Joe Castro's adobe. Castro was the military commandant serving San Juan Bautista and Monterey. The Breen family who later lived in the adobe traveled to California with the Donner Party. A mural of their journey fills one wall. Their furnishings are ornate Victorian style. On the first Saturday of each month volunteers with the California State Parks Department present reenactments of various periods in the town's history.

San Juan Bautista's streets are like a walk back in time. Wooden sidewalks lead to specialty shops, antique stores, and old-time restaurants. The rarest gem in the world and the state gem of California can be found at Tops rock shop (408/623-4441). Benitoite, the only rock that occurs as a triogonal tripyramidal natural crystalline structure, has only been found at the nearby Blue Diamond Gem mine. Most of the rock was unknowingly shattered during turn-of-the-century explosive work for quicksilver (mercury).

The west side of San Juan Bautista, reached by taking the Monterey Street exit from Highway 156, offers the opportunity to visit artisans and crafts people

Mission San Juan Bautista

in their studios and workshops. The buzz of saws crafting domestic hardwoods into rocking horses and furniture at Woodworks by Schultz Enterprises (408/623-2013) is contrasted by the gentle whir of the potters' wheels at San Juan Foothills Pottery (408/623-4305), where the owners create functional and one-of-a kind pieces of stoneware.

The passion of San Juan Bautista flows at El Teatro Campesino, 705 Fourth Street (408/623-2444). Local Luis Valdez founded the theater over two decades ago, and when not on movie location he still directs plays and workshops here. The highlight of the theater offerings is the Christmas pageant at the mission, which alternates each year between the La Pastorela and Our Lady of Guadalupe plays.

GILROY. One hundred factory outlet stores set in one center attract many bargain seekers. Take Highway 101 to the Leavesley exit for easy access.

Will Rogers joked that Gilroy was the only place you could marinate your steak just by hanging it on the clothesline. To celebrate the local top produce the annual Garlic Festival features garlic foods, entertainment, and tours. This event is very popular, with attendance figures topping the hundred-thousand mark.

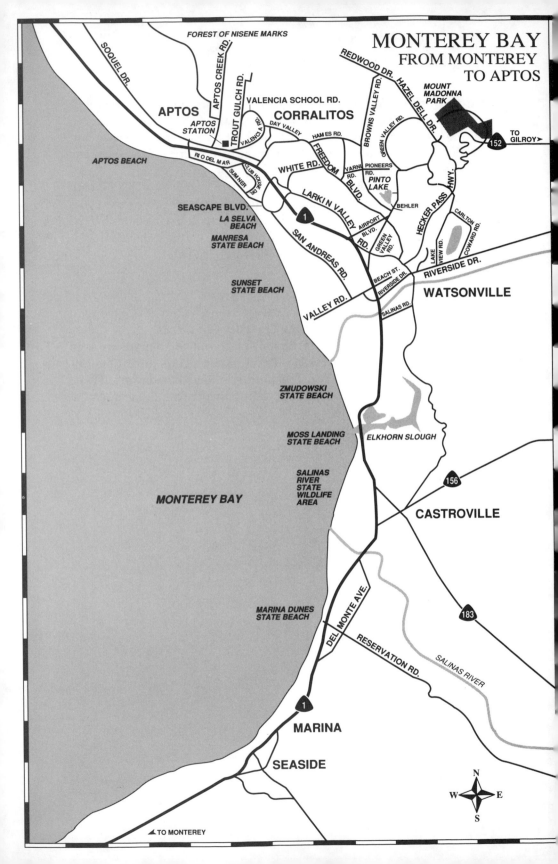

CHAPTER 8

FROM MONTEREY TO THE SANTA CRUZ BEACH TOWNS

BEACHES, ELKHORN SLOUGH, AND BACKROAD JOURNEYS

The forty-mile inner crescent of Monterey Bay curves from the city of Monterey through Santa Cruz, which itself is the focus of the next chapter. From the bay's southern tip to Capitola and the other resort communities just south of Santa Cruz, you can visit Northern California's highest sand dunes, artichoke and strawberry fields, the only national marine estuary in Northern California, historic towns filled with antique shops, expansive beaches, redwood-forested back roads, and seaside resorts.

GETTING READY

THE BEST TIMES TO VISIT AND THE SPECIAL EVENTS

Any time of the day is fine for this trip. In summer the morning and evening fog can be quite thick from Monterey to Aptos, making visibility a concern for travel at either end of the day. Highway 1 traffic can be extremely heavy especially heading north at the close of three-day weekends. Special-event weekends on the Monterey Peninsula cause heavy traffic from Castroville to near the Route 152 exit north of Moss Landing, where the road widens.

From May through November sun-loving locals and tourists flock to the sunny beaches around Capitola. Local produce ripens from May through November for productive farm-road excursions. Special events north of Monterey include the Castroville Artichoke Festival in September. The Elkhorn Slough populace celebrates National Estuaries Day in September. Moss Landing hosts a popular antique fair in July. The Antique Fly-In soars into the Watsonville Airport in May. The "World's Shortest" parade—the area's most popular—marches through Aptos on the Fourth of July. Musicians for Music turn Soquel's Main Street into an all-day Music Fest in late spring while raising funds for the town's music programs. In September, during the popular Capitola Begonia Festival, floats decorated with begonias sail down Soquel Creek.

CLIMATE AND CLOTHING

The small beach towns at either end of the bay—the Seaside-Marina and Capitola-Seacliff areas—are often gloriously sunny while the rest of the bay is cloaked in gray. Elkhorn Slough can be sunny when Moss Landing is covered as though with a dense blanket. Winters are mild but unpredictable. On any day in winter you might witness a raging storm that tosses foamy breakers onto rain-pelted beaches. A couple of days later sunbathers may relax among the driftwood on the shore. Winter storms often close the northern Elkhorn Slough road and the entrance to Salinas River Beach.

Winds can be quite strong along the stretch of beaches between Seaside and Seacliff. Swimming is not advisable for any of the beaches along this route with the exception of Capitola Beach. The water temperature is cold year-round and except for those with the thickest of skins, wetsuits are needed for swimming. Rip currents are common at most of the beaches. The Capitola and Seacliff beaches offer the best wading possibilities.

Clothing along this entire route is casual. Capitola is a sunny family resort town as well as a vibrant fun-seekers' mecca of bare chests and bikini tops. Go for comfort but dress for variable temperatures. Pack a sweater and a jacket along with shorts and swimsuit. Bring binoculars and also a camera, for fun-in-the-sun shots, panoramic vistas, surfers' moves, and those shark fins under the oaks at Elkhorn Slough.

TOUR LENGTHS

The drive from Seaside to Capitola takes forty-five minutes nonstop in light traffic. Get an early start if light traffic is key to enjoying the many places along the way. If the traffic is heavy it is best to visit the ocean side of Moss Landing during a southbound trip, as the absence of overpasses makes crossing the highway difficult. Exploring or sunbathing at beaches can fill many days. Allow at least three to four hours for hiking or kayaking Elkhorn Slough. Antiquing at Moss Landing, Aptos, or Soquel can take a full day. A county crossroads tour of the strawberry farms, apple orchards, public gardens, and ranches in the area with relaxing drives through bucolic back country and redwood groves fills a day and an ice chest. At Nisene Marks State Park a hike or bike ride can span two hours or extend to an overnight backpack camp-in. If you like jazz plan to be at the Whole Enchilada in Moss Landing by 4 p.m. on Sunday or the Capitola Wharf restaurant on weekend afternoons. Capitola, with the beach, river, shops, restaurants, and historic Victorians, is fun for an afternoon, full day, or weekend. To really relax, take advantage of weekly rentals in the northern beach towns of Capitola, Seacliff, and Rio Del Mar.

WILDLIFE WISDOM

Elkhorn Slough is a bird-watcher's heaven. Over two-hundred fifty species of birds have been observed here, including the endangered brown pelican, golden eagle, and cormorant. You have a great chance of seeing waterfowl, wading birds, and shorebirds from December through March and pelicans from spring through autumn. Egrets roost at Elkhorn Slough in April. Wednesday though Sunday the visitor's station at Elkhorn loans out binoculars and bird books to visitors. If you see a fenced-off or meshed area it could well be a protected endangered snowy plover's nest. Look for the tracks of deer, bobcat, fox, and muskrat around the slough. The estuary boasts over fifty varieties of fish, including several types of sharks, which can be seen feeding in spring and summer. Throughout the slough and Moss Landing area thirty varieties of crabs and shrimp add to thirty-eight species of oysters, clams, and mussels—part of over four hundred species of invertebrates. No wonder all those seals and sea lions swim through here.

Salinas River National Wildlife Refuge is a favorite of great blue herons, western sandpipers, and waterfowl. Allow yourself time on this trip to get absorbed in the habits or antics of some of the animals you meet along the way.

VISITOR INFORMATION

For information about the communities along this route, refer to the Chamber of Commerce listings in the Resource Guide (pp.290–291). Newspapers that cover Seaside to Moss Landing include the *Monterey County Herald*, the *Californian*, and the free *Coast Weekly*. From Moss Landing to Capitola check for information in the *Santa Cruz Sentinel*, and in the *Good Times*, which is free at newsracks.

Here is a list of information sources for some of the officially designated destinations along the bay.

ELKHORN SLOUGH NATIONAL ESTUARINE RESEARCH RESERVE, 1700 Elkhorn Road, Watsonville, CA 95076. 408/728-2822. Open Wednesday to Sunday, 9 to 5.

THE NORTHERN REGION OF THE ELKHORN SLOUGH PRESERVE: contact the Nature Conservancy Preserve, the Nature Conservancy, P.O. Box 267, Moss Landing, CA 95039. 408/728-5939. This region is open only by appointment.

CALIFORNIA STATE DEPARTMENT OF FISH AND GAME AND MOSS LANDING WILDLIFE AREA: 408/649-2870.

Moss Landing Harbor District: 408/633-2461.

Salinas River National Wildlife Refuge: U.S. Fish & Wildlife Service, 510/792-0222.

Salinas River State Beach: 408/649-2836.

Moss Landing State Beach and Zmudowski State Beach: 408/649-2836.

Palm Beach State Park and Sunset State Beach: 408/724-1266.

Forest of Nisene Marks State Park: 408/688-3241.

New Brighton State Park: 408/475-4850.

ALTERNATE TRANSPORTATION

A pedestrian and biking trail links Pacific Grove to Seaside and Seaside to Marina, in two separate segments. There are plans for a continuing eighteen-mile span to Castroville. You can pick up the trail from Pacific Grove at Lovers Point, Fisherman's Wharf, or any spot along the way. The trail continues to Roberts Lake in Seaside. You can pick up the second segment beginning in Seaside at the end of Del Monte Boulevard; it parallels portions of the freeway and continues to Marina.

PARKING

Where to park is not an issue except at the beach towns neighboring Santa Cruz. On sunny weekends and during summer, get to Rio Del Mar Beach early or don't expect to park. The Santa Cruz Metropolitan Transit District (408/425-8600) provides a fee parking lot and beach shuttle to alleviate the impossible parking situation in Capitola village. Take the Capitola exit from Highway 1 onto Bay Avenue, go one block west to Hill Street, and follow clearly marked signs at Hill Street. You can get locked in Capitola traffic for an hour and never find a parking place. Shuttle service is timely and fun. The largest parking lot in Capitola is located on Monterey Avenue near its intersection with Park Avenue.

PLACES TO STAY

THE SOUTH BAY NORTH OF SEASIDE

INN CAL, (Reservation Road exit to Dunes Road, Marina). Adjacent to Marina State Beach, 141 newer units are surrounded by dunes. Heated spa. AX, MC, V; others also accepted. 408/384-1800. For two, from $40.00 to $60.00.

THE NORTH BAY SOUTH OF SANTA CRUZ

BAYVIEW HOTEL, Bed and Breakfast Inn, 8041 Soquel Drive, Aptos (at entrance to Nisene Marks Park). This historic three-story landmark Victorian is "the heart of Aptos village." Beautifully renovated with antiques and Victorian decor, all with private baths, a few with fireplaces. Guests only breakfast in the elegant Veranda Restaurant (408/685-1881), which also serves lunch and dinner. 408/688-8654. AX, MC, V. For two, from $90.00 to $140.00.

BEST WESTERN SEACLIFF INN, (north of Highway 1, at the Seacliff exit). One-hundred forty comfortable rooms are garden landscaped. Suites with whirlpool available. Pool, whirlpool, putting green, restaurant. Full-bar lounge area featuring local musicians. Close drive or walk to beach and shops. 408/688-7300 or 800/367-2003. MC, V; others also accepted. For two, from $70.00 to $160.00.

THE INN AT DEPOT HILL,250 Monterey Avenue, Capitola. An elegant inn, with the highest Mobil-guide rating for a bed and breakfast; each distinctive suite is decorated in exacting detail to present a different place and time. The Delft Room features Dutch indulgence in blue with a huge featherbed draped in linen and lace, a private sitting room, a marble shower, and a private tulip garden with outdoor jacuzzi. The Railroad Baron Suite features a domed ceiling, red and gold fabrics, rich woods, and a large indoor soaking pool under a skylight. Full breakfast, afternoon tea or wine, hors d'oeuvres, and dessert included. VCRs, stereo systems, and FAX/modem connections in all rooms. 408/462-DEPO (3376). AX, MC, V. For two, rooms under $200.00, suites under $250.00.

K.O.A. CABINS, 1186 San Andreas Road, Watsonville. Newer-construction one-and two-bedroom log cabins, with barbecues, porch swings, and a pastoral setting. They share the full-bath-and-shower facilities of the adjacent two-hundred-plus space K.O.A. campground. One mile to Manresa State Beach. Heated pool, spas, and children's play areas. 408/722-0551. For two, $37.00. Children stay free.

SEASCAPE RESORT AND CONFERENCE CENTER (Seascape Boulevard and Sumner Avenue, Aptos-Seascape). The newest complex in the area has eighty-four guest units, studios, and one-bedrooms within a three-phase condominium development. Private balconies, ocean views, beach access by foot or golf carts, swim and racquet club, golf privileges. Spa, pool, and full service restaurant. 800/929-7727. AX, MC, V. For two, from $165.00 to $215.00.

Weekly rentals of private homes and timeshares are commonly arranged for guests and residents by real estate firms in the area. Two offices that cater to vacation renters are Bob Bailey Real Estate, 408/688-7009, and Lonagre Real Estate, 408/688-3880. Capitola home, cottage, and beach-front motel room rentals are available through Vacations by the Sea, 408/479-9360.

RESTAURANTS

THE SOUTH BAY NORTH OF SEASIDE

CENTRAL TEXAN BARBECUE, 10749 Merritt Street, Castroville. Swagger in and enjoy such favorites as smoked ribs, beef brisket, and homemade Chisholm Trail sausage. Sawdust on the floors: very casual. Ground has been broken for a new building up the street. Lunch, dinner. 408/633-2285. No cards. Entrees, mostly under $10.00.

LA SCUOLA, 10700 Merritt Street, Castroville. An 1860 schoolhouse now serves fine Tuscany cuisine. Specializing in pasta, veal, seafood, homemade gnocchi, and tiramisu. Dinner only. 408/633-3200. MC, V. Entrees, mostly under $20.00.

MOSS LANDING OYSTER BAR AND COMPANY, 413 Moss Landing Road, Moss Landing. In a friendly atmosphere, fresh fish when available, from the Moss Landing harbor vessels. Seafood pastas. Dark, rustic wood with a touch of the nautical. Lunch, dinner. 408/633-5302. AX, MC, V. Entrees, mostly under $20.00.

PHIL'S, (at the Island), Moss Landing. Casual indoor or outdoor harbor dining. Benefits from open-hearth cooking of radio-transmitter-selected fresh-catch fish. They are literally carried in from the fishing boats that are anchored across the street. Choose your fish or seafood from a large ice table; Phil or friends will prepare it. Specialties include cracked crab, stuffed prawns, creamy chowder, and cioppino in French bread rounds, to eat in or to go. Lunch, dinner. 408/633-2152. No cards. Entrees, mostly under $10.00.

THE WHOLE ENCHILADA, Highway 1 and Moss Landing Road, Moss Landing. Authentic Mexican furnishings and art add to a colorful and upbeat atmosphere. Garlic prawns and the "Whole Enchilada," a fresh filet of red snapper wrapped in a corn tortilla with spicy sauce and melted cheese, crown an extensive menu. Beginning in the late afternoon on Sundays, after lunch or before dinner at the Whole Enchilada, jazz at the adjoining lounge annex, Moss Landing Inn, packs in listeners. Lunch, dinner. 408/633-3038. AX, MC, V; others also accepted. Entrees, from $6.00 to $16.00.

THE NORTH BAY SOUTH OF SANTA CRUZ

CAFE RIO, 131 Esplanade, Rio Del Mar. Across the parking lot from the beach there is fine dining with tropical ambiance. Specializing in fresh seafood, with an oyster bar. Outdoor appetizers and drinks beginning at 3 p.m.; dinner begins at 5 p.m. 408/688-8917. AX, MC, V. Entrees, from $11.00 to $30.00.

CARPO'S, 2400 Porter Street, Soquel. Eat inside or outside on the patio, in a lively, family atmosphere. Burgers, pastas, fresh seafood, salad bar. Lunch, dinner. 408/476-6260. No cards. Entrees, mostly under $10.00.

DEER PARK TAVERN, (at Deer Park Shopping Center), Rio Del Mar Boulevard, Aptos. This restaurant combines rustic woods and cozy fireplaces with a hunting lodge motif. Steaks, seafoods, and pastas are served in the dinner house. Bright and cheery coffeehouse addition for breakfast and lunch. 408/688-5800, AX, MC, V. Entrees, from $11.00 to $25.00.

DHARMA NATURAL FOODS RESTAURANT, 4250 Capitola Road, Capitola. A casual, vegetarian restaurant, Dharma has a wonderful selection of baked goods, sandwiches, and pastas. Breakfast, lunch, dinner. 408/462-1717. No cards. Entrees, from $4.00 to $8.00.

GAYLE'S BAKERY & ROSTICCERIA, 504 Bay Avenue, Capitola. The aromas of fresh-baked breads and herbed chickens fill this take-out European style bakery/deli. Outdoor patio dining. Lunch, dinner. 408/462-4747. Delicatessen items, mostly under $10.00.

RED APPLE CAFE, (on the upper level at Deer Park Center), Rio Del Mar Boulevard, Rio Del Mar. A cozy breakfast and lunch spot, the Red Apple overlooks a green belt of grass and trees. Homemade scones and omelettes are among breakfast selections. Lunches include pasta, fresh seafood specials, and sandwiches. 408/685-1224. AX, MC, V. Selections from $4.00 to $9.00.

SHADOWBROOK RESTAURANT, 1750 Wharf Road, Capitola. Lush gardens cover the hillside above this wood-and-glass romantic hideaway along Soquel Creek. A free funicular railway carries six passengers at a time down the verdant hillside to the restaurant door. Having cocktails on the deck that meets the creek is fun by itself or as a beginning. Pasta, seafood. Reservations suggested. Dinner, Sunday brunch. 408/475-1511. AX, MC, V; others also accepted. Entrees, from $14.00 to $25.00.

THEO'S, 3101 North Main Street, Soquel. This intimate and romantic restaurant has fourteen tables and "three-hour" comfortable chairs. Impeccable service. Classic French with an eclectic touch. Fresh salmon, house-smoked trout. Surrounding restaurant garden provides the freshest greens and vegetables possible. Lunch, dinner. 408/462-3657. AX, MC, V; others also accepted. Entrees, from $12.00 to $18.00.

WATSONVILLE AREA

CILANTROS, 1934 Main Street, Watsonville. Serving Michoacan-style Mexican dishes, with a variety of sauces, Cilantros has a bright and lively tropical look. Guajillos Camarones with lingonberries is a tasty favorite. The heaping cilantro platter offers a selection of items with a tangy ceviche center. Lunch, dinner, Sunday brunch. 408/761-2161. AX, MC, V. Entrees, from $8.00 to $15.00.

GREEN VALLEY GRILL, 40 Penny Lane, Watsonville. An indoor cactus garden brings the Southwest to this popular grill located in a small shopping center off Green Valley Road. Pastas complement the grill menu, which includes baby-back ribs and grilled shrimp. Dancing on Friday and Saturday nights. Lunch and dinner. 408/728-0644. AX, MC, V. Entrees, from $5.00 to $20.00.

ZUNIGA'S, (at the Watsonville Airport) on Aviation Way, Watsonville. This local favorite moved from the downtown after the earthquake. Lunch, dinner. 408/724-5788. AX, MC, V. Entrees, from $5.00 to $13.00.

INTRODUCTION WITH HISTORICAL HIGHLIGHTS

Change is the constant for the stretch of coast that follows the crescent-shaped curve of the Monterey Bay from Monterey to Santa Cruz. Buildings, mountains, and trees disappear in front of your eyes in seasonal coastal fog. If you blink long enough or drive three hundred feet farther, bright sunlit sands may make you reach for sunglasses. Green-shrouded coastal dunes burst into color in spring, just before the last notes of migrating songbirds welcome the formations of pelicans that glide in for the summer. The pickleweed of inner estuarine waters turns bright green in summer and autumn when golden grasses cover surrounding hills. As the pelicans fly south in winter, songbirds and shorebirds return to this section of coast seeking temperate winter homes.

Changes brought by people mirror those that occur in nature. Closest to Monterey cluster the communities of Seaside, Del Rey Oaks, Sand City and Marina; for decades Seaside and Marina have been dependent on neighboring Fort Ord for a large proportion of their population and business clientele. As Fort Ord changes, with military downsizing, to civilian use, these communities are scrambling to find a new economic and social base. The evolving Fort Ord holds thousands of acres of preserved parkland and wildlife areas as well as holding potential for expansion of local university options, of housing, and of the economy.

The very course of the Salinas River that touches the northern border of Fort Ord was altered in 1908 by farmers, who diverted the river from its mouth at Moss Landing to its present outlet, some three miles south at what is now the Salinas River Wildlife Area. The 170-mile-long Salinas River flows as Demeter's shadow—often submerged in summer and autumn to emerge anew with winter and spring rains. The two- and three-foot depths of water visible at the surface cover a deeper underground stream.

Years before the flow of fresh water from the Salinas River was diverted, the waterways around Moss Landing served as a major Central Coast port. From fishing village to grain harbor, from whaling station to sardine processor, from fishing-fleet harbor to marine research site, the economic focus in Moss Landing changes with the tides of time. A row of the old port town's main-street Victorians now house "antique row."

About ten miles inland the abandoned piers of shipping ports lie silhouetted against the sky in the mudflats of the Elkhorn Slough National Estuarine Reserve. The thousands of acres of slough marshes, creeks, and wetlands keep evolving to adapt to the human imprint. In spring through summer many varieties of coastal fish, including anchovies, herring, and sharks, lay eggs or give birth in the slough and tidal creeks. As salt water levels rise the lower banks of this cradle of marine life are crumbling, causing some to wonder how the complex ecosystem of Elkhorn Slough will survive until the twenty-first century. The major research facilities at Moss Landing, which include the Moss Landing Marine Laboratory and MBARI, David Packard's nonprofit oceanic research institute, grow in importance.

Beyond Moss Landing, miles of strawberry fields cover hills where thick riparian oak forests and redwood groves grew to water's edge less than a century ago. In the mid 1800s the lumbering of the redwood forests, which extended miles back to the areas above Santa Cruz, was instrumental in the beginnings of the Santa Cruz County "mill towns" of Aptos and Soquel. La Selva Beach is the first vanguard of beach communities on the Santa Cruz side of the crescent-shaped bay. The sands of Sunset and Manresa beaches meet at the shores of this tiny hamlet. Rio Del Mar, Seacliff, and Capitola are the larger beach communities south of Santa Cruz. Capitola calls itself the oldest seaside resort on the Pacific Coast. Tourists first came to "Camp Capitola" by horse-drawn vehicles. By 1876, the railroad was extended to Capitola and brought pleasure seekers from San Francisco. The railroad's high trestle over Soquel Creek is a town landmark. In September, floats covered with begonias cruise under the trestle to cheers from crowds of adoring fans. Nightclubs, restaurants, shops, and a quintessential California beach attract the fashionable, the fun seekers, and families, who crowd together on sunny weekends.

Aptos and Soquel extend into the forested mountains above the beach communities. The historic village of Aptos is the entry point to the Forest of Nisene Marks State Park. If you hike or bike back farther into the park you can view the epicenter of the 1989 earthquake; a written plaque alerts you to the spot, since the forest itself has covered the physical evidence. Gone are the old Post Office and village square businesses. As it has since 1870, a three-story Victorian inn marks the center of town. A survivor of two major earthquakes and the changing whims of people, the Bayview Hotel has been restored regally to serve both as a quality bed and breakfast inn and as the sentinel of a century plus of changes.

TOURS

FROM SEASIDE TO MOSS LANDING

The communities of Seaside, Del Rey Oaks, Sand City, Fort Ord, and Marina lie within fifteen minutes' drive of Monterey, on the opposite side of Highway 1. Although these communities are in a transition period following the military downsizing at Fort Ord, they are basically residential, retail, and industry based.

The Del Monte exit from Highway 1 leads, with a right turn at Fremont Boulevard, to a variety of discount stores. Look for the large COSTCO sign. Continuing on Fremont Boulevard leads to the Monterey Peninsula Auto Center, which includes clusters of fourteen dealers connected by meandering paths. On the cutting edge of dealer offerings, Dan Burton's Peninsula Auto Service, located at 1661 Del Monte Avenue (408/394-6044), is one of three dealers in California who are selling the Kewet, the only production electric car that has the sanction of the U.S. Department of Transportation. Burton says he's selling the cars for his grandchildren as well as the business. He wants them to see the blue skies of Monterey rather than yellow skies, as of Los Angeles.

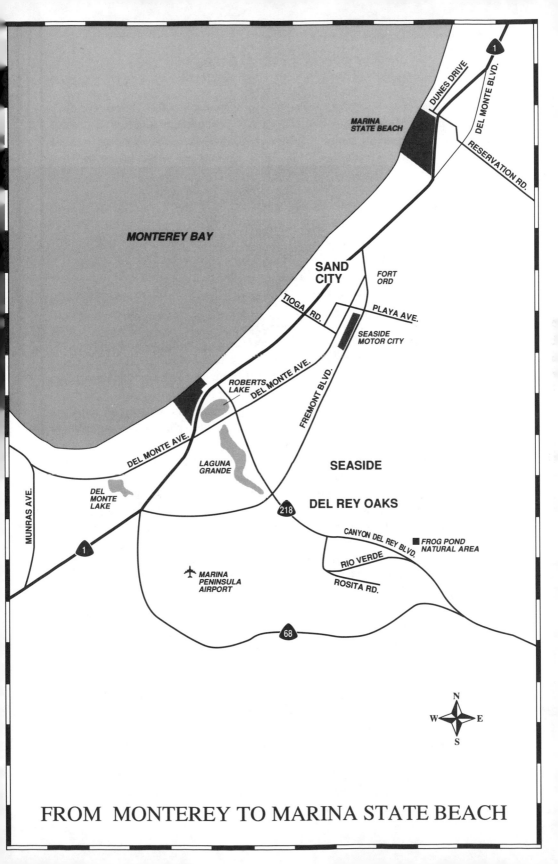

FROM MONTEREY TO MARINA STATE BEACH

About two miles south of Monterey, the Canyon Del Rey Boulevard exit from Highway 1 leads west to the Monterey Beach Hotel and expanses of beach, which rise to low dunes. The skies over the beaches here are often filled with colorful and comical kites, such as a thirty-foot-long pair of very wide jeans.

The Frog Pond Natural Area, which provides a retreat for naturalists, families, and frog lovers, is reached by traveling east on Canyon Del Rey Boulevard for two miles. You will see the city hall of the residential city of Del Rey Oaks to the right. The entrance to the Frog Pond Natural Area is kitty-corner from the next junction, Via Verde and Canyon Del Rey Boulevard. Look for a small wooden sign marking the path through the willows. Limited parking is available on the side of the road. More parking directions and nature guide books are available at city hall.

The seventeen-acre preserve with pond, actually a marsh, doesn't offer spectacular vistas, but the tranquil wetlands can soothe a family's busy agenda. In the spring, tadpoles line the water's edge. The tonal mating songs of the tiny Pacific tree frogs fill the air of December and January. Less than one inch in size, the tiny frogs may be brown or green, changing in a chameleonlike manner. They share the area with other toads and frogs, wintering wild ducks, and such upper-woodland birds as hawks, Anna's hummingbirds, sparrows, chestnut-backed chickadees, and rufous-sided towhees.

Some signs remain of a self-guided tour, and restoration of the markers is planned. A loop trail leads through dense willows. Until they were cleared for farming in the late 1800s and early part of this century, similar groves of willows were prevalent throughout much of the inland areas of the Monterey Bay and Salinas Valley. Even more historic—rather, prehistoric—are the clumps of *Equisetum,* plants that you will encounter early in your walk and that resemble, and are called, horsetails. From the true Jurassic period, these plants date back to the age of dinosaurs. Also known as scouring rush, the plants' rough stems and foliage contain silica and were used as scouring pads by early pioneers.

In addition to the pond and willow settings, trails lead through oaks, redwoods, wild roses and grassy hillsides. If you are hiking with youngsters you may want to visit Del Rey Park before you leave for the day. Located behind the city hall, the park has barbecue pits, play areas, and restrooms.

Back on Highway 1, sand mining activities have concentrated at the sand plants you can view from Highway 1 at the industrially based Sand City and north at the town of Marina. The specialty sand from this area is used in sand-blasting, foundry casting, pool filters, and the manufacture of glass.

At the northern edge of Seaside the forty-four square miles of downsized Fort Ord lands extend on both sides of Highway 1. Fort Ord was a major staging area and training center for U.S. Army troops from World War II through the Somalia missions. Possible "re-use" of Fort Ord include proposals for universities, agricultural centers, housing, and recreation, leading to speculation that Marina will develop as a college town and Seaside will join the list of golf course meccas.

The sandy hills along this tour form one of the tallest and most extensive dune systems on the California coast. Brightly colored hang gliders catch the optimum-condition winds off the dunes at fee-free Marina State Beach, which is at the end of Reservation Road off Highway 1. An Inn Cal Motel and an old sand plant mark the entrance. The hang-glider takeoff spot and a model-glider flying area are just inside the park entrance. On sunny weekends when the winds "shear" and hold at twenty to twenty-five miles an hour, the skies might fill with rainbow ribbons as thirty or forty pilots catch waves of air. Gliders can ride the wind waves above the ridge for six miles south, to Sand City. All members of the United States Hang Gliding Association who are rated three or better can register at the Western Hang Gliders' building for ramp use at the hang-gliding area. The association offers lessons for beginning through advanced hang gliders at the beach (408/384-2622).

At the northern end of Marina State Beach a wheelchair-accessible boardwalk leads from the parking lot through living dunes carpeted with native plants, such as the rare Monterey paintbrush and Menzies wallflower. Volunteer groups, neighborhood groups, and schoolchildren are replanting the shifting sands with native dune dwellers. Flowering plants help the dunes withstand pelting rain and driving winter winds. Nature's fragile balance is demonstrated by buckwheat, which roots in the dunes and serves as the food source for the endangered Smith's blue butterfly.

The Salinas River Wildlife Area is reached by the next exit from Highway 1, Del Monte Boulevard. Bring water and binoculars if you visit this birder's paradise. A dirt road (passable in the dry season, too muddy just after a storm) to the parking area traverses agricultural fields. Often muddy trails link the Salinas River, South Marsh, and a sandy beach. The two-mile trail to the beach passes a dune-sheltered brackish lagoon. Just south of the river's mouth at the beach a dune barrier separates the brackish South Marsh from the ocean. Storm-powered waves sometimes breach the barrier.

The barren, sandy beach is the preferred nesting spot of the snowy plover and the site of early morning races. The plovers' nests are nothing more than light depressions in soft sand. Their speckled eggs blend perfectly with the sand. At the crack of dawn the plovers leave their eggs to probe the wet beach for small crustaceans left vulnerable by the early morning receding tides. The plover parents hurry to gobble their daily intake of crustaceans and other tiny sand dwellers before their eggs cool. Meanwhile volunteers, roused by early morning phone calls of plover nest sightings, rush to erect plover-friendly mesh fences before the parents return. The fences shield the eggs from fox attacks and the tread of humans.

The Salinas River flows northwest for 170 miles from its headwaters in San Luis Obispo County to its mouth at the Salinas River Wildlife Area. The elusive Salinas River is one of the largest submerged rivers in the United States. Gulls, terns, and endangered California brown pelicans forage for food along the lower river. Stilts, avocets, and gadwalls nest on small islands in it. Black-shouldered kites and short-eared owls hunt over the river trail, which leads back through grasslands to your car.

Heading north again on Highway 1 after the last residential developments of Marina, the fertile fields of the Salinas Valley line the road. Many of these fields are still owned by descendants of the Cooper-Vallejo families from Mexican California days.

About three miles past the last Marina exit the road divides between the Highway 1 and Santa Cruz connection and the Highway 156 connection to Highway 101. The Highway 1 route will bypass the town of Castroville for a faster Santa Cruz connection. Backroads travelers who would like to trade inland Elkhorn Slough for coastside Moss Landing may prefer the route on 156, on Castroville Boulevard and then on Elkhorn Road, along the slough. Elkhorn Road north connects with Highway 1 via Salinas Road or, farther along at Watsonville (p. 244), via Riverside Drive.

To take the Highway 156 connecting route to Castroville is to be escorted by rows and rows of large bushy plants with club-topped spikes. Take the Highway 183 exit to "Castroville, the Artichoke Center of The World." Turn left, north, at the first street, which is Merritt. If it is early September you may be in time for the tasting, crafts booths, and music of the annual Artichoke Festival. While some claim the artichoke as an indigenous California plant, major growers say this special thistle was brought to the state's Central Coast from Italy during the late 1800s. Commemorating more recent history, each year Franco's Restaurant at 10639 Merritt Street (408/633-2090) sponsors a Marilyn-lookalike competition to pay prefestival homage to the first Artichoke Queen of Castroville, Marilyn Monroe. You might enjoy a Marilyn Monroe hamburger (with Swiss cheese and artichoke hearts) while watching the contest.

For over forty years a giant light-green replica of an artichoke has welcomed the curious and the avid artichoke fan to the Giant Artichoke, a landmark Castroville restaurant and vegetable stand on Merritt Street just beyond the freeway. In addition to a range of entrees the restaurant offers different chokes for different folks: steamed and marinated artichoke dishes, artichoke pancakes, artichoke soup, artichoke bread, artichoke quiche, and shrimp-stuffed artichokes.

Castroville reconnects with Highway 1 northbound by way of Merritt Street. The drive on Merritt passes through a town poised on a fulcrum. Across from the Giant Artichoke Restaurant, new shopping centers are branching into the historically agriculture-based town. Midway through town the original school-house now opens its doors to patrons of Tuscany-style Italian food, having become La Scuola. Older cottages, many with peeling paint and tall grasses in front yards, share the surrounding streets with freshly constructed homes and businesses. The black sign that proclaims Castroville the artichoke center of the world spans Merritt Street; just beyond the arch a colorful legitimized-graffiti art wall delivers the same message.

Artichoke plants grow between houses and stretch into fields that escort you to Highway 1, where traffic ranges from bumper to bumper on sunny weekends to one slow country truck on the midmornings of winter weekdays. On the west side, the acres and acres of artichokes, broccoli, chard, and other garden vegetables are replaced now and then by fruit and vegetable stands. The Thistle Hut at the corner of Molera Road, Springfield Farms farther up the road, the red barns of Johnny Boy, and the occasional open-bed pickup loaded with sacks and advertised with hand-lettered signs sell a wide variety of local produce, including, of course, artichokes. To turn across the highway can be dangerous; visit these stands on your southbound trips.

Ahead, always in view on sunny days, drifting in and out of the field of vision like an elusive dragon on foggy days, the five-hundred-foot-tall towers of the lighted Moss Landing Pacific Gas and Electric plant emit steam into the air. Built in 1952, it is the second-largest fossil-fuel thermal-electric power plant in the state.

The traffic jam you may be sitting in is not new to this area. Back in the 1860s grain wagons backed up for five miles waiting to be unloaded at Moss Landing. At that time the Salinas River emptied into the slough, making navigation possible. Today visitors are often surprised to learn that no river flows through Moss Landing. The seasonal estuary that surrounds Moss Landing gets fresh water after winter rains through an assortment of creeks. North of the power plant, Highway 1 crosses a wide channel created in 1946, when the Army Corps of Engineers diverted a meandering channel to cut straight through sand dunes. Two harbors, on opposite sides of the Highway 1 bridge, form a T at the mouth of the channel.

Antique stores and restaurants flank the most southern entrance to Moss Landing, at Potrero Road. The outside mural of the Moss Landing Cafe, at the intersection of Potrero Road and Moss Landing Road, depicts the village and harbor that lie ahead. Moss Landing Road travels parallel to Highway 1 and joins it again directly opposite the power plant, at an exit that is marked by a very bright pink landmark building, the Whole Enchilada Mexican Restaurant. Icpali—the traditional leather furniture from Mexico—and walls painted in the style of Frida Kahlo's kitchen, plus aromas of Mexican dishes, make the inside of the Whole Enchilada restaurant as lively as the exterior. On Sunday afternoons, sports coats replace motorcycle leathers in the lounge annex as jazz fans from miles around gather here for concerts.

For the historical and antique dealer's section of Moss Landing take the first left turn inland from the Whole Enchilada. You will be on Moss Landing Road. When I walk down the old Victorian main street and look up to the towers of the power plant I feel like a time traveler caught in two centuries at the same time.

Some twenty-five antique stores occupy old Victorians, an old refinery, a railroad car, and new construction that matches the historic buildings. This antique center is the realized vision of Cannery Row expatriate and antique dealer Roy Ami-Hamlin, who can sometimes be found working at his shop, Hamlin Antiques. "When the rents at Cannery Row quadrupled, I went in search of a reasonable place. I remembered Moss Landing, and when I saw it again I said to myself, 'That's it!'"

Hamlin designed the new yellow Chamber of Commerce building, located a couple of doors down, and lent his lot for its location. If the Chamber office is closed, just check at his store for information. Most of the antique shops in Moss Landing deal in affordable Americana. On the last Sunday in July, the Moss Landing land lubbers show their "catch" at the town's mammoth flea market. More than three hundred dealers and thousands of antique hunters converge on the town. Come early for a parking place.

If you continue straight from your turn off Highway 1 at the Whole Enchilada, or turn left at the northern end of Moss Landing Road, you will be on Sandholt Road. The harbor master's office and Tom's Sport Fishing office (408/633-2564) will be on your right. A narrow one-lane bridge crosses the Old Salinas River Slough and leads to Moss Landing Island, where the masts and colorful cabins of some four hundred commercial fishing boats, some pleasure craft, and several large research vessels, such as the 140-foot *Point Sur*, welcome you to the South Harbor. Twenty years ago the boats in the seven hundred berths were almost exclusively for commercial fishing; today only a hundred or so of the boats are regular fishing vessels. Some of the fish nabbed by the fishing boats are whisked across the street to couldn't-get-fresher fish markets.

The road continues past the Bay Marine Supply (408/633-3114), where owner Jeff Smithson will share fishing knowledge of the surrounding waters as well as sell nets, poles, striped pencil poppers, and any other fishing needs. The Monterey Bay Aquarium Research Institute (MBARI) fills the massive gray building on the left. Two other MBARI buildings are under construction, changing the core of the island from commercial to research.

The heart of Moss Landing is really found in the personage of Lillian Woodward, who has lived in Moss Landing since 1950. Her column about the history, people, and comings and goings at Moss Landing appears weekly in the *Monterey County Herald*. You might meet her at Woodward Marine (408/633-2620), which sells supplies, fishing gear, bait, and snacks. For years she has helped run a boat brokerage and launching dock. She continues to be the best source for the latest happenings in this small town.

Moss Landing Ship Yard

At the end of the island old boats, some of them rusted skeletons and some still-proud hulls with chipped paint, lie on the land next to the jetty. Fishing is permitted at the end of the jetty, and people often have fishing tail-gate picnics here.

To reach the north side of the channel, return to Highway 1 and continue north. A sign marks the entrance to the Elkhorn Yacht Club, where there are pleasure craft, kayak rentals, and a large public boat ramp. The Moss Landing Wildlife Area, a mile north of Jetty Road along Highway 1, is the newest access point on the slough. It offers four miles of trails and two wildlife viewing blinds. To reach the ocean end of the slough turn left off Highway 1 for Moss Landing State Beach. Dunes meet ocean and marsh in this location. On the beach side of the dunes anglers surfcast for ling cod and rockfishes. Slat-board walkways lead through native-plant-restored dunes and the picnic tables with barbecues that line the mouth of the harbor. You might spot the large white *Point Sur* research vessel or any of the smaller fishing boats sailing to the harbor.

Between these locations you'll pass Little Baja (408/633-2254), which offers a wide selection of Mexican imports, most notably thousands of terra-cotta pots and statues. A little farther north, J&S Surplus (408/724-0588) stocks military surplus from helmets to jeeps.

Before the antiques, before even the harbor, elk roamed the area around present-day Moss Landing. The Ohlone people shared the bounty of the tidal waters; their middens are visible along the banks of Elkhorn Slough, which extends in a branched shape from the harbor ten miles inland. Elkhorn Slough is an

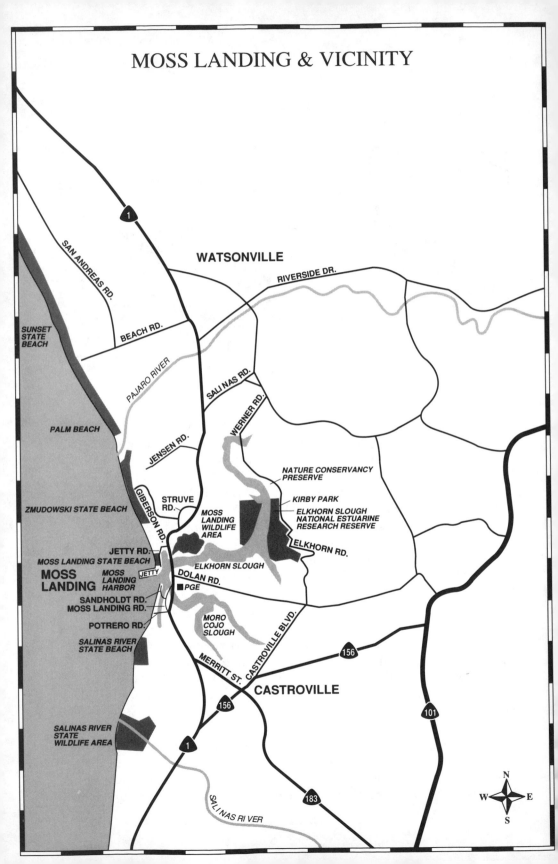

estuary; it opens to the ocean but receives fresh water from an inland source. Fresh water and brackish water, marsh, salt ponds, and mudflats cover over 2,500 acres bordered by oak woodland, strawberry fields, and grasslands. Of these, 1,400 acres are included in the National Estuarine Research Reserve. Another 500 acres are preserved through the Nature Conservancy. To view the reserve take Dolan Road at the foot of the power plant in Moss Landing east 3.5 miles to Elkhorn Road. Turn left and drive 2.2 miles to the entrance of the visitor's center. As described next the slough can be intimately observed on foot over the many trails, or in kayaks, which can be rented at the harbor and launched at Kirby Creek, above the visitor's center.

The "cradles of marine life," estuaries such as Elkhorn Slough are the fish nurseries for a number of species. Elkhorn marine babies get super formula from the offshore Monterey Bay, which sends the slough a constant supply of nutrients that mix with slough decay, such as old pickleweed, and humus from top soil to make "Elkhorn Slough stew." The stew is the first course in a food chain that passes from protozoa to plankton to young fish. Sharks, raptors, seals, otters, and humans share the harvests farther up the chain.

As you turn off Highway 1 for a moment it seems the angle of your drive will take you through the massive power plant. The gray towers that have loomed throughout your trip are just feet from your car. Twisting pipes, large fuel tanks, and megavoltage wires line the beginning of the drive, which then gently curves by cattle ranches and strawberry fields. Wooden windmills dot the land as you view the ribbon of water leading from the power plant to inland tributaries and marshes.

After turning left on Elkhorn Road, the route traverses a wooded vale of oaks; for a while the fields, wires, and cattle disappear and the forest returns. Beyond the groves of trees the winter rains soak fertile sod, and from it colorful wildflowers thrust upward in the spring to decorate bright green slopes.

About two miles north of Dolan Road turn left to the visitor's center and entrance. Before you even open your car door you might want to roll down your windows and close your eyes. Treble notes, beautiful melodies, and changed-pitch calls from surrounding trees are your invitation to watch thousands of shorebirds probing the marsh flats at low tide, or to scan pine and eucalyptus groves for the nests of the great blue heron and great egret, or to just unwind while watching harbor seals basking on the mudflats.

The visitor's center is open on Wednesday through Sunday and charges a minimal fee. It houses a relief map of the Central Coast inland and ocean region, offers free checkout of binoculars and bird books, and has checklists of birds, flowers, and animal life as viewing aids. Mystery boxes to explore through touch and the Hundred Feather Sort are examples of hands-on exhibits that help explain marsh habitats for the kids in all of us. Raptors highlight some mounted wildlife displays that aid field observation. Local guide books and wildlife books line shelves in the Elkhorn Slough Foundation gift shop. Before beginning a hike check with the ranger about any recent special slough bird sightings or activities, such as mating or fledging.

At first glance the scenery on a hike may not be breathtaking—no craggy peaks or crashing waves. As your glance lingers, fingers of fog may reach out to you. When beams of sunlight touch the slough as Midas, liquid gold surrounds you. A statuesque great egret posed on stilted legs in the mudflats brings you peaceful, deeper breaths. Then, just as you have entered the depths of meditation, the brilliant white wings of a flock of sandpipers flash before you.

The slough trail system begins just west of the visitor's center. The Long Valley loop runs 0.8 mile, the Five-Finger loop, 1.1 miles, and the South Marsh loop, 2.2 miles. Elkhorn Slough docents lead weekend walks at 10 a.m. and 1 p.m. The Five-Fingers loop trail leads to the Parson's Slough Overlook, which is the best place to watch migratory and resident bird populations that peak during the winter. This is the site of the "Big Sit" at which bird-watchers clinched the record for the most bird species seen in a single day in all of North America— 116 species, on October 31, 1982.

At the entrance to the South Marsh loop you'll pass the old Elkhorn dairy site. During Estuaries Day in September the barns are scenes of activities ranging from pressing colorful leaves to slough storytelling. Theater members dress as historical figures from the slough's past to tell the stories of the changing tidelands. The Elkhorn farm dairy operated from 1922 until the early 1970s. Rises of marshland in this area were diked and used for pasture. In 1983 the dikes were lowered in an attempt to return more of the slough to wetlands.

You can launch kayaks or hike a wheelchair-accessible trail on the eastern side of the slough at Kirby Park, which is about four miles beyond the visitor's center. The adjacent five hundred acres of nearby slough land is available for wildlife viewing by appointment only, through the Nature Conservancy, a national organization that saves the habitats of endangered animals (408/728-5939).

Rejoin Highway 1 via Elkhorn Road to Salinas Road or Riverside Drive west (left).

WATSONVILLE AND PAJARO DUNES

Highway 1 north of Moss Landing eases over miles of rolling agricultural hills shrouded with dark green enclaves of trees. The route from Watsonville to Santa Cruz is approximately the same as the Portola trail of 1769 and the Camino Real of the mission days. The Pajaro River marks the dividing line between Monterey and Santa Cruz counties. "Pajaro," Spanish for "bird," was the name given to this river during the first Portola expedition that searched for Monterey Bay. According to Father Crespi's diary of the expedition, "We saw in this place a bird which the heathen had killed and stuffed with grass. To some of our party it looked like a royal eagle....For this reason the soldiers called the stream Rio del Pajaro." The Portola party rested a day along the Pajaro River before beginning a day's march to the Corralitos region (see What Else to See and Do, p.255).

Just beyond the river the Riverside Drive exit leads inland to Watsonville and Highway 152 or, oceanside, to the Pajaro Dunes Vacation and Conference Center, Palm Beach, and San Andreas Road. This road parallels Highway 1 north to Sunset State Beach and through the community of La Selva Beach and back to Highway 1. Pajaro Dunes, a selection of deluxe private residences, rental homes, and townhomes, is situated at the site of a resort center of the 1930s named Palm Beach by developers who likened it to the style of Palm Beach, Florida. Eucalyptus and oak trees shade picnic areas here, but not a single palm tree is seen anywhere. The wave action at this public beach is gentler than most, and a lifeguard is sometimes on duty. Beachcombing yields large clam shells and sand dollars. Palm Beach melds into Sunset State Beach. This 218-acre park has ninety overnight camping sites on wooded dune bluffs above the beach.

Turn inland on Riverside Drive from Highway 1 to drive to Watsonville, which is known as the "Strawberry Capital of the World" and "Apple City of the West." Strawberries, raspberries, apples, and almost any variety of produce can be picked by you or bought fresh picked at many of the farms that surround Watsonville. You can have your apple and eat your pie too at Gizdich Ranch (408/722-1056). To reach the "Pik Yor Self Berries" part of the ranch turn left from Riverside onto Lakeview. Drive through two miles of apple orchards, berry farms, and other small farms, then turn left at Carlton Road, where signs will direct you to the five-acre picking farm. May through June is strawberry season. Olallieberries, raspberries, and boysenberries are available June through August. Tours through the family-run apple pressing plant are given by appointment at the main ranch headquarters, which is located at the next turn off Carlton at 55 Peckham Road. Picnic tables are spread out in the orchard where you can enjoy fresh pies and fresh-crushed juice. To get a free "Country Crossroads" map you can send a self-addressed envelope to the Santa Cruz County Farm Bureau, 141 Monte Vista Avenue, Watsonville, CA 95076. The map shows where to get everything from kiwi fruit to Paso Fino horses, from fresh eggs to apricots, direct from the farmer or processors in Santa Clara and Santa Cruz counties.

Besides the agricultural attractions, Watsonville boasts many Victorians and historic structures that survived both the 1906 earthquake and the 1989 temblor, which damaged much of the now-rebuilt downtown area. A "Walking and Driving Tour Map of Historic Watsonville" is available from the Watsonville Chamber of Commerce (408/724-3849).

Antique biplanes, triplanes, experimental airplanes, and stunt planes fill the skies above the Watsonville Airport during a weekend of May at the annual

Antique Fly-In (408/724-3849). While at the airport you might want to enjoy a meal at Zuniga's, a top-rated Mexican restaurant that is highly recommended by locals and visitors.

JUST SOUTH OF SANTA CRUZ

The towns and communities close to Santa Cruz, described below in some detail, begin with tiny La Selva Beach, reached by either the Mar Monte Avenue or San Andreas Road turnoffs from Highway 1. After La Selva Beach, the progression to Santa Cruz continues with Seascape, then Rio Del Mar, Seacliff, and Capitola. The general rule is, the closer you get to Santa Cruz the sooner the sun breaks through on foggy days. Aptos is to the east of Highway 1 above Rio Del Mar and melds into Soquel, which is east of Capitola and adjoins Santa Cruz. A visitor may choose to drive the back roads that parallel the freeway to connect the towns or pick and choose from direct freeway exits that are marked with the town's names. Soquel Avenue can be confusing, as it crosses the freeway and traverses Aptos, Soquel, and Santa Cruz—so if you are looking for something on Soquel Avenue, ask for the city name.

LA SELVA BEACH. Mar Monte Avenue and San Andreas Road intersect at La Selva Beach Boulevard. A row of palm trees lines this main entrance to La Selva Beach. The corner business section is anchored by a community market that offers picnic fixings and a local beach shop that offers rentals and advice. La Selva Beach Boulevard curves at a parking area along high bluffs above the bay. Just a few paces from the bluff parking, romantic benches overlook stretches of golden sand beaches and yield views across to Monterey.

MANRESA BEACH. Accessible from San Andreas Road, Manresa Beach is especially popular on sunny weekends. The fee parking lot often fills early. While the parking lot is jammed, miles of sands keep the beach from ever seeming crowded. You can walk north from Manresa to Sand Dollar Beach, where you might find the rounded white "dollar" shells of sea urchins in the sands at wave's edge. Manresa Uplands provides 64 campsites.

SEASCAPE. The spacious homes, Aptos Beach Golf Course, and open beaches of Seascape lie between the communities of Rio Del Mar and La Selva Beach. Turn at Seascape Boulevard, which runs only north from San Andreas Road. Seascape Boulevard intersects Sumner Avenue. A large community playground precedes the Seascape Resort and Conference Center on Sumner Avenue. Cement paths lead to easy beach access here. You might want first to pick up picnic items and gourmet fixings, which are available across the street at Bruno's Market in Seascape Village.

RIO DEL MAR. Continue on Sumner with a left turn at Rio Del Mar Boulevard to reach the flatlands of Rio Del Mar Beach, a popular gathering spot for beach lovers. Hot dog vendors or the steak and seafood at Cafe Rio help you play all day. You can walk to Seacliff Beach along a beachfront walkway that crosses Aptos Creek. If you turn right at Rio Del Mar Boulevard you will pass the stylish Deer Park Shopping Center before crossing over Highway 1 to the Aptos area. The traditional Deer Park Tavern, which reportedly served in early years as a bordello, is now a quality restaurant and coffeehouse. An old apple orchard and barn were preserved on the surrounding land as the center was developed.

SEACLIFF. Seacliff State Beach Park, off Highway 1 at Seacliff, five and a half miles south of Santa Cruz, is popular for day use and offers overnight spots on the beach for twenty-six trailers and campers. The eighty-five-acre park also has over a hundred one-night "en route" spots available for self-contained vehicles, but it's on a first-come, first-served basis. Ample day parking is usually available above the cliffs, which offer great vistas of surrounding beaches. Look for ancient sea fossils in the cliffs as you walk the hillside staircases.

Seacliff Beach is recognizable for miles around by the long pier that connects to the huge gray concrete ship *Palo Alto*. The cement-hulled ship was built for World War I at a cost of two million dollars as part of a "concrete fleet." The war ended before she served on the seas. She was towed to Seacliff, was ballasted to the ocean floor, and hosted a casino and dance hall for two years as part of a "floating amusement park" dream before closing during the Depression. She has since served generations as part of the fishing pier. Winter storm waves crash over the hull of the boat and have untethered her from the pier periodically. The *Palo Alto* can be viewed from the end of the wheelchair-accessible pier, which also has a snack bar and benches.

APTOS. Across the freeway roughly from Freedom Boulevard to the Seacliff exit lies the inland area of Aptos. To drive to the historic center of Aptos and entrance to the Forest of Nisene Marks State Park, exit from Highway 1 at Rio Del Mar Boulevard, then turn left at Soquel Drive. Or you can exit the beach flats of Rio Del Mar Beach on Trout Gulch Road for a woodsy drive under the freeway, then turn right at the intersection with Soquel Drive.

The stretch of land on the west side of Highway 1 between Freedom Boulevard and Rio Del Mar Boulevard often seems to be smoking on sunny days. Actually it is the steam rising from the main swampy breeding area of some five hundred of the last of the earth's long-toed salamanders. Plans to widen the freeway at this point were stopped by protests on the salamander's behalf. Cattails were planted, and salamander easements were included in the deeds of neighboring properties.

When you have reached Aptos village via Rio Del Mar Boulevard or Soquel Avenue the restored Bayview Hotel, built in 1870 and shaded by an enormous century-plus-old magnolia tree, will catch your eye as the three-storied centerpiece. In the late eighteenth century Aptos was the base of a large logging industry and held two railway stations, thirteen taverns, and three hotels. After 1900 apple orchards filled much of the cleared lowlands. A packing plant for the industry was built behind the landmark hotel. Today the large barnlike building at 417 Trout Gulch Road is home to Village Fair, a collection of antique shops and a small, old-fashioned soda fountain. The shops that surround the Bayview Hotel are known as Aptos Station.

Across the street from the hotel, wooden sidewalks lead past a variety of shops and the reasonable and locally recommended Cafe Sparrow Restaurant (408/688-6238). The old grocery and Post Office used to stand where a big gap now divides the business district. The 1989 earthquake spared the hotel but leveled this historic section.

The earthquake was centered in the Forest of Nisene Marks State Park—a sprawling ten-thousand-acre reserve of redwoods—which is directly north of Aptos village. The park entrance is located on Aptos Creek Road, next to Aptos Station. When you cross the train tracks set the "0" mileage marker for the following distances. Continuing into the park, Aptos Creek Road is paved for .8 mile, then changes to dirt. Three miles from the railroad tracks, the dirt road is closed to vehicles at a locked gate. A parking lot and the entrance to the Porter picnic area are located here. The Aptos Creek fire road past this locked gate is one of the most popular mountain biking areas along the Central Coast. Although the fire road offers an easy hike to a picturesque creek and provides people who have an interest in earthquakes the opportunity to claim they stood at the epicenter of a major one, I find it too frequented by dust-wheeling cyclists to recommend it as a good walking trail. The sign that identifies your location as close to the epicenter is 1.5 miles beyond the locked gate. Across the creek from the epicenter sign you can pick up the Aptos Creek trail that continues for a half-mile to the true epicenter. Farther on, in a canyon, Aptos Creek trail becomes the Big Slide trail, which climbs to White's Lagoon, a sag pond created during the 1906 earthquake, before it loops back to the fire road about four miles beyond the trailhead for the Aptos Creek trail. Bike racks installed at the West Ridge, Loma Prieta, and Aptos Creek trailheads provide the opportunity for a pleasant combination of hiking and biking. If you do hike or bike the Aptos Creek fire road, look at the cliffs along the way for shelves of seashell fossils, attesting to the time millions of years ago when the collision of the Pacific and North American plates and ensuing earthquakes caused the uplift of the hills from the ocean.

Over thirty miles of trails, some exclusive to hikers, lead off the main fire road to cool redwoods by meandering creeks, hillsides with sweeping views of the bay, and such vestiges of logging days as old mill sites, abandoned railroad trestles, and loggers' cabins. One of the best of these is the Loma Prieta Grade trail (a six mile round trip), which leads to the ramshackle wooden remains of a turn-of-the-century lumber camp that housed three hundred workers in its hey-day. For this trail, walk .4 mile beyond the locked gate to the Loma Prieta Grade trailhead. The trail travels above Aptos Creek for awhile, then continues along the old lumber railway bed for three miles. Your final destination is Hoffman's Historic Site. This was the last section of the park to be logged and offers hikers views of the youngest, most recently regenerated trees in the forest. You can double back on the Loma Prieta trail or take the ridge-connection trail to West Ridge trail, which connects to Aptos Creek Road, just south of the Porter picnic area.

The Forest of Nisene Marks is second-growth redwoods. The entire park was clear cut in a forty-year logging frenzy (1883 to 1923). You will not see here the ancient first-growth trees of huge circumference that have been preserved in Henry Cowell and Big Basin state parks in the Santa Cruz Mountains. The last stand of first-growth redwoods in Aptos was lumbered out in 1923. The logging industry here was then finished. Workers moved on and the narrow railroad was removed. In the 1950s the land was bought by the Marks, a family of Danish ancestry who were active in Salinas Valley farming. In 1963, Herman, Agnes, and Andrew Marks donated the land to the state of California in memory of their mother, with the stipulation that the property be left undeveloped to continue the process of regeneration. An excellent brochure produced by the Santa Cruz Mountains Natural History Association is available by writing the Forest of Nisene Marks State Park, 201 Sunset Beach Road, Watsonville, 95076, or calling 408/688-3241.

Soquel Avenue continues south, passes Cabrillo Junior College, and connects with the town of Soquel.

SOQUEL. Majestic oak trees and the white-steepled Congregational "Little White Church in the Vale" mark the antique hunter's paradise of Soquel. According to Santa Cruz mission and other local legends the original spelling of this community was Shoquel or Osocales, from an Ohlone term meaning "Place of the Willows." If you have visited the Frog Pond area in Del Rey Oaks you can superimpose that area on this landscape to imagine what Soquel looked like two centuries ago. My own most poignant memory of the town dates from the winter of 1982, when Soquel Creek rose over the streets and mud poured through restaurants and shops. Business owners, shopkeepers, and visitors grabbed shovels and wheelbarrows to trudge through the streets and dig out the town. Today the town sparkles like the eight hundred pounds of sugar that was processed here yearly in the 1870s.

Over fourteen antique shops, many with a number of dealers, line Soquel

Drive and nearby passageways. Wisteria, at 5870 Soquel Drive (408/462-2900), features furniture, French country antiques, and locally forged iron furniture. It shares an acre of gardens with Aptos Gardens (408/688-5652), where you can wander; highlights include ivy, rosemary, and lavender topiary and truly unique kelp planters, hand dried and fashioned by a local artist. Near the heart of the town, across from the steepled church, the Trader's Emporium at 4940 Soquel Drive (408/475-9201) houses over twenty-five different dealers. After Effects (408/475-5991), next door, features a wide variety of Americana.

After antique browsing, let the cool breezes of Soquel Creek soothe you at one of a selection of restaurants along Main Street. Wine tasting is available at award-winning Bargetto's Winery, 3535 North Main Street (408/475-2258), which overlooks the creek and displays old winemaking tools. Tours are given at 11 a.m. and 2 p.m. each weekday. Local musicians offer a series of concerts and local artists display work in the large tasting area.

Park Avenue, for which there is a Highway 1 exit in southern Soquel, leads both to the Park and Ride lot for Capitola and to New Brighton State Beach, where interpretive nature trails lead through wooded plateaus in the sixty-five acres of parkland. More than a hundred camping sites occupy highlands above a curving beach that is protected from pounding surf by headlands. On clear nights campers are treated to magnificent views of Monterey Bay.

CAPITOLA. The town of Capitola, toward the bay from Soquel, also borders Santa Cruz, the bay's topmost city. Greater Capitola includes a large retail shopping mall at 41st Avenue, a variety of smaller shopping centers, many residential areas, and the still-California-dreaming resort of Capitola village, where a wharf, popular sunny beach, and over a hundred shops nestle at the mouth of Soquel Creek under rows of Victorians perched on hillside bluffs. To reach Capitola village from Soquel take the convenient bus from the Park and Ride lot on McGregor Drive, off the Park Avenue exit, or drive the potentially traffic-jammed routes of Park Avenue, Capitola Avenue, Porter Street, or Wharf Road. Besides the Park and Ride, my favorite pick for an entrance to Capitola village is the woodsy creekside route along Wharf Road, which is reached by turning south on Robertson Road as you drive toward the bay from Soquel. The entrance sign for the Shadowbrook Restaurant, with its hillside tram, is to your left before Wharf Road drops to the beach area. Besides the Park and Ride lot, parking is most available in the public lot off Monterey Avenue.

As you drive down Wharf Road during the winter months you will see Soquel Creek rolling along to join the breakers of Capitola Bay. In summer, the outlet is closed with bulldozed sand and the creek becomes a lagoon for rental paddleboats, rubber rafts, and families of mallard ducks. Wharf Road curves by a century-plus-old wooden railway trestle, then meets the colorful stucco units of the circa-1920 Capitola Venetian Hotel (408/462-3004). The Italian-style hotel

CITY OF CAPITOLA

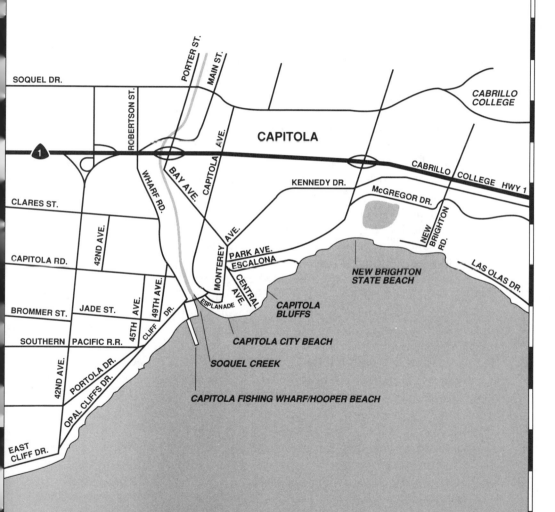

SOQUEL

CAPITOLA

CABRILLO COLLEGE

SOQUEL DR.

PORTER ST.

MAIN ST.

ROBERTSON ST.

CAPITOLA AVE.

BAY AVE.

WHARF RD.

CABRILLO COLLEGE HWY 1

KENNEDY DR.

McGREGOR DR.

CLARES ST.

42ND AVE.

CAPITOLA RD.

MONTEREY AVE.

PARK AVE.
ESCALONA

NEW BRIGHTON RD.

LAS OLAS DR.

NEW BRIGHTON STATE BEACH

CENTRAL AVE.

CAPITOLA BLUFFS

BROMMER ST.

JADE ST.

45TH AVE.

49TH AVE.

CLIFF DR.

ESPLANADE

Capitola City Beach

SOUTHERN PACIFIC R.R.

Soquel Creek

42ND AVE.

PORTOLA DR.

OPAL CLIFFS DR.

Capitola Fishing Wharf/Hooper Beach

EAST CLIFF DR.

PACIFIC OCEAN

spans the beachfront at the bottom of Wharf Road from Soquel Creek, in the heart of the village, to the Capitola wharf, which lies on the village's northern beach boundary. From Wharf Road you can veer across the road to the wharf, where limited parking is available, or merge with Opal Cliff Drive, which loops through the heart of Capitola village.

The Capitola Chamber of Commerce recommends making Capitola village your home base: five miles southeast of Santa Cruz, "this charming amalgam of beach, winding streets, restaurants, galleries and shops is so compact that your car will seem blessedly obsolete during your stay." The Capitola Historical Museum at 410 Capitola Avenue (408/464-0322) traces Capitola's past through photographs, books, and period clothing and furniture. My favorite time in Capitola begins at twilight on the night before its big event of the year—the Begonia Festival parade. Flashlights and laughter illuminate the banks along Soquel Creek as neighbors, friends, and business groups cover hand-sculpted frames with thousands of begonias. Begonia-covered barges, powered by strong arms, really float down Soquel Creek. Prizes are awarded, to the cheers of onlookers who swarm the banks and block Opal Cliff Drive. Barbecues, fishing derbies, sailboard races, and tours of begonia gardens add to the festivities. Antonelli Brothers Begonia Garden (408/475-5222), in northern Capitola at 2545 Capitola Road, displays thousands of begonias and ornamental plants in a ten-thousand-foot display greenhouse. June through October (peak months are August and September) hanging begonias cascade from the roof, lending a slightly pastel glow to the place.

The wide wooded slats of Capitola wharf lead to a fishing supply outlet, a restaurant, and sweeping views of the entire Monterey Bay. The wharf has been rebuilt after being battered by several severe winter storms in the 1980s. From the end of the wharf you can see the curve of the gentle bay to the village built alongside the mouth of Soquel Creek. The cliffs above the village are lined with the picturesque Victorians of Depot Hill. When the tide is low you can walk around the cliff and cement breakwater at the northern edge of Capitola to China Beach, where a small Chinese fishing village flourished in the late 1800s. On sunny days your view extends around Monterey Bay from China Beach and the Seacliff cement boat to the Moss Landing power plant and around to Point Pinos. No cars are permitted on the pier and the commercial ventures are limited, so the fishing and strolls for the views are very peaceful compared to the busy Monterey or Santa Cruz commercial wharfs.

Capitola Boat and Bait (408/462-2208) rents poles and boats during th calm months, March to December. On any June day you might get good reports of halibut and rockfish. The Wharf House at the end of the pier serves breakfast, lunch, and dinner, with sweeping bay views from almost every seat. On weekends, longtime resident-musician Don McCaslin and the band Warmth, "The jazz soul of the Santa Cruz Bay," play on the top deck of the restaurant. When we

Capitola Venetian Hotel

first lived in Santa Cruz, some twenty years ago, Warmth played at a restaurant in the downtown Coopers House, which was originally the city courthouse. After the 1989 earthquake, viewing the rubble that was the Coopers House shocked me to tears. Now, as sailboats bob on their moorings just a skip away, the jazz tradition continues on the wharf with the motion of the ocean.

Sailboarders, surfers, and boogie boarders glide offshore while sun worshippers, sand castle builders, volleyball players, and kite enthusiasts share the sands at popular Capitola Beach. Capitola Bay is relatively calm, as it is protected by headlands. The water is cold, but some diehards swim without wetsuits. Boogie board enthusiasts recommend this as a great beginner's beach. The first building of any importance in Capitola was a storehouse for potatoes built in 1852. If you are a beach potato, the six sand courts of volleyball team competition and the offshore surfing make great spectator sports. Bring your own picnics or simply walk to any number of eateries that offer takeout food around the village.

Above the beach, bathing suits and bare chests are common on the Esplanade, where you can get ice cream cones, slices of pizza, and cooling drinks. The grand 160-room Capitola Hotel stood, from 1895 until it burned to the ground in 1929, where now restrooms and a grassy area occupy the southern end of the Esplanade. Local artists display their work here on summer Sundays and at the Capitola Art Festival in September. Several restaurants line the upper section of the Esplanade. Mr. Toots Coffee House (408/475-3679) and Margaritaville (408/476-2263), a lively Mexican restaurant and bar, overlook both creek and ocean. The large patio of Zelda's (408/475-4900) virtually extends to the beach.

Besides enjoying the beach and sampling the restaurants, you'll want to browse through some of the unusual shops, arts and crafts galleries, and California clothing shops of the village area, which fills several blocks between Monterey Avenue and Capitola Avenue and extends uphill along Capitola Avenue. A row of beach houses and small rental cottages line the beachfront and a lawn area between the shops. A California Registered Historical Landmark plaque identifies the large Victorian that fills the corner of Capitola Avenue and Bay Avenue as the first superintendent's building of the fifteen-acre resort community of Camp Capitola, which was established in 1869. Mr. Wonderful (408/462-1233), a men's clothing store, presently occupies the lower level. While walking through the village you will pass several California-style women's clothing stores, including Oceania Imports (408/476-6644) at 204 Capitola Avenue and Clothes Garden (408/475-7648) at 131 Monterey Avenue. The Village Mouse (408/476-7566) features a world of miniatures, thousands of figurines, and locally handcrafted gifts. Owners Bobbie Moore and Steve Austen have a wealth of information about the area if you have questions. The background music you hear in the store is probably from the tapes of local musicians, such as *Music to a Wild Rose* by Linda Gauthier. The entrance to the Craft Gallery (408/475-4466) is just off Capitola Avenue at 126 San Jose Avenue. Sand castle sculptures and an extensive selection of drums highlight an extensive array of pottery, paintings, and handicrafts, many of which are created by local artists. At Latta's Jewelry as Art (408/475-1771) you may enjoy watching Jay Latta craft jewelry on his forge, or viewing the paintings by local artists that are displayed at this gem of Capitola. You can also grab a cookie at the Mercantile, which is a bright collection of shops on Monterey Avenue.

The narrow wedge of streets between Capitola Avenue and Bay Avenue is home to a variety of Victorians and resort homes that are squeezed together on narrow lots. At 202 Cherry a blue plaque awarded by the Santa Cruz County Historical Trust recognizes an 1887 Victorian of distinction, built in Queen Anne and Eastlake styles. Before you leave Capitola village you may want to drive by the row of picturesque Victorians on Depot Hill. You can also make reservations to tour or stay at The Inn at Depot Hill (408/462-DEPO [3376]), the turn-of-the-century railroad depot that has been transformed into a four-star Mobil-rated bed and breakfast inn. To reach Depot Hill travel toward Highway 1 on Bay Avenue and turn right on Central Avenue. From Depot Hill you will enjoy a panoramic view of Capitola village north to Santa Cruz.

WHAT ELSE TO SEE AND DO

HIGHWAY 152. Coming to the Monterey Bay from Highway 101, twisty Highway 152, which exits Highway 101 at Gilroy and winds over Hecker Pass, offers you a bird's eye view of Elkhorn Slough, the city of Watsonville, and stretches of coast south to Point Lobos and north to Santa Cruz. Take advantage of the few viewing-area pulloffs, and drive slowly. If you are already at the bay it may well be worth a couple of hours of your time to drive from Watsonville to the summit of Highway 152, enjoy a walk through the redwood groves of Mount Madonna County Park, and wind back down the very curvy road. Mount Madonna County Park also offers many camping possibilities, nature trails, and a small herd of white deer.

BACKROADS FROM WATSONVILLE TO APTOS. The backroads between Watsonville and Aptos, popular with bicyclists and adventurous Highway 1 travelers, pass bucolic hillsides and through vales dappled with apple orchards, turn-of-the-century farmhouses, flower sheds, and occasional vineyards. Redwood groves shade the roads as they wind along the foot of the Santa Cruz Mountains.

One of my favorite routes (a twenty-one-mile excursion from Watsonville to Aptos) begins at the Green Valley Road exit just north of Riverside Drive, Watsonville's main exit. Turn northeast on Green Valley Road. This route can be a pleasant forty-minute drive or a full-day excursion. The road is basically urban and busy until you cross Freedom Boulevard. (If you want a road that parallels Highway 1 and gives you a feel for the countryside but is not so lengthy, turn left—northeast—at Freedom Boulevard.)

Continuing on Green Valley Road, you pass the Watsonville Hospital at the corner of Airport Boulevard. The first entrance to Pinto Lake (408/722-8129), a small lake with wooded shores, is one-half mile north of the hospital. If you miss the first entrance a second one is a little farther up Green Valley Road. You can rent boats, sail, and picnic or barbecue, but no swimming is allowed at this time. Trout are planted twice monthly for anglers. There is a small fee for day use. Overnight parking of trailers and RVs is permitted on the lake shore. In recent years the park has become a mecca for the devoted who come to pray at an oak tree, which they feel holds an image of Mary, mother of Jesus.

At 17 Behler Road, across from the first entrance to Pinto Lake, the Desert Theater (408/728-5513) presents five greenhouses full of one of the "coolest" cacti collections in Northern California. The *Cephalocereus almerii* sprouts a topping of wooly hair to protect it from the snow of its native Peru. The artistic owner, Kate Jackson, the self-proclaimed "Donald Trump of Succulents," is originally from Australia, which accounts for the "Watch for Kangaroo" signs. Kate explains that her specimens are not field collected but are originally from estate sales or nurseries, or propagated on the premises. If you call ahead Kate will lead you on a fascinating tour of her exotic specimens as well as her propagation greenhouses.

As you climb the foothills past Pinto Lake, you view orchards and surrounding small farms that are interspersed with groves of eucalyptus and redwoods. This is a slow, winding country road with an occasional tractor to really compel you to slow down and take it easy. About eight miles past Pinto Lake you enter a thick redwood forest. About a half mile farther Green Valley Road ends at Hazel Dell Road, where you turn left.

A fern-lined stream meanders alongside Hazel Dell Road for part of this stretch, and an occasional sunny dell peeks through the forested road. After about two miles veer left on Browns Valley Road. Deep redwood stands and fern grottos grow along the roadside creek.

Roses of Yesterday and Today (408/724-3537), at 802 Browns Valley Road, specializes in old, rare, and unusual roses. In May and June the acre demonstration garden with close to three hundred varieties from "wide parts of the world" is a mass of colorful blooms and sweet fragrance. Roses in the garden are labeled with introduction or discovery dates. Ancient musk rose and eglantine roses form the beginning of a "Shakespeare corner." The delicate pink blossoms of Cecile Brunner (1894) climb into a backdrop of redwood trees. Maiden's Blush, also called Passionate Nymph's Thigh (1797), entices visitors with the palest of blush pink buds and a sweet fragrance. The public is welcome to walk through the garden and relax on garden benches, seven days a week. A catalog for mail order, which doubles as a guide to the garden, is available at a retail outlet that operates from 9 p.m. to 3 p.m. on weekdays. On Mother's Day weekend the gardens host an open house when rare roses can be purchased.

Browns Valley Road leads to the mountain village of Corralitos. People often pack ice chests with the old-fashioned apple-wood smokehouse products available at the Corralitos Market & Sausage Company (408/722-2633), including cheesy Bavarian, Cajun, and fifteen other varieties of sausages, along with smoked salmon, smoked cornish game hens, beef jerky, and ham. The grocery includes a full-service market. You might be there when a local farmer brings in crates of fresh double-yolk turkey eggs. A picnic spot under the redwoods is located behind the community center, three buildings back on Browns Valley Road.

At the market junction jog right onto Hames Road. In springtime, roll down your windows for the fragrant apple-blossom breezes that surround the Apple Barn (408/724-8119), one-and-a-half miles past Corralitos at 1765 Hames Road, Aptos. Family owned and operated since 1882, the farm outlet sells eighteen varieties of apples and fresh cider at a large 105-year-old redwood-planked barn, between August and November. You might be lucky enough to catch the cider mill in operation. The cider is popular; people often call ahead to reserve ten gallons for freezing. Beyond the Apple Barn Hames Road merges briefly with Pleasant Valley Road, then intersects Freedom Boulevard (which continues to Aptos). After you turn onto Freedom Boulevard, an immediate right turn on Day Valley Road leads through softly rounded hills and farms. Merge with Valencia Road; pass the first turn signed "Valencia Road" and continue along until the road just changes names. Valencia Road leads through a thick redwood forest, crosses a bridge, and delivers you to Aptos village.

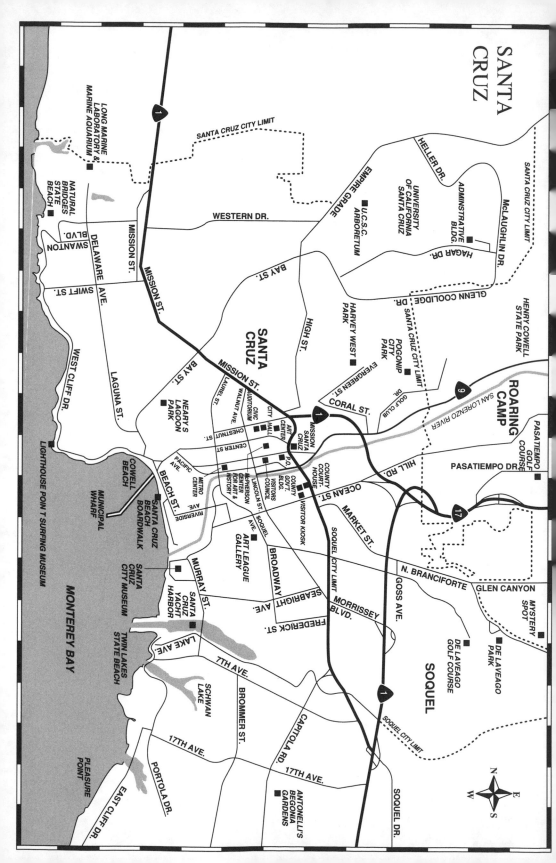

CHAPTER 9

SANTA CRUZ

THE CITY, THE MOUNTAINS, AND
POINTS NORTH

S anta Cruz anchors the northern curve of the Monterey Bay. With a University of California campus and the boardwalk amusement park the city vibrates with energy. Redwood forests line the inland side of this city of many beaches.

GETTING READY

THE BEST TIMES TO VISIT AND THE SPECIAL EVENTS

Santa Cruz is beautiful year-round. Summer brings tourists seeking sun and the beach. The weather in spring and fall is just as nice and the crowds are few. Traffic to Santa Cruz is very heavy during weekends in the summer and commute hours year-round. Santa Cruz activities start with waterfront breakfasts and continue to late night.

CLIMATE AND CLOTHING

Santa Cruz is the sunniest city on the bay. Wear fun and casual clothes here. Bring shorts, a hat, a bathing suit, and suntan lotion. Wear comfortable walking shoes for hillside hikes. The water is cold, so if you plan more of a swim than just a quick dip you will need a wetsuit.

TOUR LENGTHS

Plan to spend at least three hours downtown. Adding the boardwalk and beach can fill your whole day. West Cliff Drive takes about an hour to walk and five minutes to drive (not including the time you will want to spend at various stops along it). Try to allocate at least a half-day for the monarch butterflies, tidepools, and lovely beach at Natural Bridges State Park, with an extra hour tagged on for Long Marine Lab. You can spend all day at the university, especially if special activities are scheduled. The drive to Davenport takes about fifteen minutes; to experience a turn-of-the-century farm or enjoy coastal and wooded hikes, stop and experience Wilder Ranch along the way. You can fill a full week with Santa Cruz tours, shopping, and restaurants.

WILDLIFE WISDOM

Seals and sea lions can be seen at many places along the coast, especially along the West Cliff Drive tour. Natural Bridges State Park tidepools are among the best in California. Remember to never turn your back on the ocean. After observing and holding the tidepool creatures remember to return them to their own pools. Schwan Lake, off East Cliff Drive, and Neary Lagoon, a freshwater marsh located near the center of town, attract many birds, such as herons, coots, willets, and mallards. At Waddell Creek Marsh and Bird Sanctuary, gulls, waterfowl, and shorebirds such as willets and sanderlings overwinter on the dunes. Avocets, stilts, herons, and egrets are sighted in the marsh preserve. There is a harbor seal rookery south of the beach. Rockfish, halibut, and salmon frequent the bay. In the mountains you can see deer and squirrels. Raccoons will visit your campsite during the night.

VISITOR INFORMATION

Santa Cruz County Conference and Visitors Council, 701 Front Street (408/425-1234), is very helpful in meeting visitors' needs for information about lodging, restaurants, events, and the general area. The *Good Times* is a free weekly guide to news and entertainment. The *Santa Cruz Sentinel* also provides information about the area. Santa Cruz Walking Tours with Capitola native Ross Gibson (408/423-1932) offer informative introductions to all areas of the county.

PARKING

The beach and boardwalk area gets very congested with cars in the summer. On weekends a shuttle bus parking lot is open at the government center on Ocean Street. Parking at the boardwalk usually costs five dollars a day. Downtown parking is free but is limited to two hours, unless you park farther away on side streets.

ALTERNATE TRANSPORTATION

Santa Cruz Metro Center is located at 920 Pacific Avenue. Buses serve all of Santa Cruz County. Regular fares are one dollar, and day passes are three dollars. A free beach bus shuttles between Ocean Street downtown and the beach boardwalk area.

PLACES TO STAY

IN TOWN

BABBLING BROOK INN, 1025 Laurel Street, Santa Cruz. A bed and breakfast inn set under redwoods in town has twelve individually decorated rooms with garden views, private decks, and a lovely old waterwheel. Private baths, fireplaces, jet tubs. 408/427-2437 or 800/866-1131; fax, 408/427-2457. AX, MC, V; others also accepted. Two-night minimum for Saturday accommodations. For two, from $85.00 to $150.00.

DARLING HOUSE, 314 West Cliff Drive, Santa Cruz. Eight units in an elegant oceanside 1910 mansion have wood-accented interiors with Chippendale furnishings, Tiffany glass, orchids, and fresh roses. Breakfast included. Private and shared baths. 408/458-1958. AX, MC, V; others also accepted. For two, from $80.00 to $225.00.

THE DREAM INN, "On the Beach," 175 West Cliff Drive, Santa Cruz. The Cowell Beach–front hotel has an ocean view for each of the 164 units. Large rooms, decorated with soft pastels. Restaurant, cafe, and lounge on premises. Pool, hot tub, and sauna. In-room coffee and mini-refrigerators. 408/426-4330 or 800/662-3838; fax, 408/427-2025. AX, MC, V; others also accepted. For two, from $175.00 to $275.00.

IN THE MOUNTAINS

BOULDER CREEK LODGE AND CONFERENCE CENTER, 16901 Big Basin Highway, Boulder Creek. Set in the redwoods adjacent to eighteen-hole Boulder Creek Golf Course are forty-three condominiums. All units have fireplace, kitchen, dining room, deck, and daily maid service. Golf, tennis, swimming pools, and restaurant with lounge on premises. 408/338-2111; fax, 408/338-7862. AX, MC, V. For two, from $96.00 to $107.00. Larger units available.

GRIFFIN'S FERN RIVER RESORT, 5250 Highway 9, Felton. Four acres of redwoods surround these thirteen units. Private river beach. Near Henry Cowell State Park and Roaring Camp Railroad. Some fireplaces, kitchenettes, suites. 408/335-4412. AX, MC, V. For two, from $60.00 to $120.00.

RESTAURANTS

IN TOWN

COCONUT GROVE SUN ROOM, (at the Santa Cruz Beach Boardwalk). Sunday brunch only is served here. Private parties or public events at other times. The buffet, of a wide selection of items, was voted the best in town. Ocean views from the glass-domed sun room. 408/423-2053. AX, MC, V. $14.00 for adults and $8.00 for children.

THE CREPE PLACE, 1134 Soquel Avenue, Santa Cruz. You can create your own wholesome crepes. Salsa crepes, shrimp creole crepes, and dessert crepes too. Lunch, dinner, and late night. 408/429-6994. MC, V. Dinner crepes, mostly under $10.00.

CROW'S NEST RESTAURANT, (at the Santa Cruz Harbor). Wood-highlighted interior, fresh breezes, and ocean views make a wonderful atmosphere. Deck or indoor dining. Watch the sailboats and small craft while you enjoy fresh seafood, vegetarian, or meat dishes. Lunch, dinner. Upstairs lounge with dancing. 408/476-4560. AX, MC, V; other also accepted. Entrees, from $7.00 to $15.00.

INDIA JOZE RESTAURANT, 1001 Center Street, Santa Cruz. Watch for this restaurant's events, especially the Squid Festival in August. Voted best in the county for Mediterranean-to-Middle East, Indian, and Southeast Asian cooking. Art shows by locals give this a living-museum atmosphere. Lunch, dinner. 408/427-3554. MC, V; others also accepted. Lunch, dinner. Entrees, from $6.00 to $13.00.

MEMPHIS MINNIES, 1415 Pacific Avenue, Santa Cruz. Hand-painted Victorian pressed ceilings highlight this popular Creole New Orleans restaurant. On the mall, with bistro atmosphere. Lunch, dinner. 408/429-6464. AX, MC, V. Entrees, from $6.00 to $11.00.

SEABRIGHT BREWERY, 519 Seabright Avenue, #107, Santa Cruz. On an open deck with afternoon music (on weekends), enjoy American bistro cuisine. Award-winning beers brewed on premises. Lunch, dinner. 408/426-2739. MC, V. Entrees, from $6.00 to $15.00.

SUNSET DINING ROOM AT CHAMINADE, 1 Chaminade Lane, Santa Cruz. Panoramic views of the bay enhance casual dining, with a different buffet theme each night, such as Mediterranean or seafood. Breakfast, lunch, and dinner. 408/475-5600. AX, MC, V; others also accepted. Dinner buffets, from $16.00 to $25.00.

ZOCCOLI'S PASTA HOUSE, 2017 North Pacific Avenue, Santa Cruz. Try the homemade Genovese pasta and sauces, California seafood ravioli and Gorgonzola lasagna, and Southern Italian sauces as well. Excellent service. Lunch, dinner. 408/423-1717. MC, V. Entrees, from $6.00 to $10.00.

IN THE MOUNTAINS

SCOPAZZI, 13300 Big Basin Highway, Boulder Creek. Italian-French fare is served outdoors or in a rustic yet semiformal redwood dining room where patrons have gathered since 1912. I admit I crave the Caesar salad. Pastas, veal dishes, and fresh seafood complete the offerings. Lunch, dinner. 408/338-6441. AX, MC, V. Entrees, from $11.00 to $25.00.

TYROLEAN INN, 9600 Highway 9, Ben Lomond. Classic German cooking is served here in a Bavarian setting. Lunch, dinner. 408/336-5188. MC, V. Entrees, from $8.00 to $11.00.

ON THE NORTH COAST

NEW DAVENPORT CASH STORE RESTAURANT (Highway 1 and Davenport Avenue), Davenport. Enjoy soups and hearty California and international dishes in the friendly atmosphere of a large inn. Ocean views. Breakfast, lunch, and dinner. Bed and breakfast available. 408/426-4122. MC, V; others also accepted. Entrees, from $8.00 to $15.00.

INTRODUCTION TO SANTA CRUZ WITH HISTORICAL HIGHLIGHTS

You can't put Santa Cruz in a capsule. Its spirits are too free, waves too wild, and energy too eclectic. On a walk downtown you'll rub shoulders with those dressed to shock and high-tech highbrows. You can revisit the 1960s and 1970s in the multitude of coffee shops here, where you'll find the most politically correct and artistically knowing of 1990s conversations. You can also walk along quiet streets lined with Victorians and spend the day with families at the beach where you can watch timeless waves and their "Surf City" riders.

Ocean Street divides the original section of Branciforte and surrounding residential areas from the Government Center next to the San Lorenzo River. Across the river you'll find the newly revitalized downtown shopping and business area, which formed the Pacific Garden Mall before the devastating earthquake of 1989. Ocean Street with a turn at Beach Street leads to Santa Cruz Beach Amusement Park, the only one left on the West Coast. You can ride to a superb view at the top of the rollercoaster, a National Landmark, but your adrenalin will probably shut those eyes tight before they can look north to the streets of old Victorians and, farther still, to the University of California at Santa Cruz, set in the northeast section of the city.

If you drive to Santa Cruz on Highway 17, you will pass through the flat-lands of Scotts Valley. Up to 7000 years ago, an immense lake covered this region. The oldest archaeological records here date to 10,000 years ago when local tribes lived in the abundance of the lakes. Following the dispersion of the lake by unknown causes, the tribes moved toward Santa Cruz with major population centers developing around the San Lorenzo River and Soquel Creek. The wind-swept waterless highlands of what is now La Selva Beach separated the peoples of this region from the those further south. In 1769 while searching with Portola, Jose Ortega led a scouting party into this land of several tribes. Although each tribe had a word for the Creator, (in Rumsen, "Parataruk"), the people were labled as heathens, baptized, and set up as a labor force for the Santa Cruz mission which was completed in 1794. Their numbers declined so rapidly due to attacks on their safety and health that by 1806 Yokuts from the Central Valley were recruited as a labor force for the mission. The town that prospered in conjunction with the mission was the pueblo of Branciforte, now part of Santa Cruz.

Even before Santa Cruz was officially a city, it was an important port on the Monterey Bay. Potato growers used the first wharf during the "spud rush" of 1852 when potatoes sold for an ounce of gold each. After the spud rush went bust, the lime industry and then lumber mills boomed. While Monterey slumbered as a peaceful village in the late 1880s, Santa Cruz vibrated with industry. Also a center for local ranchos, the city has the longest-operating tannery on the West Coast. Nowadays the city is a resort, residential center for the neighboring high-tech Silicon Valley, and center for higher education as host for the University of California. Although the largest cannery in the city has been converted into the largest indoor recreational climbing facility in the world, light industry continues in the tourists' shadows.

Historian Sandy Lydon likens the symbol of Santa Cruz to a Phoenix. Through recurring floods, massive fires, and destructive earthquakes Santa Cruz has risen each time in a somewhat metamorphosized state. A devastating fire in 1894 resulted in a brick building code for the downtown. Many of these brick structures toppled in the 1906 earthquake and more recently in the 1989 quake. Floods covered the city regularly, most notably by a devestating 1955 flood that resulted in the dredging and present levee design of the lower San Lorenzo River. The 1989 Loma Prieta earthquake devastated the city but has united the community, with the rebuilding of a strong and vital downtown, referred to by Neil Coonerty, Santa Cruz mayor in 1992 and 1993, as a "civic living room." He speaks with warmth and pride of the rebuilt downtown which, as recently as 1992, consisted mainly of deep holes, trenches, piles of bricks, and tent businesses.

TOURS

The first tour leads through downtown, with a look at buildings and places that were important to the city's past or are important in their own right—just as survivors. Bicycle or walk to fully experience the West Cliff Drive tour that leads past stately Victorians and also to the premier surfing spot for both thrillseekers and thrillwatchers. Dress for tidepools and rock-hiking, since the tour continues to Natural Bridges State Park. The mountain tour is accessed by Highway 9 and leaves the city for ancient redwood forests and small mountain towns. Many of the Santa Cruz County wineries are nestled in the mountains. The North Coast tour begins at the western border of Santa Cruz and continues along beaches that, along with spectacular rock formations, hold a recreated Victorian farm park and the old lumber and whaling town of Davenport.

THE DOWNTOWN TOUR

Pacific Avenue is the main street of downtown Santa Cruz. More than two-hundred fifty restaurants and retail shops fill the twenty-nine-block business district bordered west to east by Laurel and Water streets and north to south by Cedar and Front streets.

Free parking lots are plentiful throughout the area. At most of the lots however, parking is allowed only for two hours, which is the bare minimum you should set aside for the downtown area. If you can walk or take bus connections from your lodging, all the better. On the weekends you can park at the County Government Center on Ocean Avenue and walk across a footpath and bridge to downtown. You can get directions at a kiosk information booth in the parking lot.

The original downtown once extended no farther than Cooper Street; over the decades it advanced block by block farther south on Pacific Avenue. As a result, one could take a walk southward on Pacific and see the architectural history of Santa Cruz revealed in chronological order. The 1989 earthquake disrupted this "Heritage Walk." Original brick buildings that withstood the 1989 quake, replicated facsimiles of historic structures, new buildings with complementary architecture, and vacant excavated lots now fill downtown. The clock tower on Pioneer Plaza is a good place to begin a renewed heritage tour.

Overlooking what was once known as the "American Plaza," the clock tower stands at the northern head of Pacific Avenue, where it intersects Water Street. The tower marks the spot where the downtown was born. In 1848 potato magnate Elihu Anthony built the first building, which was a combination blacksmith shop and general store, as well as the first foundry in California outside of San Francisco.

The clock tower was built into a freestanding tower in 1976 as the city's American Bicentennial project. Look for donors' names in "honorary bricks."

Across Water Street from the clock tower, a bronze eagle on a marble pedestal honors World War I veterans and symbolizes the spirit of what was previously known as the "Pacific Garden Mall." This downtown area was first saved from blight in the 1960s, through the efforts of photographers Esther and Chuck Abbott. Brick planters and flowering nooks highlighted the outdoor mall.

Don Gardener, a longtime local, reflected about the downtown's new 1990s character: "It's newer, cleaner. It seems wider, open, lighter. But in other ways it seems more distant." The sidewalks on the sunny side of the street have been widened. For sidewalk enjoyment, kiosks sell flowers and refreshments such as Mexican agua frescas and Italian calzones.

Zoccoli's Deli, at 1504 Pacific Avenue, is one of the prequake-business survivors. This building, with a 1925 stucco facade, was first built in 1852 as a stagecoach barn.

Across the street at Espresso Royale Cafe, 1545 Pacific Avenue, you can view the unreinforced brick construction that was typical of many prequake buildings. Why this building stayed erect while the neighboring one housing Bookshop Santa Cruz collapsed is a mystery. The Espresso Royale Cafe is one of some fifteen popular coffeehouses that now fill the cups of what some call the "Java Garden Mall." Cafes range from cozy to upbeat, from hippy to upscale. The cafes are a telling sign of the times, as people tend to socialize more in coffeehouses than in bars like the very popular Lulu Carpenters, which used to serve drinks here and was known as the best bar in town.

Cafe Pergolesi, situated in the Victorian-era Dr. Miller's Building on Cedar Street, is a favorite gathering place for students and artists. According to old-timers, you order coffee at what used to be the waiting room of one of the first dentists in Santa Cruz. The Cafe Bene, on the north end of Cedar, is a small, cheery cafe with a scrumptious selection of pastries and coffees. Soft lighting and wooden tables are conducive to conversation at the Java House on Union Street. You'll find people playing board games or conversing after the movies at the Santa Cruz Roasting Company on the southern end of Pacific Avenue. Logos, Gateways, and the Bookshop Santa Cruz have coffee shops or outside bars where you can enjoy your newly acquired book and a favorite cup of coffee.

Nearby the Espresso Royale Cafe, a little walkway called Plaza Lane leads from Pacific Avenue to Cedar Street. One of the businesses along the walkway, Rhythm Fusion (408/423-2048) carries imported and locally crafted percussion instruments including congas, kalimbas, rainsticks, and marimbas.

It was behind this area that Bookshop Santa Cruz operated out of a huge tent for several years following the 1989 quake. With tens of thousands of books, plush chairs, private alcoves, garden benches, and an adjoining coffee shop, the new Bookshop Santa Cruz, farther south at 1520 Pacific Avenue, now occupies a building with a Saint George Hotel exterior facsimile. A luxury hotel had opened here in 1893 and burned a year later. It was rebuilt and reopened as the Saint George Hotel because Saint George had defeated the fire-breathing dragon, and the owner wanted to emphasize that the hotel was fireproof. It contained the first elevator in town, had a lobby with an Italian mosaic floor, and once housed the offices of the mayor. Its Wisteria Dining Hall had French panel paintings of dancing nymphs in floral bowers and a glass-roofed "tea room" called the Garden Court.

The hotel survived first the 1906 and later the 1989 earthquakes, but the fire dragon prevailed and it burned a year later in 1990. Most of its external features have been incorporated into its new design, and the Garden Court skylight was partially replaced in one of the interior spaces.

The Bookshop Santa Cruz (408/423-0900) is one of several bookstores located downtown. Others feature specialty collections and used-book buyer discounts: Logos, 1117 Pacific Avenue (408/426-2106), features religious and used books. Literary Guillotine, 204 Locust (408/457-1195), specializes in rare and out-of-print books. Gateways, 1018 Pacific Avenue (408/429-9600), offers a selection of metaphysical books.

Outside the Bookshop Santa Cruz, flowers usually fill the metal hands of a lively man with a bent saw. Music seems to flow from the metal bow and tapping toe of the likeness of Tom Scribner, to whom this sculpture was dedicated in the late 1970s, before his death in 1982. When Scribner played on the mall, crowds would often gather, just as they do nowadays around exceptionally talented street musicians and performers who frequent Pacific Avenue. However, crowds also move away from some off-key hawkers who also perform on the street. The dilemma of what constitutes art and what constitutes music often is brought to the discussion table at city hall. What constitutes art in downtown Santa Cruz was the basis for an actual civic election that resulted in the selection of the eight sculptures now "living" on Pacific Avenue.

Following the Great Fire of 1894, the rebuilding effort focused on quality architecture inspired by the Renaissance. This effort produced, among others, the 1895 Romanesque Court House, which was known as the Cooper House at the time it was destroyed in the quake of 1989; the 1910 "I.D. Building," which is still standing at the north corner of Pacific and Locust streets; and the 1911 main Post Office on the upper plaza. The Post Office's design was modeled after the Foundling Hospital in Florence—the building that began the Italian Renaissance.

Locust Street offers a snapshot of the many shops downtown. The spacious Integrand Design—I.D.—Building (408/426-4717) stocks household design items beneath its high, antique tin ceilings. At 1534 Locust, Tom Bihn Packs (408/423-5659) offers about two hundred varieties of day packs, fanny packs, and beverage packs. Imagine (408/427-0240) lets you walk into the world of the Beatles, offering everything from Beatle figurines to John Lennon art cards and T-shirts. Next step into Pilot International (408/457-8200), which features furniture and clothing from Bali and Indonesia.

A side trip three blocks west on Church Street takes you to the 1937 city hall, a Monterey-colonial-style building designed by C. J. Ryland and built by Hearst Castle's contractor, George Loorz to duplicate the architecture of a provincial governor's palace from Old California. Here, a Spanish-style garden entreats you to reflect awhile and enjoy year-round fragrances and blooms.

Across the street, the Santa Cruz Civic Auditorium offers concerts. During July the Cabrillo Music Festival offers the public free practice performances before two weeks of memorable concerts. It's a treat to watch a practice, prior to enjoying a concert, with a greater understanding of the hours expended and nature of the preparation.

You can continue on this side tour or come back for dinner at India Joze Restaurant, 1001 Center Street, where squid mobiles hang from the ceiling as reminders of the annual Squid Festival that was dreamed up as a lark and has grown into an event. Five- to six-foot-tall squid take your orders and present the "Squid Review." Along with squid tastings, a highlight of the event includes Squid Art Festivals, where entries have ranged from elaborate squid sculptures to underwater squid photography to a lone bottle labeled and filled with squid ink. Other festivals celebrated throughout the year at India Joze include the Fungus Faire and Chick Pea Week.

Actors Theater (408/425-Play) is located in the same building and draws large crowds to performances by locals. At receptions and during rehearsal evenings you might meet directors such as Clifford Henderson, who enjoys the opportunity to direct plays featuring strong women's roles for local audiences.

When you continue along Pacific Avenue you have the opportunity to view art at the McPherson Center for Art and History. The red-brick Octagon Building at the south corner of Pacific Avenue and Cooper Street is part of the downtown's new museum complex and features rotating art exhibits. The Octagon Building was erected in 1882 as the Hall of Records. When the architect asked what sort of design the city wanted, the town fathers handed him a twenty-dollar gold piece featuring a picture of the U.S. Treasury Building. The architect, however, thought that the octagonal shape of the coin was what was wanted (since octagonal construction was experiencing a brief vogue). The building is now a gallery for changing exhibits.

Behind the Octagon Building, the former County Jail building has been converted to the McPherson Center for Art and History. Its history gallery on the second floor has a complete exhibit on Santa Cruz County that will give you a new appreciation for the local places you visit.

You will find a variety of local artists' work for sale at Artisans (408/423-8183), 1364 Pacific Avenue. Artisans is located along a part of Pacific Avenue that was redeveloped by F. A. Hihn in the 1880s and 1890s. He produced San Francisco Eastlake and Italianate architecture to the point that Santa Cruz was nicknamed "Little San Francisco" in the 1880s. The lower half of his development became an early theater district, while the north half came to be called "College Corners." By the time the town had rebuilt after the Great Fire of 1894 it was promoting itself as the "Florence of the West."

As Rhythm Fusion anchors the music scene on the north end of Pacific Avenue, a local tradition packs in music fans at the southern end. In business for over thirty years, the Catalyst (408/423-1336) still books top bands in Santa Cruz. Rock and roll, reggae, and occasional country and western music keeps the beat.

You can walk to the Santa Cruz Wharf from the end of Pacific Avenue, but you will be passing empty lots vacated by car dealerships. Extra police patrols have been added to the beach flats area at the time of this writing because of increased need for security.

If the post-quake vision continues, downtown Santa Cruz will extend two blocks past its present terminus to connect with the wharf and boardwalk area. In the words of Neil Coonerty, "I see Santa Cruz's shops, cafes, bookstores, and neighborhoods close to downtown, keeping it for real. Santa Cruz will continue to evolve."

WEST CLIFF DRIVE TOUR

Architectural treasures, pleasing surf and a surfers' museum, Natural Bridges State Park, and Long Marine Lab are found along the one-and-a-half-mile route that begins on West Cliff Drive. An adjoining pathway makes this one of the Central Coast's best city-and-seashore walking tours.

The initial stretch of West Cliff Drive before the lighthouse was once known as "Millionaire's Row." Each block was a private estate. The block between Gharkey Street and Santa Cruz Street was owned by Bishop Henry W. Warren, whose estate was called "Epworth by the Sea." When he and his wife divided their estate between their children, the daughter received the original house and son William Warren got the horse pasture. On it he constructed the 1905-10 "Warren House," designed by William Weeks. In the 1980s the Mission Revival style home was renamed "The Darling House" and converted to a bed and breakfast.

On the cliff at the end of Pelton Street a statue of a 1930s surfer stands in front of his ten-foot-long surfboard and scans the waves. In 1885 Santa Cruz became the birthplace of mainland surfing. The Hawaiian royal family was visiting Mrs. Lyman Swan, a former chamberlain of the queen, for the summer. Prince David Kwananakoa and his brothers milled the first redwood surfboards and surfed the San Lorenzo river mouth. Supposedly, the fifteen-foot planks weighed one hundred pounds apiece! Their redwood creation and the decline of koa wood generated a fad in Hawaii for redwood surfboards from Santa Cruz.

The original beacon on Lighthouse Point was constructed as a wooden Stick-style building in 1867. The Coast Guard installed an automated beacon on a tripod at the point in 1941, and demolished the historic lighthouse in 1948. In the 1960s nationally known photographers Chuck and Esther Abbott lobbied for city officials to construct Pacific Garden Mall. In the midst of their triumph, their son was killed in a surfing accident. In memoriam the Abbotts built the Mark Abbott Memorial Lighthouse in 1968.

In the 1980s Lighthouse Museum (408/429-3429) opened as the nation's first surfing museum. Photographs, memorabilia, and a ceiling of surfboards display the prominent Santa Cruz connection in the development of the sport of surfing. When the legislator for a Southern California city introduced a bill to the state legislature in 1993 for the rights to the name "Surf City," there was no contest. The rich heritage of surfing in Santa Cruz convinced lawmakers that no other city could exclusively claim the title "Surf City."

The surfer monument stands in front of a stretch of coast called Steamer Lane. Once a busy shipping lane, today it ranks as one of the premier big-wave surfing spots in California. Jack O'Neill invented wetsuits in Santa Cruz to block "the cold and ice cream headaches." The big waves that do roll in here are for experienced surfers like Zach Acker, who lives around the corner, has been surfing thirteen-plus years, and says, "In winter, big ground swells coming from the Gulf of Alaska kick up and you'll see surfers way out about one-half mile, where the movies film those monster waves." Waves that break one-half mile out top twenty feet. The waves in the everpresent pile of sea plants you can see from in front of the museum are known as the middle peak and can reach heights of fifteen feet in winter. "You've got to be mentally and physically fit to surf here. When the waves are that big, you run on adrenaline. You just go. Never hesitate. You put your head down and paddle as hard as you can. You feel the wave take you. Aim for the bottom. Make a bottom turn and ride out the wave. When you kick out, you're still shaking 'cause you rode a giant wave. And you go out and do it again."

In summer the waves are from the south, and surfing by the point predominates. You can sometimes see surfers "tube" in the hollow waves of the slot between the cliffs and middle peak. While watching surfers you'll notice those with the shorter boards making quick turns. Watch for the fancy footwork of the smooth-riding longboarders.

Lighthouse Field State Park was originally the large, forested estate of James Duval Phelan and was known as Phelan Park. Phelan's estate was a Bohemian retreat for artists and writers well known in California, such as Jack London, Ambrose Bierce, Gertrude Atherton, Joaquin Miller, and Isadora Duncan.

The historic Eastlake-style mansion and artists' cabins were bulldozed during the planing stage of a 1960s hotel complex of eleven-story Las Vegas–style skyscrapers. This concept drew opposition from a grass-roots coalition that wanted to see California's last open headland in a metropolitan area preserved. Citizens voted the complex project down two to one, in favor of making the site a state park.

Small beaches and sheltered coves mark West Cliff Drive. A stretch of cliffs between Lighthouse Beach and Woodrow Street is called "Seasculptors" because, when the pounding surf hits these crags, the breakers form ephemeral sculptures. The waves along this section have sculpted caves, natural bridges, and figural rock formations. Offshore, sea lions bark commands and share the surfers' spotlight.

NATURAL BRIDGES. At the end of West Cliff Drive you reach Natural Bridges State Park, which can also be reached by car if you exit Highway 1 on Swift Street and follow the signs. There is a state park day-use fee if you bring your vehicle into the park. Plan to spend at least three hours here.

Natural Bridges was named for three natural arches along its seawall. The last of these bridges collapsed after the quake of 1989. This special park has myriad opportunities for the day visitor. Plan to be here for low tide if you want to visit one of the best tidepool areas on the Central Coast. The tidepools are located about a five-minute walk down the beach on a rock ledge. Several rocky outcroppings must be traversed to reach the tidepool area from the beach. Between the beach and tidepools you pass the Secret Lagoon; great blue herons and ducks galore are spotted here.

On calm days this beach is very pleasant, but winds can pick up in the afternoons. You might find yourself heading for the sheltered picnic tables back on the bluffs.

MONARCH BUTTERFLIES. From October through March, in a "good year" you might see upwards of two hundred thousand monarch butterflies clustering or fluttering in the eucalyptus trees above the beach area. A signed monarch trail begins by the park's small interpretive center. It branches to a self-guided nature trail that ends in a grove of Monterey pines. Docents also lead tours during peak months.

LONG MARINE LABORATORY AND MARINE AQUARIUM. The lab (408/459-2883) is reached by continuing past Natural Bridges State Park to turn right on Swanton Street and left at Delaware Avenue. The University of California, Santa Cruz, which operates it, opens the lab to the public Tuesday through Sunday, 1 p.m. to 4 p.m., with ongoing docent tours. This marine research and instructional facility features facinating tidepool aquariums, touch tanks, the skeleton of an eighty-five-foot blue whale, a dolphinarium, and a glimpse of current research.

THE HIGHWAY 9, INTO-THE-MOUNTAINS TOUR

Highway 9 leads through redwoods to connect with the mountain towns of Felton, Ben Lomond, and Boulder Creek. Highway 9 was one of the original stagecoach roads to Santa Cruz. Multi-laned Highway 17 now provides the major transit connection and Highway 9 is still the same slow-paced, narrow, winding road.

If you are in downtown Santa Cruz, you can take River Street north until it merges with Highway 9. If you are driving Highway 1, take the Highway 9 exit. South of Felton, Highway 9 winds through dark groves of redwoods and intermittent bright sun. You can also drive Graham Hill Road or Highway 17 to Mount Hermon Road to connect with Highway 9 in Felton. Although these routes appear longer on the map than taking Highway 9 to Felton, their time traveled is less. If you have the time to enjoy a back road through the redwoods, slow down and enjoy all of Highway 9.

Pogonip Park, a relatively new open-space park operated by the city of Santa Cruz, stretches along the lower reaches of Highway 9. Access it by parking at a turnout of Highway 9 just past the railroad tracks. A relatively flat trail leads along four miles of open meadows, redwood groves, oak, and madrone. Incredible ocean views, probably the best, overlook Santa Cruz. A walking-trail map is available at the Santa Cruz City Information Office, 323 Church Street (408/429-3777), Monday to Friday, 9 a.m. to 6 p.m.

Halfway between Santa Cruz and Felton a line of parked cars will lead you to the Garden of Eden, a legendary swimming hole in a bend of the San Lorenzo River. In the late nineteenth century Highway 9 was a toll road. The old Toll House still stands at a bend in the road, just past the Garden of Eden. The Toll House used to be the south entrance to Big Trees Grove.

Other summer swimming holes occur along the length of the San Lorenzo River. After Memorial Day the town of Ben Lomond dams up the river at Ben Lomond Park, and lifeguards sit in watch. In Boulder Creek, a popular local swimming hole is found in town at the corner of Middleton and Junction streets; "the dam" is located a half-mile up at Irwin and Middleton.

Heading up 9 you soon approach the southern entrance to Henry Cowell Big Trees State Park. Rising from massive trunks, redwoods grow to be the tallest trees in the world. The Henry Cowell redwoods are some of the few first-growth redwoods preserved in the heavily logged Santa Cruz Mountains and make this park a highly recommended stop on your trip. Some trees here are 285 feet tall. The widest tree has a 52-foot circumference. Henry Cowell Park was preserved as a Victorian showplace of some unusual tree formations that you can still view. Near the ranger kiosk off Highway 9 a type of deciduous redwood, the dawn redwood, has been planted from seeds brought from China, where it was rediscovered in 1944.

HIGHWAY 1 NORTH FROM SANTA CRUZ
AND
HIGHWAY 9 INTO THE SANTA CRUZ MOUNTAINS

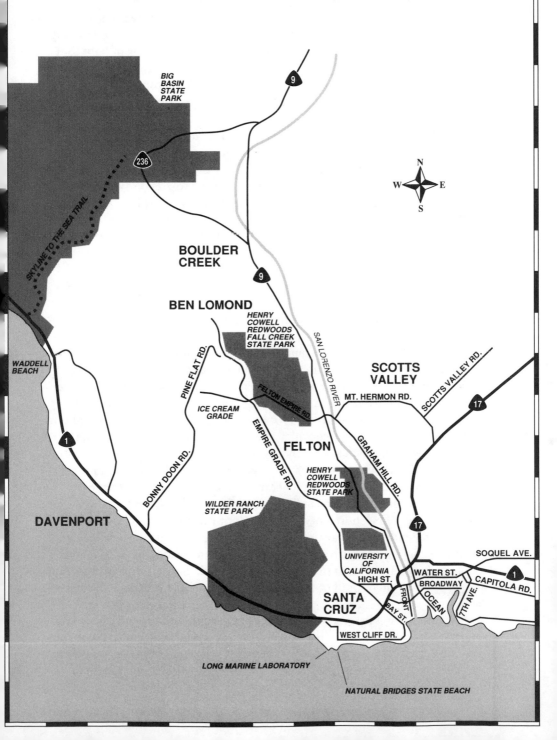

Redwoods have the unusual adaptation of being able to sprout new shoots from damaged roots, particularly when they are damaged by fire. Each of these shoots then grows to maturity as an exact clone of the parent tree. The Rincon trail, which starts at a parking lot at the southern end of the park, leads to a ring of these cloned trees. When the sun is hidden behind them, rays of light that filter through the shady forest rim them with a luminescence, so it is apropos that this ring of haloed trees is called the Cathedral Redwoods. Throughout redwood country you can see similar rings of young clones growing from a single parent base.

The Redwood Grove is an easy circular hike. If you feel the bark of redwoods you'll see it is soft and fibrous. This fiber is relatively fire resistant. Trees here have lifespans up to eighteen hundred years. Over their lifetimes these trees have lived through many fires. Many have partially burned trunks. Fifty people can fit inside the largest hollow tree in the park. Legend has it that Fremont camped inside this tree on his 1846 expedition. You aren't allowed to sleep in a hollow tree, but you can picnic at grounds overlooking the San Lorenzo River or, if you get your reservations in early enough with Mistix (800/444-7275), you will be able to camp at one of 113 sites.

All aboard! Directly adjacent to Henry Cowell Big Trees is Roaring Camp and Big Trees Narrow Gauge Railroad, on Graham Hill Road (408/335-4400). At this living railroad museum you can ride authentic narrow-gauge locomotives to the top of Bear Mountain, or take the old broad-gauge line through Rincon Gorge for an hour-and-a-quarter trip from Roaring Camp to the Santa Cruz Beach Boardwalk. Along the way conductors comment on the history of railroading along the Central Coast. This train continues as a round trip between the boardwalk and Roaring Camp, allotting time for you to explore before returning. Beach trains are scheduled for two round trips each day. Throughout the year the Roaring Camp schedules events, such as loggers' contests, the Mountain-Men Rendezvous, and Civil War reenactments.

The railroad park was named for the first power sawmill in California. Built near Felton, it was named for the racket it produced. Famous Western writer Bret Harte had a summer home in Santa Cruz in the 1860s and borrowed the mill's name for his first short story, "The Luck of Roaring Camp." Although you can see the railroad's steam billowing and recognize the whistle from Henry Cowell Park, you need to drive Highway 9 to the intersection of Graham Hill Road for access. Travel east on Graham Hill Road. The entrance to Roaring Camp is one-half mile south of the Mount Hermon and Graham Hill roads intersection.

Felton, although it lies at the crossroads between the San Lorenzo Valley to the north and Scott's Valley to the east, has not developed as a tourist center and still has the aura of a logger's town. They still serve logger-size pancakes at Dales Diner, 6560 Highway 9, (408/375-2000). Set in a rambling old house this

Henry Cowell Redwoods

Felton Covered Bridge

restaurant consistently wins "Best Place for Breakfast" contests. Most people enjoy eating on the porch that encircles the whole house. The Felton Bowl was the greatest draw for crowds before Salawinski Auctions, 6192 Highway 9 (408/335-9000), opened its doors. The antique auctions are favored by collectors and other dealers. Other antique stores are found along Highway 9 through Ben Lomond and Felton. Past Glass and Crafts, 722 Highway 9, Felton (408/335-7202) specializes in Depression Glass, kitchen collectibles, and rhinestone jewelry while the group of co-operatives at Before My Time, 6221 Highway 9, south of Ben Lomond, (408/335-1142) offer a gamut of items. Coming up 9, north from Santa Cruz, if you turn left on Graham Hill Road you will travel a saddle through the redwoods to Fall Creek State Park, Bonny Doon, then descend a grade to Highway 1. (See the Highway 1 north coast tour, p.279.) If you turn right on Graham Hill Road you will eventually follow a large bow to Roaring Camp Railway and, continuing, return to Santa Cruz. The Felton Covered Bridge County Park is the first right turn you can make on Graham Hill Road from Felton. There, redwood slats let sunlit reflections of water slip through the cracks. The thirty-five-foot height of the roof, built so high to allow passage of log-filled wagons heading for the mills, makes this the tallest covered bridge in the United States. Nearby, a redwood-sculpted ox strains to pull a giant log. Picnic tables and restrooms aid mountain travelers.

Farther on this route a side trip up Zayante then Lompico Road will take you to Loch Lomond Reservoir (408/335-7424), a fishing and boating lake surrounded by redwoods. In 1992, after being closed to the public through five years of drought, fishing enthusiasts camped overnight at the park entrance to get a spot on opening day at the renewed, rain-swollen lake.

At Loch Lomond, you can rent paddle boats or rowboats for the day and picnic on Cleir Innish Island in the middle of the lake. According to the chief ranger Walt Cacace, while the streams are running, "You can take a boat up the canyon to see Newell Creek and McFarland Creek Falls. The walls are all mossy and the ferns are overgrown. It's like an E ticket ride at Disneyland."

Back on Highway 9 you will curve north through the narrow San Lorenzo Valley. Because of the large number of Scottish settlers, many of the valley's place names are of Scotch origin. North of Felton, you pass through Brackney and Glen Arbor before seeing Highlands Park on the river side. This was a mill site that in 1902 became Highlands Ranch, which included a Scottish-Tudor farmhouse and outbuildings.

If you are traveling with kids Highlands Park might help you out, with a wide expanse of grass, play equipment, nature trails, and a pool with a use fee that opens to the public in summer. Delis and restaurants, antiques and castles, a motel with an indoor trout stream, and a lake with trout are all situated around the town of Ben Lomond.

Around some curves in the road you'll pass Brookdale Lodge (408/338-6433), once a world-famous resort. It still has enough eccentric charm and delightful details to make it worth a visit, and the new owners have been slowly restoring. Still existing are the "Mermaid Room," which has a window in the wall giving an underwater view of people in the swimming pool, and a brook that flows through the dining room.

Highway 9 could be called the Dr. Jekyll and Mr. Hyde of roads. In summer, the redwoods dapple or completely carpet the curvy road with shady patterns, the river babbles along, and an occasional deer or squirrel peeps from an opening in the serene forest canopy. In winter storms, shallow-rooted redwoods slide down mud-soaked cliffs, the river roars, and camouflaged creek waterfalls plunge from rocks. Through it all—flood, fire, quake, or hundred-year snowstorm—Highway 9 is Boulder Creek's link to the outside. The redwoods are special, as are the river, wildlife, restaurants, hundred-year-old buildings, shops, artists' studios, creekside cabins, and views, but the real defining core of Boulder Creek is its people, individuals who are survivors and contributors. Probably the most recognized face in town belongs to Craig Barker, whom many consider the community father figure of Boulder Creek. In 1992, he retired after serving for twenty distinguished years as principal first of the town's only kindergarten-through-sixth-grade school and then, during his last two years, of Redwood Elementary (the new school up Highway 9). He helped design Redwood to accommodate the town's one thousand elementary children (up from four hundred when he started in the early sixties). "I have a real warmth for this town....It began when my wife slipped and broke her ankle on the eve of my first teaching assignment. Our kids were five months and two years old at the time and she was in the hospital for a week. The home and school club took care of my kids, cooked, cleaned, you name it...that kind of giving stays with you for a long time....A horrendous hundred-year snowstorm closed the schools later that year and roads were so bad, kids and bus drivers were lodged in a combination of each other's homes for up to a week. In 1976 the drought was so bad we couldn't open school on schedule. In 1982 the floods closed the road for over a week. Every time there's trouble the community pulls together. My son Karl's a volunteer fireman in town now and every time he hears the whistle, he drops what he's doing and he goes."

Boulder Creek was first settled in the mid 1860s. But it was the coming of the railroad that turned it into a boomtown. By 1884 twenty-five lumber mills surrounded the town, making it one of the busiest rail shipping points in California. Today people settle here for many reasons: some to get away from the smog and traffic of Silicon Valley, just over the "hill"; some to live in beauty; some for a back-hills lifestyle that may seem more like the 1890s than the 1990s, and some because it's the last mountain town on the highway. Take a three-block walk down the main street in Boulder Creek and add some side jaunts to visit the bakeries, bookstore, galleries, and other hometown businesses.

With miles of trails and cascading waterfalls, Big Basin Redwoods State Park is a worthwhile camping or day trip. The Highway 9 route above Boulder Creek to Big Basin is a narrow, roundabout approach to the park. For a more direct route turn left at the corner past the Boulder Creek Market, onto Highway 236, and follow it to the park. If you are planning to hike the Big Basin skyline-to-the-sea trail, described next, you might consider taking a Santa Cruz Metropolitan Transit bus (408/425-8600) that drops off hikers at Big Basin and picks them up at Waddell Beach, the end of the trail. If you are driving back to Santa Cruz, Boulder Creek is the turnaround point.

Various trails traverse Big Basin Park. Several begin from the camping sites, which are well spaced under redwoods. The most memorable trail, the eleven-mile walk from the skyline to the sea, begins at the center of the park. You will need to first ascend the Opal Creeks Basin trail and cross over several other trails before descending, alongside Kelly Creek, through a shaded, damp section of redwoods. The bright orange banana slug thrives in this cool, moist environment and is often seen along the trails. Four miles from the trailhead you'll hear and then see the cascading waters of Berry Falls. (If you want a shorter hike than the full eleven miles you may want to choose the next waterfall, named Sunset Falls, as your turnaround point, and loop back to where you started.) Next you'll descend through Waddell Valley, a picturesque setting of redwoods, pines, firs, and meadows. When you reach Twin Meadows Camp you'll be a mile and a half from the ocean. Near the end of the trail, land meets water and birds find a resting place at Waddell Creek Marsh and Bird Sanctuary.

THE NORTH COAST TOUR

North of Santa Cruz ranches, farms, and pristine wilderness stretch to the Santa Cruz County line and into San Mateo County beyond. On the ocean side sheer cliffs and meandering dunes drop to expansive beaches that are swallowed whole by morning and evening mists. White clouds rise from the cement factory in the old whaling and lumber village of Davenport, the last town left along the beach in Santa Cruz County as you head north. Roll down your windows for the strange mix of fresh ocean breezes and pungently sweet Brussels sprout aromas. When the sun shines the beaches along the way glisten and the eery ghost-like mists vanish. Yet Highway 1 remains now a ghost of stretches of California's past.

Four miles north of Santa Cruz an old coastal dairy, Wilder Ranch (408/426-0505), has been preserved as a historic cultural reserve, featuring an 1897 Victorian farmhouse, an 1830s adobe from earlier rancho days, a blacksmith shop, and various farm buildings.

Costumed docents recreate the atmosphere of a working Victorian ranch, with plenty of livestock: goats, cattle, horses, pigs, and chickens. The ranch buildings formed a self-contained community that included its own working blacksmith forge, and innovations abounded. The dairy barn was built over a stream to provide natural air-conditioning. Butter churns were automated by waterwheel power. In the 1890s a waterwheel powered a generator, making the Wilder house the first outside the city limits to have electricity. The house is outfitted with innovative electric gizmos. For example, an electric foot button helped anyone with their arms full unlatch a door. The ranch is open Wednesday through Sunday, 10 a.m. to 5 p.m, with the possibility of winter schedule changes. Demonstrations, such as of Victorian-style baking, pieced-quilt making, and sheep shearing, are presented on Saturdays and Sundays. Docents also lead trail walks; excellent stands of some rare native plants grow at Wilder Beach. Trails traverse the thirty-five-hundred acres that surround the ranch and extend beyond, east of Highway 1. You can take your pick of walks on the beach, on grasslands with ocean-overlook views, and on redwood forest trails. During the summer the trails are open daily from 8 a.m. to sunset.

Two miles north of Wilder Ranch, a red, white, and blue painted mailbox of 1960s vintage marks the entrance to one of several clothing-optional beaches along the coast. Most others are marked by lines of cars parked along fields or bluffs with no one in sight. For a fee, the Red, White, and Blue Beach (408/423-6332) offers day use for families and adults. Volleyball, picnic tables, barbecue areas, restrooms, and overnight camping facilities are available.

Four miles north of Wilder Ranch and one mile south of Davenport, Bonny Doon County Beach offers picnic facilities for everyone opposite the turnoff to Bonny Doon Road. Known for its geological formations, this sheltered cove includes steep cliffs and natural bridges.

You can take the backroad Bonny Doon route inland through miles of redwoods, by occasional ocean vistas and the exclusive community of Bonny Doon, and on to Felton and Highway 9. This is also the northwest edge of Santa Cruz County wine country. Bonny Doon Vineyard (408/425-3625), located at the Pine Flat Road intersection with Bonny Doon Road, offers tastings and picnic facilities from noon to 5 p.m., Thursdays through Mondays. After passing the close-knit but spread-out community of Bonny Doon you arrive at the intersection of Bonny Doon Road and Empire Grade Road. If you turn left on Empire Grade Road here, you ascend a sinuous back route to Highway 236, which leads to Big Basin Redwoods State Park. Turn right on Felton Empire Grade Road to continue on to Felton, with connections to Highway 9 or Mount Hermon Road. Along the way you pass trailheads for Fall Creek State Park. Limekiln facilities that operated here provided lime for the bricks and cement in the rebuilding of San Francisco after the 1906 earthquake. Trails lead to ruins of the old lime tunnels and brick furnaces. After about an hour's journey from Highway 1 you see the entrance of Hallcrest Vineyards to your right (408/335-4441). The tasting room opens to a redwood deck with views of a half-century-old vineyard and Henry Cowell State Park. The winery also hosts special events featuring a variety of musicians, and you can rent horses here for picnic trail rides.

Highway 1 North to Davenport

If you have not detoured into the redwoods and are continuing north on Highway 1 you soon arrive at the town of Davenport, and may soon be hollering "Thar she blows!" The original town was built around a whaler's cove formed to the north by El Jarro Point and called Davenport Landing. The settlement was named by a Rhode Island sea captain, John P. Davenport, who is credited with establishing the state's first on-shore whaling operations.

Besides whaling the wharf was used for the shipment of lumber, by the San Vicente Lumber Company, which logged the old rancho grant. As the whale populations have somewhat bounced back, Davenport again is a whaler's town, but only for watching.

A huge demand for Davenport cement and for San Vicente lumber followed the earthquake of 1906. Davenport cement was also used in the 1930s to construct the south pier of the Golden Gate Bridge, as well as a fleet of cement boats, such as the one at Seacliff.

The 1914 Davenport jail was famous for never being used. Prisoners were sent to Santa Cruz instead! Today, the jail is the Davenport Historical Museum

(408/425-7278). Exhibits explore topics such as the local environment and the days of loggers, whalers and rum-runners.

We used to make a yearly trek to Davenport for the annual Big Creek Pottery open house, but a year now seems too long to wait. The pottery is sold along with other wholesome items at the McDougals' New Davenport Cash Store (408/423-4122), which combines a store and restaurant. The store sells collectible imports—toys, clothing, and musical instruments, as well as environmentally friendly posters, puppets, crafts, and of course Big Creek Pottery. The new Davenport Bed and Breakfast Inn operates above and adjacent to the store and restaurant.

Artists and craftspeople of exceptional talent seem drawn to Davenport. The Lundberg Studio usually opens the three weekends before Christmas to display its selection of blown-glass lampshades, goblets, and paperweights. When I visited the glass studio in Cambria I had only to whisper the name "Lundberg" and people put down their paperweights to hear any news. Custom woodwork is sawed at the Davenport Mill, 433 Marine View Avenue (408/423-8577), a veritable museum of antique woodworking tools. If you can haul yourself over to the nearby Aeolus Boat Works (408/423-5681) you might catch owner Bill Grunwald at work handcrafting a custom-order boat.

Other businesses in Davenport are close together on Highway 1. You can get sandwiches at the delicatessen to enjoy on the cypress-shaded bluff across the highway. The general store in town sells fishing gear. Fishing at this beach is recommended at low tide only. The tides here can catch you unaware. People are frequently stranded on the rocky outcroppings.

Speaking of rocks, the large "Greyhound Rock," five miles north of Davenport, has been a popular fishing area for years and is now run by the state as a seventy-acre "Fishing Access." It is named for a rock formation that extends into the ocean, forming a point. There is a paved walkway that leads down to the beach from the parking area. The endless stretch of beaches and the rock formations that meet the sands at Greyhound Rock are well worth every step back up.

This stretch, between Davenport and northern Pescadero, was once known as the Graveyard of Ships, and many points, coves, and rocks were named for the ships that were wrecked here. This was a major shipping route for freighters carrying gold from the 1849 rush, lumber, lime, supplies for the gold camps, and passengers. Pigeon Point was named for the 1853 wreck of the clipper *Carrier Pigeon*; Franklin Point, for the 1865 wreck of the *Sir John Franklin*.

Just north of Greyhound Rock you might see people completing the skyline-to-the-sea trail. Seventeen-hundred acres of this region known as Rancho del Oso, "Ranch of the Bears" are today a subunit of Big Basin State Park and include the popular skyline-to-the-sea trail. The trail descends 1,200 feet and 11 miles, from park headquarters at Big Basin, or descends 30 miles from Castle Rock

State Park at the summit, to the terminus of Waddell Creek at Waddell State Beach. Hikers can catch a Santa Cruz Metro bus back to their cars (see page 260 for more information).

Herons, egrets, and legions of shorebirds welcome the hiker or Highway 1 traveler to Waddell Creek and marsh. The freshwater marsh at the trail's end is a prime stopover for birds on the Pacific flyway. The Theodore J. Hoover Natural Preserve here protects over two hundred kinds of native and migratory birds. A small interpretive center and weekend hikes add to awareness of the area.

Beyond Waddell Creek, crumbling cliffs rise as sheer walls near Highway 1. Winter storms used to block wagon travelers along this stretch from their polling places in Santa Cruz County. Now the cliffs form a natural and political separation between Santa Cruz and San Mateo counties, and between the Central Coast and parts north in California.

WHAT ELSE TO SEE AND DO

SPECIAL SANTA CRUZ ATTRACTIONS: SANTA CRUZ BEACH BOARDWALK. (408/423-5590): Whiffs of corndogs and shrill cries of thrillseekers may be calling you to the Santa Cruz Beach Boardwalk (408/423-5590), home to the Big Dipper, a sunny beach with swimming lagoon, and crowds of summer fans. This oceanside park is the only remaining coastal amusement park in California and a registered National Historic Monument.

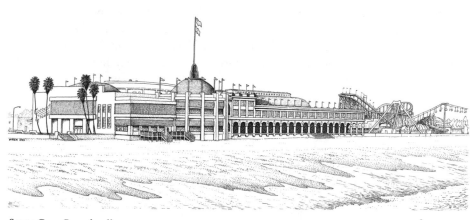

Santa Cruz Boardwalk

My favorite time to visit the boardwalk is from October through March. If you are joining the summer crowds, catch the shuttle from the government center on Ocean Street. Parking at the boardwalk is five dollars daily. Traffic is slow and hot. Steps lead from the boardwalk to the beach, so dress is as casual as you want. You can put on your better clothes for the Sunday brunch at the Coconut Grove, which also offers special events and weekend concerts.

Fred Swanton brought electricity to Santa Cruz in 1889. In 1903, he laid plans for a Moorish "pleasure casino," a tent-city campground, boardwalk attractions, and a river-bend "Neptune Park" for water carnivals.

The Swanton boardwalk opened in 1904 to great success. Then two years later, after surviving the 1906 earthquake, his casino and a previously built bathhouse burned to the ground. Undaunted, he rebuilt the casino and "plunge" larger than before, with John Philip Sousa providing music for the opening ceremonies.

Swanton sold the boardwalk in 1915 to the Seaside Company, which has operated it ever since. The merry-go-round was created by master designer Adolph Looft, and it is the last "brass ring" merry-go-round in North America. Looft also designed the Big Dipper Roller Coaster in 1924, with the intent of combining in one ride all the thrill experiences he could think of. The ride after the ascent is powered by the coaster's own momentum.

The old saltwater plunge has today been replaced with a miniature golf attraction, and a museum exhibit depicting the history of the boardwalk.

The San Lorenzo River mouth is north of the boardwalk area. In summer the offshore steelheads are frustrated but calm-water swimmers delighted when sand blocks the river's course, which provides a swimming lagoon. The lagoon is sometimes closed to swimming due to high bacteria counts; watch for posted warnings.

SANTA CRUZ MUNICIPAL WHARF AND COWELL BEACH. At the wharf and the beach (408/429-3628) you can kick back and relax. The half-mile-long wharf is lined with shops, fish markets, and seafood restaurants. Fish off the wharf, spend some time at the "main beach" between the boardwalk and the wharf, get a bite to eat or enjoy a fancy meal, join a charter boat trip with the long-established Stagnaro Family Boat Charters (408/423-1020), or rent your own boat and line at Santa Cruz Boat Rentals (408/423-1739). Parking on the pier is available for seventy-five cents an hour, with twelve-hour meters designated by blue poles. The wharf separates the main beach from the also-public Cowell Beach in front of the Dream Inn. In summer, the Richard Schmit Surf School (408/423-0928) offers the premier surfing lessons on the West Coast at this beach. Schmit, one of the world's top five big wave riders, has pioneered a unique method in which he rides out to waves with you, then the two of you catch the waves together. He lifts you up and you are riding on the first day.

KUUMBWA JAZZ CENTER. The nonprofit organization at 320 Cedar Street, Number 2 (408/427-2227), presents jazz concerts by both internationally known and local talent. On weekends an eclectic mix of music adds to the concert series. Theater-style seating and a jazz art gallery add to the concert experience. Seriously, several locals have told me Kuumbwa is the reason they moved to town.

THE LAST SUPPER. The life-size wax figures at 1927 Ocean Street Extension (408/ 426-1601), on the grounds of Santa Cruz Memorial Park, are an interpretation of Leonardo Da Vinci's famous painting.

MISSION SANTA CRUZ. The mission at 196 High Street in Santa Cruz (408/426-5686) was founded in 1791 as the twelfth in California. The original buildings were destroyed in 1857. In 1931 a half-size replica was built about seventy-five yards from the original site, where the Holy Cross Church now stands. Nearby is Casa Adobe, Santa Cruz's oldest building, which is undergoing extensive archaeological research and reconstruction. The mission chapel is open daily, 9 a.m. to 5 p.m.

MYSTERY SPOT. At 1953 North Branciforte Drive in Santa Cruz (408/423-8897) balls roll uphill and visitors find themselves leaning at precarious angles in a place where the laws of gravity appear to be reversed. Guides lead thirty-minute fee walking tours daily from 9:30 a.m. to 4:30 p.m.

PACIFIC EDGE INDOOR CLIMBING FACILITY. The facility at 105 Bronson Street, Suite 5012 (408/454-9254) is the largest indoor climbing gym in the world. Fifty-foot tall artificial cliffs rise from the floor of a former cannery. Lessons are offered to beginners.

A. K. SALTZ TANNERY. On River Street not far inland from its intersection with Highway 1 the old tannery dates back to the 1800s and is still operating. Tours are given (408/423-4470) and fine leather goods can be purchased.

SASH MILL. The diverse businesses found at 303 Potrero Street in buildings that housed the turn-of-the-century Sinkinson Sash Mill are on the other side of the tracks but worth the effort of discovery. In summer you can sit on the deck of the Sash Mill Cafe (408/425-8720) and wave to the engineer of the Roaring Camp Suntan-Special as the train passes on its way to redwoods or the Boardwalk. Down the Sash Mill walkway you will find Storrs Winery (408/458-5030), the only winery in the Santa Cruz city limits. Winery tours and tastings, highlighted by their award-winning Chardonnay, are offered here. You can sample the difference in coopering between domestic and French barrels, and Pamela and Stephen Storrs will share their intimate knowledge of grape growing in Santa Cruz County with you. Light manufacturing continues at Annie Glass (408/426-5086), where eleven lines of dinnerware including their signature Roman antique and frosted lines of slumped glass are created. Call in advance to arrange a tour. Their showroom has moved to 109 Cooper Street, downtown. The William James Foundation (408/426-2474) is found in the upstairs office space; and visitors can view a small gallery of prison art that is an outgrowth of the foundation's work with artists in prisons. Kayakers at the Sash Mill? For true adventure walk to the back of the mill where Adventure Sports (408/458-3648) uses a large pool to teach kayaking, scuba diving, and other aquatic sports. It also carries the necessary sports equipment and organizes scuba, kayaking, and camping trips.

SANTA CRUZ CITY MUSEUM. The museum at 1305 East Cliff Drive (408/429-3773) features six rooms of collections and exhibits dedicated to the natural sciences, history, and art of Santa Cruz County. Working exhibits include a beehive and fossil dig. Special tours and lectures, including the popular Spring Garden Tour of Victorian homes, are offered throughout the year. The museum is open Tuesday through Saturday, 10 a.m. to 5 p.m., and Sunday, noon to 5 p.m.

THE UNIVERSITY OF CALIFORNIA AT SANTA CRUZ. UCSC (408/459-0111) has at present eight colleges with an enrollment of about ten thousand on the two-thousand-acre campus. Each college is self-contained, with a complex of classrooms and student and faculty lodging. Libraries and laboratories are examples of shared facilities. Each college has its own focus and style. Students have a history of vocal participation in city politics. Several graduates have been elected to the city council. Some permanent residents "off the hill" feel that the transient nature of student voting weakens consistency in local government, and other people enjoy the energy and volunteerism that the students offer to the community.

To reach UCSC, turn inland from Highway 1 (Mission Street) onto Bay Street. Maps and guides are available at an entrance kiosk. The weathered buildings were originally part of the Cowell Ranch. If you visit the campus on a weekday you can hop on and off the campus shuttle bus—The Banana Slug.

When I talked with campus architect Frank Zwark he had just conducted a tour with top Tokyo architects who had traveled to the United States to view the best architecturally designed college campuses—including Harvard, MIT,

Stanford, and UCSC. When visitors come to UCSC to view the architecture, Zwark suggests they view Cowell Hall: "For two reasons, one because I graduated from Cowell College, so I have an added pride, and two because it exemplifies what the architecture at UCSC seeks to achieve. It's located at the edge of the forest and fields. You have a sense that the campus and the campus landscape are the same. It's not what you see at UCSC, its what you don't see—the architecture blends with the surrounding landscape. You have views over the fields of the whole city and beyond, to the bay. When The Cowell Foundation donated the college it was with the understanding that this college would be located in a spot where it could see the city and the city see it, to symbolize the interconnectedness of the two. "Cowell College is typical of architecture by Wurster, Bernardi, and Emmons, which blends the use of industrial materials with traditional standbys, such as tile roofs and planked timbers.

You are welcome to wander through the campus and in the buildings to appreciate the architecture. While on campus be sure also to visit the science complex, most notably the Earth Science Building completed in 1993 and the Science Library, which was designed by the architectural firm of Esherick, Homsey, Dodge, and Davis—the same architectural firm that designed the Monterey Bay Aquarium. The large bay and corner windows invite the forest inside. The library fits the environment so well that, in the Zwark's words, "It looks like they helicoptered it in among the trees."

The campus forest paths and bookstore areas as well as the coffee shops and restaurants are exploration points for tourists. The campus arboretum off Empire Grade displays an international selection of plants, especially those of Australia and South America. Docents are usually on hand to answer questions.

APPENDICES

RESOURCE GUIDE

TRANSPORTATION

Airports

Monterey Peninsula Airport. On Highway 68. Served by one major carrier, United, and four regional carriers.

San Francisco International Airport. Served by all major airlines and regional carriers.

San Jose International Airport. Served by all major airlines and regional carriers.

Ground Transportation

To and from all Airports

A-1 Limousine Service Inc., 408/649-1425.

Adventure Tours Unlimited and Airport Shuttle, 408/375-2409.

Airport Executive Limousine, 408/372-5555.

Central Coast Limousine, 408/636-5988.

Otter-Mobile Tours & Charters, 408/625-9782.

To San Francisco and San Jose Airports

Santa Cruz Airporter, 408/423-1214.

A Sea Coast Safari, 408/372-1288.

Monterey Airport Taxi Service

Joe's Cab/Carmel Taxi, 408/626-3333.

Yellow Cab, 408/646-1234.

Charter Coaches

Discovery Tours, 408/722-5010.

Pacific Monarch Ltd., 408/429-6600.

Local Buses

Santa Cruz Metropolitan Transit District, 408/425-8600.

Monterey-Salinas Transit, Monterey, 408/899-2555. Salinas, 408/424-7695.

San Luis Obispo County Area Transit (SLOCAT) Buses, 408/541-2277.

Rail Line

Amtrak, 800/872-7245.

VISITOR'S CENTERS

Monterey County

Monterey County Parks Department Tourist Center, 1160 Broadway (in San Lorenzo Park), King City. Open daily, 10:00 a.m. to 5 p.m. 408/385-1484.

Monterey Peninsula Chamber of Commerce and Visitor's and Convention Bureau, 380 Alvarado Street, Monterey. Monday through Friday, 8:30 a.m. to 5 p.m., 408/649-1770.

Monterey Visitor Center, Information Center for the City of Monterey, 401 Camino El Estero, Monterey. Open seven days a week, for walk-ins only.

Santa Cruz County

Santa Cruz County Visitor's Information, Conference, and Visitor's Council. Three locations: 701 Front Street, Santa Cruz, 408/425-1234. Open seven days a week, all year. Kiosk location in front of county buildings at 701 Ocean Street, Santa Cruz; Open from Memorial Day to Labor Day. Summit Visitor's Center (at the top of

Highway 17, by the Summit Inn Garden Restaurant); open seven days a week, all year.

Gilroy

Gilroy Visitor's Bureau, 7780 Monterey Street, Gilroy, 408/842-6436. Information center for areas around Gilroy including Morgan Hill, local wineries, and garlic events. Open seven days a week.

In addition, many individual cities offer visitor's centers in their Chamber of Commerce or business-association offices.

CHAMBERS OF COMMERCE

Monterey County

Big Sur Chamber of Commerce, P.O. Box 87, Big Sur 93920, 408/667-2100.

Carmel Business Association, in the Eastwood Building on San Carlos Street between Fifth and Sixth avenues, or P.O. Box 4444, Carmel 93921, 408/624-2522.

Carmel Valley Chamber of Commerce, 9 Delfino Place or P.O. Box 288, Carmel Valley 93924, 408/659-4000.

Castroville Chamber of Commerce, California Artichoke Advisory Board, P.O. Box 744, Castroville 95012, 408/633-6545.

Del Rey Oaks: contact the Monterey Peninsula Chamber of Commerce.

Gonzales Chamber of Commerce, City Hall, 109 Fourth Street, Gonzales 93926, 408/675-9019.

Greenfield Chamber of Commerce, City Hall, 215 El Camino Real or P.O. Box 333, Greenfield 93927, 408/674-3222.

King City Chamber of Commerce: 203 Broadway, King City 93930, 408/385-3814.

Marina Chamber of Commerce: phone contact welcome, 408/384-0155.

Moss Landing Chamber of Commerce: information available at By-a-Button, 345 Moss Landing Road, P.O. Box 41, Moss Landing 95039, 408/633-5202.

Pacific Grove Chamber of Commerce, Forest Avenue and Central, or P.O. Box 167, Pacific Grove 93950, 408/373-3304.

Salinas Chamber of Commerce, 119 East Alisal, or P.O. Box 1170, Salinas 93902, 408/424-7611.

(Salinas) Old Town Salinas Chamber of Commerce, 408/758-9272.

Seaside Chamber of Commerce, 505 Broadway Avenue, Seaside 93955, 408/394-6501.

Soledad Chamber of Commerce, City Hall, 248 Main Street, or P.O. Box 335, Soledad 93960, 408/678-2278.

Santa Cruz County

Aptos Chamber of Commerce, in Redwood Village, 9099 Soquel Drive, #12, Aptos 95003, 408/688-1467.

Capitola Chamber of Commerce, 621 Capitola Avenue, Capitola 95010, 408/475-6522.

Pajaro Valley Chamber of Commerce (Watsonville), P.O. Box 1748, Watsonville 95077, 408/724-3900.

San Lorenzo Chamber of Commerce, serving the cities of Ben Lomond, Felton and Boulder Creek, 408/335-2764.

Santa Cruz Area Chamber of Commerce, 1543 Pacific Avenue, Santa Cruz 95060. 408/423-1111.

Santa Cruz Downtown Association, 1543 Pacific Avenue, Suite 212, Santa Cruz, 95060 408/429-8433.

Scotts Valley Chamber of Commerce, P.O. Box 66928, Scotts Valley 95066, 408/438-1010.

Soquel Village Business Association, 4633 Soquel Drive, Soquel, 95073 408/475-1702.

Cambria and San Simeon

Cambria Chamber of Commerce, 767 Main, Cambria 93428, 805/927-3624.

San Simeon Chamber of Commerce, 9255 Hearst Drive, San Simeon 93452, 805/927-3500.

San Juan Bautista and Gilroy

Gilroy Chamber of Commerce, 7471 Monterey Street, Gilroy 95020, 408/842-6437.

San Juan Bautista, 402-A Third Street or P.O. Box 1037, San Juan Bautista 95045, 408/623-2454.

GUIDED TOURS

Adventure Tours Unlimited and Airport Shuttle, Pacific Grove, 408/375-2409.

The Bicycle Rental and Tour Center, Santa Cruz, 408/426-8687.

Gourmet Food & Wine Tours of Monterey Bay, Carmel by-the-Sea, 800/924-WINE; in California, 408/655-TOUR.

Otter-Mobile Tours & Charters, Carmel, 408/625-9782.

A Sea Coast Safari, Pebble Beach, 408/372-1288.

Trolley Connection, fourteen shops along the Monterey Peninsula, 800/634-1115.

SPECIALIZED TOURS

Airplane Tours

Wings Over Paradise Biplane Tours, at the Watsonville Airport, Watsonville, 408/662-WING.

Hot Air Balloon Tours

Balloons By-the-Sea, 71 Myrtle, Salinas, 408/424-0111.

Kayak Tours

Adventures by the Sea, 408/372-1807.

Adventure Sports, kayaks and scuba diving, 303 Potrero Street, #15, Santa Cruz, 408/458-3648.

Kayak Connection, Santa Cruz, 408/479-1121, Moss Landing, 408/724-5692.

Monterey Bay Kayaks, 623 Del Monte Avenue, Monterey, 408/373-5357(KELP).

Semisubmersible Submarine Tours

Nautilus Monterey, Fisherman's Wharf, No. 1, Monterey, 408/647-1400.

Walking Tours

Bio-Tours with Todd Bliss, 408/375-5089.

Cannery Row Walking Tours, 408/373-5571.

Monterey State Historic Park Walking Tour, 408/649-7118.

Santa Cruz Walking Tours with Ross Gibson, 408/423-1932.

Whale-watching Tours and Fishing Trips

Chris's Fishing Expeditions,
48 Fisherman's Wharf No. 1, Monterey,
408/375-5951.

Monterey Sport Fishing, 96 Fisherman's
Wharf No. 1, Monterey, 408/372-2203.

Randy's Fishing Trips, 66 Fisherman's
Wharf No. 1, Monterey, 408/372-7440.

Sam's Fishing Trips, Municipal Wharf
No. 1, Monterey, 408/372-0577.

San Simeon Landing, William Randolph
Hearst State Beach, San Simeon,
805/927-1777.

WINERIES

The following listings of wineries offer
tours and/or tastings. Call in advance of
your visit for special arrangements, days,
and times.

Monterey and Vicinity

Bargetto's Santa Cruz Winery, 700
Cannery Row, Monterey 93940,
408/373-4053.

Chalone Vineyard, Highway 146,
Soledad 93960, 408/678-1717.

Chateau Julien Winery, 8940 Carmel
Valley Road, Carmel Valley 93923,
408/624-2600.

Cloninger Cellars, 1645 River Road or
P.O. Box 5, Salinas 93902, 408/758-
1686.

Lockwood Vineyard, Steinbeck Station,
P.O. Box 1997, Salinas 93932, 800/753-
1424.

The Monterey Peninsula Winery Tasting
Room, 786 Wave Street, Monterey
93940, 408/372-4949 or 408/394-2999.

The Monterey Vineyard, 800 South Alta
Street, Gonzales 93926, 408/675-2316.

Paraiso Springs, 38060 Paraiso Springs
Road, Soledad 93960, 408/678-1593.

Paul Masson Wine Tasting Room and
Museum, 700 Cannery Row, Monterey
93940, 408/646-5446.

Ventana Vineyards, 2999 Monterey-
Salinas Highway, Monterey 93940,
408/372-7415.

Santa Cruz and Vicinity

Ahlgren Vineyard, P.O. Box M, Boulder
Creek 95006, 408/338-6071.

Bargetto Winery, 3535 North Main
Street, Soquel 95073, 408/475-2258.

Bonny Doon Vineyard, 2 Pine Flat Road
or P.O. Box 8376, Santa Cruz 95061,
408/425-3625.

Byington Winery and Vineyard, 21850
Bear Creek Road, Los Gatos 95030,
408/354-1111.

Crescini Wines, P.O. Box 216, Soquel
95073, 408/462-1466.

David Bruce Winery, 21439 Bear Creek
Road, Los Gatos, 408/354-4214.

Devlin Wine Cellars, 3801 Park Avenue
or P.O. Box 728, Soquel 95073, 408/476-
7288.

Hallcrest Vineyards, 379 Felton Empire
Road, Felton 95018, 408/335-4441.

River Run Vintners, 65 Rogge Lane,
Watsonville 95076, 408/726-3112.

Roudon-Smith Vineyards, 2364 Bean
Creek Road, Santa Cruz 95066,
408/438-1244.

Santa Cruz Mountain Vineyard, 2300
Jarvis Road, Santa Cruz, 95065,
408/426-6209.

Storrs Winery, 303 Potrero Street, #35, Santa Cruz 408/458-5030, 408/458-5030.

Zayante Vineyards, 420 Old Mount Road, Felton 95018, 408/335-7992 or 408/335-5770.

SHOPPING CENTERS AND DEPARTMENT STORES

Monterey County

American Tin Cannery Outlet Center, 125 Ocean View Boulevard, Pacific Grove, 408/372-1442. Forty factory outlet stores with items ranging from baby clothes to jewelry, from fine china to toys, offer discounts in the spaces of this former cannery.

The Barnyard, 26400 Carmel Rancho Lane, Carmel, 408/624-8886. Beautiful gardens surround barnlike buildings which house a collection of fifty shops including clothing boutiques, a bookstore cafe, art galleries, and restaurants.

Carmel Plaza Associates, Ocean and Junipero, Carmel, 408/624-0137. Fifty stores, including twenty clothing stores, gift shops, a bookstore, and specialty shops, cover a two block area at the eastern entrance to Carmel.

The Crossroads, 159 Crossroads Boulevard, Carmel, 408/625-4106. Cobblestone walkways lead to eighty specialty stores and restaurants that win many local taste awards. A Safeway and Longs Drugs anchor the collection of shops.

Del Monte Shopping Center, 1410 Del Monte Shopping Center, Monterey, 408/373-2705. Large wall murals, gardens, and special events add ambiance to this major shopping center with over one hundred stores in an open mall setting.

Harden Ranch Plaza, 1762B North Main Street, off Highway 101, Salinas, 408/449-6672. This new plaza houses thirty-five stores including major department and discount stores.

Northridge Mall, 796 Northridge Mall, off Highway 101, Salinas, 408/449-7226. A hand-carved carousel and over one hundred forty stores including major department stores, electronics stores, and home furnishing stores line this indoor mall.

Major shopping areas are located in the downtown areas of Carmel, Monterey, Pacific Grove, and Salinas. Cannery Row in Monterey is a shopping mecca with over one hundred fifty stores and new centers planned. Carmel Valley has shopping at Mid-Valley and Carmel Valley Village. Large discount stores are located in Marina and Sand City. Seaside also offers retail stores. Moss Landing Village includes forty businesses, among them twenty-five antique stores.

Santa Cruz County

Brown Ranch Marketplace (Clares Street, off 41st Avenue), 408/464-3555. The newest shopping center in the Santa Cruz area includes discount gourmet food stores, discount toy stores, and quality clothing stores as well as popular restaurants.

Capitola Mall, 1855 41st Avenue, Capitola, 408/476-9749. Over one hundred fifty stores anchored by major department stores fill this inside mall.

Downtown Santa Cruz includes a major shopping area along Pacific Avenue and adjacent streets. New shopping complexes are centered in Scotts Valley. Shops are also located along Highway 9. Various stores are located in downtown Watsonville, and small shopping centers are located on the outskirts of town.

Cambria and San Simeon

These two enclaves include small town shopping areas as well as a variety of galleries, craft stores, and specialty shops.

Gilroy

The Outlets at Gilroy, 8300 Arroyo Circle, Gilroy, 408/848-7228. Over one hundred factory outlet stores for almost every need cover several acres here.

COLLEGES AND UNIVERSITIES

Monterey

Hartnell Community College, 156 Homestead Avenue, Salinas, 408/755-6721/6700.

Monterey Peninsula College, 980 Fremont Street, Monterey, 408/646-4000.

San Jose State, Monterey County Campus, 893 Blanco Circle, Salinas, 408/755-8600.

Santa Cruz

Cabrillo College, 6500 Soquel Drive, Aptos, 408/479-6100. A community college.

University of California at Santa Cruz, 1156 High Street, Santa Cruz, 408/459-0111.

MUSEUMS

In addition to these museum listings, many visitor locations such as libraries, missions, wineries, and state parks offer museums on their sites. Monterey and San Juan Bautista State Historic Parks include several museums in their parameters.

Monterey County

Boronda History Center, 333 Boronda Road at Calle de Adobe, Salinas, 408/757-8085.

Center for Photographic Art, in the Sunset Center, San Carlos Street and Ninth Avenue, Carmel, 408/625-5181.

Maritime Museum of Monterey, in the Stanton Center at Custom House Plaza near Fisherman's Wharf, 408/373-2469.

Monterey Peninsula Museum of Art, 559 Pacific Street, Monterey, 408/372-7591. La Mirada addition, 720 Via Mirada, Monterey, 408/372-3689.

Museum of Natural History, 165 Forest Avenue, Pacific Grove, 408/372-4212.

Monterey County Agricultural and Rural Life Museum, 1160 Broadway, in the San Lorenzo Park just outside King City, 408/385-5964.

Tor House and Hawk Tower, 26304 Ocean View Avenue, Carmel, 408/624-1840.

Santa Cruz County

Art Museum of Santa Cruz County, 224 Church Street, Santa Cruz, 408/429-3420.

Capitola Historical Museum, 410 Capitola Avenue, Capitola, 408/646-0322.

Lighthouse Surfing Museum, West Cliff Drive, Santa Cruz, 408/429-3429.

Octagon Museum, 118 Cooper Street, Santa Cruz, 408/425-2540.

Santa Cruz City Museum of Natural History, 1305 East Cliff Drive, Santa Cruz, 408/429-3773.

William Volck Museum, 261 East Beach Street, Watsonville, 408/722-0305.

PERFORMING ARTS

Monterey County

Music and Theater Festivals

The following is a list of major annual festivals which have continued for several years.

Carmel Bach Festival, Carmel Sunset Center and the Carmel Mission Basilica, Carmel, 408/624-1521.

Dixieland Monterey, Main Street, downtown Monterey and Fisherman's Wharf, Monterey, 408/649-1770.

Mariachi de Alta California, Western Stage at Hartnell College, 408/755-6980.

Monterey Blues Festival, Monterey Fairgrounds and Exposition Park, 408/649-1770.

Monterey Jazz Festival, Monterey Fairgrounds and Exposition Park, 408/373-3366.

Mozart Monterey, 408/624-8792. Summer concert series at several locations including the Monterey Conference Center.

Symphony Orchestras

Monterey Bay Symphony, P.O. Box 146, Carmel, 408/372-6276. This symphony offers free outdoor concerts on the lawns of the Naval Postgraduate School on Memorial Day, July Fourth, and Labor Day, as well as an August concert for children at the Del Monte Shopping Center in Monterey.

Monterey County Symphony, P.O. Box 3965, Carmel, 408/624-8511. This symphony offers a series of six concerts from October through May at the Sunset Center in Carmel and at Sherwood Hall in Salinas.

Theaters

There are ongoing musical and performing arts events throughout the year presented at the following locations:

California's First Theatre, Scott and Pacific Streets, Monterey, 408/375-4916.

Carl Cherry Foundation, Guadalupe and Fourth, Carmel, 408/624-7491.

Forest Theater, Mountain View and Santa Rita, Carmel. Indoor and outdoor performances, Children's Experimental Theatre, 408/624-1531.

Grovemont's Monterey Playhouse, Hoffman and Lighthouse, Monterey, 408/649-6852.

Hidden Valley Music Seminars, Carmel Valley and Ford Roads, Carmel Valley, 408/659-3115.

Monterey Peninsula College Theatre, 980 Fremont Boulevard, Monterey, 408/646-4213.

Sherwood Hall, Salinas Community Center, 940 North Main Street, Salinas, 408/758-7351.

Steinbeck Forum, Monterey Conference Center, 1 Portola Plaza, Monterey, 408/646-3770.

Sunset Center Theater, San Carlos Street between Eighth and Ninth, Carmel, 408/624-3996.

Western Stage, Hartnell College Performing Arts Center, 156 Homestead Avenue at Alisal Street, Salinas, 408/756-6816.

Wharf Theater, Old Fisherman's Wharf, Monterey, 408/649-2332.

Santa Cruz County

Music and Theater Festivals

The following is a list of major annual festivals which have continued for several years.

Cabrillo Music Festival, summer concerts in Santa Cruz and at Mission San Juan Bautista, 408/662-2701.

Dickens Players, Kresge College, University of California at Santa Cruz, Santa Cruz, 408/459-2103. Year-round performance schedule of high-spirited vignettes culled from the works of Dickens, highlighted by productions in conjunction with summertime Shakespeare Santa Cruz Festival and Dickens Universe conference.

Santa Cruz Baroque Festival, Santa Cruz, 408/459-3418 or 408/476-2313. An annual concert series with a focus on the Baroque period and a range of music from medieval through classic and early romantic. Season runs February through May.

Shakespeare Santa Cruz, Performing Arts Complex, University of California at Santa Cruz, Santa Cruz, 408/429-2121. Year-round performance events, highlighted by a six-week summer festival of Shakespeare and contemporary theater masterpieces.

Symphony Orchestra

Santa Cruz County Symphony, 6500 Soquel Drive, Aptos, 408/462-0553.

Theaters

The Cultural Council of Santa Cruz County, 408/476-2313, offers informa-tion about performing arts groups and presentations. There are ongoing musical and performing arts events throughout the year presented at the following locations:

Hallcrest Vineyards, 379 Felton Empire Road, Felton, 408/335-4441.

Kuumbwa Jazz Center, 320 Cedar Street, Number 2, Santa Cruz, 408/427-2227.

Mountain Community Theater, 1000 Alba Road, Ben Lomond, 408/336-2278. Regular season of live family-oriented theater.

Santa Cruz Civic Auditorium, 307 Church Street, Santa Cruz, 408/429-3444.

Santa Cruz County Actor's Theatre, 1001 Center Street, Santa Cruz, 408/425-PLAY. A year-round production company offering dramatic and musical perfor-mances, as well as a play-reading series held one Wednesday of each month. Call for performance and ticket information.

UCSC Performing Arts Concert Hall, University of California at Santa Cruz, Santa Cruz, 408/459-2787. Offers a wide range of performing arts events, from classical to ethnic music, from drama to ballet, as well as lectures.

Cambria and San Simeon

Pewter Plough Playhouse, 824 Main Street, Cambria, 408/927-3877.

San Juan Bautista and Gilroy

El Teatro Campesino, 705 Fourth Street, San Juan Bautista, 408/623-2444.

Gavilan College Theatre, 5056 Santa Teresa Boulevard at Mesa Road, Gilroy, 408/848-4860.

BEACHES

The Monterey Bay, from Monterey north to Santa Cruz, has wide expanses of sandy beaches. Along the northern and southern ends of the bay and open ocean there are rockier shores, some of which hide coves, interspersed with wide beaches. Most beaches are known to have rip currents and undertows. Ask rangers and lifeguards about surf conditions. Large, erratic waves are common along many of the beaches. There is camping at some beaches in Santa Cruz County and along Big Sur. The following list includes the major beaches, as there are hundreds of small intimate beaches in this area.

South of Carmel

Andrew Molera State Park Beach. On Highway 1, twenty-one miles south of Carmel. Primitive walk-in meadow campsites (no showers). 4,786 acres of beach and woodland hiking and riding trails. 408/667-2315.

Garrapata State Beach. On Highway 1, 6.7 miles south of Carmel (18 miles north of Big Sur). 3,000 acres. Activities include fishing and hiking. 408/667-2315.

Julia Pfeiffer State Beach. From Highway 1, one mile south of Pfeiffer Big Sur State Park, turn right toward the coast on Sycamore Canyon Road. Part of Pfeiffer Big Sur State Park. Beautiful, windy beach. 408/667-2315.

Limekiln Creek Beach. On Highway 1, fifty-three miles south of Carmel. At this writing ownership access is in dispute, and beach visitors must pay at the Limekiln Creek Campground. Some campsites here are on the sands. In the summer, waders dip their feet in pleasant Limekiln Creek and kayakers glide over the waves in the cove. 404/667-2403.

Monastery Beach. On Highway 1, one mile south of Carmel. Strong undertow; be careful near the water at this beach. Great view of Point Lobos State Reserve and the Carmelite Monastery.

San Simeon State Park and Beach. On Highway 1, five miles south of William Randolph Hearst State Beach. One hundred thirty campsites are located on an inland expanse of grass. Walking trails lead from the campground and from turnoffs along Highway 1 to sandy stretches interspersed with tidepools. Farther south, San Simeon State Beach merges with Leffingwell Landing State Beach and then Moonstone State Beach, where quartz agates can be gathered after large tides. 805/927-2035.

William Randolph Hearst State Beach. At San Simeon Landing, near the entrance road to William Randolph Hearst Castle. Usually sunny, this sheltered beach, with a fishing pier and a creek for wading, is a Central Coast favorite. San Simeon Landing (805/927-1777), a fishing and whale-watching business, operates near the parking lot. 806/927-2035.

Monterey and Vicinity

Asilomar State Beach and Conference Center. Along Asilomar Avenue, Pacific Grove. 105 acres. Conference grounds are available. Rocky shoreline surrounds a wide expanse of beach. 408/472-8016.

Carmel River State Beach. From Highway 1 in Carmel, take Ocean Avenue and Scenic Road. 106 acres. Wetlands and sandy beach. Strong undertow. 408/624-4909.

Lovers Point Beach. Along Ocean View Boulevard, Pacific Grove. A man-made cove with two sheltered beaches, picnic areas, kayak rentals, diving access, and snack vendor. 408/373-3304.

Marina State Beach. At the foot of Reservation Road in Marina, ten miles north of Monterey. High dunes; wind-surfing and sailing areas. Strong rip currents. 408/384-7695.

Monterey State Beach. In Monterey, take Del Monte Avenue and Camino Aguajito. A long stretch of beach; two sections interspersed with city beaches. Continues to wharf area. 408/384-7695.

Mid-Monterey Bay

Moss Landing State Beach. From Highway 1 in Moss Landing take Jetty Road. Within close view of the PG&E plant. Picnic tables along a jetty, a sandy dune beach; en route camping for self-contained vehicles. 408/384-7695.

Salinas River State Beach. From Highway 1, one mile south of Moss Landing, take Potrero Road. Remote sandy beach that stretches south to a National Wetlands. Strong rip currents. 408/384-7695.

Zmudowski State Beach. From Highway 1, one mile north of Moss Landing, take Struve Road. 220 Acres. Coastal dunes and sandy beach, primitive parking, chemical toilets. Strong currents. Fishing and bring-your-own horse riding, 408/384-7695.

Santa Cruz and Vicinity

Capitola State Beach. Beside Capitola Wharf and the Esplanade. A sunny popular beach volleyball, restrooms, lifeguards.

Cowell Beach and the Main Santa Cruz Beach. Along the Dream Inn and Boardwalk. A sandy stretch of beach; volleyball, surfing, lifeguards. Cowell Beach has gentle waves. In the summer, the mouth of the San Lorenzo River is blocked by sand walls here to create a swimming lagoon.

Davenport Landing. Off Highway 1 some ten miles north of Santa Cruz. No lifeguards or amenities. Whale watching area. Be aware of the tides so as not to get stranded here.

Greyhound Rock. At Swanton Road and Highway 1, some fifteen miles north of Santa Cruz. A paved walkway leads downhill to a scenic beach and popular fishing access.

Manresa State Beach. From Highway 1 north of Watsonville take Mar Monte from the exit with that name, then San Andreas Road. At La Selva Beach the first parking lot is a day-use area. Manresa Uplands, with sixty-four walk-in tent campsites, is located a half mile north of the day use area. Turn toward the coast on Sand Dollar Drive. Both sections offer wide expanses of beach with breathtaking cliff views, frequent morning fogs. 408/724-1266.

Moran Lake Beach. Along East Cliff Drive at 26th Avenue in Live Oak, an unincorporated section of Santa Cruz County, just south of the city of Santa Cruz. A cove beach, popular with surfers.

Natural Bridges State Beach. At the end of West Cliff Drive in Santa Cruz. Picnic areas, marshes, hiking trails, a monarch butterfly grove, interpretive center, and rocky tide pools. Docents lead interpretive walks. 408/423-4609

New Brighton State Beach. Off Park Avenue in Capitola. Camping on wooded bluffs above sandy beach. 408/475-4850.

Pleasure Point. Along East Cliff Drive, near 41st Avenue in Live Oak. Popular with surfers.

Red, White, and Blue Beach. Along Highway 1 (at red, white, and blue mailbox), some six miles north of Santa Cruz.

Private Beach. Swimsuit optional; admission fee. Camping available. 408/423-6332.

San Lorenzo Point/Castle Beach. Along East Cliff Drive between the San Lorenzo River and the Yacht Harbor in Santa Cruz. Summer lifeguards, restrooms; less populated than the main Santa Cruz beach.

Seacliff State Beach. Off Highway 1 at the Seacliff exit in Aptos. Popular sandy beach, home of World War I cement boat. Picnic areas, hiking trails, fishing, RV and trailer camping only. 408/688-3222.

Sunset State Beach. From Highway 1 north of Watsonville take Mar Monte from the exit with that name, then San Andreas Road south about three miles to a brown sign at Sunset Beach Road, Watsonville. Large dunes, camping. 408/724-1266.

Twin Lakes Beach. Along East Cliff Drive, east of the Yacht Harbor. A sunny crescent beach with fire pits. Restrooms, nature walks across the street at small lakes and bird refuge.

Waddell Creek Beach. On Highway 1 just south of the San Mateo County line. Sea to Skyline trail from Big Basin Park connects near the marsh on the inland side of Highway 1. The marsh is a popular bird refuge, while the offshore waters are frequented by large-winged, mammalian windsurfers.

CAMPING

Big Sur

State Parks

Andrew Molera State Beach, 408/667-2423. Walk-in, primitive campsites only.

Pfeiffer Big Sur State Park, Big Sur, 408/667-2423, Mistix 800/444-PARK for campsite reservations.

Julia Pfeiffer Burns State Park, 408/667-2423, Mistix 800/444-PARK for campsite reservations. Four walk-in campsites.

Los Padres National Forest Campgrounds

Five Big Sur Campgrounds and several back country camps are under this jurisdiction, 408/385-5434. The campgrounds with water are Kirk Creek and Plaskett. Ponderosa and Nacimiento campgrounds are set on the eastern side. Bottchers Camp no longer can provide quality water.

Private Parks

Riverside Campgrounds and Cabins, Big Sur, 408/667-2414.

Ventana Campgrounds, Big Sur, 408/667-2331, or 408/624-4812.

Carmel Valley

Private Parks

Riverside RV Park, Schulte Road, Carmel Valley, 408/624-9329.

Saddle Mountain Recreation Park, Schulte Road, Carmel Valley, 408/624-1617.

Marina

Marina Dunes RV Park, 3330 Dunes Drive, Marina, 408/384-6914.

Monterey and Vicinity

Monterey County Park at Laguna Seca Recreation Area, 1025 Monterey Road, Salinas, 408/422-6138.

Veterans Memorial Park (municipal), Jefferson Street and Skyline Drive, Monterey, 408/646-3865.

Southern Monterey County

Camping is available near King City at San Lorenzo Park and at Lake San Antonio with the Monterey County Parks, 408/647-7795.

Santa Cruz and Vicinity

State Parks

Big Basin State Park, off Highway 9 north of Boulder Creek, 408/338-6132. 147 camping sites; nature trails, natural history museum.

Henry Cowell Redwoods State Park, Highway 9, Felton, 408/438-2396. 105 developed campsites; hiking trails and nature walks along the San Lorenzo River.

Manresa State Beach, the uplands. Sand Dollar Drive. From Highway 1 north of Watsonville take Mar Monte from the exit with that name, then San Andreas Road. 408/724-1266. Sixty-four walk-in campsites.

New Brighton State Beach, 1500 Park Avenue, Capitola, 408/475-4850. 115 campsites

Forest of Nisene Marks State Park, Aptos Creek Road, Aptos, 408/688-3241. Backcountry camping only.

Seacliff State Beach, 235 Santa Cruz Avenue, Aptos, 408/688-3222. Recreational vehicle camping only. Reservations needed.

Private Parks

Carbonero Creek Travel Park, 4556 Scotts Valley Drive, Scotts Valley, 408/438-1288. Daily, weekly, monthly rates.

Cotillion Gardens RV Park, 300 Old Big Trees Road, Felton, 408/335-7669.

Redwood Rest Resort, 150 East Grove Road, Boulder Creek, 408/338-3413.

River Grove Park, 4980 Highway 9, Felton, 408/335-9155. RV, trailer, and camper park near Henry Cowell Redwoods.

Santa Vida Travel Park, 1611 Branciforte Drive, Santa Cruz, 408/425-1945. Trailers, RVs, tents; by day, week, or month.

Watsonville

Private Parks

KOA Campground, 1186 San Andreas Road, Watsonville, 408/722-0551. Pool, hot tubs, tennis courts, and laundry.

Loma Linda RV Park, 890 Salinas Road, Watsonville, 408/722-9311.

Marmo's Pinto Lake, 1324 Amesti Road, Watsonville, 408/722-4533.

Pinto Lake, 757 Green Valley Road, Watsonville, 408/722-8129. 34 developed RV campsites.

State Parks

Sunset State Beach, 201 Sunset Beach Road, Watsonville, 408/724-1266. 90 campsites among sand dunes.

San Simeon

San Simeon State Park, located on Highway 1 just south of San Simeon, 408/927-2020.

San Juan Bautista

Fremont Peak State Park, at the top of San Juan Canyon Road, 11 miles south of Highway 156, 408/623-4255.

BICYCLE RENTALS

Monterey

Adventures by the Sea, 299 Cannery Row, Monterey, 408/372-1807.

Bay Bikes, 640 Wave Street, Monterey, 408/646-9090. Also on Lincoln between 5th and 6th, Carmel, 408/625-BIKE.

Monterey Moped Adventures, 1250 Del Monte Avenue, Monterey, 408/373-2696.

Santa Cruz

The Bicycle Center and Tour Center, 415 Pacific Avenue, Santa Cruz, 408/426-8687.

Dutchman Bicycles, 3961 Portola Drive, Santa Cruz, 408/476-9555.

BOAT RENTALS

Monterey County

El Estero Boating, Lake El Estero, Monterey, 408/375-1484. Pedal boats for paddling around lake.

Lake San Antonio Resort, South Shore, 805/472-2313. Jet skis, fishing boats, and pontoon boats.

Santa Cruz County

Loch Lomond Reservoir for boating, fishing, exploring, 408/335-7424.

Pinto Lake Park in Watsonville for boating, 408/423-9703.

DIVING

Monterey

Aquarius Dive Shop, 2240 Del Monte Boulevard, Monterey, 408/375-1933.

Bamboo Reef, 614 Lighthouse Avenue, Monterey, 408/372-1685.

Dive Monterey, 598 Foam Street, Monterey, 408/655-3483.

Santa Cruz

Adventure Sports, 303 Potrero Street, #15, Santa Cruz, 408/458-3648.

Scuba Ventures, on the beach at the Yacht Harbor, Santa Cruz, 408/476-5201.

GOLF

Monterey County

Carmel Valley Ranch Resort, 1 Old Ranch Road, Carmel, 408/625-9500.

Laguna Seca Golf Club, York Road, Monterey, 408/373-3701.

The Links at Spanish Bay, Inn at Spanish Bay, 17 Mile Drive, Pebble Beach, 800/654-9300.

Old Del Monte Golf Course, 1300 Sylvan Road, Monterey, 408/373-2436.

Pebble Beach Golf Links, 17 Mile Drive, Pebble Beach, 408/624-3811, ext. 239.

Poppy Hills Golf Course, 3200 Lopez Road, Pebble Beach, 408/625-1513.

Quail Lodge Golf Club, 8025 Valley Greens Drive, Carmel, 408/624-1581.

Rancho Cañada Golf Club, Carmel Valley Road, Carmel, 408/624-0111.

Ridgemark Golf and Country Club Resort, 3800 Airline Highway, Hollister, 408/637-8151.

Santa Cruz County

Aptos Par 3, 2600 Mar Vista Drive, Aptos, 408/688-5000.

Aptos Seascape Golf Course, 610 Clubhouse Drive, Aptos, 408/688-3213.

Boulder Creek Golf and Country Club Golf Shop, 16901 Big Basin Highway, Boulder Creek, 408/338-2121.

Casserly Par 3 Golf Course, 626 Casserly Road, Watsonville, 408/724-1654.

De Laveaga Golf Course and Lodge. De Laveaga Park. Golf reservations, 408/423-7212. Pro shop, 408/423-7214.

Golf Course at Seascape Resort and Conference Center, 1 Seascape Resort Drive, Aptos, 800/929-7727.

Pajaro Valley Golf Club Inc., 967 Salinas Road, Watsonville, 408/724-3851.

Pasatiempo Golf Club, 555 Highway 17 (take Pasatiempo exit off Highway 17), 408/426-3622.

Scotts Valley Course (same as Valley Gardens Golf Course), 263 Mount Hermon Road, Scotts Valley, 408/438-3058.

Spring Hills Golf Course, 31 Smith Road, Watsonville, 408/724-1404.

Cambria and San Simeon

Cambria Adult Recreation Golf Association, 408/995-0911.

HORSEBACK RIDING AND TRAIL RIDES

Monterey County

Barlocker's Rustling Oak Ranch, 25252 Limekiln Road, Salinas, 408/659-9121.

The Holman Ranch, Carmel Valley, 408/659-2640.

Molera Trail Rides, Andrew Molera State Park, Highway 1, Big Sur, 408/625-8664.

Monterey Bay Equestrian Center, 19805 Pesante Road, Salinas, 408/663-5712.

Monterey County Equestrian Center, 225 River Road, Salinas, 408/455-1336.

Pebble Beach Equestrian Center, Portola Road and Alva Lane, Pebble Beach, 408/624-2756.

Ventana Wilderness Ranch, Carmel Valley, 408/659-0433.

Santa Cruz County

Hallcrest Vineyards, 379 Felton Empire Road, Felton, 408/335-4441.

KAYAKING

Adventures by the Sea, 299 Cannery Row, Monterey, as well as Lovers Point, Pacific Grove, 408/372-1807.

Adventure Sports, 303 Potrero, #15, at the Old Sash Mill, Santa Cruz, 408/458-3648.

Kayak Connection, 413 Lake Avenue, Santa Cruz, 408/479-1121. Moss Landing, 408/724-5692.

Monterey Bay Kayaks, 693 Del Monte Avenue, Monterey, 408/373-5357.

PARASAILING AND HANG GLIDING

Para Sail, Santa Cruz, 408/423-3545.

Western Hang-gliders, Reservation Road and Highway 1, Marina, 408/384-2622.

SAILING

Chardonnay II Cruise, Santa Cruz, 408/423-1213. Monterey, 408/373-8664.

SKATES AND SURFBOARD RENTALS

Monterey

Adventures by the Sea, 299 Cannery Row, Monterey, 408/372-1807.

On the Beach Surf Shop, 693 Lighthouse Avenue, Monterey, 408/646-WAVE. Also at Ocean and Mission, Carmel, 408/624-7282.

Sunshine Surf and Sport, 443 Lighthouse Avenue, Monterey, 408/375-5015.

Santa Cruz

Freeline Design Surfboards, 821 41st Avenue, 408/476-2950.

Go Skate, 601 Beach Street (across from the boardwalk), 408/425-8578.

O'Neill's, 1149 41st Avenue, Santa Cruz, 408/475-4151.

Seabright Surf Shop, 541 Seabright Avenue, 408/423-1451.

SPORTS CENTER

Monterey Sports Center, 401 East Franklin, Monterey, 408/646-3700.

TENNIS

Monterey

Carmel Valley Inn and Tennis Resort, Carmel Valley Road and Los Laureles Road, Carmel Valley, 408/659-3131.

King City Park Tennis Courts, South Vanderhurst Avenue (next to golf course). Racquetball Courts, 401 Division Street. King City, 408/385-3575.

Hyatt Hotels, 1 Old Golf Course Road, Monterey, 408/372-1234.

Monterey Tennis Center, 401 Pearl Street, Monterey, 408/372-0172.

City of Pacific Grove Tennis Courts, 515 Junipero Avenue, Pacific Grove, 408/372-2809.

Sherwood Tennis Center, 930 North Main Street, Salinas, 408/758-7318.

Santa Cruz

Aptos High, 7301 Freedom Boulevard, Aptos, 408/688-6565.

Cabrillo College, 6500 Soquel Drive, Aptos, 408/479-6266.

Cabrillo Courthouse, 6200 Soquel Drive, Aptos, 408/475-5979.

Harbor High, 300 LaFonda, Santa Cruz. Near Soquel and Capitola roads.

Neary Lagoon Park, Bay and California streets.

Soquel High, 401 Old San Jose Road, Soquel, 408/429-3919.

Cambria and San Simeon

Cambria Tennis Club, Cambria, 408/927-1041

CALENDAR OF EVENTS

Exact dates of events may change. Check the local papers and visitor's guides for a complete listing of events. Call the appropriate Chambers of Commerce for additional phone information.

January

Gray whales migrate to lagoons in Baja. You can watch them from overlooks along the coast and on whale-watching expeditions. Good viewing days also in December and February.

Usually in the First Two Weeks:

Rio Resolution Run, Carmel, 408/642-4112. January 1. A cross-country run on trails, beaches, and roads surrounding Carmel. Proceeds benefit the Family Resource Center.

El Dia de Los Reyes, 408/375-0095. January 6. Hispanic celebration to honor the three kings. Candlelight procession down Calle de Principal, musicians, treats for children, traditional *roscas* bread.

Often Later in the Month:

AT&T Pro-Am Golf Tournament, Pebble Beach, 800/541-9091. First week in February, sometimes in last week of January. Well-known professionals are paired with celebrities and amateurs for this crowd-pleasing event.

Fungus Festival and Fungus Fair, celebrated at the Santa Cruz Natural History Museum, 408/429-3760, and Santa Cruz India Joze Restaurant, 408/427-3554. Features mushroom-enhanced art and tastings, too. Weekends for exhibits; food and art for two weeks.

February

Millions of lady bugs are hatching in the sun-specked valleys of the Santa Lucia Mountains. Canadian geese trim the greens at Pebble Beach.

Usually in the First Two Weeks:

Masters of Food and Wine, Carmel Highlands Inn, 408/624-3801. International star chefs and vintners present cooking classes and tastings.

Natural Bridges Migration Festival, Natural Bridges State Beach Park, Santa Cruz, 408/423-4609.

Often Later in the Month:

Annual John Steinbeck Birthday Party, Monterey, 408/372-8512. February 27. Music, play excerpts, readings, and impersonations help celebrate John Steinbeck's birthday.

Monterey County Hot Air Affair, Monterey, 408/649-6544. Balloons fill the air above Laguna Seca in a "fox and hounds" race. Balloon rides, food, and entertainment.

March

Wildflowers begin painting hillsides. Peak viewing may be next month or in May. Songbirds fill gardens and glens with their calls and melodies.

Usually in the First Two Weeks:

Dixieland Monterey, Monterey, 408/443-5260. A selection of the nation's finest Dixieland bands parade and play in cabaret locations throughout downtown Monterey and Fisherman's Wharf.

Colton Hall Birthday, Monterey, 408/646-5640. Celebrate Monterey's birthday with historic plays, free birthday cake, and punch.

Often Later in the Month:

Monterey Wine Festival, Monterey, 800/525-3378. The festival features tastings of over eight hundred wines from two hundred wineries, gourmet luncheons, and seminars.

Beacon House Art Auction, Monterey, 408/372-2334. Artwork by well-known local artists is auctioned off at this evening event. All proceeds benefit Beacon House.

California Chocolate Abalone Dive, Monterey, 408/375-1933 or 408/375-6605. Divers search for chocolate abalone in the bay to benefit the Pacific Grove Marine Rescue Unit and Divers Alert Network.

April

Harbor seals give birth and snowy plovers nest on selected beaches.

Usually in the First Two Weeks:

The Bellas Artes del Valle with the Festival de Mariachi de Alta California at Hartnell College, Salinas, 408/755-6980. Spotlights Hispanic arts, music, and dance.

Monterey Outdoor Recreation Show, Monterey, 408/649-6544. The show features RVs, boats, recreational equipment, and water sport exhibits.

Annual Wildflower Show, Pacific Grove, 408/648-3116. Over six hundred types of local wildflowers and plants on exhibit.

Good Old Days Celebration, Pacific Grove, 408/373-3304. A celebration of a

bygone era. Events include a parade, arts and crafts fair, and annual quilt show.

Often Later in the Month:

Rhododendron Show, Antonelli Brothers Begonia Garden, Capitola, 408/475-5222. Hundreds of trusses of rhododendrons in colorful display.

Annual Adobe Tour, Monterey, 408/372-2608. Local guides dressed in period costume escort you through Monterey history, in twenty-five adobes and gardens.

Big Sur International Marathon, Big Sur, 408/625-6226. April 25. One of the most beautiful and challenging foot races along the coastline of the Pacific Ocean. Walking and shorter running courses are also offered.

Springtime at La Mirada, Monterey, 408/372-5477. April 29 and 30. Afternoon tea and tour of the historic home and gardens of La Mirada as well as other beautiful gardens of the Monterey Peninsula.

Wildflower Festival and Triathalons, Lake San Antonio, 408/755-4899. A weekend festival combining the county's most extensive wildflower exhibits with entertainment, an arts and crafts fair, and two world-class triathalons.

May

Pelicans fly in formation and dive bomb submerged fish from above. They will be seen commonly through early autumn.

Usually in the First Two Weeks:

Soquel Country Fair, Porter Street, Soquel, 408/475-1702.

Monterey County Artists Studio Tour, Monterey County, 408/625-4175 or 375-6165. A self-guided tour through local artists' studios in Monterey County. Participants can interact with emerging and well-established artists in their working environments.

Santa Cruz County Fair Spring Festival, County Fairgrounds, Watsonville, 408/724-5671.

Spring Fair, San Lorenzo Park, Santa Cruz, 408/425-1234. Arts and crafts booths and entertainment bring a festive atmosphere to the park.

Monster Truck Race/Tractor Pull, Salinas, 408/757-2951. Major tractors and monster trucks go head to head.

Often Later in the Month:

Cooper-Molera Garden Day and Plant Sale, Monterey, 408/649-7118. Enjoy the beauty of plants typical before 1865. Seeds and plants from the garden will be on sale.

Memorial Day Weekend:

Boulder Creek Art and Wine Festival, Boulder Creek, 408/335-2764. Fourteen area wineries share tastings amid food and crafts booths. Designated drivers recommended.

The Great Monterey Squid Festival, Monterey, 408/649-6544. A one-of-a-kind event featuring squid every which way. Entertainment, arts and crafts, cooking demonstrations, and more.

West Coast Antique Fly-In Air Show, Watsonville Municipal Airport, Watsonville, 408/496-9559.

Felton Remembers Parade and Fair, downtown Felton, 408/335-2764.

Santa Cruz Longboard Invitational, Steamer Lane, Santa Cruz, 408/458-5360. The best longboard surfers in the world ride the waves at Steamer Lane.

Annual Civil War Memorial, Roaring Camp, Felton, 408/335-4484. Costumed Union and Confederate soldiers reenact the parades and conflict of the Civil War.

June

Sharks swim up Elkhorn Slough to pup. Does emerge with young fawns in Pacific Grove, Pebble Beach, and mountain areas. Strawberries and raspberries are ripening on rural vines.

Usually in the First Two Weeks:

Northern California Volley Tournament, main beach, Santa Cruz, 408/429-3665.

Monterey's Birthday Party, Monterey, 408/655-8070. A celebration of Monterey's birthday sponsored by the Old Monterey Business Association. Along with the parade, a four-block fair along historic Alvarado Street features more than a hundred booths.

Redwood Mountain Faire, Highlands Park, Ben Lomond, 408/338-2669. A gathering of local vintners, arts and crafts booths, and entertainment—all to benefit nonprofit organizations.

Often Later in the Month:

Early Days in San Juan, 408/623-4526. A celebration of San Juan Bautista's founding includes costumed docents and an 1860s dance.

Outdoor Summer Art Festival, Carmel, 408/624-3996. Art by local artists, photographers, and sculptors is displayed and for sale in a beautiful outdoor setting.

Monterey Bay Theaterfest, Monterey, 408/649-0340. An arts and crafts fair begins a summer series of free performances that feature fairy tale theater, comic opera, Shakespeare, musicians, and arts and crafts.

California Golf Association Amateur Championship, Pebble Beach and Monterey, 408/625-4653. The top amateurs in California play Pebble Beach Golf Links.

Santa Cruz Japanese Cultural Fair, Mission Park Plaza, Santa Cruz, 408/429-3778. Martial arts exhibitions, rice pounding, flower arranging, the tea ceremony, and Japanese dancing are featured.

Monterey County Strawberry Festival, Monterey, 408/663-4166. Continuous entertainment, arts and crafts, a food fair, and 10K race pay tribute to the strawberry at Laguna Seca.

Berry Festival, County Fairgrounds, Watsonville, 408/724-5671.

Monterey Bay Blues Festival, Monterey, 408/394-2652. This festival celebrates the best of blues music amid the lawn and oak trees of the Monterey Fairgrounds.

Father's Day Weekend:

Pops for Pops Annual Free Concert, Henry Cowell State Redwood Park, Felton, 408/462-0553. The Santa Cruz Symphony Orchestra honors fathers with classical pops in the park.

July

Coastal fog lingers as inland valleys heat up. Halibut and salmon swim along the coast.

Summer programs begin at local parks. At Wilder Ranch State Park, two miles north of Santa Cruz, 408/426-0505, docents dressed in Victorian attire present crafts and farming demonstrations of yesteryear. Rangers and docents lead guided walks and share their knowledge

of natural wonders and local history at Seacliff State Beach, 408/688-7146; Big Basin Redwoods State Park, 408/338-6132; and Big Sur State Park, 408/667-2315.

Some Fourth of July Celebrations:

World's Shortest Parade, Rancho Del Mar to Aptos Village, Aptos, 408/688-1467.

Celebration and Firecracker 10K, Harvey West Park, Santa Cruz, 408/429-3477.

Granite Rock's Independence Day Concert, Quarry Road, Aromas, 408/724-5611. The Monterey and Santa Cruz County symphonies and local rock bands accompany firecrackers over a lake in the area's largest quarry.

Hometown activities in the park and fireworks galore at Cambria, 805/927-3624.

Parade and City Celebration, Monterey, 408/646-3866. A hometown flag-raising parade down Alvarado Street features marching bands, clowns, jugglers, military units, and more.

Usually in the First Two Weeks:

Handcar Races and Steam Festival, Roaring Camp, Felton, 408/335-4484.

Sloat Landing Ceremony, Monterey, 408/373-2469. July 10. Commemorates anniversary of Commodore Sloat's landing with the laying of wreaths, military band performances, and a gun salute.

Theodore Sanders Memorial Northern California Monopoly Game Tournament, Santa Cruz Beach Boardwalk. 415/221-8813. All players can take a walk on the Boardwalk and the one who accumulates the most wealth wins this officially sanctioned tournament.

California Rodeo, Salinas, 408/757-2951. America's best cowboys compete for world championship points on the wildest broncos and bulls in the country. Also trick riders, horse races, and horse show competitions.

Beach Street Revival, Watsonville, 408/438-1957. Nostalgic car show and festival with live entertainment, car races. "Twilight Time Cruise," car auction, contests, kids' activities, and a variety of food and special interest booths.

Often Later in the Month:

Carmel Bach Festival, Carmel, 408/624-1521. A three-week celebration of classical music, highlighting J. S. Bach. Includes concerts, recitals, educational events, children's concerts, and a candlelight concert at the Carmel Mission Basilica.

Shakespeare Santa Cruz, University of California, Santa Cruz, 408/459-2159. Over two weeks of classic and modern interpretations of the bard's work.

Monterey National Horse Show, Monterey, 408/372-1000. Features exciting high jumping, team roping, and more by show horses, cutting horses, and cattle-working horses.

Santa Cruz Open Volleyball Tour, main beach, Santa Cruz, 408/423-1111.

Vintners' Festival, 408/479-9463. Tours of and tastings from a variety of Santa Cruz wineries. Special restaurant presentations.

Wharf to Wharf Race, Santa Cruz to Capitola, 408/475-2196. A 10K race for true athletes and fun runners including bands, bird callers, and six-foot-tall squid.

Gilroy Garlic Festival, Gilroy, 408/842-1625. The garlic capital of the world celebrates with three days of food and fun.

Moss Landing Annual Antique and Flea Market, Moss Landing, 408/633-5202. Vendors from all over the West Coast display and sell their treasures.

August

Poison oak turns fiery red along paths and up the trunks of trees. Be extra careful with fire this time of year.

Usually in the First Two Weeks:

The Annual San Juan Bautista Flea Market and Antique and Collectible Show. 408/623-2454. For over thirty years this show has presented some of the best collections in California.

Cabrillo Music Festival, Civic Auditorium, Santa Cruz, 408/662-2701. The Santa Cruz Symphony presents classic and modern themes in a week of concerts that include a children's concert in the park and concerts in Mission San Juan Bautista. Includes an arts and foods festival.

Calamari Festival, India Joze, Santa Cruz, 408/427-3554. Contest for best squid art, squid tasting, and squid review entertainment.

Carmel Valley Fiesta, Carmel Valley, 408/659-4000. A weekend celebration featuring food, games, music, parades, entertainment, arts, crafts, and a Saturday night street dance.

Monterey Scottish Festival & Highland Games, Monterey, 408/649-1770. This traditional gathering of Scottish clans and families includes a parade, live bagpipe music, Highland and country dancing, Scottish food, and athletic competitions.

Often Later in the Month:

Monterey County Fair, Monterey, 408/372-1000. Carnival rides, agricultural displays, livestock exhibits, and home arts are the hallmarks of this county fair.

Pro Volleyball Tournament, main beach, Santa Cruz, 408/429-3665.

Annual Monterey Historic Automobile Races, Monterey, 408/648-5100 or 800/327-SECA.

Pebble Beach Concours d'Elegance and Christie's Auction, Pebble Beach, 408/624-3811. Considered the world's most prestigious Concours, the Pebble Beach event showcases more than a hundred of the world's finest classic automobiles. Auction proceeds benefit local charities.

September

Sycamore leaves turn golden. Round pods hang from the bare branches of buckeye trees. Summer fog retreats and clear days prevail.

Usually in the First Two Weeks:

Annual Carmel Shakespeare Festival, Carmel, 408/649-0340. Performances are presented at the historic outdoor Forest Theater.

California All-Indian Market, San Juan Bautista, 408/623-2379. A celebration of native tribes featuring tribal artists, dancers, food, and fashion.

Greenfield Broccoli Festival, Greenfield, 408/674-3222. Enjoy over thirty arts and crafts booths, entertainment, and a variety of broccoli delicacies.

Santa Cruz County Fair, Santa Cruz County Fairgrounds, 408/724-5671. Carnival rides, local agriculture, displays by artists.

Annual Greek Festival, Monterey, 408/424-4434. Festivals feature authentic Greek food, live music, traditional dancing, a taverna, and crafts.

Begonia Festival, Capitola Village, 408/475-6522. Two-week festival; the high point is a parade of begonia-covered floats down the San Lorenzo River.

Santa Rosalia Festival, Monterey, 408/373-2628. An all-day Italian event includes a parade, procession down Main Street to Custom House Plaza, blessing of the fishing fleet, outdoor mass, food, and entertainment.

Often Later in the Month:

Monterey Jazz Festival, Monterey, 408/373-3366. The oldest continuous jazz festival in the United States, starring some of the greatest jazz performers in the country. Music, clothing, and food booths. Outdoors during the day and under the stars to the morning hours.

Festival del Pueblo de Monterey, Monterey, 408/375-0095 or 625-5056. Contributions of the indigenous people of the Americas are celebrated with a coronation ball and a fiesta.

Estuaries Day, Elkhorn Slough, 415/728-2822. Guided walks, historical theater, and nature activities.

Annual Artichoke Festival, Castroville, 408/633-2465. At the artichoke capital of the world, this festival provides ongoing entertainment, a crafts fair, a parade, and food.

Capitola Art and Wine Festival, Capitola Village, 408/475-6522. Art in the park and a long beach promenade. Tastings of local vintners' wines.

Monterey Bay 10K Run for the Beacon, Monterey, 408/372-2334. A 10K race along the coastline, including a Kids' Fun Run. All proceeds benefit the Beacon House, a drug-and-alcohol rehabilitation program.

Annual River Inn Resort Oktoberfest, Big Sur, 408/625-5255, 667-2700. Features authentic German food and beer, arts and crafts, and live entertainment. Proceeds benefit the Beacon House.

Swanton Pacific Country Picnic, Swanton, on the North Coast, Santa Cruz, 408/476-6116.

Ohlone Day, Henry Cowell State Park, 408/335-3174. Ohlone stories, music, food, and crafts under the redwoods.

October

Monarchs fly in for the winter. Look for them at Pacific Grove and at Natural Bridges and Andrew Molera state parks.

Usually in the First Two Weeks:

California International Airshow, Salinas, 408/754-1983. Top civilian and military aerobatic performers take to the sky to benefit local charities.

Indy Car World Series at Laguna Seca Raceway, Monterey, 408/648-5100 or 800/327-SECA. The final stop on the 1993 PPG/INDY car world series, featuring some of the great race stars of our time.

Octoberfest, Monterey, 408/649-6544. Authentic German food, wine, beer gardens, bands, folk dancers, and German arts and crafts await festival goers. Proceeds benefit the Monterey Jaycees.

Open Studios, Santa Cruz, north county, 408/688-5399. Arts and Crafts studios

open their doors to display their work. Meet local artists, visit studios, and purchase one-of-a-kind pieces, for two weekends.

Butterfly Parade, Pacific Grove, 408/646-6520. Elementary school children parade in butterfly costumes and different themes to welcome the return of the Monarch butterfly.

Pacific Grove Victorian Home Tour, 408/373-3304. Visit impeccably restored Victorians often featuring artwork of owners and antique furnishings.

Gorda Jade Festival, Gorda, 805/927-5574. The largest gathering of jade artists in the country.

California Constitution Day, Monterey, 408/375-9944. October 13. Festivities celebrate the signing of California's Constitution in Colton Hall.

Often Later in the Month:

Big Sur River Run, Big Sur, 408/624-4112. A 10K Run through the redwoods and oak groves of beautiful Pfeiffer Big Sur State Park.

November

Shorebirds and waterfowl flock to Elkhorn Slough. The first of the migrating gray whales are spotted off the coast.

Usually in the First Two Weeks:

Pacific Grove Band Review, 408/646-6520. High school bands from throughout Northern California compete in marching and performance competitions.

Robert Louis Stevenson's "Unbirthday," Monterey, 408/649-7118. November 13. Join young and old alike to wish Robert Louis Stevenson a "Happy Unbirthday."

Often Later in the Month:

Christmas Craft & Gift Fair, Cocoanut
Grove, Santa Cruz, 408/423-5590.

December

Christmas tree lighting ceremonies and
holiday festivals brighten the coast from
Cambria to Santa Cruz. Northern storms
send gifts of large waves to beaches.
Eagle tours begin at Lake San Antonio.

Usually in the First Two Weeks:

Festival of Trees, Monterey, 408/372-
5477. View lovely Christmas trees at the
Museum of Art, each uniquely decorated
with handcrafted ornaments.

Lighted Boat Parade, Santa Cruz Yacht
Harbor, 408/423-9680. Features boats
with yule lights and holiday themes.

Christmas in the Adobes, Monterey,
408/649-7118 or 408/649-7111.
Monterey's historic buildings are candlelit and enhanced by period Christmas
decorations, musical entertainment, and
the presence of costumed volunteers.

Christmas at the Inns, Pacific Grove,
408/373-3304. Victorian bed-and-breakfast
inns decorated for the holidays hold open
house.

La Posada, Monterey, 408/646-3866.
December 10. A traditional Christmas
candlelight parade led by carolers in
Spanish and English. A piñata party follows the parade.

BIBLIOGRAPHY

Ansel Adams. *Ansel Adams: An Autobiography*. Boston: Little Brown and Company, 1985.

Clark, Donald Thomas. *Monterey County Place Names: A Geographical Dictionary*. Carmel Valley, California: Kestrel Press, 1991.

Dana, Richard Henry. *Two Years before the Mast*. New York: Penguin Books, 1981.

Fink, Augusta. *Monterey County: The Dramatic Story of Its Past*. Santa Cruz, Western Tanager Press/Valley Publishers, 1972.

Gebhard, David, Eric Sandweiss, and Robert Winter. *A Guide to Architecture in San Francisco and Northern California*. Santa Barbara, California: Peregrine Smith, 1976.

Gilliam, Harold, and Ann Gilliam. *Creating Carmel: The Enduring Vision*. Salt Lake City, Peregrine Smith, 1992.

Gordon, David, and Alan Baldridge. *Gray Whale*. Monterey, California: Monterey Bay Aquarium, 1991.

Gordon, Burton L. *Monterey Bay Area: Natural History and Cultural Imprints*. Pacific Grove, California: The Boxwood Press, 1977.

Hart, James D. *A Companion to California*. New York: Oxford University Press, 1978.

Howard, Donald M. *Early Man of the Monterey Peninsula*. Carmel, California: Antiquities Research Publication, 1978.

Howard, Donald M. *Ranchos of Monterey: The Hacen Dados and Their Land*. Carmel, California: Antiquities Research Publication, 1978.

Koch, Margaret. *Santa Cruz County: Parade of the Past*. Fresno, California: Valley Publishers, 1973.

Lydon, Sandy. *Chinese Gold: The Chinese in the Monterey Bay Region*. Capitola, California: Capitola Book Company, 1985.

McLane, Lucy Neely. *A Piney Paradise: A Pictorial Story of the Monterey Peninsula*. Monterey, California: Herald Printers, 1975.

Miller, Henry. *Big Sur and the Oranges of Hieronymus Bosch*. New York: New Directions, 1957.

Muir, John, and J. R. Fitch. *Picturesque California: The Rocky Mountains and the Pacific Slope*. San Francisco and New York, J. Dewing Company, 1887.

Schaffer, Jeffrey P. *Hiking the Big Sur Country*. Berkeley, California: Wilderness Press, 1992.

Silberstein, Mark, and Eileen Campbell. *Elkhorn Slough*. Monterey, California: Monterey Bay Aquarium Foundation, 1989.

Steinbeck, John. *Cannery Row*. New York: Bantam Books, 1945.

Steinbeck, John. *East of Eden*. New York: Viking Press, 1952.

The Sunset Authors. *The California Missions: A Pictorial History*. Menlo Park, California: Lane Publishing, 1979.

Margolin, Malcolm. *The Ohlone Way: Indian Life in the San Francisco Monterey Bay*. Heyday Books, 1978.

INDEX

Grateful acknowledgement is made to the following:

Pebble Beach Company for permission to use images of the Lone Cypress tree, which are trademarks and service marks of Pebble Beach Company. Used by permission of Pebble Beach Company.

Viking Penguin for excerpts from *Cannery Row*, by John Steinbeck. Copyright © 1945 by John Steinbeck, renewed © 1973 by Elaine Steinbeck, John Steinbeck IV, and Thom Steinbeck. Excerpts from *East of Eden*, by John Steinbeck. Copyright © 1952 by John Steinbeck. Material used by permission of Viking Penguin, a division of Penguin Books USA, Inc.

New Directions for excerpts from *Big Sur and The Oranges of Hieronymus Bosch*, by Henry Miller. Copyright © 1957 by New Directions Publishing Corporation. Material used by permission of New Directions Publishing Corporation.